Ransoming the Waste Land

Ransoming the Waste Land

Papers on C.S. Lewis's Space Trilogy, Chronicles of Narnia, and Other Works

Volume I

by

Nancy-Lou Patterson

Editors

Emily E. Auger

and

Janet Brennan Croft

Valleyhome Books

First Printing 2016
Ransoming the Waste Land Volume I
Hardcover ISBN 978-1-987919-00-4
Paperback ISBN 978-1-987919-03-5
Epub ISBN 978-1-987919-04-2

Ransoming the Waste Land Volume II
Hardcover ISBN 978-1-987919-01-1
Paperback ISBN 978-1-987919-05-9
Epub ISBN 978-1-987919-06-6

Table of Contents

Abbreviations for C.S. Lewis's Fiction

PR *The Pilgrim's Regress*. 1933. Illus. by Michael Hague. 1981. Grand Rapids, MI: William B. Erdmans, 2000. [ISBN 0-8028-0641-4 with matching kindle edition.]

OSP *Out of the Silent Planet*. 1938. Hammersmith, London: HarperCollins*Publishers*, 2005. [EPub Edition ISBN 0-00-715715-0, with page nos. matching print edition ISBN 0007157150].

ST *The Screwtape Letters with Screwtape Proposes a Toast*. With a New Preface. New York: Geoffrey Bles, 1961. [New Preface 5-13. Original Preface 19-20. *The Screwtape Letters* (1942) 23-138. *Screwtape Proposes a Toast* (1959) 139-57.]

PER *Perelandra*. 1943. Hammersmith, London: HarperCollins*Publishers*, 2005. [EPub Edition ISBN 0-00-7157169, with page nos. matching print edition ISBN 0684833654].

THS *That Hideous Strength*. 1945. Hammersmith, London: HarperCollins*Publishers*, 2003. EPub Edition ISBN 978-0-007-33227-4, with page nos. matching print edition ISBN 0684833670].

LWW *The Lion, the Witch and the Wardrobe*. 1950. Collector's Edition with Illustrations by Pauline Baynes. New York: HarperCollins, 2010. [E-Pub Edition 978-0-06-197415-1; with page nos. matching print edition ISBN 0064409422].

PC *Prince Caspian: The Return to Narnia*. 1951. Collector's Edition with Illustrations by Pauline Baynes. New York: HarperCollins, 2010. [E-Pub Edition ISBN 978-0-06-197422-9 with page nos. matching print edition ISBN 0060234830].

VDT *The Voyage of the Dawn Treader*. 1952. Collector's Edition with Illustrations by Pauline Baynes. New York: HarperCollins, 2010. [E-Pub Edition ISBN 9780061974267, with page nos. matching print edition ISBN 0064471071].

SC *The Silver Chair*. 1953. Collector's Edition with Illustrations by Pauline Baynes. New York: HarperCollins, 2010. [E-Pub Edition ISBN 978-0-06-97423-6, with page nos. matching print edition ISBN 0064409457].

HB *The Horse and His Boy*. 1954. Collector's Edition with Illustrations by Pauline Baynes. New York: HarperCollins, 2010. [E-Pub Edition 978-0-06-197413-7, with page nos. matching print edition ISBN 006023489X].

MN *The Magician's Nephew* (1955). Collector's Edition with Illustrations by Pauline Baynes. New York: HarperCollins, 2010. [Epub Edition ISBN 978-0-06-197416-8, with page nos. matching print edition 0064409430].

LB *The Last Battle*. 1956. Collector's Edition with Illustrations by Pauline Baynes. New York: HarperCollins, 2010. [E-Pub Edition ISBN 978-0-06-197414-4, with page nos. matching print edition ISBN 0060234938].

TWF *Till We Have Faces: A Myth Retold*. Illus. Fritz Eichenberg. 1956. New York: Harcourt, Brace and Company, 1980. [ISBN 0156904365 with matching kindle edition].

Preface

Nancy-Lou Patterson's (b. 1929) many accomplishments include works of visual art, poetry, and fiction, and numerous scholarly papers published in *Mythlore* and other journals and anthologies. Of the Inklings, about whom she wrote most often, she particularly favored C.S. Lewis, whose work she read and enjoyed over a period of many decades.

> I have to admit to a very peculiar point of view. *That Hideous Strength* is my favorite book for adults. Not merely my favorite book for adults by C.S. Lewis, but my favorite book, period! Oddly, I don't remember exactly when I first read it. It must have been during the academic year 1953/1954 because that was when I read *Out of the Silent Planet* and *Perelandra*, but I have read it so often since then that I can't pinpoint the exact place where I first read it, as I so often can, having a powerful visual memory, with other books more seldom read. What I do remember is the impact of the book, its wonder, its delight, which for me—even after the word-for-word reading I gave it this year to prepare to discuss it with you—is what makes it the best of the trilogy. I say nothing against the cool masculine vision of *Out of the Silent Planet* and the warm feminine vision of *Perelandra*: these numinous "other" worlds are forever encoded in my memory as encounters with wonder. But my favorite book—not only of the trilogy, but of all books for adults, is *That Hideous Strength*. The more I read it, the more it speaks to me. I am here to tell what I think it says.[1]

Patterson's enthusiasm for the writings of C.S. Lewis is part of a widespread and long-lived flourishing of academic and popular studies of his work.[2] The strength of her analyses of Lewis's fiction derives from her recognition—perhaps inspired by her own creative work as a fiction author—that the power of his images, motifs, and symbols derives from his ability to use his extensive knowledge of literature and his own lived experiences to develop them in relation to broader cultural archetypes.

Patterson's most frequent approach is what is today popularly called "source criticism." When source criticism developed in the eighteenth century, it was called literary criticism and involved the analysis of texts in relation to probable antecedents. "Source criticism," E.L. Risden (2011) writes, "in current parlance implies different notions in different fields [...] It began as a subset of biblical criticism, to discern the various sources behind canonical (or non-canonical) books and stories, in part to understand the process of canonization and in part to understand the movement of story and the cultural influences of the ancient world."[3] Today, beyond its role in the actual preparation of books from manuscripts, source criticism generally

> considers relative chronology, authorship, and intention (if we can determine them), settings of the works, themes, patterns of organization of the whole works or of plot, common literary units such as borrowed characters, motifs, or "memes" (e.g., linguistic elements or even "narremes," repeated sections of narrative or similar digressions), parallel passages, points of view, and stylistic peculiarities. [...] Documenting sources provides readers a powerful tool to gain insight into authors, how they thought and worked, and to use in the interpretation of texts, so that we may find, enjoy, appreciate, and teach better and fuller (though not exclusive) readings. It helps us understand how all writers experience the pressures of the past as well as contemporary exigencies.[4]

Source criticism has become one of the most favored approaches to the study of Tolkien's fiction,[5] although, as Tom Shippey (1982) observes, Tolkien did not approve of it.[6] Numerous scholars have demonstrated the influence on him of "Beowulf and everything else in Old English [...]; medieval Romance, Arthurian and otherwise [...], but those examples only slightly less than the Bible [...]; fairy tales, fables, and folksongs [...]; Classical myth [...]; and the readings and discussions with his fellow Inklings."[7] Apparently Lewis, who drew on no fewer sources than Tolkien, sometimes disapproved of source criticism too;[8] yet he was without question interested in the approach, as papers such as his "What Chaucer Really Did to [Boccaccio's] *Il Filostrato*" indicate.[9]

Patterson comments on an "annotated Lewis" as a wonderful book yet to be written,[10] but her primary goal in studying and writing about Lewis's sources, both literary and biographical, was to show the importance of the themes he addressed. The papers included in the first volume of *Ransoming the Waste Land* examine Lewis's treatment of salvation in Arthurian and biblical forms, his hierarchy of beings from divine to inanimate, and his representation of the feminine in relation to a purportedly masculine divinity. Some of those in the second volume also address these subjects, but emphasize Lewis's representation of spatial and temporal realities, including directional symbolism, northerness, and environmentalism, and some of his character types, including anthropomorphized animals, deities, witches, and others.

Both volumes include papers that Patterson herself identified as part of a series on the representation of evil:

1. "'Banquet at Belbury': Festival and Horror in *That Hideous Strength*" (1981) Volume I
2. "'Halfe Like a Serpent': The Green Witch in *The Silver Chair*" (1984) Volume II
3. "Letters from Hell: the Symbolism of Evil in *The Screwtape Letters*" (1985) Volume II
4. "'The Bolt of Tash': the Figure of Satan in C.S. Lewis's *The Horse and His Boy* and *The Last Battle*" (1990) Volume II
5. "'Always Winter and Never Christmas': Symbols of Time in Lewis's Chronicles of Narnia" (1991) Volume II
6. "'This Equivocal Being': The Un-Man in C.S. Lewis's *Perelandra*" (1995, 1996) Volume I

The seventh paper, "The Holy House of Ungit" (1997), was not yet written in 1996 when Patterson identified this series. It is, as she describes it, about "Lewis's last novel *Till We Have Faces* [in which] no character specifically embodies or symbolizes evil, including the great goddess Ungit [...]"[11] By contrast, many of Patterson's papers outside this series are about Lewis's good or saved characters.

Patterson's approach to Lewis's fiction by way of the images that he brought to life is validated by Lewis's own creative process. Lewis believed that in writing stories "images always come first."[12] In a frequently cited passage, he wrote,

> All my seven Narnian books, and my three science fiction books, began with seeing pictures in my head. At first

> they were not a story, just pictures. The *Lion* all began with a picture of a Faun carrying an umbrella and parcels in a snowy wood. This picture had been in my mind since I was about sixteen. Then one day, when I was about forty, I said to myself: "Let's try to make a story about it."
>
> At first I had very little idea how the story would go. But then suddenly Aslan came bounding into it. I think I had been having a good many dreams of lions about that time. Apart from that, I don't know where the Lion came from or why He came. But once he was there He pulled the whole story together, and soon He pulled the six other Narnian stories in after Him.[13]

The starting point for *Perelandra*, he writes, "was my mental picture of the floating islands. The whole of the rest of my labours in a sense consisted of building up a world in which floating islands could exist."[14] This authorial sense of the importance of the image translated readily for Lewis into an understanding of symbolism: "It [symbolism] makes its first effective appearance in European thought with the dialogues of Plato. The Sun is the copy of the Good. Time is the moving image of eternity. All visible things exist just in so far as they succeed in imitating the Forms."[15] Whereas the allegorist "leaves the given [...] to talk of that which is [...] fiction. The symbolist leaves the given to find what is more real." In his own writing, Lewis specified that "the attempt to read that something else through its sensible imitations, to see the archetype in the copy, is what I mean by symbolism or sacramentalism."[16]

C.G. Jung's understanding of the archetype was interesting to Lewis, if not absolutely compelling, as he commented in his paper on science fiction: "I am not sure that anyone has satisfactorily explained the keen, lasting, and solemn pleasure which such stories can give. Jung, who went furthest, seems to me to produce as his explanation one more myth which affects us in the same way as the rest. Surely the analysis of water should not itself be wet?"[17] Of course Lewis greatly admired mythology, and his conversion to Christianity was, for him, very much about accepting that "the story of Christ is simply a true myth: a myth working on us in the same way as the others, but with this tremendous difference that *it really happened*."[18]

He found the images in "Pagan" stories to be evidence of God working with what "He found there."[19] Readers may thus understand the emphasis and importance that Lewis placed on the "image" as what he "found" and as the starting point of all of his stories. Similarly, if, on a few occasions, some of Patterson's readers find the perspectives offered on the gender-specific aspects of archetypes and marriage a little old-fashioned, they might recall the recentness and changeability of modern perceptions related to these matters and that, like many literary critics, Patterson always begins with the text and what there is to be found in it. She shares her discoveries, particularly about Lewis's debt to biblical narrative, in thoughtful, in-depth, and beautifully written papers. Her explorations of other subjects and themes, such as anti-semitism, environmentalism, evil, feminism, and Tarot, in the work of George MacDonald, Dorothy Sayers, and Charles Williams are equally intriguing.

Her scholarly goals—unfortunately, in my opinion—never extended to the treatment of Lewis's work or the Bible as sources for the tropes and conventions of more contemporary examples of fantasy and science-fiction genres, or the ease with which archetypes become stereotypes and stereotypes become the basis for misogynistic fantasy fiction. The essential aspects of Jane's character and story are certainly all too familiar today, as they are endlessly repeated and caricatured in novels, films, and television shows: she is the independent woman who must be tortured and burdened by associates with a wildly exaggerated concern for her failure to procreate in a timely fashion:

> "Sir," said Merlin, "know well that she has done in Logres a thing of which no less sorrow shall come than came of the stroke that Balinus struck. For, Sir, it was the purpose of God that she and her lord should between them have begotten a child by whom the enemies should have been put out of Logres for a thousand years."
>
> "She is but lately married," said Ransom. "The child may yet be born."
>
> "Sir," said Merlin, "be assured that the child will never be born, for the hour of its begetting is passed. Of their own will they are barren [...] For a hundred generations in two lines the begetting of this child was prepared; and unless God

> should rip up the work of time, such seed, and such an hour, in such a land, shall never be again."
>
> "Enough said," answered Ransom. "The woman perceives that we are speaking of her."
>
> "It would be great charity," said Merlin, "if you gave order that her head should be cut from her shoulders; for it is a weariness to look at her." (THS 275-76; ch. 13)

Jane ultimately relinquishes her pre-marital plans for her life entirely, and gives herself over to the demands of a heterosexual relationship, conceived of in the most conventional of terms. Patterson occasionally shows her awareness of the imperfections in Lewis's characters and plot developments—these may or may not coincide with the flaws perceived by her readers—but the definitions and implications of genre and cultural stereotyping obviously paled for her in comparison with the rich reverberations of biblical narratives in Lewis's fiction.

Further to the archetype (not the stereotype) in particular, rather than the image in general, Lewis acknowledged that "for Jung, fairy tale liberates the archetypes which dwell in the collective unconscious, and when we read a good fairy tale we are obeying the old precept, 'know thyself.'"[20] While Lewis might not have agreed with all of Jung's theory, he thought enough of it to suggest adding to it such non-human beings as talking animals for their power to convey "psychology, types of character, more briefly than novelistic presentation and to readers whom novelistic presentation could not yet reach. Consider Mr Badger in *The Wind in the Willows* [...]."[21] Lewis also specifically identified the image of God "as a grave old king with a long beard" as "a Jungian archetype [that] links God with all the wise old kings in the fairy-tales, with prophets, sages, magicians. Though it is (formally) the picture of a man, it suggests something more than humanity. At the very least it gets in the idea of something older than yourself, something that knows more, something you can't fathom."[22]

In December of 1938, Lewis responded to a fan letter: "I like the whole inter-planetary idea as a mythology and simply wished to conquer for my own (Christian) point of view what has always hitherto been used by the opposite side. I think Wells's *First Men in the Moon* the best of the sort I have read [...]"[23] Later, in 1944, he wrote that "The real father of my planet books is David Lindsay's *Voyage to*

Arcturus"; this was because it gave him "the idea that the 'scientific-tion' appeal could be combined with the 'supernatural' appeal."[24] Certainly, Lewis had no second thoughts about writing fantasy and science fiction, as opposed to a more "realist" fiction, as he believed that "Good stories often introduce the marvelous or supernatural,"[25] and admired its effects in H.G. Wells's *First Men in the Moon* and *War of the Worlds*,[26] and Walter Miller's *Canticle for Leibowitz*, as well as in Lindsay's novel, and others.[27] With regard to children's stories, which have an entirely "local and accidental" association with fairy tales and fantasy, he thought Tolkien's essay "the most important contribution to the subject that anyone has yet made."[28] He denied deliberately choosing fiction for didactic purposes, describing such assertions as "pure moonshine,"[29] and thought "that a book worth reading only in childhood is not worth reading even then."[30]

Although Lewis regarded much of the theology people later found in his stories to be of their own invention, he must have been pleased when readers of *Out of the Silent Planet*, such as the one Dorothy Sayers wrote to him about in 1953, recognized the Christian story it contained: "He said it was a most wonderful experience, as though two entirely different worlds had suddenly come into focus together, like a stereoscope, and it's a thing he can never forget."[31] Patterson's papers work on Lewis's fiction in a manner that is also much like a stereoscope, adding dimensions to the experience of reading that the reader—whether Lewis's work is new or familiar to them, whether his biblical sources are unfamiliar or already known to them—might have otherwise passed by without even knowing they existed.

——Emily E. Auger

Notes

[1] Nancy-Lou Patterson, "Ransoming the Wasteland: Arthurian Themes in C.S. Lewis's Interplanetary Trilogy, Part I," *The Lamp-Post of the Southern California C.S. Lewis Society* 8.2 (November 1984): 16. This statement was taken from the draft Patterson prepared for a proposed anthology on C.S. Lewis's fiction, which is the version presented in the first part of the present collection.

Notes

[2] William Calin counted "more than 150 books and hundreds of articles devoted to him, in whole or in part," as well as "three scholarly journals devoted entirely to the Inklings' current in modern literature plus four semi-scholarly journals published by the most important of the C.S. Lewis societies that came into existence after the writer's death and have grown in strength and in numbers ever since." The former include "*Seven* (ceased publication after 1991), *Mythlore*, and *Inklings Jahrbuch*." The latter include *CSL: The Bulletin of the New York C.S. Lewis Society*, *The Lamp-Post of the Southern California C.S. Lewis Society*, *The Canadian C.S. Lewis Journal* [OP], and *The Chronicle of the Portland C.S. Lewis Society* [OP]." "C.S. Lewis and the Discarded Image of the Middle Ages and Renaissance," *The Twentieth-Century Humanist Critics from Spitzer to Frye* (Toronto, ON: University of Toronto Press, 2007) 85, 202. C.S. Lewis's life has been made the subject of numerous biographies and his relationship with Joy Davidman the subject of a film *Shadowlands* (1994) with Anthony Hopkins and Debra Winger in the starring roles.

[3] E.L. Risden, "Source Criticism: Background and Applications," *Tolkien and the Study of His Sources*, ed. Jason Fisher (Jefferson, NC: McFarland, 2011) 22.

[4] Risden 24.

[5] Jason Fisher, "Preface," *Tolkien and the Study of His Sources*, ed. Jason Fisher (Jefferson, NC: McFarland, 2011).

[6] Tom Shippey, "Appendix A: Tolkien's Sources: The True Tradition," *The Road to Middle-earth: How J.R.R. Tolkien Created a New Mythology, Revised and expanded edition* (Hammersmith, London: HarperCollins*Publishers, 1982*).

[7] Risden 18.

[8] Richard B. Cunningham, *C.S. Lewis, Defender of the Faith* (Philadelphia, PA: Westminster Press, 1967) 91.

[9] C.S. Lewis, "What Chaucer Really Did to [Boccaccio's] *Il Filostrato*," *Selected Literary Essays by C.S. Lewis* (Cambridge: Cambridge UP, 1969) 27-44.

[10] Patterson wrote an enthusiastic review of Paul F. Ford's *Companion to Narnia* (1980), a book which some readers might consider coming

Notes

close to achieving the goal of an "annotated Lewis." See "From Adam to Zardeenah," *Mythlore* 8.1 (1981): 31-32.

[11] Nancy-Lou Patterson, "'This Equivocal Being': The Un-Man in C.S. Lewis's *Perelandra*," *The Lamp-Post of the Southern California C.S. Lewis Society* 19.3 (Fall 1995): note 1; see notes at the end of the second part of the article 19.4 (Fall-Winter 1995-96) 18.

[12] C.S. Lewis, "On Three Ways of Writing for Children," *Of Other Worlds Essays and Stories*, ed. Walter Hooper (New York: Harcourt Brace Jovanovich, 1966) 33.

[13] C.S. Lewis, "It All Began with a Picture," *Of Other Worlds Essays and Stories*, ed. Walter Hooper (New York: Harcourt Brace Jovanovich, 1966) 42.

[14] C.S. Lewis, Kingsley Amis, and Brian Aldiss, "Unreal Estates," *Of Other Worlds Essays and Stories*, ed. Walter Hooper (New York: Harcourt Brace Jovanovich, 1966) 87. See also Roger Lancelyn Green and Walter Hooper, *C.S. Lewis A Biography* (London: St. James's Place, 1974) 162-66.

[15] C.S. Lewis, *The Allegory of Love: A Study in Medieval Tradition* (1936; Oxford UP, 1967) 46-47.

[16] C.S. Lewis, *The Allegory of Love* 46.

[17] C.S. Lewis, "On Science Fiction," *Of Other Worlds Essays and Stories*, ed. Walter Hooper (New York: Harcourt Brace Jovanovich, 1966) 71. Jung also had a moment in the 1930s at which he recognized that the roots of his work lay in esoteric Christianity. See Gerhard Wehr, "C.G. Jung in the Context of Christian Esotericism and Cultural History," *Modern Esoteric Spirituality*, eds. Antoine Faivre and Jacob Needleman (New York: Crossroad, 1992) 386-87.

[18] Green and Hooper 118.

[19] Green and Hooper 118.

[20] Lewis, "On Three Ways of Writing for Children" 27.

[21] Lewis, "On Three Ways of Writing for Children" 27.

[22] C.S. Lewis, *A Grief Observed* (New York: Seabury Press, 1961) 27.

[23] Green and Hooper 163. He also wrote in this letter that Olaf Stapledon's *Last and First Men* (1931) was one of the inspirations for *Out of the Silent Planet* because it is one of those with "the desperately immoral outlook which I try to pillory in Weston" 163.

Notes

[24] Green and Hooper 164.

[25] C.S. Lewis, "On Stories," *Of Other Worlds Essays and Stories*, ed. Walter Hooper (New York: Harcourt Brace Jovanovich, 1966) 13.

[26] C.S. Lewis, "On Stories" 9, 11.

[27] C.S. Lewis, "On Science Fiction" 88-89.

[28] C.S. Lewis "On Three Ways of Writing for Children," *Of Other Worlds Essays and Stories*, ed. Walter Hooper (New York: Harcourt Brace Jovanovich, 1966) 26. See also J.R.R. Tolkien, "On Fairy-stories" (1947), *The Tolkien Reader* (New York: Balantine, 1966) 33-99.

[29] C.S. Lewis, "Sometimes Fairy Stories May Say Best What's To Be Said," *Of Other Worlds Essays and Stories*, ed. Walter Hooper (New York: Harcourt Brace Jovanovich, 1966) 36. See also "Unreal Estates" 87.

[30] C.S. Lewis, "Sometimes Fairy Stories" 38.

[31] Green and Hooper 165.

Editorial Notes

In finalizing this collection I have followed Nancy-Lou Patterson's original anthology design for Volume I with regard to general content, organization, and thematic emphasis. I added later papers to the sections they obviously belong in, and altered some paper and section titles to eliminate repetition and improve clarity in the context of the updated collection. I chose the epigraphs from the original papers, from Patterson's revisions to those papers, and from the citations within the papers. The papers included in Volume II have been organized according to theme and subject matter. I added an abstract and a credit paragraph at the beginning of each paper.

I edited the previously published papers in Volume I in general accordance with the revisions Patterson herself worked on with only a few exceptions. I removed or revised a few statements of faith to improve the uniformity of the scholarly authorial "voice," which varied slightly according to the original publishing venue, to satisfy my own scholarly expectations as well as those of the reviewers and future readers. I restored some of the sections included in the published "Anti-Babels" that were edited out of the archive draft of "The Unfathomable Feminine Principle," either to the main text or the notes; but otherwise this paper follows Patterson's more recent work on the subject. I changed the title of "The Unfathomable Feminine Principle" to "Archetypes of the Feminine" in recognition of the restored content and to allow "The Unfathomable Feminine Principle" to stand, as it appropriately does, as the concluding section title.

The other changes or corrections that I made were minor or of a technical nature. Among those worth noting are minor alterations to introductions and conclusions, including the removal of some extended and overly discursive paragraphs, as well as some that became redundant in the context of the collection; and slight revisions necessitated by the treatment here of papers originally published in parts as continuous essays. I added a few citations from the novels to support and clarify Patterson's arguments, as in the explanation of the "bent one" in "Thesis, Antithesis, Synthesis." I also changed the various references to C.S. Lewis's Trilogy as the Cosmic, Interplanetary, Ransom, and Space Trilogy to a uniform "Space Trilogy" or just plain

Trilogy.[1] I changed the various British, American, and Canadian English patterns applied in the papers in accordance with their original publishing venues to a uniform American English. I updated the citations to C.S. Lewis's fiction to the matching print and ebook (kindle) editions. There is currently—at the time of my writing of this preface—only one complete Space Trilogy matching print and ebook set and it is in British English; the only complete Chronicles of Narnia matching print and ebook set has been Americanized. I adjusted the quotations in Patterson's papers so that they are consistent with these volumes.

Wherever possible, I checked quotations and sources, with the exception of the Bibles and dictionaries, which have been left as Patterson gave them with her notes regarding the versions and editions used. The software for checking sources in ebooks is very good, but I did find that rechecking for a phrase sometimes resulted in different page numbers (by a variation of only one page), depending on which part of the quotation I put in the query box and whether or not the passage extended over two pages. I hope these or other discrepancies in source editions are not problematic for readers; the task of rechecking all of Patterson's references to the novels in particular, which she used in various editions, would have been more or less impossible without the ebook software. In the few instances where corrections to other citations and sources were required and editions were in doubt, I updated the edition or added citations to that which was available.

By way of acknowledgements, I want to thank my co-editor Janet Brennan Croft, editor of *Mythlore*: without her interest in Patterson's work and generous contributions this collection would simply never have come to publication. E Palmer Patterson and his daughters Fanny, Melanie, and Samantha have also been very supportive and generous with their time and interest. In addition, the Special Collections Librarians at the University of Waterloo (Waterloo, Ontario, Canada) provided access to the relevant papers, and all of the librarians with whom I came in contact at the Universities of Guelph, Waterloo, and Sir Wilfrid Laurier were extraordinarily helpful and interested in supporting this project. And last, but by no means least, I am very glad my nephew Mathew just happened to be available to brainstorm some pre-intel computer software into service when it was needed.

Notes

[1] The British collection is titled *The Cosmic Trilogy*. C.S. Lewis himself, however, frequently referred to the collection as the "Ransom Trilogy." See, for example, some of his letters in *The Collected Letters of C.S. Lewis*, including two to Sister Penelope. On September 6th, 1945, he wrote "Yes, I've finished another book wh. concludes the Ransom trilogy" (624); and on January 3rd, 1945, he wrote "Yes, I have written a story […] wh. concludes the Ransom trilogy" (635). *The Collected Letters of C.S. Lewis Volume II: Books, Broadcasts, and the War, 1931–1949,* ed. Walter Hooper (New York: HarperCollins, 2004). He also wrote to Rosamond Cruikshank on July 2nd, 1959, about "the Ransom trilogy." *The Collected Letters of C.S. Lewis, Volume III: Narnia, Cambridge and Joy 1950–1963*, ed. Walter Hooper (New York: HarperCollins, 2007) 1063.

Arthurian and Biblical Themes

To one who said that myths were lies
and therefore worthless, even though "breathed through silver."
—Tolkien, Dedication of "Mythopoeia"

Nancy-Lou Patterson. "The Fisher King." First reproduced on the back cover of *Mythlore* 21.3 (Summer 1996). Further reproduction prohibited.

1. Thesis, Antithesis, and Synthesis in the Space Trilogy

Have no fear; for I have paid your ransom;
I have called you by name and you are my own.

—Isaiah 43.1-2, New English Bible

Patterson identifies the primary elements linking C.S. Lewis's Space Trilogy novels, including the Waste Land, the recurring good and villainous characters, and the use of substitution or "ransoming" to direct the narrative action; and shows how they are emphasized by Lewis's specific and deliberate use of names, particularly that of Ransom and the devil. Patterson highlights Lewis's premise—one easily missed in a superficial reading of the novels—that Thulcandrians lose the things they desire or value the most and shows it to be essential to the overall plot about the relationship of good to evil and to the motivations and actions of the individual characters. Thus Thulcandrians have lost true communication, which still exists on the Malacandra/Mars of Out of the Silent Planet*; and true innocence, which still exists on the Perelandra/Venus of* Perelandra*; but in* That Hideous Strength*, the Thulcandrian Waste Land is redeemed by ransom by Ransom and Merlin and by love. Patterson further argues that Lewis develops the Space Trilogy in conformity to biblical and Arthurian patterns and uses the dynamic and dialectical form of thesis—antithesis—synthesis to resolve the problem of good and evil.*

Patterson also took up the thesis–antithesis–synthesis narrative patterns in Lewis's fiction in her paper "'Always Winter and Never Christmas': Symbols of Time in C.S. Lewis's Chronicles of Narnia" and in "The Holy House of Ungit," both of which may be found in Ransoming the Waste Land Volume II. *She discusses the premise that loss leads to light again in "This Equivocal Being."*

An earlier version of this paper was published as "Thesis, Antithesis, Synthesis: the Interplanetary Trilogy of C.S. Lewis" in CSL: The Bulletin of the New York C.S. Lewis Society *16.8 (June 1985): 1-6. It was revised by Patterson for a proposed anthology of papers about Lewis's fiction.*

The central symbol uniting the novels of C.S. Lewis's Space Trilogy is the Waste Land, the physical world threatened with sterility and desolation through the loss of spiritual integrity, but the heart of the Trilogy is the promise of salvation, of the ransom, beyond hope, of what is most loved and seems most irrevocably lost. Again and again the most ravishing images of purity and beauty, at once supernal and fragile, are painted with unforgettable poignancy, threatened, and, at the last, rescued and renewed. This theme of ransom and rescue, of salvation and retrieval, is posed in classical Christian terms. One must risk one's life if it is to be saved, and that to which one clings most tightly will be the most inevitably lost. The Space Trilogy books are figures for our fondest hopes and most hopeless dreams. True communication between species has been one of humankind's most profound desires: on Malacandra the philologist Ransom learns original language from an array of intelligent species. Never to have lost our innocence, never to have known fear, evil, malice, need, or bereavement: this desire of fallen humankind is fulfilled on Perelandra where Ransom is privileged to intervene in the temptation of the Perelandrian Eve. In *That Hideous Strength* the bureaucratic nightmare that has afflicted not only our complex contemporary society, but also the ancient urbanized societies of the Near East, the Mediterranean, Mesoamerica, the Andes, and the Far East, is resoundingly dismantled, destroyed, and replaced with a celebratory paroxysm of conjugal love.

Malacandra

Out of the Silent Planet begins with a man, aptly named Ransom, who grants a boon to a lady. She is seeking her retarded son, who has been unaccountably delayed, and sends the holidaying don in search of him. Ransom stumbles on the scene of the son's kidnapping in a farmyard despoiled by conversion to a rocket launching pad. Inside the farmhouse, which is strewn with evidence of bachelor housekeeping, he is drugged and rapt away on a spaceship to Mars, drafted into the role of a substitute sacrifice by the ideological scientist Weston and the self-seeking financier Devine. Ransom's chivalrous act of "taking the adventure" has placed him in danger of his life.

When the spaceship lands on Malacandra, its exquisite landscape already bears the blight of human occupation left by Weston and Devine on their previous visit. The Waste Land motif is vividly expressed in a scene littered with packing cases and disfigured by a deserted hut, reminding a latter-day reader of the trash left on the moon by its human visitors in 1969!

How is Ransom to survive in this impossible situation? In the Old Testament a beautiful promise is made, which Lewis no doubt had in mind when he was developing the plot and action of this and later novels:

> Have no fear; for I have paid your ransom;
> I have called you by name and you are my own …
> When you pass through deep waters, I am with you. …
> … walk through fire and you will not be scorched.
> (Isaiah 43.1-2, New English Bible)

Throughout his sojourn on Malacandra, Ransom is under this protection. But he does not know this; thus his acts of bravery, of self-abandonment and self-mastery, are real and hard-won. His name reiterates the gift of the Christian ransomer, whose role is made explicit in the New Testament. Christ, in the Authorized Version, is said to be not only "a ransom for man" (Matthew 20.28), but even "a ransom for all" (I Timothy 2.6). As a ransomed soul, Ransom moves through real dangers and makes real decisions, even while under a real protection. As one thus enabled to act as an *alter Christus*, he offers himself as a ransom first for an idiot boy, but latterly for a whole planet, even a whole solar system.

His ransoming role on Malacandra turns out to be one of interpreter. The fallen characters on this unfallen planet—Weston and Devine—cannot speak directly to its archon, the Oyarsa Malacandra. They do not speak Old Solar, the original language of the solar system. Ransom does, for he has been taught by the native inhabitants of the planet, among whom he has sojourned after fleeing from his two human captors. In his efforts to explain the situation to his benefactors, he finds that the nearest adjective to "bad" is "bent," thus his kidnappers are "'bent' men" (OSP 82; ch. 11). This sojourn is a necessary and perhaps even commanded adventure, even though Ransom becomes momentarily delinquent by lingering too long in that paradisal world, thus causing the death of one of its denizens. Lewis often spoke against the desire to linger, to seek again a pleasure that is given only once or at the will of an outside power. He derived these preoccupations from his own experience, when as a youth he had mistaken his occasional intimations of immortality for ends in themselves. Ransom, when turning aside from his true task, causes death instead of life. When recalled from his necessary sojourn, he is ready to mediate between the two interplanetary imperialists and the leader of their intended victims.

Weston and Devine, speaking a patronizing pidgin, think they have brought Ransom as a human sacrifice to propitiate the natives, perceived by them as ignoble savages to whom nothing is too repulsive. We see that these men are projecting, attributing to the unfallen Malacandrians what are actually traits characteristic of themselves. Naturally the two men see only their own finest traits, and in fact there are elements of nobility in the character of Weston. He does serve what he regards as a high cause—the salvation, as he understands it, of humankind. His fall is thus a spiritual one: Lewis believed that spiritual sins are the worst and that the most evil acts are carried out in an atmosphere of affable camaraderie. The "silence" of Thulcandra, as Ransom learns from the Oyarsa of Malacandra, is due to the "fall" of its Oyarsa. This "Bent One" tried to destroy worlds other than his own; in a great war, he was fought, defeated, and bound to Thulcandra (OSP 153-54; ch. 18).

In *Perelandra*, Weston, seduced by the tempter's spiritual promises, becomes the vehicle that carries the evil archon—the "bent" Oyarsa—of Thulcandra into space so that he can attempt to spread his spiritual infection to Perelandra. There, when resting from his efforts, he occupies himself by tearing frogs to pieces, littering this celestial landscape too with scattered debris, in this case pathetic animal corpses and body parts, and turning it too into something of a wasteland.

Not surprisingly, Lewis's first portrayal of Weston in *Out of the Silent Planet* suggests his greater qualities in an ironic manner:

> "May I ask," said the thicker and taller of the two men, "who the devil you may be and what you are doing here?" His voice had all the qualities which Ransom's had so regrettably lacked. (OSP 8; ch. 1)

The word "devil" is ready on his tongue: Lewis never places such language in the mouths of his characters without reason. In the end, Ransom defeats Weston through hand-to-hand combat in a terrifying scene underground, where the dying man, now a mere shell for the satanic presence which has possessed him, marks his killer with a bite on the heel.

Devine is a smaller person spiritually and hence, in the novels, physically:

> He was nearly as tall as the other, but slender, and apparently the younger of the two, and his voice sounded vaguely familiar to Ransom. (OSP 8; ch. 1)

While Weston becomes the tempter of Tinidril, the unfallen "Eve" of Perelandra, and the antagonist of Ransom, Devine becomes the tempter of Mark Studdock on Thulcandra/Earth. In *That Hideous Strength*, Merlin takes the place of Ransom, just as Ransom had replaced the "idiot boy" (OSP 5; ch. 1) in *Out of the Silent Planet*, in a stately dance of substitutions. As his last act, Merlin forces Devine, now Lord Feverstone, to return to the doomed Edgestow and perish there under the great upheaval of earth which swallows that unfortunate town, the inhabitants of which have all fled.

The two wicked explorers of Malacandra are thus reintroduced, and ultimately dispatched—underground—on Perelandra and Thulcandra respectively. Their characters are used to tie the Trilogy together. They are evil not so much because of their evil actions as because by their intentions they have become the vehicles or agents of diabolical forces. Weston's imperialistic actions on Malacandra are frustrated by Ransom's ironic translations, and his spiritual intentions on Perelandra are ended by Ransom's physical interception. Devine's desires have been merely for wealth and social advancement, in which he has certainly had his reward, but his recruitment of Mark for the N.I.C.E., with the disguised intention of obtaining Mark's wife Jane in order to make use of her visionary gifts, comes close to what would have been a disastrous success. These men—Weston and Devine—have made themselves, each according to his capacities, fit vessels from which may be poured out truly fatal poisons upon all whom they encounter, even as they are themselves destroyed by the processes which they have invited. This is a stern warning delivered by Lewis to his own culture, and it is addressed not only to the various intellectual, scientific, and social sciences of his era, but to all spiritual adventurers who hope, by their "own" powers, to surpass the limits of human capacity and privilege.

Perelandra

Perelandra begins with its ending: in the first chapter, Lewis, a character in his own novel, travels across a blasted heath and an industrial wasteland to supervise the departure of Ransom for Perelandra, and prepares in the second chapter to receive the interplanetary traveler when he returns. It is therefore in chapter two of *Perelandra* that we learn of Ransom's extraordinary change as he steps out of his "coffin" onto the grass of Earth:

> I was silent for a moment, astonished at the form which had risen from that narrow house—almost a new Ransom, glowing with health and rounded with muscle and seemingly ten years younger. In the old days he had been beginning to show a few grey hairs; but now the beard which swept his chest was pure gold. (PER 27; ch. 2)

The language of this passage is the language of resurrection: the "new Ransom" rises from the "narrow house" of the "coffin," "younger" and with a beard of "pure gold." Thus in *Perelandra* the apotheosized Ransom of *That Hideous Strength* is presented to the careful reader. And he is already wounded: "Hello, you've cut your foot," says Lewis's doctor companion, Humphrey (a figure drawn from an actual friend of the author's). We hear no more of the wound until Tor, the Adam of Perelandra, remarks, "There is a red dew coming up out of your foot, like a little spring," and Ransom replies, "Yes [...] it is where the Evil One bit me" (PER 188; ch. 17). The language used here is that of the fountain of blood, a wound inflicted by the power of evil but pouring out life for ransomed souls!

Thulcandra

In *That Hideous Strength* Ransom appears as the wounded survivor of physical and spiritual combat, and takes his place as the spiritual and physical center of resistance to the diabolical infestation of Edgestow by a malignant bureaucracy, the N.I.C.E. A small Company of people and animals assembles itself around him and he lies on his couch, a wounded Fisher King, bearing in his own body the wound which now begins to afflict the land. Thus immobilized, he continues his role as mediator. He mediates between the archons of the unfallen planets of the solar system and Earth, whose defecting archon seeks to destroy it. And he mediates in the marriage relationship of the two central characters of the novel, Jane and Mark Studdock, an all-too-human couple of the twentieth century. Most of the events are seen through the eyes of this pair: Jane meets and experiences the members of the Company, and through her visionary capacities sees the innermost secrets of the N.I.C.E. Mark, seduced by Lord Feverstone (Devine), tries to become a member of the N.I.C.E. His salvation comes through thoughts of Jane, while Jane's love for her husband is quickened by her encounter with the gloriously renewed Ransom, which leads her to an encounter with her Creator, whom she meets, appropriately, in a garden.

Merlin, whose enchanted sleep the N.I.C.E. desires to interrupt in hopes of recruiting him and his power over the chthonic forces of the Earth, chooses instead to join the little Company around Ransom at St. Anne's Manor. At the climax of the novel it is Merlin into whose body the heavenly powers descend. Merlin is consumed by the spiritual forces of which he is the focus, and is, like a denizen of Malacandra, un-made and released at last from the magical prolongation of his earthly life.

The Problem of Good and Evil

Thus far I have explored three sets of motifs by which the novels of the Trilogy are interlocked: the Waste Land theme, the recurring villains, and the complex sequence of substitutions of which the character of Ransom is the central figure. There is another and deeper layer, that of structure, by which the fundamental themes of the novels are embodied and set forth. On this level, the Trilogy follows the precedent of the central Christian narrative, which, as D.W. Ingersoll argues in his profound and enlightening essay "Why a Yellow Ribbon?" (1985), is not a duality but a trinity; that is, "a whole series of mediate oppositions," of which the Holy Trinity is the foremost but not the only example. Ingersoll formulates a variety of these trinities with the mediating element in the middle: most significant here are these:

Male / one flesh / female
Man / Christ / God[1]

Set forth in this manner, the mediating element is flanked by the members of an opposed pair of polarities. The three elements are placed in a synchronous relationship and the result is a stasis, a perfect, eternal triad, which can admit of no terminus. The example of "Male/one flesh/female" explains why Christians regard true marriage as indissoluble. The example of "Man/Christ/God" reiterates Jesus Christ as the same yesterday, today, and forever.

Lewis described his personal image of the relationships between his various written works in one of his letters, one not written for a child, in a manner that invites comparison with the Christian tripartite structure:

> It's fun laying out all my books as a cathedral. Personally, I'd make *Miracles* and the other "treatises" the cathedral school: my children's stories are the real side-chapels, each with its own little altar.[2]

In terms of this exquisite metaphor, the Narnian Chronicles become chapels around the apse, and the central figure of that apse, the high altar, is surmounted by a magnificent triptych: the three volumes of the Space Trilogy. The two wings present the polar pair of the masculine *Out of the Silent Planet* on one side and the feminine *Perelandra* on the other. These wings flank the central and mediating *That Hideous Strength*, with its emphatic emphasis on marriage. Marriage, as Lewis knew, is also used as the image of the relationship between Christ and his Church: this Church itself is identified as the body of Christ such that Christ and his Church are understood to be one.

Malacandra, of the *Out of the Silent Planet* wing of the Space Trilogy triptych, is a bracing, chilly, masculine world of sharp contrasts and poignant comradeships. Its population is small: we meet the primitive, poetic *hrossa*; the wise, ascetic *seroni*; the busy, artistic *pfifltriggi*; and the evanescent, spiritual *eldila*. Its scenery, sketched with delicate but masterful touches, extends from the purple-stemmed, rose-crowned forests and warm blue waters of the Malacandrian valleys to the airless highlands whose petrified forests were blasted by Satan when he and his angels rebelled. It is a very mature world: Lewis told a child in 1957: "I was picturing a world in its extreme old age-like an old man tranquilly and happily proceeding to his end."[3] In rich and voluptuous contrast, Perelandra, of the *Perelandra* wing is, by contrast, a feminine world of melting loveliness, vivid, warm, and provided with a chthonic underworld of equal elaboration. Its population, at least above ground, consists of Tor and Tinidril, the original couple of their green race, together with a multitude of enchanting heraldic animal forms which range from dragons to singing beasts. Golden clouds hang low over endless mild seas on which fecund islands, covered with copious and exquisitely evoked vegetation, undulate and sail. It is a very young world, with a very young population, as Tinidril is fond of saying.

The centerpiece of this triptych, *That Hideous Strength*, mediates between the two wings. Ransom, who has tasted of both worlds and ransomed them both one way or another, from the spoliation of earthly visitors, now returns to Earth to save it too. This time he lies wounded while the Waste Land begins to spread from its center at Belbury out toward Bragdon Wood and Bracton College with a felling of trees, a choking of rivers, and the rumble of bulldozers over rose gardens and lawns. The Waste Land, evoked in each of the preceding novels, becomes the central paradigm. The population of this novel is large. There are eight major villains (one of whom is a villainess) at Belbury. There are twelve companions at St. Anne's Manor, a suggestive number in the context of a Christian novel. The masculine and feminine images of unfallen Mars and Venus appear here in an ancient wood, a venerable college, a large country garden, and a rambling country house, and most particularly in the married couple whose renewed nuptials conclude the novel and the Trilogy. Finally, there are five planetary intelligences whose descent, focused through Merlin, drives back the diabolical outbreak of the N.I.C.E. Our Trilogy triptych might well depict Jane and Mark Studdock holding hands on the central panel, and the Oyéresu of Malacandra and Perelandra flanking them on the side-panels (Lewis depicts them in the visionary conclusion of *Perelandra*), while the multitude of personages invented by Lewis look on from the Martian, Venusian, and Earthly landscapes in which these figures are set.

The metaphor of the triptych is of course only a metaphor, a structural parallel, but it dramatizes the contrast between dialectical structures, such as characterize the Space Trilogy, and the synchronous and static structure which most characterizes visual art. Somebody has written that "painting is frozen poetry," and visual artists often struggle against this gelid restraint, at once the glory and the limitation of their trade. Indeed, a triptych is a kind of kinetic art form: by moving the side panels from the closed to the opened position a sequence can be introduced. On the other hand, sequence is the primary structure of the literary arts. Every such work must be written one word at a time, and even the most rapid reader can take in no more than a fragment at a time, and that sequentially. The adage of the White Queen, to "begin at the beginning, go on till you come to the end, and then stop," still applies. Novels, with their classical construction of conflict and climax, develop in a sequential and diachronic manner.

The Christian narrative structure always expresses itself in a dialectical form; that is to say, the fundamental Christian narrative begins with the Creation as a thesis, goes on to the Fall as antithesis, and concludes with the Passion and Resurrection as a synthesis. A good (the Creation) is marred (by the Fall) and order is restored by means of a new good, which takes account of both thesis and antithesis (in a new Creation even better than the first). This dialectical structure is dynamic, diachronic, and irreversible. A static system cannot resolve the problem of the binary pair of good and evil. As some theologians, including C.S. Lewis, point out, the two elements "good" and "evil" are not true polarities but successive terms: evil is a marred good. Lewis therefore uses the word "bent" to describe the situation and follows biblical precedent by using a tripartite dialectical structure to resolve the problem of good and evil in the Space Trilogy.

Notes

[1] D.W. Ingersoll, "Why a Yellow Ribbon?" *Anthropology and Humanism Quarterly* X (February 1985): 13.

[2] *C.S. Lewis's Letters to Children*, eds. Lyle Dorsett and Marjorie Mead (1985; New York: Touchstone, 1995) 3 (epigraph).

[3] C.S. Lewis, "Letter July 10th, 1957," *C.S. Lewis's Letters to Children* 70.

2. Adventure and Exchange in the Space Trilogy

You must throw yourself in. There is no other way.
—George MacDonald, *The Golden Key*

Patterson shows how C.S. Lewis treats the Arthurian theme of the knightly quest or "taking the adventure" in the Space Trilogy as a form of ransom, or what Charles Williams called "Exchange." In this context, she compares Ransom and Weston in Out of the Silent Planet *and* Perelandra *and Jane and Mark in* That Hideous Strength, *and discusses the Tramp as a substitute for Merlin. This paper also introduces the subject of Lewis's symbolic treatment of food, a subject addressed at greater length in "Miraculous Bread ... Miraculous Wine."*

An earlier version of this paper was published as "Ransoming the Wasteland: Arthurian Themes in C.S. Lewis's Trilogy Part I," including sections subtitled "Introduction" and "Adventure and Exchange," in The Lamp-Post of the Southern California C.S. Lewis Society *8.2-3 (November 1984): 16-26. It was revised by Patterson for a proposed anthology of papers about Lewis's fiction.*

It has become almost a commonplace to attribute "Arthurian" motifs in *That Hideous Strength* to Lewis's friendship with Charles Williams; T.S. Eliot is another frequently cited source; and Lewis's borrowing of Tolkien's "Numenor," which he equated with Atlantis and spelled "Numinor," has also not gone unnoticed. Logres and the Pendragon are found in Williams's *Arthuriad* and in Lewis's Space Trilogy, while the Waste Land appears in Eliot's poem of that name twenty years before Lewis published *That Hideous Strength*, and we know that Lewis heard Tolkien read aloud from *The Lord of the Rings* and perhaps from portions of *The Silmarillion.* In my opinion, the influence of these men on Lewis's work is not in dispute; what is in dispute is the belief that Arthurian elements are peculiar to *That Hideous Strength* and represent intrusions into the planetary mythology of the Trilogy.

John H. Timmerman (1977), for example, writes, "the direct Arthurian impetus to *That Hideous Strength* clearly derives [...] from Lewis's association with Charles Williams's masterful *Taliessin*

Through Logres and *The Region of the Summer Stars,"* and adds, "it is not difficult [...] to recognize these elements which lie beneath the structure of *That Hideous Strength*."[1] This expresses the idea of Lewis's indebtedness in a relatively neutral tone. Margaret Hannay (1981) is more negative: "Lewis's Arthurian scholarship and his historical imagination are evident, but the Arthurian elements fit awkwardly into the story."[2] A more balanced treatment of the relationship of the Arthurian materials to the full Trilogy is given by Charles Moorman in his pioneering study *Arthurian Triptych* (1960): "Hints thrown out in the first two novels that the great battle to rescue Earth was shortly to begin are developed here [in *That Hideous Strength*]."[3] In this third novel of his Trilogy, Lewis "deliberately deemphasizes the silent planet myth" and "introduces another myth to take the place of the cosmic adventure story—the Arthurian myth."[4] Moorman clearly finds Lewis's images vital to the argument he poses in the Trilogy.[5]

Lewis's use of these materials is indeed not only deliberate and meticulously structured, but he also combines perfectly traditional elements, seriously treated, with interpretations that, while entirely consonant with his sources, are richly original. The "Arthurian material" is part of a complete *schema* around which all three novels are organized and hence neither an afterthought nor a case of mismanagement. The problem of its interpretation seems to arise thusly: the "silent-planet myth" is perceived as being original, while the "Arthurian material" is not. In fact, the silent planet motif, which is indeed original, turns on a conceptualization of the cosmos which is not at all original with Lewis, as he himself knew, and which he had addressed in his book, *The Discarded Image*, the first of all works which ought to be read in concert with the Trilogy and the Narnian Chronicles. In all ten of these works the basic supposition of the fantasy is this: what if, in ways heretofore unimaginable, aspects of ancient and medieval mythology were *true*?

Now, I am not saying that Lewis thought or even wished, as we are sometimes told that Tolkien did, that the myths of gods, nymphs, dragons, tree-spirits, and fauns, were true, though we cannot say the same for the specifically Christian concepts, such as angels and devils, and indeed, Adam and Eve, though he was no literalist and (I hope) not a Creationist. Rather, I am saying that Lewis used elements from Western mythology as fantasy motifs because he thought that they could continue to do in his art what they had already done in human history: act as bearers or conduits of truth. He had long since abandoned his boyhood notion that myths are "lies breathed through silver" and acted as if he now thought them truth sung through gold! Tolkien had persuaded him that in Christianity, myth had become fact: the dying gods of ancient myth had been precursors or prefigurations of the real Dying God. This idea is not of course original with Tolkien either; medieval people thought the same. What Lewis has really done in his Trilogy is to marshal the conceptual past of Western culture for his own purposes.

In particular, he borrowed richly from the full Arthurian ethos, which was itself saturated in medieval conceptualizations, and also reached back into the primal past, the root world of shamanism, year-kings, ritual sacrifice, ceremonial combat, and fertility magic. Evidence of this borrowing appears throughout the Trilogy and the name of the central character—Ransom—is a central clue to the meaning of these elegant works. Lewis used two major themes or sets of interrelated themes which are Arthurian in form, but which are also found throughout the history of Western thought. The first of these begins with the concept of knightly quest as the acceptance of a challenge, as "taking the adventure." This element presents a moral challenge to the reader to do likewise. Related to and arising from this is the role of the substitute, the sacrifice, who engages in what Charles Williams called "Exchange," which is what Lewis *really* learned from Williams.

Ransom and Devine

In *Out of the Silent Planet*, Ransom, a "fellow of a Cambridge college" (OSP 2; ch.1) who is on a walking tour, accepts a quest by granting a boon to a lady. She is a farm wife, a version perhaps of the "loathly lady." She lives in "a very small cottage of ugly nineteenth-century brick" (OSP 2; ch. 1) and has a "humbly fretful voice" (OSP 3; ch. 1), but her need is real: her retarded son has gone missing and she fears for his safety. At her request the reluctant Ransom proceeds to a farmhouse further down the road. "The last thing Ransom wanted was an adventure," Lewis writes, portraying his philologist hero as a kind of Bilbo Baggins.

But he breaks through the hedge of the farm—having committed himself by tossing his backpack over the locked gate—and ends up as a substitute for the boy, kidnapped and transported to Mars to become, his captors think, a human sacrifice. Most of the novel describes Ransom's adventures on Malacandra, trying to escape this supposed fate, and in the end he does indeed play the role for which he has actually been invited, that of interpreter or go-between. In so doing he plays the role of mediator, like the Son of God who mediates between fallen humankind and God the Father. In the novel he acts as translator for Weston and Devine, whose attempts to address the supernatural in pidgin are a rich parody, I suppose, of much human prayer; the divine world in this case is the planetary intelligence or *Oyarsa* who is not God but is certainly a god.

Among the intelligent life-forms or *hnau* species invented by Lewis to inhabit Malacandra, speech is the common denominator. The highest of them are the *eldila*, and the *Oyarsa* is a kind of arch-*eldil*. *Eldila* are almost all speech—a speech based on light rather than blood. The identity of the human being is thus established by speech. This element is not fantasy. We regard speech as the fundamental mark of the human. As Ransom is a philologist, he can learn any language and thus communicate with any being who can speak. The concept of Old Solar in the Trilogy implies a fundamental structure or grammar of which all verbal communication is a variation. The doom of nonsense—babble—which provides the climax of *That Hideous Strength*, is the antithesis or reversal of this unifying motif.

After Ransom's return from this adventure, where he learns the language of the three Malacandrian species, he is taken again from Earth, this time willingly, to Venus or Perelandra. Now he mediates between Tinidril the Green Lady, the Eve of her planet, and the Tempter who has broken through the hedge of the Moon's orbit (previously broached, you recall, by Weston and Devine) by riding in Weston's own body. These tasks have a way of escalating. First Ransom is only asked to find an old woman's straying son. Then he mediates between a pair of interplanetary imperialists and a supposed witch-doctor who is really the masculine principle of the solar system, Mars himself. Now he is expected to challenge the fallen archon of his own planet, who is on an interplanetary foray of his own, to despoil the unfallen world of the feminine principle, Venus. Ransom uses rational argument as long as he can, and finally comes—midway in the Trilogy—to wrestling, literally, with the fallen angel inhabiting the shell of Weston's body. This ritual combat, taking the challenge of an adversary, is, like the taking of a quest as a boon to a lady, a ubiquitous motif in the Arthuriad.

The physical combat of Ransom and the Un-man, whose mount, the scientist Weston, is first bridled and broken by Satan, not only takes place on another planet and hence "out of this world," but even there, in the underworld. It is in fact a *bellum intestinum*, a war within, a psychic battle in Ransom's own soul. In Jungian terms the temptation of the Lady is his temptation, for she is his own *anima* or feminine self, and in the end he wrestles with the *Shadow* (an intellectually inclined adversary of his own gender) to win through to wholeness. I am making a distinction here between Weston as a shadow-figure for Ransom and Satan, who is no man's shadow, and who escapes the meshes of Ransom's psyche to do mischief again in the third volume of the Trilogy.

After Ransom descends into the Perelandrian underworld, he ascends again, to a mountaintop. At the end of *Perelandra* the entire Creation is presented to him in his Perelandrian Paradise atop Mount Purgatory. It appears, despite the title of the Great Dance commonly applied to it, in the image of a seamless web. It actually uses the language associated with weaving and pattern formation. This imagery is taken from an essentially feminine mythological motif, the Great Web: Creation as a huge woven pattern of intricacy. Lao Tze said of the Tao that it has wide meshes but nothing is lost. Marie Louise von Franz (1980) speaks of the unconscious (which is an image of the cosmos) as a vast network of interrelated meanings in which eventually everything is related to everything.[6] Moreover Lewis makes the strands of this web represent individuals and their intersecting events, not the other way around. Individuals, persons, even things are real and eternal, he is saying. Events, histories, the so-called "forces" of culture and all other time-factored phenomena are only the concatenations of these everlasting strands or threads in the woven pattern of the web.

After this climactic visionary experience Ransom is returned to earth. There, in *That Hideous Strength*, he appears in apotheosized form as a wounded king who must in his turn be saved by others.

Wounded in the heel during his battle with the Un-man, he has become the maimed Fisher King of Arthurian myth. On earth, the combat against the macrobes or evil *eldila* and their leader, the Bent *Oyarsa* of Thulcandra, is carried out by the combined *Oyéresu* of the solar system through the agency of Merlin, who is broken and "used up" by the experience. Merlin thus takes the place of Ransom, and by Exchange does his work for him. Ransom is translated to Perelandra to be healed, and Merlin dies in a state of sanctity. The novel concludes with a final motif, the ritual marriage, between Mark and Jane. The Waste Land—which we will discuss below—is restored to fertility and the life of the Earth goes on.

Jane and Mark Studdock

The problem presented to Mark (whose name may suggest *Marche* or border) and Jane (Janus or threshold) is to relate correctly to a proffered adventure. Mark must unlearn *cupiditas* and retreat from Belbury, the center of death, to which he has mistakenly gone in response to the invitation offered him by Devine (Lord Feverstone). Jane must, in contrast, accept the invitation offered her by a model young couple, Arthur and Camilla Denniston, and go to St. Anne's, the center of life, there to learn *caritas*. One by one they cross the threshold to their marriage chamber at the end of the novel, and there they are united.

Mark has gone to the N.I.C.E. for the wrong reason—his mere desire to belong; and Jane has resisted St. Anne's for the wrong reason—her desire not to be "taken in." Both have undergone temptations against taking the adventures as Providence presents them, freely in trust with confidence in Grace to support them and without looking for reward. When adventures are taken in this spirit, unlooked for rewards will come and disregarded fears will be mercifully unfulfilled. Lewis had experienced both of these attractions—toward what he called the "inner Ring" and against being "taken in" by God. Mark and Jane are alike drawn from life: Lewis's own life. He once wrote that it was easy to write about sinners because one can use one's self for an example. And the root of sin is traditionally said to be Pride.

In *The Pilgrim's Regress*, Lewis's only allegorical work, in which he described his conversion, *Superbia* (Pride) is presented as an anorexic specter who scrabbles at what appears to be a mirror but "was only the rock itself scraped clear of every speck of dust and fibre of lichen and polished by the continual activity of this famished creature" (PR 182; ch. V). Superbia expresses her attitude in a poem which prefigures the ideas of Filostrato, one of the members of the N.I.C.E:

> I have scraped clean the plateau from the filthy earth,
> Earth the unchaste, the fruitful, the great grand maternal,
> Sprawling creature, lolling at random and supine.
> (PR 182; ch. V) [7]

Filostrato explains to Mark: "The world I look forward to is the world of perfect purity. The clean mind and the clean minerals. What are the things that most offend the dignity of man? Birth and breeding and death" (THS 171; ch. 8). In profound contrast with this repugnance to the natural, Lewis makes *That Hideous Strength* and his Trilogy culminate in a grand celebration of life, fecundity, and flowering materiality. It is a validation not only of nature but also of her Creator which knows no parallel in my reading experience, outside of Genesis.

By separating herself from all that is physical, Pride, too prudish for earthly attachments of any sort, has starved herself almost to death. She will not allow others either to enjoy or obtain any good thing from her, nor will she gain or receive any good thing from them. And since all goodness for any individual comes from Exchange with others, Pride is perforce denied the essentials of both physical and psychic life. This is a matter which goes far beyond male-female relationships and which in human life is literally true.

Now, both Jane and Mark are depicted in *That Hideous Strength*, though not in such extreme terms, as hungering. He hungers for acceptance. She hungers for freedom. He is always trying to get *in*. She is always trying to stay *out*. What they are called upon to do is to offer Exchange to each other, to ransom each other. The need of each can be fulfilled by the other. Each offers the other salvation. She can save him by giving herself as a center for his selfhood; he can rescue her from her solitary self-centeredness by offering her relationship. He longs to give himself, to be taken in. She longs to keep herself, not to be taken in. Lewis has used various sets of images to depict these polar problems. Mark, who has gone bursting into the garden of Jane's cool, prim elegance, is taken to Belbury by Lord Feverstone, who drives at terrible speed through a benign countryside endangered by his male arrogance and contemptuous disregard. We note that Feverstone's demise at the end of the novel follows an episode in which *he* is the helpless passenger in a car madly driven by Merlin down an ancient Roman track across a countryside even more remote and antique! Of course we know that Lewis disapproved of automobiles at least as the ideal form of travel, and preferred walking tours to motor holidays. But as we shall see, he was capable of making a motor vehicle an instrument for good in the right hands.

In contrast with Mark's ride in the fast lane (to use our own parlance) Jane goes to St. Anne's very slowly. She takes the train. This trip is based on at least one experience of Lewis's which he described in a letter to his father, 20 June, 1918:

> On Sunday […] I made my pilgrimage. Even to go to Waterloo was an adventure full of memories, and every station that I passed on the way down seemed to clear away another layer of the time that passed, and bring me back to the old life.[8]

The same sense of return to a fundamental good is given in Jane's train ride. At every stop she sees the charms of the country life; every moment of the ride shows her the goodness of the natural world and its denizens: animals and people alike. Her reluctance, insofar as it represents a kind of virginal hesitation, is no bad thing in itself, or so this passage seems to say. What is recommended for her is not a mad impulsive gesture. But she must at least *take* the train, not remain enclosed in her lonely rooms at home. I do not think Lewis meant to say that she was wrong to resent her empty life in her apartment. He wanted her to come out, to engage in human contact, to bear children, and to participate in the human race.

As for Mark, the N.I.C.E. want *him* entirely because he is married to Jane. He is enticed to come to them so they can get hold of his wife, whose psychic powers they simultaneously fear and wish to use for their own purposes. She is, as it were, the best part of him, and even his enemies know it. What is most pathetic about his situation is that he does *not* know it; all the time he thinks he is being invited at last into the circle whose center he has sought all his life, he is not even wanted for himself, and the center to which he is being sucked is that of absolute annihilation, absorption into the diabolical maw. He is saved in fact by his wife, by his own dawning comprehension of her qualities, by the salvation she has offered to him.

She on the other hand wished to keep *out* of the bodily relationship which calls to her. She has never given to Mark the full welcome he so desperately needs, and which he has pathetically gone to seek elsewhere. She has lacked the Charity to see his pitiful weakness and needfulness. He is not a monster, only a human. In him she can find, now that he has come to himself again, a full appreciation of her own qualities. She cannot know them save in the mirror of his response. She offers resistance to everything—St. Anne's Manor, Mark, even her own body, which she wishes to deny. Her problem is truly a form of *Superbia*—Pride: this is why Ransom prescribes humility for her, note: not humiliation. Mark for his part has been too humble. He has to be driven to resist and to draw back.

The invitations to salvation both Mark and Jane receive are partly embodied in a most unlikely symbol, a picnic. And each is physically rescued by a motor ride to a place near St. Anne's Manor, freely offered to them by strangers. The picnics and other simple meals, shared with compassionate strangers and offered along the wayside, are figures of the Eucharist, certainly another manifestation of the Exchange. The Last Supper was a celebration of the Passover, which is precisely a commemoration of the meal taken in haste by the children of Israel as they prepared to make their escape from slavery, offered salvation by the sacrifice of blood in anticipation of the ultimate ransom of the whole world through the Blood of one of their descendants.

The invitation to join the Company at St. Anne's Manor is offered to Jane by the Dennistons at a site beyond Sandown, on "a rather foggy day in a wood in autumn" (THS 111; ch. 5). They tell her that they like "Weather," all kinds of weather. This is a taste Lewis shared and approved. He often wrote to Arthur Greeves to describe his delight in similar scenes, and the autumnal theme, he tells us in *Surprised by Joy*, brought him one of his earliest pleasures, as it appeared in Beatrix Potter's *Squirrel Nutkin*. In this idyllic setting, the ideal young couple, Arthur and Camilla, share a picnic with Jane—"sandwiches and a little flask of sherry, and finally hot coffee and cigarettes"—enjoyed in a "little grassy bay with a fir thicket on one side and a group of beeches on the other," with "a rich autumnal smell all round them" (THS 111; ch. 5). This offer of a safe harbor at St. Anne's is refused by Jane, who is frightened by the idea of giving herself, without knowing why, to a group of people she barely knows. She cannot (and in good sense perhaps should not) take the adventure.

It is much later that she finally goes, altogether willingly, to stay. By this time she has plenty of reason to do so, but the actual means of her going is a goodwill act of rescue by a stranger. She is found alone and exhausted where her torturers have left her in an Edgestow sidestreet after the riot. A car stops, a man asks "Are you all right?" and a woman inquires "Were you hurt in the riot?" To Jane, "It seemed so long [...] since she had heard kind, or even sane, voices that she felt like crying. The unknown couple made her sit in the car and gave her brandy and after that sandwiches" (THS 156; ch. 7). And they drive her toward Birmingham to her stop near St. Anne's. She is saved, you will note, in the context of a second picnic. How did people seeking to escape a riot come to have brandy and sandwiches in their car? Possibly they are passersby, perhaps "day trippers" who, from a surrounding England not yet poisoned by the N.I.C.E., have stopped at Edgestow to see where the riot took place. In any event they act the part of angels met unawares, offering literal salvation to the distraught and victimized Jane.

A similar rescue is proffered to Mark. First of all, he enters his first true inner circle in company with the Tramp, a comic figure who is the substitute for Merlin whom the N.I.C.E. actually receives in place of the real object of their plot to gain control of Bragdon Wood. In wakening, Merlin has met the Tramp in his hut in the countryside and taken away his clothing and horse. The naked vagrant is brought by N.I.C.E. agents to Belbury where their superiors anxiously try to communicate with their captive guest, who wisely remains silent in their presence. Mark is set to guard him, between bouts of the psychically dissociating initiation rites under the tutelage of Frost. Alone with the Tramp, Mark partakes of "toasted cheese" (THS 309; ch. 14) and other homely delicacies, in a "sort of continual picnic which the two shared" (THS 310; ch. 14). Along with his visions of Jane as a haven of natural refreshment, these child-like meals become a symbol of the normal and the straight when compared with the grotesque puerilities of ritual desensitization which Mark is alternately forced to undergo.

Mark, Merlin, and the Tramp

We may meditate for a moment on the role of this Tramp. In the first place he is a perfectly free man. Unlike Mark he has neither need nor desire to be included in a group. It is not that the Tramp has no need of other people: as an itinerant he is constantly dependent upon handouts. He accepts whatever happens to him with equanimity and even satisfaction. He is, in a sense, his own center, at home wherever he finds himself. Mark could learn from him! And indeed, Lewis suggests that Mark experiences his first truly disinterested friendship with this extremely common but essentially innocent man. The Tramp, perhaps a fool or trickster figure, substitutes for Merlin until the real Merlin arrives and is able to have his will with the N.I.C.E. Merlin controls the Tramp, causing him to speak as he chooses, and then translating the words he has put into his puppet's mouth. In this way, in his guise of a Basque priest, he is able to say to the N.I.C.E. exactly what he chooses. Basque is a language traditionally held to be without relationship to any other known language and the Basques are famous in popular folklore for their magicians. In Merlin, magus and priest are combined. The Tramp, used as Merlin's ventriloquist's dummy, comes to no harm and makes his escape in the end, humble and riding upon a donkey!

Mark, for his part, is given final rescue from the vicinity of Belbury in the same manner as Jane, by the aid of a stranger, in his case a lorry-driver who stops on the snow-covered road to offer him a lift: "A big lorry, looking black and warm in that landscape, overtook him." Like the unnamed couple, the lorry driver is headed for Birmingham, and drops Mark off near St. Anne's, "beside a little country hotel" (THS 357; ch. 17). Here Mark bathes, eats "a capital breakfast," and later takes "a boiled egg with his tea." These humble traveler's meals taken in a hotel are parallels for Jane's autumnal picnics. After this day of rest and contemplation, Mark walks through the melting snow toward St. Anne's to meet his wife.

Clearly the Arthurian motifs of accepted adventure and sacrificial exchange are not foisted on the Trilogy novels; they are integral to the motivations and actions of the major characters, notably Ransom and Weston, and Mark and Jane, who define the plot structure of the entire series. But this is only the first of the constellated Arthurian motifs at work in the Space Trilogy. The second, which provides the context for the first, is the Waste Land. With this, we may turn to the most commonly cited source of Lewis's Arthurian motifs, T.S. Eliot, and to the second part of my discussion of this subject, "Waste Land and Fisher King in the Space Trilogy."

Notes

[1] John H. Timmerman, "Logos and Britain: the Dialectic of C.S. Lewis's *That Hideous Strength*," *The Bulletin of the New York C. S. Lewis Society* 9.9 (November, 1977): 2. A similar point is made by Gunnar Urang, *Shadows of Heaven* (Philadelphia, PA: Pilgrim Press, 1971): "The concluding work of the Trilogy, *That Hideous Strength*, seems to have been influenced by the fictional techniques of Charles Williams" (21) and "The influence of Charles Williams may be discerned in more than just the 'novelistic' handling of setting and character. It is also reflected in the Arthurian materials which Lewis integrates with his own 'silent planet' myth by way of the dichotomy of Britain and Logres and the figure of Merlin" (24). Needless to say, I do not agree with Urang's interpretation.

[2] Margaret Patterson Hannay, *C. S. Lewis* (New York: Frederick Ungar, 1981) 105. Hannay further suggests that Merlin is tenuously related to the "interplanetary myth" by his "association with neutral spirits or *eldila*" (105). If I read this phrase correctly, this is a mistake: there are no neutral *eldila*. *Eldila* are angels, and for Lewis's angels the battle lines are clearly drawn, as in *Paradise Lost*. The neutral spirits in *That Hideous Strength* are nature spirits like those depicted in loving detail in the Narnian Chronicles. Lewis wrote in his last great scholarly work, *English Literature in the Sixteenth Century* (London: Oxford UP, 1954), of the "high magic" of that era, that it was not the "faerie" magic which was "part of the furniture of Romance" to the medieval reader, but a magic that "might be going on in the next street" (8). It was centered upon "the belief that there are many potent spirits besides the angels and devils of Christianity" (9). He explained: "The Arabs say that men can rise above their corporeal and their sensitive powers and in that state receive into themselves 'the perfection of heaven and of the diuine intelligences'" (9). These megalomaniac ideas were based upon a special conception of humanity which was not Christian: "He could become a saint but

Notes

not an angel: a swinish man but not an animal" (12), but which rather aimed at "the performance of 'all things possible'" (14). These are the dreams of Weston and the N.I.C.E., which are ironically realized only by Merlin, who perishes in the process.

[3] Charles Moorman, *Arthurian Triptych* (Berkeley, CA: University of California Press, 1960) 111.

[4] Moorman 112-13.

[5] Moorman 102-26.

[6] Marie-Louise von Franz, *On Divination and Synchronicity* (Toronto, ON: Inner-City Books, 1980) 61-64.

[7] This source was suggested by Judith Brown, "Pilgrimage from Deep Space," *Mythlore* 4.3 (March 1977): 13-15.

[8] *The Letters of C.S. Lewis*, ed. W.H. Lewis (London: Geoffrey Bles, 1966) 42.

3. Waste Land and Fisher King in the Space Trilogy

> [T]he Director had at last come to a certain conclusion. Dimble and he and the Dennistons shared between them a knowledge of Arthurian Britain which orthodox scholarship will probably not reach for some centuries.
>
> ——C.S. Lewis, *That Hideous Strength*

Patterson examines the Waste Land and Fisher King motifs in the Space Trilogy. While acknowledging the similarities between T.S. Eliot's "The Waste Land" and C.S. Lewis's Space Trilogy, as well as the likelihood that both authors studied Jessie Weston's From Ritual to Romance *(1920), she argues that Lewis's development of Arthurian themes was uniquely his own. She discusses the Trilogy's numerous Arthurian elements: the wounding and passivity of the Fisher King, the activity of the Fisher King's agent for good, the role of the sister, the failure of the knight (Perceval/Jane) to ask questions, the Waste Land, and others; and shows how Lewis integrated some images of personal significance to him, such as lorries, bachelor-style housekeeping, academic life, and pollution, into these contexts.*

An earlier version of this paper was published as "Ransoming the Wasteland: Arthurian Themes in C.S. Lewis's Trilogy Part II," with the subsection titled "Waste Land and Fisher King," in The Lamp-Post of the Southern California C.S. Lewis Society *8.4 (December 1985): 3-15. It was revised by Patterson for a proposed anthology of papers about Lewis's fiction.*

In a recent study devoted entirely to the influence of Eliot's poem *The Waste Land* on twentieth-century British novelists, Fred D. Crawford (1982) remarks of Lewis that "he would be unlikely to concede the extent to which his novels resembled *The Waste Land*."[1] Indeed, Crawford adds that "His disapproval of Eliot's attitudes suggest that resemblances between *The Waste Land* and Lewis's novels may result from common sources, such as Jessie Weston's *From Ritual to Romance* rather than from direct borrowing on Lewis's part."[2] And he admits that Lewis's Mr. Fisher-King—Ransom in *That Hideous Strength*—differs "significantly from Eliot's," as in fact he does.

Crawford cites two convincing coincidences of language, both of which are two-word phrases, as evidence of the influence of Eliot's poem on the Space Trilogy. First, in line 22 of *The Waste Land*, Eliot uses the phrase "A heap of broken images." In *Perelandra* the worshipping Ransom cries out at the feet of Tor and Tinidril that "I have lived all my life among shadows and broken images" (PER 176; ch. 17). Second, Eliot writes of the polluted Thames:

> The river bears no empty bottles, sandwich papers,
> Silk handkerchiefs, cardboard boxes, cigarette ends
> Or other testimony of summer nights. (lines 177-179)

In *That Hideous Strength* Lewis describes the ruined river Wynd at Edgestow in much the same language: "sailed on by endless fleets of empty tins, sheets of paper, cigarette ends and fragments of wood" (THS 118; ch. 6). A similar passage is found by Crawford in *All Hallows' Eve* by Charles Williams, in which the Thames appears to the dead Lester as "dirty and messy. Twigs, bits of paper and wood, cards, old boxes drifted in it."[3] At this point one thinks of Williams's exasperated remark quoted from *Collected Plays* by one of his commentators: "Mr. Eliot has made choruses a little difficult. I know all about the Greeks, but they do not prevent one being told one is copying Mr. Eliot."[4] As we shall see below, Lewis was quite capable of putting "cigarette ends" where he liked, from what must have been his own experience.

The Waste Land Myth

In fact, the theme of the Waste Land can be traced throughout the Trilogy. First, however, it will be useful to set forth the Waste Land myth. The Waste Land lies waste—desert, dry, infertile—because its king, the "Fisher King," has been wounded. This motif appears, naturally, in Eliot's poem, in lines 424-426 in the Section entitled "What the Thunder Said":

> I sat upon the shore
> Fishing, with the arid plain behind me
> Shall I at least set my lands in order?

In his footnotes Eliot refers his readers to "Miss Weston's book," which is, as Crawford has told us, *From Ritual to Romance* (1920). In it she says that in Chretien de Troyes "the name [Fisher King] is connected with his partiality for fishing, an obviously *post hoc* addition."[5] For Weston, the Fisher King is a cult figure from an ancient mystery, surviving past the period when his meaning could be understood. In his version, Chretien wrote this:

> The Maiden said, "Fair sir, a king he is, well do I dare say it to you; but he was wounded and maimed without fail in a battle so that he has not been able since to help himself, for he was wounded with a javelin through both his hips. He is still so in anguish because of it that he cannot mount a horse; but when he wishes to disport himself or undertake any amusement he has himself put in a boat and goes fishing with a hook; for this he is called the Fisher King."[6]

The young knight to whom the maiden gives this reply has asked his questions too late: she remonstrates with him for his former silence: "how unfortunate you were then when you did not ask all this, for you would have bettered so much the good king who is maimed, for he would have wholly regained his limbs and could hold his land, and so great good would come of it."[7]

In this first "purely literary" treatment of the theme, the king is wounded through the thighs—that is, in the generative organs—and still retains the link to the fertility of his land which marks him as an embodiment of ritual kingship. John Darrah (1914; 1981), a student of archaic motifs in the Arthuriad, writes that "The reality which underlies many well-known inhabitants of Camelot [...] is not to be found in the meagre chronicles of the Dark Ages but in an oral tradition which has remembered the actions of cult figures from the heyday of the native paganism—a paganism already in decline by the time of the Roman occupation."[8] A central feature of this ancient paganism is the Sacred King. Quoting Freud, who was following Frazer, Darrah tells us that "Kings, crushed by the burden of their holiness, became incapable of exercising their power over real things and had to leave this to inferior but executive persons who were willing to renounce the honors of royal dignity."[9] Charles Moorman (1960) has pointed this out very clearly: "Merlin becomes the active form of good in the novel [*That Hideous Strength*], Mr. Fisher-King the passive. It is Merlin who goes to Belbury, confounds the scientists with the curse of Babel, releases the beasts, and prepares the destruction."[10]

Writing of Merlin, Darrah says "the cult belief was that Merlin represented lightning and that his spouse was the goddess of the sacred grove and spring."[11] This spouse is presumably the enchantress who confined him to his long sleep near a well—Merlin's Well—in a wood—Bragdon Wood; these are the sacred grove and spring in *That Hideous Strength.* As to Merlin's relation to lightning, read Jane's eighth and final dream:

> It looked as if he was on fire … I don't mean burning, you know, but light—all sorts of lights in the most curious colours shooting out of him and rushing up and down him. (THS 359; ch. 17)

Darrah states that the "matter of Britain" describes "the Late Neolithic/Beaker Accommodation," that is, the invasions of the Beaker People, which strongly influenced all Britain from their cult center in Wessex,[12] when Indo-European language was introduced along with a male sky deity (one who wields lightning) where heretofore there had been "a mother goddess."[13]

Darrah's description of the Waste Land situation is most useful:

> As a result of a wound to the Fisher King the land of Logres fell under an enchantment, so that neither peas nor wheat were sown, no children were born, marriages did not take place, plants and trees did not turn green and birds and animals did not reproduce, "so long as the king was maimed."[14]

This is a good depiction of conditions in Edgestow as described in *That Hideous Strength*, where it is first autumn and then winter; where Jane and Mark are deliberately childless; and where, when Ransom is taken away to be healed, the animals and birds are mating and Mark and Jane meet for the first time in true Charity.

Lewis's description of the Mr. Fisher-King in *That Hideous Strength* reads as follows:

> He had a married sister in India, a Mrs Fisher-King. She has just died and left him a large fortune on condition that he took the name. She was a remarkable woman in her way; a friend of the great native Christian mystic whom you may have heard of—the Sura. And that's the point. The Sura had reason to be-

> lieve [...] that a great danger was hanging over the human race. (THS 112; ch. 5)

The Sura has disappeared, and "Mrs Fisher-King more or less handed over the problem to her brother, to our chief [...] He was to collect a company round him to watch for this danger, and to strike when it came" (THS 112; ch. 5). We have heard of this sister before, in *Out oj the Silent Planet*, when Ransom innocently tells Devine and Weston that he has little family to be concerned should he disappear: "Only a married sister in India" (OSP 14; ch. 2). The distinguishing features of the new holder of her name is that "He is a great traveller but now an invalid. He got a wound in his foot, on his last journey, which won't heal" (THS 112; ch. 5).

It has been noted by various commentators that Mr. Fisher-King, whom we know to be Ransom and now also Pendragon of Logres, is wounded not in the thighs like the Fisher-King of Chrétien, but in the foot. This element is related to the Celtic aspect of the Arthurian tradition, for the figure of Bran in Welsh literature is wounded in the foot, in fact, in the heel.[15] Ellen Rawson (1983) also notes that Jane is like the Knight Perceval in confronting the Fisher King. As we have seen above, the knight fails to ask his questions on this occasion. Perhaps there is also a question which Jane has failed to ask: "How, Sir, does your name fit your role?" This matter has in fact been dismissed by Robert Plank (1972): after stating that "'fisher-king' is specifically the title of the master of the knights of the Holy Grail in the medieval legend," he finds it odd that Jane, a graduate student of English, working on a doctoral thesis on Donne, does not recognize the meaning of the words "Mr. Fisher-King." It is necessary to the plot that she must not understand its meaning when she hears it at first. Indeed, Plank thinks this is one of Lewis's jokes.[16] Richard West (1972), taking Lewis more seriously, notes that like "le Riche Roi Pecheur," Ransom is now rich. His sister, Mrs. Fisher-King, has left him her fortune on the promise that he take her name.[17] We recall that she had lived in India as a disciple of the Sura: Sarras was the name of the land to which the Grail was taken in Malory's *Morte d'Arthur*, and this place is sometimes held to have been located in India. Nevertheless, in another article, Robert Plank (1969), who admits that he (like Jane) missed the Fisher-King allusion, jeers "Sister in India indeed!"[18]

In fact, both India and sister are related to the Fisher-King tradition. In the first place, the motif of the "great native Christian mystic" reminds us that Jessie Weston stated in her classic study—almost certainly read by Lewis—that "[t]he first Avatar of Vishnu the Creator is a Fish. At the great feast in honour of this god, held on the twelfth day of the first month of the Indian year, Vishnu is represented under the form of a golden Fish, and addressed in the following terms: 'As Thou, O God, in the form of a fish saved the Vedas who were in the Underworld, save me also.'"[19] Furthermore the fish-god who descended to aid his followers reminds us of Jane's fifth dream, of a bearded man "divinely young [...] golden and strong and warm coming with a mighty earth-shaking tread down into that black place" (THS 133; ch. 6). In this dream she sees a prefiguration of Ransom as Fisher King, playing a role played by Jesus in the Harrowing of Hell when he descended into Hell to rescue the souls imprisoned there.

The relation of the fish motif to the acronym for Christ, ICHTHYS, and to Christ's disciples as fishers of men has not, of course, been lost on Lewis's commentators, nor has the wounded heel failed to be related to the wounding of the serpent's head by the "seed of woman" in Genesis 3.15. So much is certainly intended by Lewis. But what *has* been missed heretofore is his use of the motif of the sister, which has its doublet in the character of Myrtle, Mark's twin sister, in *That Hideous Strength*. Myrtle was the center of that circle into which Mark never felt himself able to be admitted, though Jane saw her as totally devoted to her brother, and indeed, as a potential rival for his affections.

In Malory we read of "How Sir Percival's sister bled a dish full of blood for to heal a lady, wherefore she died."[20] Her body is sent in a boat to "the City of Sarras," defined as "that spiritual place."[21] She sacrifices herself in exchange for the other, offering her example to her brother. The place to which she goes is clearly an "otherwhere," not perfectly part of the physical universe. In this context, an association with India is a similar tactic to an association with Perelandra as an image of "a spiritual place," and Lewis uses the image of the "sister in India" in this manner. She is the source of Ransom's identity. She has given him her name and her fortune. His original name—Ransom—has been related to his role as sacrifice. His new name—

Mr. Fisher-King—derived from his sister, is thus also to be interpreted as related to sacrifice. Although the Fisher King in Malory is healed by the Knight, Ransom/Mr. Fisher-King cannot be healed on earth. He must be translated (like the sister in Malory) to another world. Ransom is taken away to Aphallon (Avalon) on Perelandra as the Space Trilogy, of which he is central, comes to an end.

Lewis's "Silent Planet"

The Waste Land situation of the Space Trilogy is the work of the Bent One, the *Oyarsa* of Thulcandra or Earth. This theme is introduced in the first chapter of *Out of the Silent Planet.* In that novel, we learn, much later, that Thulcandra is silent to the rest of the solar system because of the Fall of the rebellious *eldila*: Earth is in a kind of solar quarantine while the other denizens of the Field of Arbol circle in their seven heavens and communicate in melodious discourse. Like the quiet on the western front in World War I this silence is—or its maker wishes it to be—the silence of death. The progress of death against life leads to the creation of a Waste Land where once there was florescence and fecundity. The garden of Earth has been made into a waste place of brambles, a desert place where wild animals howl and monsters prowl at their will. Or such will be the case when the Bent One's companions, the macrobes who infest Tellus, have totally had their way. This quarantine has been occasioned by a previous foray in which the Archon of Earth reached out to blast Malacandra, turning his upper regions into airless deserts of cold and confining life to the canals or *handramits* of the lowlands. This is the "silent planet myth" which is thus itself predicated on a Waste Land theme.

When the Waste Land first appears in *Out of the Silent Planet* it is presented as a significant feature of an earthly experience. Exactly as in *That Hideous Strength*, it is rationalized as a part of the plot. Ransom has broached the hedge of the farmhouse in carrying out his boon to the farmwife. Here is what he sees:

> It was lighter on the drive than it had been under the trees and he had no difficulty in making out a large stone house divided from him by a width of untidy and neglected lawn. The drive branched into two a little way ahead of him—the right-hand path leading in a gentle sweep to the front door, while the left ran straight ahead, doubtless to the back premises of the

> house. He noticed that this path was churned up into deep ruts—now full of water—as if it were used to carrying a traffic of heavy lorries. (OSP 5; ch. 1)

The "right-hand path" is associated with the house, which appears at first glance to suggest welcome, comfort, and rest, while the "left" path suggests an intrusive destination, in accord with the negative associations of left-handedness. The "ruts," caused by the "traffic" of "lorries," are presented as an act of spoliation, on what ought to be a tranquil rural scene. We know that Lewis disliked the traffic of motor cars. He had also experienced the miserable, mud-filled trenches of the First World War in France. Throughout *That Hideous Strength* lorries or trucks are associated with violence and destruction, with the exception of what might be called "the good lorryman" who gives Mark a lift out of Edgestow to a country hotel on the way to St. Anne's Manor, thereby saving not only his sanity but his life.

When Ransom succeeds in entering the house, he finds that it has been turned into a Waste Land too:

> The room into which he had been shown revealed a strange mixture of luxury and squalor. The windows were shuttered and curtainless, the floor was uncarpeted and strewn with packing cases, shavings, newspapers and books, and the wall-paper showed the stains left by the pictures and furniture of the previous occupants. (OSP 12; ch. 2)

Out of the Silent Planet is dedicated "To my brother W.H.L., a life-long critic of the Space-and-Time story," and Warren Lewis, in his Memoir included in his collection of *The Letters of C.S. Lewis*, speaks feelingly of the pain caused to his brother by frequent moves during his years with Mrs. Moore, only cured when they settled at the Kilns. Here we have a vivid description of the empty or abandoned house as Waste Land.

But there is more to come in a quote that Crawford missed:

> On the other hand, the only two armchairs were of the costliest type, and in the litter which covered the tables, cigars, oyster shells and empty champagne bottles jostled with tins of condensed milk and opened sardine tins, with cheap crockery, broken bread, teacups a quarter full of tea and cigarette ends. (OSP 12; ch. 2)

Who are the occupants of these unattractive quarters, the consumers of this, to use my Eucharistic image, black mass or anti-picnic? Who can afford cigars, oysters, champagne, but will also buy condensed milk, bread, tea and cigarettes? The scientist Weston and his cohort Devine. We see them in the dishevelment of their daily lives, in its "squalor," which is "strewn" full of "litter" and afflicted with "stains," both "jostled" and "cheap." Surely Lewis wrote here from some personal observation of bachelor behavior: the cigarette ends in the teacups speak volumes. This disagreeable tableau is surely a dress-rehearsal for the ruined banquet at Belbury.

These are the men who take Ransom away to Mars. There, his first sight, after his vision and comprehension simultaneously clear, is of his kidnappers' hut, built on Malacandra during a previous visit. The Waste Land has been spread to outer space in this sequence, and I invite you to think about the litter left on the Moon by your astronauts as you contemplate this passage:

> They behaved as one might have expected. They walked into the hut, let down the slats which served for windows, sniffed the close air, expressed surprise that they had left it so dirty, and presently re-emerged. (OSP 47; ch. 7)

"Littered" again: it is almost a treatise against pollution! And we are witnessing the would-be pollution of a planet by potential exploiters who intend, and indeed proceed, to kill the inhabitants in order to take their remnant of the planet from them. They will, if they can, finish the work of destruction which their mentor (of whom they are as yet unconscious) has in some remote age begun. At the end of *Out of the Silent Planet* they are sent home, thwarted but unrepentant, to reappear in the two subsequent novels.

I do not wish to make Lewis more calculating than he was: I know that he interrupted himself at the completion of the first part of his Trilogy with a false start, toying with the idea of following his space travel with a time travel novel, the torso of which we know as *The Dark Tower*, Like the "Lefay Fragment" which was the false dawn of *The Magician's Nephew*, this profoundly dystopic work contains the germ of *That Hideous Strength*, presented in an otherworld, together with some of the characters (in germ) of the later novel, including the resident skeptic MacPhee and Arthur Denniston. Abandoning this effort, Lewis wrote the second volume, *Perelandra*, which many readers regard as the most perfect portion of the trilogy.

This book begins, like the first, on Earth. This time the pollution is, first, more broadly spread across the landscape, and second, boldly hinted as being diabolical in origin. Lewis, the narrator who will report Ransom's account of his Venusian adventure, is on his way to meet his fellow don in a country house, and suffers a psychic attack intended to prevent him from reaching his goal.

> I was now coming to the end of the heath and going down a small hill, with a copse on my left and some apparently deserted industrial buildings on my right. (PER 12; ch. 1)

Naturally he traverses a "heath"—one thinks of the blasted heath where the witches of *Macbeth* foregathered. And of course he sees "deserted industrial buildings," surely the most derelict sort of ruin! Industrial architecture, the "dark, satanic mills" of Blake, have been the target of romantic disapproval for nearly two centuries. And now the narrator Lewis begins to doubt his sanity.

> Wasn't there some mental disease in which quite ordinary objects looked to the patient unbelievably ominous? ... looked, in fact, just as that abandoned factory looks to me now? Great bulbous shapes of cement, strange brickwork bogeys, glowered at me over dry scrubby grass pock-marked with grey pools and intersected with the remains of a light railway. (PER 12; ch. 1)

Here abandonment and monstrosity are linked in powerful evocation of certain surrealistic works of art with which readers in the early 1940s were familiar. But the scene is realistic enough, for the obsolescence of industrial structures is by now a deep part of the Western experience.

Even a small domestic structure appears malevolent to the disturbed consciousness of the narrator Lewis:

> There was a little empty house by the side of the road, with most of the windows boarded up and one staring like the eye of a dead fish. (PER 13; ch. 1)

Here we have not only the Waste Land but fish! These passages, in the first chapter of *Perelandra* both chime with the beginning of the previous novel and provide a background for events which occur much later in the heart of *Perelandra*, where the subject is not merely a diabolically produced psychic attack, but total devilish infestation.

In Chapter Nine, Weston, who comes to Perelandra not only as a devotee but as a host of the Bent Archon of his native planet, calls his Master fully into himself. Satan is now present in the Un-man, the occupied corpse which has become a mere vehicle for the ultimate malevolence. Here is the first physical evidence of that terrible presence: "It was a damaged animal," Lewis writes, "so damaged that the frog could not leap" (PER 93; ch. 9). Ransom's response comes from deep sources in Lewis's childhood experience and has special significance for present day victims of industrial pollution: "It was like the first spasm of a well-remembered pain warning a man who had thought he was cured that his family have deceived him and he is dying after all" (PER 94; ch. 9).

To Ransom, "the thing was an intolerable obscenity which afflicted him with shame." But worse is to come: "a trail of mutilated frogs lay along the edge of the island." And after twenty-one frogs, he finds Weston:

> He did not look like a sick man: but he looked very like a dead one. The face which he raised from torturing the frog had that terrible power which the face of a corpse sometimes has of simply rebuffing every conceivable human attitude one can have towards it. (PER 95; ch. 9)

Weston here is as much a ruin as the industrial buildings which open the same novel. And who will dare to say that *That Hideous Strength* is not built upon this symbolic foundation?

In the third novel, we are back on Earth again. This time, instead of traveling away to other planets, we remain in Thulcandra. One of the great Tellurian myths, that of the Waste Land, only visible on Mars and Venus where the wanton Weston has carried its evidence with him, now reveals itself in its native place. At first we receive only a hint, but what a hint! Mark has been carried by Lord Feverstone (the Dick Devine of *Out of the Silent Planet*) to Belbury, headquarters of the N.I.C.E. There he sees buildings with a division of traits like those of the farmhouse used by Weston and Devine at the beginning of the Trilogy:

> a florid Edwardian mansion which had been built for a millionaire who admired Versailles. At the sides, it seemed to have sprouted a widespread outgrowth of newer cement buildings […] (THS 49; ch. 2)

The mixture of "luxury and squalor" is indeed familiar. The cement excrescence, which sprouts after the same fashion as the industrial ruin which produced "great bulbous shapes of cement" in *Perelandra*, is called the "Blood Transfusion Office." Blood suggests life, even if only spilled life, but the transfusion here is false and dead, for the head within is the remnant of a corpse, serving like Weston's body as a vehicle for Satan.

After this hint we are led into the narrative. After several chapters of academic intrigue in which the dons of Bracton College are bored, tricked, and bullied into agreeing to the sale of Bragdon Wood, the first notice of the results of this apparently minor action are revealed, not in the Wood itself, but in the front yard of the Dimbles, a couple who are close to Jane and, in the end, to Mark. Mrs. Dimble tells the story, and the first clue-word is "lorry," just as it was in *Out of the Silent Planet*:

> The first thing we saw […] this morning was a lorry on the drive with its back wheels in the middle of a rose bed, unloading a small army of what looked like criminals, with picks and spades. Right in our own garden! (THS 72; ch. 4)

We have already been told that "The Dimbles' garden was famous" (THS 27; ch. 1). The gardens of the English are their sanctuaries. In the cities one sees miniscule plots at the front doorstep between sidewalk and foundation. Gardens have become a central preoccupation of their symbolism (as in many other cultures). The violation of a rose bed reminds us that the plucking of a rose is an image of the sexual act in the *Roman de la Rose*. This beautiful little household garden has been, in a word, raped. And it is a gang-rape: a lorry-full of criminals have committed this act. And what is more,

> the big beech that you used to be so fond of had been cut down, and all the plum trees. (THS 73; ch. 4)

If the first outrage is rape, the second is emasculation, the cutting off of rooted life; indeed, the murder of trees. Other commentators have been reminded of Tolkien's lament for a beautiful tree of his acquaintance whose only offence had been that it was alive. Lewis used the murdered woodland as a motif again in *The Last Battle*. The beech tree and the plum trees: do you know the beech? A magnificent tall tree with a straight grey trunk and large leaves that turn bronze and copper in the fall—and the plum has a springtime blossoming of praeter-natural whiteness and purity. These outrages are followed by the awful event of which they are harbingers: the destruction of Bragdon Wood.

We have been prepared for this act of sylvacide by a long description of the Wood as recalled by the narrator "Lewis." This passage is full of symbolic overtones. The first result of its acquisition of the N.I.C.E. is

> the conversion of an ancient woodland into an inferno of mud and noise and steel and concrete [...] (THS 88; ch. 4)

This "ancient woodland" was so old that the narrator Lewis has told us "a sixteenth-century Warden of the College [used] to say that 'we know not by the ancientest report of any Britain without Bragdon" (THS 19; ch. 1). Now it is "an inferno." Exactly. It will become a focal point of diabolic activity, a hell on earth.

The first of its featured elements is "mud," as in the path "churned up into deep ruts—now full of water" in *Out of the Silent Planet* and the land "pock-marked with grey pools" in the novel *Perelandra*. Before its sale, Bragdon Wood had a surface of "quiet turf." Now, we read of "noise"—Screwtape calls his homeland "the Kingdom of Noise" (ST 135; Ltr. 31), as you may recall. Lastly, we read of steel and concrete, two obviously related materials associated with modem industrial architecture. In *Perelandra* we have already read of "great bulbous shapes of cement" (PER 12; ch. 1) and we know that Belbury itself has "sprouted [...] cement buildings" (THS 49; ch. 2). As to steel, the head of the department of the N.I.C.E. which Mark particularly wishes to join is named Steele! And his initiator into the Institute's arcanest mysteries wears on his cold face a pair of pince-nez which reflect the light like a mirror, showing to Jane the evil within. This motif was prefigured by *Superbia* in *The Pilgrim's Regress* when she that "I have made my soul (once filthy) a hard, pure, bright mirror of steel" (PR 182; ch. V).

The Dimble's garden and Bragdon Wood are but two of the anachronisms which are to be—or are planned to be—liquidated by the N.I.C.E. A full list would require a greater ransacking of *That Hideous Strength* than a short study will bear, but a selected list can be suggested. It would include Bill Hingest, the one true scientist we meet at Belbury, who dies trying to get away from it; Mary Prescott, reported to have been raped and murdered; Cure Hardy, the sturdy heart of England in the form of a country village; Mark's job at Bracton; the east window of that college's most beautiful room; and in the end the entire town of Edgestow, suburbs, abbey, public houses, woodland, train stations, colleges, river, and all.

The last motif on this list, the river, is given an especially long description in *That Hideous Strength*. It presents us with a before and an after, in a single paragraph, and is the set piece of comparisons with Eliot's *The Waste Land*.

> [A]ll beyond the Wynd was now an abomination. [...] The river itself which had once been brownish green and amber and smooth-skinned silver, tugging at the reeds and playing with the red roots, now flowed opaque, thick with mud, sailed on by endless fleets of empty tins, sheets of paper, cigarette ends and fragments of wood, sometimes varied by rainbow patches of oil. (THS 118; ch. 6)

The description of the river Wynd in its purity most surely owes something to the river in Kenneth Grahame's *The Wind in the Willows* (1908)—"this sleek, sinuous, full-bodied animal, chasing and chuckling, gripping things with a gurgle and leaving them with a laugh."[22] And its terminal illness, choked nearly to death by pollution, is a catalogue of modern society's ills: "empty tins," used to enclose artificially preserved and flavored and colored food and drink; "fragments of paper," presumably produced by the endless bureaucratic paper chase; "cigarette ends," as we have seen from their presence in the tea cups of *Out of the Silent Planet*; "fragments of wood," presumably from the murdered woodland; and "rainbow patches of oil," an ironic but natural inversion of the rainbows seen in the sky.

According to the plan of the N.I.C.E., "There was to be no river in Edgestow." Of course: now it will really be a waste, that is to say a dry and desertous land. And indeed, "Twenty-four hours later the N.I.C.E. boarded over the doomed Wynd and converted the terrace into a dump." This terrace was a narrow strip of the riverbank beyond Bracton College and its acquisition and destruction marks the doom, indeed, not only of Bracton but of all Edgestow. Its conversion to a "dump" seems to me especially terrible and apt. Hell is a kind of dump or junkyard of the human spirit and its guardian Cerberus is the meanest of all junkyard dogs. In modern life the dump is the true Waste Land, a foretaste of what our planet may become. If Lewis had added poisonous industrial and radioactive waste, his picture would have been complete.

But Lewis is not finished with the Waste Land at this point in his narrative. Having established it in physical form, he now turns to its spiritual significance. Above I have noted a symbolic element related to Frost of the N.I.C.E. He has a co-equal in his evil organization, the Deputy Director Wither, who bears a Waste Land Name. Wither's spirit as well as his simulacrum has a way of wandering, "through formless and lightless worlds, wastelands and lumber rooms of the universe" (THS 185; ch. 9). In Britain a "lumber room" is a storeroom. The word "lumber" in this context is derived from "Lombard," and the original meaning is of a pawnshop or storeroom of pawned objects. To Lewis it meant a pile of discarded objects in a seldom-used space.

Now we come to the use of this motif, so carefully prepared, both in the personal lives of the novel's main characters—Jane and Mark Studdock—and second in the life of humankind, who are the only literally real characters in this "fairytale for grownups." Mark, in meditating upon his life, uses Lewis's images of dump, wasteland, and lumber room: he sees at last that he has "chosen the dust and broken bottles, the heap of old tin cans, the dry and choking places" (THS 244; ch. 11).[23] The dry and choking places are the places of the Waste Land, so central to the theme that they are almost immediately reiterated. Four times, Mark recalls, there had been "invasions of his life by something from beyond the dry and choking places."

The first was Myrtle, Mark's twin sister, whom he had turned into a "flower [...] planted among the tin cans" (THS 244; ch. 11). Second was Pearson, a schoolmate, whom he had "thrown away" like a piece of unwanted trash. Third was Denniston, whom he had known as an undergraduate and had abandoned and even eventually displaced by receiving in his place the appointment he has held at Bracton College. Fourth and finally was Jane, his wife, whom he had—he now sees—hoped to keep entirely to himself as "a secret hostess." In contrast to these Waste Land images we have his vivid apprehension of his wife's true qualities: "She seemed to him […] to have in herself deep wells and knee-deep meadows of happiness, rivers of freshness, enchanted gardens of leisure" (THS 244; ch. 11). This is a veritable catalogue of the repeated motifs that are a litany of feminine images of wholeness: for "deep wells," read Merlin's Well; for "knee-deep meadows," read the quiet turf of Bragdon Wood: for "rivers of freshness," read the River Wynd; for "enchanted gardens," read the garden of St. Anne's Manor.

After he has escaped from Belbury, Mark is reluctant to go to Jane. He remembers "when she first crossed the dry and dusty world which his mind inhabited she had been like a spring shower," bringing renewal to the waste places of his spirit. But up till now his marriage had not given him "either power or title to appropriate that freshness" (THS 358; ch. 17). Only at the end of the novel, will he meet her and she him at the beginning of their true marriage, and she will freely welcome him to the place of refreshment, light, and peace, there to see herself in the mirror of his grateful eyes.

The richly sensual passages with which the novel concludes are prefigurations of a restored world of prelapsarian perfection. Our world is not yet quite like that. In a conversation between Merlin and Ransom, Lewis provides a view of the goal of the N.I.C.E., a goal toward which its late twentieth-century counterparts still point their ambitions as I write:

> However far you went you would find the machines, the crowded cities, the empty thrones, the false writings, the barren beds: men maddened with false promises and soured with true miseries, worshipping the iron works of their own hands, cut off from Earth their mother and from the Father in Heaven. (THS 290; ch. 13)

In this awful vision, "The shadow of one dark wing is over all Tellus." This situation is not, surely, to be permanent, The devastations of Belbury's demise, the mixture of luxury and squalor, of blood and banquet, that demolishes the N.I.C.E., and the avalanche of earth that swallows up Edgestow, are followed by a restoration of both Eros and Charity at St. Anne's Manor.

Notes

[1] Fred D. Crawford, *Mixing Memory and Desire: The Waste Land and British Novels* (University Park, PA: Pennsylvania State University, 1982) 97.

[2] Crawford 99.

[3] Quoted from Charles Williams, *All Hallows' Eve* in Crawford 94.

[4] Quoted from Charles Williams, *Collected Plays* in Agnes Sibley, *Charles Williams* (Boston, MA: Twayne Publishers, 1982) 18.

[5] Jessie L. Weston, *From Ritual to Romance* (1920; Garden City, NY: Doubleday Anchor Books, 1957) 116.

[6] Chretien de Troyes, *The Story of the Grail*, trans. Robert White Linker (Chapel Hill, NC: University of North Carolina Press, 1952) 75.

[7] Chretien de Troyes, *The Story of the Grail* 76.

[8] John Darrah, *The Real Camelot: Paganism and the Arthurian Romances* (1914; London: Thames and Hudson, 1981) 7.

[9] Quoted from Freud's chapter "The Taboo upon Rulers" in *Totem and Taboo* (1955) by Darrah.

[10] Charles Moorman, *Arthurian Triptych* (Berkeley, CA: University of California Press, 1960) 121.

[11] Darrah 134.

[12] Darrah 143

[13] Darrah 144.

[14] Darrah 54.

[15] Ellen Rawson, "The Fisher King in That Hideous Strength," *Mythlore* 9.4 (Winter 1983): 31.

[16] Robert Plank, et al, "*That Hideous Strength*," *The Bulletin of the New York C.S. Lewis Society* 3.7 (May 1972): 8; Plank quotes from his essay "Some Psychological Aspects of Lewis's Trilogy," *Shadows of Imagination, The Fantasies of C.S. Lewis, J.R.R. Tolkien, and Charles Williams*, ed. Mark R. Hillegas (Carbondale, IL: Southern Illinois UP, 1969) 28.

[17] Richard West, et al, "*That Hideous Strength*," *The Bulletin of the New York C.S. Lewis Society* 3.7 (May 1972): 8.

Notes

[18] Robert Plank, "Some Psychological Aspects of Lewis's Trilogy," *Shadows of Imagination, The Fantasies of C.S. Lewis, J.R.R. Tolkien, and Charles Williams* (Carbondale, IL: Southern Illinois UP, 1969) 28.

[19] Weston 126.

[20] Sir Thomas Malory, *Le Morte D'Arthur*, vol. II (Harmondsworth, UK: Penguin, 1969) bk XVII, ch. 11, 348.

[21] Malory, *Le Morte D'Arthur* vol. II, bk. XVII, ch. 11, 349.

[22] Kenneth Grahame, *The Wind in the Willows* (1908; New York: Ariel Books, 1980) 2.

[23] A detailed analysis of these passages in the context of Mark's conversion is given by Jeannette Hume Lutton, "A Passion of Patience: Ransom in the Waste Land." [Editor's note: Patterson's reference here appears to be to a conference version or draft of the paper later published as "Wasteland Myth in C.S. Lewis's *That Hideous Strength*," *Forms of the Fantastic*, ed. Jan Hokenson and Howard D. Pearce (Westport, CT: Greenwood, 1986) 69-86.)

4. "Miraculous Bread ... Miraculous Wine"

> Anything which renders to a certain extent the intangible tangible is certainly not useless and not a sin.
>
> ——Albert Lewis, 6 May 1831[1]

Patterson analyzes Lewis's use of food symbolism as it relates to the Bible and the Eucharist and to Lewis's own statements on the subject, which range from his comments about his personal food preferences, to his study of ancient myths, and most importantly here, to his observations on Christian practice and perception of the sacrament as "objective efficacy." She examines the related symbolism in Lewis's eleven fiction novels, considering not only the salvational aspects of food rituals but also other associations, such as the "anti-mass" in That Hideous Strength *and the contrasts between familiar and exotic foods in* The Horse and His Boy. *The section "Bread and Wine" deals primarily with the Space Trilogy; "The Breakfast of the Lamb" is about the Chronicles of Narnia with frequent comparisons to the Space Trilogy; and "Honey Cakes and Red Wine" addresses* Till We Have Faces. *The Conclusion is an extended discussion of Lewis's ways of making food symbolism, notably the fruits associated with the Tree of Life and the Tree of Knowledge and the various aspects of the Eucharistic pattern, part of the overall structure of his novels.*

"Miraculous Bread" expands the discussion of food symbolism introduced in "Adventure and Exchange" and may be read as a companion piece to "Banquet at Belbury." The salvational aspect of time associated with Father Christmas is also treated in "'Always Winter and Never Christmas': Symbols of Time in C.S. Lewis's Chronicles of Narnia" available in Ransoming the Waste Land Volume II.

This paper was previously published in Mythlore *22.2 (Summer 1998): 28-46. It has been added to the original roster of papers that Patterson included in this section of her proposed anthology about Lewis's fiction because of its relevance to the theme of ransoming or salvation.*

In her remarkable study of formal behavior at the dinner table, Margaret Visser (1992) states that the Eucharist "is undoubtedly the most significance-charged dinner ritual ever devised."[2] "In this ritual," she says, "Christ, who for believers is both God and human, enters not only into the minds but the bodies of the congregation; the people present at the table eat God. No animals and no new death are needed, no bridges required; God enters directly. The Eucharist is the ritual perpetuation of the incarnational relationship with humankind that God initiated through Christ."[3] In his eleven fantasy novels, C.S. Lewis's use of eucharistic motifs in particular, and of symbolic food in general, unfolds as the reader moves from the Space Trilogy to the seven Chronicles of Narnia, to the single tale of Glome, *Till We Have Faces*.

The Trilogy begins with scattered allusions to the Eucharist in *Out of the Silent Planet*, proceeds to paradisal parallels in *Perelandra*, and culminates in the complex indications of good and evil—from the salvational picnic to the banquet from hell in Belbury, to the explicit repast of the Pendragon at St. Anne's, who only takes bread and wine—in *That Hideous Strength*. The rich vocabulary of allusions developed in the Trilogy recurs in the Narnian Chronicles, with eucharistic imagery expressed in a variety of fairy tale forms, especially in the first four novels. In *The Lion, the Witch and the Wardrobe*, the self-sacrifice of Aslan sets forth the fundamental paradigm of which all Eucharists are in some way an embodiment. *Prince Caspian* reiterates the sacrifice motif with its reference to the Stone Table, but reaches its climax, in terms of eucharistic symbolism, in the revels of Bacchus with its miraculous wine. *The Voyage of the Dawn Treader*, with its Magician who, like Ransom, takes only bread and wine, also includes the motifs of Aslan's Table and the Breakfast of the Lamb. In *The Silver Chair*, the water of life and the propriety of eating body and blood are explored. In *The Horse and His Boy*, the contrast between sensuality and simplicity—certainly an issue in terms of religious practice—is sharply drawn. In *The Magician's Nephew*, the idea of salvational fruit—the apple of life—emerges as a major motif, as Digory visits the newly made Garden of Narnia, plucks a silver apple, and takes it to his mother, who is healed. Finally, in *The Last Battle*, the incapacity of the unbeliever to recognize the sacred in the ordinary—food and wine perceived as "hay" and "dirty water"—is presented, and there is a glimpse in Aslan's Country of the miraculous apple tree.

Standing alone, *Till We Have Faces* presents imagery of body and blood, bread and wine, in the context of religious worship traced to its origins. At the climax of this last novel, Lewis turns again to the meaning of a sacrament as "the outward and visible sign of an inward and spiritual grace" (as the *Book of Common Prayer* has it), when Psyche attempts to offer her sister divine food and sacred drink, and Orual blindly rejects this gift of life, refusing to ask, as she is later to say, "for an apple from the tree that fruited the day the world was made." All of Lewis's novels are eucatastrophic, however, and in the end, Orual meets, face to face, the God who has accepted Psyche's sacrifice. For the author of these eleven novels, it is this God whom the Christian meets in the Bread and the Wine.

Objective Efficacy

Most scholars attempting to discern what C.S. Lewis taught and believed about Holy Communion have resorted to the short list of statements he made about it in his letters, diaries, biographical books, and apologetic writings. A review of the majority of these is interesting and informative, but by no means conclusive. Nevertheless, any study of his teachings on this subject must begin by examining his recorded remarks. Lewis did not particularly care for formal dinners. Several touching early comments of his about food and drink indicate his pleasure in simple repasts; on 27 May 1922, he wrote in his diary that he, his house companion Mrs. Moore, and her daughter Maureen had eaten a "Supper of boiled eggs, plums and cream in the garden. We all decided that it was the only meal for this weather";[4] and on 29 June 1922, he recorded that "at supper I drank cowslip wine for the very first time in my life. It is a real wine, green in colour, bittersweet, as warming as good sherry."[5]

A decade later, on 17 January 1932, he wrote to his brother Warren about his approach to the Eucharist: "I see (or think I see) [...] a sense in which *all* wine is the blood of God—or all *matter*, even, the body of God, that I stumble at the apparently special sense in which this is claimed for the Host when consecrated. George MacDonald observes that the good man should aim at reaching the state of mind in which all meals are sacraments. Now that is the sort of thing I understand."[6] At the end of his life, Lewis expressed a similar openness regarding the role of the eucharistic elements: "I do not know and can't imagine what the disciples understood Our Lord to mean when, His body still unbroken and His blood unshed, He handed them the bread and wine, saying *they* were His body and blood."[7]

Between 1942 and 1964 he wrote from time to time regarding the Eucharist, but all his comments have this same import—that he finds it impossible to say precisely what the Eucharist is, does, and signifies, but that it is essential to the Christian life. Part of this reticence—I do not believe he found the matter incomprehensible—probably comes from the wide range of eucharistic practices and styles characteristic of Anglicanism. Lewis made Screwtape gloat that "The real fun is working up hatred between those who *say* 'Mass' and those who *say* 'holy communion' when neither party could possibly state the difference between, say, Hooker's doctrine and Thomas Aquinas,' in any form which would hold water for five minutes" (ST 77; Ltr. 16) and made him add that without the ceaseless labor of himself and his fellow demons, "the variety of usage within the Church of England might have become a positive hotbed of charity and humility" (ST 78; Ltr. 16).

In 1947, Lewis published his most explicit meditation on the Eucharist. "Miraculous wine will intoxicate," he wrote; "miraculous bread will be digested. The divine art of miracle is not an art of suspending the pattern to which events conform but of folding new events into that pattern."[8] In talking about bread and wine, which are the two elements of the Eucharist, he discusses what he calls "Miracles of *Fertility*,"[9] stating that "The earliest of these was the conversion of water into wine at the wedding at Cana. This miracle proclaims that the God of all wine is present. The vine is one of the blessings sent by Jahweh: He is the reality behind the false god Bacchus. Every year, as part of the natural order, God makes wine."[10] Again, he discusses bread: "Other miracles that fall in this class are the two instances of miraculous feeding. They invoke the multiplication of a little bread and a little fish into much bread and much fish."[11] In her superb commentary on these passages, Janine Goffar (1995) states that "The Sacraments show the value of matter and the senses in God's scheme,"[12] thus echoing and validating my epigraph from Albert Lewis, the father of C.S. Lewis, above.

Furthermore, Lewis notes that "once in the desert Satan tempted [Jesus] to make bread of stones. He refused the suggestion

[…] Little bread into much bread is quite a different matter. Every year God makes a little corn [grain] into much corn: the seed is sown and there is an increase."[13] Finally, Lewis reiterates his evocation of an ancient divinity; "Here, at the feeding of the five thousand, is He whom we have ignorantly worshipped: the *real* Corn-King who will die once and rise once at Jerusalem during the office of Pontius Pilate."[14] Cana and the Feeding of the Five Thousand are both used by Christians as symbolic prefigurations of Holy Communion; also relevant to this discussion is Bacchus, whose appearance in *Prince Caspian* is a significant element in Lewis's developing treatment of the theme. His argument in these passages was extremely close to his heart; he had been converted (that is, literally, turned back) to the religion of his father and mother through his renewed understanding that these ancient myths—of Bacchus and the Corn-King—were prefigurations of Christ.

In *Transposition* Lewis wrote that "Put in its most general terms our problem is that of the obvious continuity between things which are admittedly natural and things which, it is claimed, are spiritual; the reappearance in what professes to be our supernatural life of all the same old elements which make up our natural life and (it would seem) of no others."[15] He told a correspondent in 1950 that "The only rite which we know to have been initiated by Our Lord Himself is the Holy Communion ('Do this in remembrance of me.' 'If ye do not eat the flesh of the Son of Man and drink His blood, ye have no life in you.') This is an order and must be obeyed."[16] About a decade after making this absolute affirmation, he wrote in *A Grief Observed* that "Tomorrow morning a priest will give me a little, round, thin, cold, tasteless wafer. Is it a disadvantage—is it not in some ways an advantage—that it can't pretend the least resemblance to that with which it unites me?"[17]

The posthumously published *Letters to Malcolm*, from which I have already quoted, contains Lewis's longest series of meditations upon the Eucharist, albeit disguised in a fictitious voice. We need not, for instance, believe that he is quite precise when he says "You may ask me why I've never written anything about the Holy Communion. For the very simple reason that I am not good enough at Theology."[18] In this book, in fact, he makes the statement upon which, taking Janine Goffar as my guide, I base my argument in this essay: "Actually my ideas about the sacrament would probably be called 'magical' by a good many modern theologians."[19] Readers who wonder what "magic" means in this context can recall that he explained, "I should define magic in this sense as 'objective efficacy which cannot be further analysed.'"[20]

Where analysis is impossible, imagination—the use of imagery and symbolism—comes to the rescue. What defies reason becomes comprehensible in art, as in religious practice. To "take" and "eat" is to understand, at a level far deeper and hence more lasting and more profound than any form of ratiocination. Therefore, an examination of the eleven fantasy novels of C.S. Lewis may well yield still more information about his understanding of the Eucharist than is available in his letters or apologetic works. My analysis will include not only positive but negative symbols, not only, that is, the Mass, but the anti-Mass. Further, I will consider not only the elements of the Eucharist—bread and wine—in particular, but food in general, as it figures in the fantasies.

It seems to me clear that the matter of the Holy Communion—including the literal sense of "matter" as physical material—lies at the heart of Lewis's understanding of reality, as it must for any member of a liturgy-centered branch of Christianity. His statements about the Eucharist are exactly synchronized with his belief—one of his most important and least mentioned beliefs—in the sacrality of the physical creation. He says in one place that all ground is holy and every bush a Burning Bush, and in another place that aside from the Blessed Sacrament, our neighbor is the holiest object ever presented to our gaze. These were not by him hyperbolic statements but declarations of fact. To Lewis, the physical act of eating food that is concrete and actual is as important as the spiritual act of eating food that is sacred, and vice versa. When Christ says "This is my Body," Lewis takes him to mean it, and to mean it in both the above senses.

Bread and Wine

The use of eucharistic symbolism begins with a bang in *Out of the Silent Planet* with a dystopic parody of the eucharistic elements. The despicable Devine describes Weston (who will in the second novel of the Space Trilogy become possessed by the Devil) in these terms: "You know. The great physicist. Has Einstein on toast and drinks a pint of Schrödinger's blood for breakfast" (OSP 9; ch. 1). The body of Einstein is presented on toasted bread, and the blood of Schrödinger provides the wine, in this infernal parody. Most mentions of food in the early phase of this novel, as Devine and Weston take the kidnapped Ransom from Earth to Mars, suggest disgust and malaise. When his captors have eaten, Ransom sees "cigars, oyster shells and empty champagne bottles jostled with tins of condensed milk and opened sardine-tins, with cheap crockery, broken bread, teacups full of tea and cigarette ends" (OSP 12; ch. 2). The "jostled" wine and the "broken bread"—both, surely, eucharistic references—are cast aside here among the remnants of a perfectly agreeable picnic, presented as garbage.

During the trip to Mars food and drink become obstacles: "all he [Ransom] ever remembered of his first meal in the spaceship was the tyranny of heat and light" (OSP 30; ch. 4); "Food was snatched as best they could, and drinking presented great difficulties" (OSP 44; ch. 6). Readers sixty years later will note, from observing the flight of American, Canadian, and Russian astronauts, that Lewis has not exaggerated the inconveniences, including cramped space and unpleasant food, that apply to this form of travel.

Soon after arriving on Mars, Ransom escapes his captors and the mood changes from infernal to paradisal, as he meets his first Martian, or, as we learn to call it, Malacandrian, a *hross*, who offers him a cup; "Whatever had been added to the water was plainly alcoholic; he had never enjoyed a drink so much" (OSP 67; ch. 9). This combination of water, and, as it were, wine, constitutes Ransom's first communion with a Malacandrian. After a series of adventures among the three intelligent life forms of Malacandra, he reaches Meldilorn, the island of the *eldila*, where he is to meet the *Oyarsa* of Malacandra, a being for whom "Light is instead of blood" (OSP 151; ch. 18). When Ransom meets this extraordinary being (whether a planetary divinity or an archangel is intended is never completely clarified) he explains that he has been sent as a human sacrifice by men who "think the *eldil* drinks blood" (OSP 154; ch. 18). This combination of sacrifice and the drinking of blood resonates with eucharistic symbolism, where "This is my Body" and "This is my Blood" are applied to bread and wine.

The conclusion of the novel, in which the three space travelers, now bound for Earth, endure "the agony of thirst" (OSP 189; ch. 21), contains an allusion to the utterance of Christ on the Cross: "I thirst" (John 19.38). Ransom in particular thirsts "for grass and meat and beer and tea and the human voice," like a dead person remembering the joys of life (OSP 191; ch. 21). When, finally, he lands safely and alive, he enters a pub, and asks for his favorite Tellurian (earthly) drink: "A pint of bitter, please" (OSP 194; ch. 21), and is finally able to assuage his thirst. In these passages, food and drink are presented as the daily pleasures of both Earth (Tellus) and Mars (Malacandra); the sacramental import of these natural and lawful pleasures will appear again and again in the fantasies that follow this beginning.

The second novel of the Trilogy, *Perelandra*, begins this characteristic inclusion of food references when Lewis, after struggling through demonic assault on his way to meet Ransom, finds a note telling him that there are "Eatables in [the] larder" (PER 15; ch. 1). Ransom, as promised, returns to Earth from a second trip, this time to Venus (Perelandra). "I somehow don't feel like bacon or eggs," he tells Lewis, and asks, "No fruit? […] Bread or porridge or something?" (PER 27; ch. 2). On this feminine planet he has lost his taste for meat, and prefers fruit and grain. As his experiences are described, we learn that "To say that [the smells in the forest] made him feel hungry and thirsty would be misleading; almost, they created a new kind of hunger and thirst, a longing that seemed to flow over the body into the soul and which was a heaven to feel" (PER 37; ch. 3). Hunger and thirst, satisfied in the Eucharist by sacramental bread and wine, are in fact held to feed soul and body, and as these motifs end *Out of the Silent Planet*, so here they introduce *Perelandra.*

The association of food and Paradise, a female Paradise not unrelated to the joys provided by the womb and the nursing breast, are emphasized in this novel about the feminine planet, Venus. On Perelandra, Ransom encounters "great globes of yellow fruit" and finds that "It was like the discovery of a totally new genus of pleasures […] out of all reckoning, beyond all covenant" (PER 37; ch. 3). The word "covenant" is defined "In biblical translations and allusions," according to *The New Shorter Oxford English Dictionary*, as "an engagement entered into by God with a person, nation, etc.," specifically, in

Christian terms, as "the engagement with God that is entered into by believers at their baptism." On Perelandra, the fruit-globes shower the naked (newborn) Ransom in a new kind of baptism with liquid that is not only cleansing but also delicious to drink, welcoming him into a new covenant which is "beyond all covenant."

Bread as well as drink is provided on Perelandra: Ransom picks "oval green berries" of which the "flesh was dryish and bread-like," offering "the specific pleasure of plain food—the delight of munching and being nourished" (PER 44; ch. 4). Readers of Lewis's letters, diaries, and biographical works will recall that to call food "plain" is to pronounce it good.

At last, after a paradisal period during which he meets the Green Lady, the Eve of Perelandra, he encounters his old adversary, Dr. Weston. His interest is in the local animals, particularly the hapless Perelandrian frogs, whom he enjoys torturing and killing. As prefigured by this very pronounced difference in taste, the central portion of the book consists of a battle to the death between the two men, or rather, between the man Ransom and the Un-Man Weston, who has invited Satan to inhabit his body. The survivor, Ransom, is afterwards fed "a grape-like fruit" (the sort of fruit, one may imagine, from which eucharistic wine might be made) for an incalculable time. Healed as well as nourished, he recovers.

The third novel of this trilogy, *That Hideous Strength*, takes place on Earth (Thulcandra). Here the eucharistic references and parallels become more numerous, being apparent in daily meals, picnics, bread and wine, an evil banquet and a good dinner (in both the moral and the aesthetic sense). On the very first page of *That Hideous Strength*, we read of "breakfast [...] lunch and tea" (THS 11; ch. 1) in the context of Jane Studdock's housewifely life. This dailiness is, in Lewis's view, a positive good, and Jane is, albeit reluctantly, the heroine of the novel. When we read later that "During lunch Dr. Dimble talked about the Arthurian legend," we rightly sense the same aura of goodness about him. Chapter Two, significantly titled "Dinner with the Sub-Warden," is a harbinger of evil to come. It begins with "James Busby [...] Lord Feverstone and Mark [...] all drinking sherry before dining with Curry" (THS 32; ch. 2), at Bracton College where Mark is employed. Lord Feverstone is the egregious Devine of *Out of the Silent Planet*; as Weston died in Perelandra, so Feverstone/Devine will die in *That Hideous Strength*. The dinner progresses successfully (in its own terms): "The good wine was beginning to do its good office" (THS 35; ch. 2). The narrator Lewis says, ironically, in an allusion to the remark of the diners at Cana: "Thou hast kept the good wine till now" (John 2.10), and adds of Busby that "wine and candlelight loosened his tongue" (THS 35; ch. 2).

When Mark is, in fact, enticed from his college to Belbury, partly as a result of the above dinner, he goes to lunch feeling vulnerable and insecure, not certain what he will find at this Edwardian mansion which houses the diabolically-sponsored N.I.C.E. "Although the food and the drinks were excellent, it was a relief to Mark when people began getting up from table" (THS 54; ch. 3). People who dine at Belbury do not enjoy themselves. At dinner with Fairy Hardcastle, the head of the N.I.C.E. Secret Police, Mark's meal is spoiled by her "disagreeable" stories and "esoteric" inside information about police life. The word "esoteric" has a double meaning here, including references not only to what is hidden in general, but also in the occult sense of forbidden knowledge. William Hingist, the good scientist, goes from this table to his death, a guest betrayed, in a clear allusion to Jesus, who went from the Last Supper to betrayal by his fellow diner Judas.

The gradual descent of Mark is recorded in a series of references to meals: "It [a report he has been assigned to write] took them the rest of the day, so that Cosser and he came in to dinner late and without dressing. This gave Mark a most agreeable sensation. And he enjoyed the meal too" (THS 84; ch. 4). Next day he visits a village slated for destruction by the N.I.C.E., and in "The Two Bells," a country pub, he sees "Two labourers [...] sitting with earthenware mugs at their elbows, munching very thick sandwiches" (THS 86; ch. 4), as is only right and proper. Mark's companion finds this scene undesirable and unsanitary, but Mark (not yet lost) thinks "it had its pleasant side" (THS 86; ch. 4). So far, his participation in the Belbury regime consists of boyish rebellion (against dressing for dinner) and a commendable incapacity to disapprove of humble food.

Returning the narrative to the little college, Lewis reports, "That evening the Fellows of Bracton sat in Common Room over their wine and dessert" (THS 88; ch. 4). The college, like the country town, is slated for extinction; outside, the N.I.C.E.'s heavy machinery destroys the adjacent woodland. Among the diners are Curry and Feverstone; as the latter "was pouring himself out another glass of wine," the "famous east window" of the room is struck by a machine and destroyed (THS 91; ch. 4). The light from the east is the rising sun, a major symbol of Christ. Mark, meanwhile, is still at Belbury, unaware that his former place of employment is being destroyed. All unknowing, he "ate his breakfast by artificial light"—everything at Belbury aims toward artificiality—and takes "his second cup of tea" (THS 100-101; ch. 5), just as Feverstone had taken another glass of wine. Attentive readers will remark the allusion here to the wonder-fruit on Perelandra where one drink was enough.

At the same time, Camilla and Arthur Denniston, another couple who, like Jane and Mark, have been associated with Bracton College (Arthur had failed to get the job that was won by Mark), attempt to recruit Jane to the Company at St. Anne's Manor, the novel's opposite to Belbury. They do this in the context of a picnic, one of several picnics which, as I have argued elsewhere, "are figures of the Eucharist."[21] I would associate the picnics in this novel with the Seder, the meal prescribed by God which features unleavened bread because the Israelites came "out of the land of Egypt in haste" (Exodus 12.8), and with the wilderness situation in which God fed the traveling Israelites with manna, "bread from heaven" (Exodus 16.4). This particularly significant picnic scene finds Camilla, Arthur, and Jane "in a sort of little grassy bay with a fir thicket on one side and a group of beeches on the other"—a setting of the kind Lewis most loved and praised—and "there was some unstrapping of baskets, and then sandwiches and a little flask of sherry" (THS 111; ch. 5). This is a picnic at which the food consists of bread and wine, the exact elements of the Eucharist.

We get a glimpse of the Bracton College chapel (where the Eucharist would have been celebrated) on the occasion of the murdered Hingist's funeral. Outside, fog presses everywhere and the noise of heavy machinery persists. "Inside the chapel the candles burned with straight flames, each flame the centre of a globe of greasy luminosity, and cast almost no light" (THS 122; ch. 6). In an Anglican chapel, all ceremonies from Holy Communion to Morning Prayer to Evening Prayer to the funeral service, are accompanied by lighted candles, signifying in yet another way—by the natural substance of bees' wax—the presence of God. Here, in these circumstances, this light is very dim.

Mark finally crosses the boundary into illegality in "the library," where "Never had the fire seemed to burn more brightly nor the smell of drinks to be more attractive" (THS 125; ch. 6). The word "seemed" in the sense of falseness is operative here, for in this context he learns that the N.I.C.E. has created its own riots, and he allows himself to be persuaded to write false press releases to deal with the matter. Miss Hardcastle closes her persuasions thus: "Time for one more drink and you and I'd better go upstairs and begin. We'll get them to give us devilled bones and coffee at three" (THS 127; ch. 6). Again, this false behavior will take place after "one more drink," which, as we have seen, signals danger.

The reference to "devilled" food here, an intentional one, I am sure, has caused some puzzlement among North American readers. The *New Shorter Oxford English Dictionary* explains that in British usage, one sense of "devil" is "a highly seasoned, peppery dish of broiled or fried meat; peppery season for meat," and, again, "to coat with peppery condiments." Margaret Fulton (1984), another British source, describes it as "a hot, spicy mixture used to coat food for grilling."[22] The term "devilled bones" thus refers to the British equivalent or parallel to the North American dish, barbecued ribs, which are indeed bones. This meal, shared with a murderess, offers a perfect anti-Mass. The body will be comprised of highly seasoned bones, and the blood will be replaced by coffee, drunk, one has no doubt, without sugar or cream.

Lewis says of Mark in this bizarre context that "all the while the child inside him whispered how splendid and how triumphantly grown up it was to be sitting like this, so full of alcohol and yet not drunk" (THS 132; ch. 6), anticipating what is actually a perfectly innocent (although perhaps not perfectly digestible) repast of spiced meat and black coffee. It is the company he is keeping, and the task at which he is engaged that are the signs of his corruption, not really the food—to which his attention has deliberately been turned—or even the hour, though people will do at three in the morning what they might not do at three in the afternoon. Lewis's point is that Mark is seduced by the chance to be included in a small and select group, and that the idea of being an insider will make people do things they otherwise would not.

It is at this point of crisis that Jane "sees" the corpse of Merlin in his tomb, and pictures someone "divinely young [...] all golden and strong and warm coming with a mighty earth-shaking tread down into that black place" (THS 133; ch. 6). This passage evokes the Descent into Hell (now more weakly called the "descent to the dead") as well as the Raising of Lazarus, and shows in visionary terms—Jane is a visionary—the awakening of Merlin from his long enchanted sleep, the turning point of the plot of *That Hideous Strength*, since it is Merlin who will overthrow the N.I.C.E.

Afterward, as Jane travels by train she moves toward the light, to "a little green sun-lit island looking down on a sea of white fog" which marks a sacred center—St. Anne's Manor—which cannot be overcome by the diabolical fog. Another sacred center is also revealed to her: "the wooded hills above Sandown where she had picnicked with the Dennistons" (THS 135; ch. 6). When Jane arrives at St. Anne's, she is served tea (as opposed to coffee) and then ushered into the presence of the Pendragon, the Director of the Company of St. Anne's, who is Ransom, returned from Perelandra. She meets him, and sees "the gold hair and the gold beard of the wounded man" (THS 139; ch. 7).

In their meeting, the symbolism of the Holy Communion becomes explicit:

> Mrs Maggs presently returned with a tray, bearing a glass, a small flacon of red wine, and a roll of bread. She set it down on a table at the Director's side and left the room.
>
> "You see," said the Director, "I live like the King in *Curdie*. It is a surprisingly pleasant diet." With these words he broke the bread and poured himself out a glass of wine. (THS 146; ch. 7)

These actions are precisely those of a priest. They are based in part on George MacDonald's fantasy, *The Princess and Curdie* (1883): "with eager hands she broke a great piece from the loaf, and poured out a full glass of wine."[23] This food is intended to save the aged King, who has been secretly poisoned; "Every now and then he asked for a piece of bread and a little wine, and every time he ate and drank he slept, and every time he woke he seemed better than the last time."[24] The wounded Ransom is also, presumably, aided by this eucharistic repast as he lies disabled by a bite to his heel inflicted by Weston on Perelandra.

There is here, in both MacDonald and Lewis, an allusion to the story of Melchizedek in the Bible: "And Melchizedek king of Salem brought forth bread and wine, and he was the priest of the most high God" (Genesis 14.18); also alluded to in Psalms 110.4, "Thou art a priest for ever after the order of Melchizedek," a figure echoed and reinterpreted in Hebrews 7.2 as "King of Salem, which is, King of Peace," and repeated in Hebrews 5.21 as "Thou art a priest for ever after the order of Melchizedek."

On her way home from this life-changing encounter with someone enacting the role of the King of Salem, Jane, or rather, in her meditations upon herself, "This fourth and supreme Jane was simply in the state of joy" (THS 149; ch. 7). For Lewis, "joy" was a word of the most profound significance and there is some reason to suggest that Jane is modeled, as is Mark, on aspects of himself. As Jane, who like Lewis had homely tastes, "rejoiced also in her hunger and thirst and decided that she would make herself buttered toast for tea—a great deal of buttered toast" (THS 149; ch. 7) she echoes a notion which was no joke for Lewis—"God never meant" humankind "to be a purely spiritual creature. This is why He uses material things like bread and wine [or toast and tea] to put the new life into us. We may think this rather crude […] God does not: He invented eating. He likes matter. He invented it."[25]

What Jane actually meets on her way home, however, is Fairy Hardcastle, who submits her to torture. Set free, she is rescued by a man and a woman in a car, and her wish for tea and toast is in the end rewarded by a second salvational picnic. They "made her sit in the car and gave her brandy and after that sandwiches" (THS 156; ch. 7), and returned to "the Manor at St. Anne's." When Jane awakens there next morning, she is given breakfast, and asks for "the *Curdie* books, please" (THS 160; ch. 8), presumably to look up the Director's allusion regarding his diet of bread and wine. After a full day of rest and recovery from her ordeal, she is offered "a nice cup of tea," and, somewhat recovered (one may think that Lewis underestimated the lastingness of the effects of being tortured, however superficial the wounds may be), she joins the household in the kitchen where the women and men take turns preparing meals.

Mark, meanwhile, "sat down to lunch that day in good spirits" (THS 166; ch. 8), and, in the afternoon, "while he was having tea, Fairy Hardcastle came and leaned over the back of his chair" (THS 168; ch. 8). Later, Mark "was late for breakfast, but that made little difference for he could not eat. He drank several cups of black coffee" (THS 183; ch. 9) instead, which in this symbolic structure is clearly an ominous sign. Later still, the evil Deputy Director of the N.I.C.E. calls for him: "I would not have kept you from your breakfast unless I felt that in your own interests you should be placed in full possession of the facts at the earliest moment," he says, ominously (THS 203; ch. 10). In a bracketing structure, he informs Mark that he is to be blackmailed into forcing his wife Jane to come to Belbury, and concludes the interview by saying, "You must be hungry for your breakfast [...] Don't let me delay you" (THS 209; ch. 10).

The result of this terrible interview is that Mark actually walks away from Belbury; as he makes his escape he encounters a pub (an event prefigured in his visit to the doomed pub): "He thought sometimes about Jane, and sometimes about bacon and eggs, and fried fish, and dark, fragrant streams of coffee pouring into large cups. [...] He went in and ordered a pint and had some bread and cheese" (THS 211; ch. 10). Clearly, this repast, including coffee, is a symbol of goodness. When he goes home, he finds that Jane is not there. This is made clear by his discovery that "The bread in the cupboard was stale. There was a jug half full of milk, but the milk had thickened and would not pour" (THS 213; ch. 10). This image of stagnation and loss embodies precisely the precarious nature of Mark's and Jane's relationship at that moment, despite the fact that at the pub he had thought of her hopefully, along with bacon and eggs. Lewis reminds us here of Mark's need, both psychological and physical, for Jane, a need that in the end, literally, on the last page, will be his salvation.

Distressed, he goes to Dr. Dimble, who, not surprisingly, will not reveal Jane's whereabouts. Rejected, Mark stumbles away in the rain, and is arrested for "the murder of William Hingest," an act of which the reader knows he is not guilty. Returned to St. Anne's, Dr. Dimble reports Mark's approach; again, food images reinforce this location as good: "There were signs that everyone else had had an early supper," and he too is given something to "eat and drink." Every occupant of St. Anne's feeds well, according to need and desire; even the resident bear, Mr. Bultitude, can feast: "The bear is kept in the house and given apples and golden syrup till it's near bursting" (THS 259; ch. 12), the gardener complains.

Meanwhile, back at the N.I.C.E., a tramp has been mistaken for Merlin, and invited to dine; he "devoted his attention entirely to cold beef, chicken, pickles, cheese and butter," along with "a second pint of beer" (THS 264; ch. 12). His choice of foods, resembling those of a very good pub meal, marks this man as blameless, as indeed he is. Merlin, on the other hand, has made his way to St. Anne's Manor. Most of the household are put into a magical sleep including those who had been engaged in the kitchen, the women, on this particular day, as it happens. Ransom directs that they be awakened and welcome this guest: "Ask them to bring him up refreshments. A bottle of Burgundy and whatever you have cold" (THS 278; ch. 13). The reference to cold food is based on a British custom of preparing hot roast meat once a week and eating the cold leftovers sliced for several days thereafter.

Mark, meanwhile, is undergoing an attempt to brainwash and then initiate him into the diabolical center of the N.I.C.E., which is not a truly scientific enterprise after all, but a cult, in order to compel him to bring in his wife. In the process he is led to the room where the false Merlin (the tramp) is sleeping near a table where the "light gleaming on glasses and silver" reveals "all sorts of delights" (THS 297; ch. 14). Here Mark is left alone with the tramp, whose conversation turns largely upon "toasted cheese" (THS 309; ch. 14), a sure sign of his benignity.

In enormous contrast to this innocent and prolonged "sort of continual picnic which the two shared" (THS 310; ch. 14), is the high point of horror in *That Hideous Strength*, the Chapter titled "Banquet at Belbury," which presents a true anti-Communion, during which no communication of an intelligible sort takes place, as the doom of Babel falls upon the denizens of the N.I.C.E. The people who come to eat at the banquet are themselves eaten by wild animals (who had been caged in order to undergo vivisection). Their bodies and blood mix with the food and wine of an entirely unholy communion, a banquet in hell like the one concluding *The Screwtape Letters* in which the demons devour both the damned souls and their unsuccessful tempters.

The Banquet at Belbury is a scene presenting the reverse of communion, where no communication takes place. A similar set of motifs appeared in the film *Cool Hand Luke* (1967), in which Luke, the holy fool (Paul Newman), who eats eggs (life) to excess and sings about his "plastic Jesus," is finally killed. The comment of the prison camp guard from hell (the unforgettable Strother Martin) is this: "What we have here is a failure to communicate." Luke is, in this film, an *alter Christus*, an innocent person who suffers and dies. The people at Belbury's banquet who die are not innocent; although, in the context of Mercy, death does not always lead to damnation. The scene of these bloodied tables and their ruined plenty may be based on the *Odyssey*, in which Odysseus kills his wife's suitors as they are being entertained in his house, "spilling all the vittles on the ground—meat and bread in a mess,"[26] so that the victims "fell sprawling over a table; vittles and cup went scattering over the floor."[27]

From this scene of destruction, Mark is saved by Merlin, who sends him to Jane and St. Anne's with a clap on the back that he is to remember for the rest of his life. On the road in daylight he is offered a ride by a lorry-driver (a trucker in North American parlance) and, dropped off at "a little country hotel," which as we know by now is a good place, he eats "a capital breakfast," and later, "a boiled egg with his tea" (THS 357; ch. 17).

As the novel draws to its close we note that "Dinner was over at St. Anne's and they sat at their wine in a circle about the dining-room fire" (THS 365; ch. 17), a sure sign that all shall be well. And, as the prisoners, animals and human, of the N.I.C.E. are released, Ivy feeds her husband Tom, at last a free man, and reports that "I gave him the cold pie and the pickles [...] and the end of the cheese and a bottle of stout, and [...] a nice cup of tea" (THS 375; ch. 17). By this time we know that such a meal, simple and good, is for Lewis a figure for that most holy and frugal meal of all, which, though it consists of a thin wafer and a sip of wine, prefigures a place at the table of the Lamb in Paradise.

The Breakfast of the Lamb

In considering the Narnian Chronicles, Doris T. Myers (1984) says that "the Breakfast of the Lamb [is] the analogue of communion."[28] She regards "Aslan's Table on Ramandu's island" as "quite different" from "the homely, almost routine attitude associated with communion" among Anglicans. "The meal is a simple breakfast," she says, "a meeting with Aslan, neither a remembrance of him, nor a re-enactment of Christ's death [but rather] a meeting with the resurrected Christ."[29] The interpretation of a scene in *The Voyage of the Dawn Treader* to be discussed in that context below, clearly reinforces my thesis that all or at least many of Lewis's homely meals in his fantasies are meetings with the Creator in the Creation.

The first significant meeting in *The Lion, the Witch and the Wardrobe* (1950), the first of the seven Chronicles of Narnia, finds Lucy, the seeress of the Chronicles as Jane is the seeress in *That Hideous Strength*, having tea with Mr. Tumnus the faun, the first person she meets in Narnia. "And it really was a wonderful tea. There was a nice brown egg, lightly boiled, for each of them, and then sardines on toast, and then buttered toast, and then toast and honey, and then a sugar-topped cake" (LWW 15; ch. 2). The boiled eggs suggest the supper of "boiled eggs, plums and cream" Lewis ate in 1922. This tea in general, with its emphasis on boiled eggs, sardines and other good things on toast, is a eucatastrophic reversal of the dystopic "Einstein on toast" imagined by Devine on Earth (OSP 9; ch. 1), and the discarded "opened sardine tins" of the Malacandran picnic (OSP 12; ch. 2).

In great contrast to eggs, sardines, toast, butter, honey, and cake, when Edmund meets his first person in Narnia, she is, unfortunately for him, not a Narnian, but the White Queen. She gives him an evil drink, not tea, but "a jeweled cup full of something that steamed [...] very sweet and foamy and creamy, and it warmed him right down to his toes" (LWW 36; ch. 4), and evil food, "a round box, tied with green silk ribbon, which, when opened, turned out to contain several pounds of the best Turkish delight. Each piece was sweet and light to the very center" (LWW 36; ch. 4). This food proves to be addictive, and makes Edmund a slave of the White Witch.

The Pevensie children, whom the now corrupted Edmund has rejoined, find their way to the house of Mr. and Mrs. Beaver, where

Edmund slips away after hearing news of Aslan, and the other children and the Beavers prepare to make their escape; Mrs. Beaver, wise creature, takes along "a packet of tea, [...] sugar, [...] and two or three loaves" (LWW 100; ch. 10) in order to insure a minimal tea, including bread, the basic necessities of life in British terms. As they hide in a cave during their flight, they are provided by Father Christmas, who has more business being in Narnia than does the White Witch,[30] with a splendid tea, "a large tray containing five cups and saucers, a bowl of lump sugar, a jug of cream, and a great big teapot all sizzling and piping hot" (LWW 109; ch. 10). Mrs. Beaver's tea supplies are useless in a cave in the snow, since she has brought nothing with which to make a fire; the tea provided by Father Christmas is, as it should be, miraculous. In very sad contrast to all this bounty, all that the now-captive Edmund gets is "an iron bowl with some water in it and an iron plate with a hunk of dry bread on it" (LWW 111; ch. 11), the traditional punishment food of western culture, in stark contrast not only with the marvelous tea of Father Christmas but with the seductive and enslaving food by which the witch entrapped him.

Soon after, the witch, with the wretched Edmund in tow, encounters another group who have had the benefit of Father Christmas's bounty.[31] This is the "merry party" of small Narnians. "Edmund couldn't quite see what they were eating, but it smelled lovely and there seemed to be decorations of holly and he wasn't at all sure that he didn't see something like a plum pudding" (LWW 115; ch. 11). There is drink as well as food, of course: "the Fox [...] had just risen to its feet, holding a glass in its right paw" (LWW 115; ch. 11). When the fox attempts to "drink [her] Majesty's very good health," she turns them all to stone, including the "stone table on which there were stone plates and a stone plum pudding" (LWW 115-16; ch. 11).

The motif of the stone table is to recur; Aslan, in order to save the betrayer Edmund, is sacrificed on a Stone Table. Richard Sturch (1995) has said of this episode that "Lewis [...] avoided adherence to any *theory* of the Atonement [... but] the death of Aslan [...] is a straight substitution."[32] Walter Hooper (1996) agrees that the Table of Stone is indeed "the Narnian equivalent of Calvary,"[33] and that Aslan "offers his life for Edmund's."[34] Lewis, on the other hand, seems to have stood as far away from specificity on eucharistic doctrine in his fiction as he did in his apologetics: "I did not say to myself 'Let us represent Jesus as He really is in our world by a Lion in Narnia': I said 'Let us *suppose* that there was a land like Narnia and that the Son of God, as He became a Man in our world, became a Lion there, and then imagine what would happen.'"[35] In the case of Aslan's death, then, we cannot identify Lewis's understanding of the theory of the Atonement, let alone of the precise role, structure, and meaning of the Eucharist. On the other hand, the striking combination of miracle and homeliness is conveyed with unforgettable numinosity and poignancy.

In *Prince Caspian* (1951) Lewis continues his references to food, beginning with "the sandwiches mother gave us for the journey" (PC 6; ch. 1), in a reiteration of the "unleavened bread" (Exodus 12.18) eaten "in haste"—a motif characteristic of the Seder—"Seven days shalt thou eat unleavened bread [...] for thou cameth forth out of the land of Egypt in haste" (Deuteronomy 16.3). Paul specifically refers to this motif when he says in I Corinthians 5.8, "Let us keep the feast [...] with the unleavened bread of sincerity and truth." While the sandwiches were not made of unleavened bread per se, they were certainly eaten in the circumstances of a "journey," like the similar meals eaten in a car or a lorry in *That Hideous Strength*.

Trapped temporarily on an island in Narnia, the children "had to content themselves with raw apples" (PC 18; ch. 2), perhaps a delicate reference to the biblical phrase, "Comfort me with apples" (Song of Songs 2.5). Apples will continue to play a major role in the later Chronicles. Edmund, now redeemed, longs for "a good thick slice of bread and margarine" (PC 18; ch. 2), a desire that contains a touch of World War II austerity, at least for those who remember the period; readers should recall that *The Lion, the Witch and the Wardrobe* begins when the Pevensie children come to the house where they find the Wardrobe during World War II, having been sent away from an area more likely to suffer air-raids.

As they explore the place to which they have returned on this second visit to Narnia, they discover a treasure trove, where Lucy finds "the magical cordial which would heal almost every wound and every illness" (PC 28; ch. 2) which had been presented to her by Father Christmas along with the tea, discussed above. Since it heals rather than enslaves, it is the positive counterpart of the negative drink the witch gave to Edmund in *The Lion, the Witch and the Wardrobe*.

In company with a Narnian Dwarf, the children eat "fresh pavenders [roasted] in the embers" of a campfire (PC 38; ch. 3). Pavenders are a species of fish, and are enjoyed here along with apples and water. This meal of fish prefigures the "Breakfast of the Lamb," which has its roots in *The Voyage of the Dawn Treader* and is based on John 21.9, but it can also be seen as an allusion to those "miracles of *fertility"* discussed by Lewis in *Miracles*, which included not only bread and wine, but fish; specifically the feeding of the multitude, mentioned in all four gospels, which combined bread and fish, and in the miraculous draft of fishes in Luke and John.

Now, we read of Aslan's "How," described as "a perfect maze" built of "stones" with "strange characters and snaky patterns, and pictures in which the form of a Lion was repeated again and again" (PC 92; ch. 7), which suggest a sort of Narnian tumulus on the order of New Grange or some other site that Lewis may have seen or known. "In the center was the Stone itself—a stone table, split right down the center" (PC 94; ch. 7). This table, however, is not to be the site of a eucharistic event; quite the contrary. Instead a procession of dancers of the great and ancient divinity Bacchus arrives: "One was a youth, dressed only in a fawn-skin, with vine-leaves wreathed in his curly hair. His face would have been almost too pretty for a boy's, if it had not looked so extremely wild" (PC 157; ch. 11). And, "There were a lot of girls with him, as wild as he." Lewis wrote of "Euripides' picture of Dionysus [in *The Bacchae*]," as "something Mediterranean and volcanic [...] perhaps unconsciously connected with my own growing hatred of public school orthodoxies and conventions," in *Surprised by Joy*.[36] Thus, the being who arrives at the stone in *Prince Caspian* is the very Dionysus who, in *The Bacchae*, meets Pentheus's soldiers:

> Laughing, he told us to come on, bind him,
> lead him away.[37]

Pentheus, suicidally, taunts the god:

> [...] bodily you are not bad looking, stranger,
> in a seductive way [...]
> Those locks of yours are long,
> for lack of sport, cascading along your cheek,
> full of enticement.[38]

Pentheus pays with his life for a sight of the Dionysian revels; in *Prince Caspian* we are able to read of them and live.

As Bacchus begins his revels in *Prince Caspian*, Lucy sees "a bunch of grapes," and soon "Everyone began eating, and [...] you have never tasted such grapes. Really good grapes, firm and tight on the outside, but bursting into cool sweetness" (PC 159; ch. 11). Here, surely, is both the literal and figurative source of the wine in the Holy Communion, in terms of Lewis's symbolic intentions. This is the very "miraculous wine" to which Lewis refers in *Miracles*, the wine offered by the One who is "the reality behind—Bacchus." Later, after mentions of marching rations—"a lump of hard cheese, an onion, and a mug of water," instead of "venison pasties" or "buttered eggs and hot coffee" (PC 174; ch. 12)—available in the ruler "Miraz's tent" (PC 181; ch. 13), we hear again, and finally, of Bacchus, who gives to Caspian's old nurse the revivifying wine, "the richest wine, red as red-currant jelly, smooth as oil, strong as beef, warming as tea, cool as dew" (PC 204; ch. 14).

The novel moves toward its conclusion with a banquet, rhapsodically described in the same terms: "roasted meat [...], wheaten cakes and oaten cakes, honey and many-colored sugars and cream as thick as porridge and as smooth as still water, peaches, nectarines, pomegranates, pears, grapes, strawberries, raspberries" and finally, "the wines; dark, thick ones like syrups of mulberry juice, and clear red ones like red jellies liquefied, and yellow wines and green wines and yellow-green and greenish-yellow" (PC 211; ch. 15), all mandated and permitted, in this ecstatic catalog.

A last delightful touch reminds us that life emerges from the Earth: at this universal banquet, "the trees were going to eat *earth* [...] They began with a rich brown loam that looked almost exactly like chocolate"; then, "an earth of the kind you see in Somerset, which is almost pink [...] lighter and sweeter," followed by "a chalky soil" and "delicate confections of the finest gravels powdered with choice silver sand." Finally, along with "very little wine" (one thinks of the endless libations of wine poured upon the Earth in ancient Greece, or perhaps of Paul's advice to "use a little wine" in I Timothy 5.23) "they quenched their thirst with deep drafts of mingled dew and rain," surely the very water of life (PC 211; ch. 15). If all ground is holy ground, then all food is holy food.

The Voyage of the Dawn Treader begins its catalogue of foods with a list of provisions aboard the Dawn Treader, in keeping with the imagery of food eaten on the way, for this beautiful ship is setting off on a voyage of exploration that will take them to the uttermost East. Listed are "sacks of flour, casks of water and beer, barrels of pork, jars of honey, skin bottles of wine, apples, nuts, cheese, biscuits, turnips, sides of bacon, [...] hams and strings of onions" (VDT 25; ch. 2). Also aboard is Lucy's cordial; "a drop from her flask" (VDT 27; ch. 2) cures the seasickness of Eustace, the boy villain of this Chronicle, as Edmund was of the first.

The keg of water taken aboard the Dawn Treader is a necessity; one cannot drink seawater. Thus, one of Eustace's significant offences is to sneak drinks of what truly becomes the water of life when the supply is rationed during a long passage between widely separated islands. Finding landfall at last, the selfish Eustace finds himself turned into a dragon; this time, even Lucy's magic cordial cannot heal him. At this moment of despair, accompanied by repentance, Aslan un-dragons Eustace by means of water;

> "I knew it was a well because you could see the water bubbling up from the bottom of it: and it was a lot bigger than most wells—like a very big, round bath with marble steps going down into it." (VDT 114; ch. 7)

In fact this passage exactly describes the baptismal fonts of certain churches in Rome built after the legalization of Christianity; this is the water of life, contained in the well of life.

Lucy too will have an adventure, as she visits the house of the Magician, where she will attempt to enhance her divinely given gifts as a seer by using a magic spell instead. The voyagers land on the island of the Dufflepuds, a race of beings miraculously changed into monopods, and are served a banquet of "mushroom soup and boiled chickens and hot boiled ham and gooseberries, redcurrants [sic], curds, cream, milk, and mead" (VDT 156; ch. 10), a list of foods relished in the English countryside, but not, in post-war England, nearly so readily available. The meaning is simple and straightforward; this is good food, well-chosen. However, during a meal served by the Magician himself, while Lucy is given "an omelette, piping hot, cold lamb and green peas, a strawberry ice, lemon-squash to drink [...] and a cup of chocolate" (VDT 175; ch. 11), we are told that "the Magician himself drank only wine and ate only bread" (VDT 176; ch. 11). This, in the context of the food eaten by Ransom as the Director of the Company at St. Anne's in *That Hideous Strength*, as well as by the Old King in *The Princess and Curdie*, may make readers wonder if this Magician is not, in fact, a sort of priest-king, after the order of Melchizedek.

The most significant table in this novel, which presages its climax, is "a long table laid with a rich crimson cloth" (VDT 207; ch. 13), "There were turkeys and geese and peacocks, there were boars' heads and sides of venison, there were pies shaped like ships in full sail or like dragons and elephants, there were ice puddings and bright lobsters and gleaming salmon, there were nuts and grapes, pineapples and peaches, pomegranates and melons and tomatoes," and "the smell of the fruit and the wine blew toward them like a promise of all happiness" (VDT 208; ch. 13). Reepicheep, the valiant mouse, alone is bold enough to eat and drink at this idealized medieval banquet:

> "Sire," he said to Caspian, "of your courtesy fill my cup with wine from that flagon: it is too big for me to lift. I will drink to the lady." (VDT 217; ch. 13)

It is significant that of all the bounty available, Reepicheep selects only the wine, and that in order to engage in a courteous act. This lady is the Star's daughter, whom Caspian will later marry.

"Why is it called Aslan's Table?" Lucy asks, and receives the answer (she, unlike the various characters in the Arthurian cycle, knows that she should ask): the lady answers, "for those who come so far" (VDT 217; ch. 13). The phrase "set here by his bidding" does encourage a eucharistic interpretation, as does the statement that this food is "eaten, and renewed every day" (VDT 218; ch. 13), but again we have a suggestion of some other intention or at least some note of contrast between this banquet scene for exhausted travelers, and what Lucy, always the visionary, alone sees: "one bird fly to the Old Man with something in its beak that looked like a little fruit, unless it was a little live coal, which it might have been, for it was too bright to look at. And the bird laid it in the Old Man's mouth" (VDT 223; ch. 14). There is a strong suggestion here of the seraphim "having a live coal in his hand" who lays it upon the lips of the prophet in Isaiah 6.6.

Myers believes that "critics mistakenly consider the Narnian analog of communion to be the feast at Aslan's Table on Ramandu's Island. Despite the many details that suggest communion [...] the mood is simply wrong."[39] Why? Because, she argues, Lewis talks about Holy Communion from his own experience as an Anglican: "The feelings aroused by the episode are quite different from the ones Anglicans associate with communion. [...] [T]he discomfort of having to eat fancy, 'evening' food at breakfast, and the absence of Aslan himself from the meal—all these suggest feelings quite opposed to the homely, almost routine attitude associated with communion."[40] This apparent conflict may be reconciled through a comparison of festival Eucharists such as Christmas and Easter, and early or daily services, a possibility I explore in the conclusion of this paper.

In any event, the birds from the Sun consume the feast, leaving "the table pecked clean and empty" (VDT 224; ch. 14); the fruit is a "fire-berry from the valleys in the Sun" (VDT 226; ch. 14) which makes the Old Man grow daily younger. It is, then, a fruit of life, like the apples which become important in the last two novels of this cycle. After this encounter, the ship races eastward, eventually reaching waters so "strong" that nobody will "need to eat anything now" (VDT 249; ch. 15). The water, now "sweet" and hence drinkable, is clearly the "water of life."

The book ends with the sight of "a Lamb," reminiscent of Jesus's resurrection and appearance in John 21: "Then they noticed for the first time that there was a fire lit on the grass and fish roasting on it. They sat down and ate the fish, hungry now for the first time for many days. And it was the most delicious food they had ever tasted" (VDT 268; ch. 16). Aside from the theme of miraculous fish, discussed above, and the presence of what was a very long-used symbol, the fish, as a figure for Christ, as well, of course, as the lamb as a symbol of the Lamb of God, again, Christ; there is here the essential requirement set forth by Myers for a true Anglican communion: the presence of Jesus. The Lamb turns into Aslan, and tells the children frankly that he is sending them home so that they can learn to know him under another name—obviously, Jesus of Nazareth—there. As Myers says of this scene, "It is a meeting with the resurrected Christ," and "is consonant with the aspect of communion most often emphasized in Anglican spirituality."[41]

The theme of the water of life, emphasized in several places in *The Voyage of the Dawn Treader*, recurs in *The Silver Chair*, as Jill, also in Aslan's country, feels an overwhelming thirst but dares not approach "the stream, bright as glass, running across the turf" (SC 21; ch. 2), because Aslan, a great lion, is lying in front of it. This stream is almost certainly based upon the stream in *At the Back of the North Wind* (1868) by George MacDonald, which runs over the grass in the land at the back of the North Wind.[42] Finally, told that "There is no other stream," she drinks, and finds that "It was the coldest, most refreshing water she had ever tasted" (SC 23; ch. 2). The symbolism is of the stream that runs through Paradise, and the motif of water that flows over the grass is distinctive to MacDonald's version, though he derived the stream itself, as he says, from *The Divine Comedy*. This stream is the water of life, the living water that Jesus promises in John 4.10-11 and that flows in Revelation 21.16 and 22.1.

The concept of the water of life plays a role in Holy Communion whenever wine is used. Eucharistic wine is customarily mixed with water, and hence the act of combining blessed water with wine before the eucharistic formula, "This is my blood," is pronounced over it. This practice derives from the ancient Mediterranean custom of mixing water with wine, but it is also based on biblical symbolism: when the Roman soldier thrust his spear into the side of Jesus, both water and blood came forth (John 19.34). This motif is sometimes used to express the role of baptism (in water) as well as of Holy Communion (water and wine), but in both cases the Eucharist is implicit because in liturgical churches the Eucharist is available only to those who are baptized.

The concept of water as associated with the afterlife is presented again as a reversal when Jill is told the story of Prince Rilian's mother's death. The mother had been the Star's daughter who married Prince Caspian: "where a fountain flowed freshly out of the earth [...] there they dismounted and ate and drank and were merry"; as she rests, she is stung to death by "a great serpent" (SC 57; ch. 4).

A water-related food is introduced when Eustace and Jill eat eels in the house of Puddleglum, who lives in a marsh; the eels here are not symbols of disgust, because the eel, whether smoked or fresh, is regarded as a delicacy in Britain. "When the meal came it was delicious and the children had two large helpings each," followed by "tea, in tins," and, on the next day, by the party setting out with "a large bit of bacon […] the remains of the eels, [and] some biscuit" (SC 76; ch. 5), reiterating Lewis's long theme of food associated with travel, indeed, as most of these sequences eventuate, of pilgrimage.

The main explicitly identified vegetarians in the Narnian Chronicles are Eustace's parents, whose other beliefs involve the wearing of certain prescribed underwear, but the complex issue of humans eating the Body of Christ, is raised as the children visit Harfang, the Castle of the Giants. Here, they are welcomed as guests, as Jill announces her party's arrival; "The Lady of the Green Kirtle […] has sent us two Southern Children and this Marsh-wiggle […] to your Autumn Feast" (SC 105; ch. 7). Next day, the children discover the truth; first, they learn that they are being fed upon something more than venison: "So we've been eating a *Talking* Stag" (SC 128; ch. 9). On realizing this, they "felt as you would feel if you found you had eaten a baby" (SC 129; ch. 9). Soon after, they find "an open book" (SC 131; ch. 9). This proves to be a "cookery book" (SC 131; ch. 9), and it contains recipes for preparing two foods. The first is

> MAN. This elegant little biped has long been valued as a delicacy. It forms a traditional part of the Autumn Feast, and is served between the fish and the joint. Each Man—
> (SC 131; ch. 9)

The next entry is a recipe for "MARSH-WIGGLE" (SC 132; ch. 9). This discovery is followed by the escape of the prospective entrees.

Their escape takes them to Underland, where they discover Prince Rilian in captivity. Here, too, diet plays a role: "When the meal (which was pigeon pie, cold ham, salad, and cakes) was brought" (SC 156; ch. 11), the prince tells them that he suffers daily periods of delusion during which he must be bound to a silver chair for his own safety. Actually he is deluded all the time except for these periods. His false revelations are punctuated by references to food, as he addresses each of his guests (rescuers) in turn: "Honest Frog-foot, your cup is empty. Suffer me to refill it"; and "Sir, be pleased to take another breast of pigeon, I entreat you," and finally, "Little lady, eat one of these honey cakes, which are brought for me from some barbarous land in the far south of the world" (SC 157; ch. 11). The association of the empty cup with the personage whose native habitat is a marsh;

of the pigeon, a form of game, with the boy, whose parents are vegetarians; and the association of the honey cakes, symbolic of Aphrodite, with the girl, are not perhaps, entirely accidental.

This poisonous hospitality comes to an end as Rilian is bound in the Silver Chair; he knows himself, and begs to be released. Because he invokes the name of Aslan, he is freed, because Aslan has decreed that anyone asking for anything in his name is to be aided. The Queen of Underland proves to be that very serpent who has killed Prince Rilian's mother and has made him her captive and dupe. In a reversal of all these terrible ironies, the name of Aslan sets him free. Managing to kill the Green Witch in her serpent form (a different matter, one assumes, from killing her in her humanlike form) they set out to escape from Underland.

In one wonderful moment, the sad gnomes who have also been captives there—they have been forced to go upwards to their slavery, unlike the Prince, who had been forced to go downwards—make their escape too, leaping joyously down into the Land of Bism ("abyss") where Golg, a gnome, tells the children and the Marsh-wiggle that "There I'll pick you bunches of rubies that you can eat and squeeze you a cup full of diamond juice" (SC 206; ch. 8). Bism is not Hell, in an endearing bit of directional correctness.

At last the three travelers emerge from the Narnian underworld into the delights of a dance performed by Narnians with snowballs—"The Great Snow Dance." Afterwards they enjoy a supper of "sausages [...] real meaty, spicy ones, fat and piping hot and burst and just the tiniest bit burnt," made, one presumes, from non-talking pigs. "And great mugs of frothy chocolate, and roast potatoes and roast chestnuts, and baked apples with raisins stuck in where the cores had been, and ices just to freshen you up" (SC 228-29; ch. 9). Next day they dine on "scrambled eggs and toast" (SC 230; ch. 12), and learn that a Centaur (who as half human and half horse has a more complex set of needs than most) dines on "porridge and pavenders and kidneys and bacon and omelette and cold ham and toast and marmalade and coffee and beer" as well as "grazing for an hour or so and finishing up with a hot mash, some oats and a bag of sugar" (SC 231; ch. 16). The sense of food as being specific, appropriate, and licit, in accordance with a rule of behavior, is very strongly present in this novel, which deals with reversals of identity and position as a major theme.

The Horse and His Boy, which follows the Caspian-related sequence, turns the narrative back to the period of *The Lion, the Witch and the Wardrobe*, describing events which follow Aslan's resurrection. Escaping from captivity with the horse Bree as his companion, Shasta breakfasts upon "a meat pasty, [...] a lump of dried figs and another lump of green cheese [and] a little flask of wine" (HB 21; ch. 2). When he first encounters Narnians, in the great city of the Calormenes, "he was given iced sherbet in a golden cup to drink" (HB 63; ch. 4) by Tumnus, who reappears in the novel and continues his role as an amiable host.

The main symbolism of food in this novel concerns discernment of the customary diet. Most of the Calormene foods resemble Near Eastern diet, and we meet many well-remembered Narnian repasts. The major theme is one of contrast, not between evil and good, but between exotic and familiar, at least from the British point of view. Of course British cuisine included food from throughout the British Empire, not only in Lewis's Edwardian childhood, but even today, when it is if anything more varied. The contrast is embodied in Calormene food, the food of a culture that is to be distinguished from the food of Narnia, which Lewis always expressed in terms of his personal tastes.

In *Orientalism* (1978), Edward W. Said describes the breadth of the Western concept of the so-called Orient as "a prodigious cultural repertoire whose individual items evoke a fabulously rich world: the Sphinx, Cleopatra, Eden, Troy, Sodom and Gomorrah, Astarte, Isis and Osiris, Sheba, Babylon, the Genii, the Magi, Nineveh, Prester John, [...], monsters, devils, heroes, terrors, pleasures, desires," and lists the writers "between the Middle Ages and the eighteenth century" who drew upon these themes: "Ariosto, Milton, Marlowe, Tasso, Shakespeare, Cervantes, and the authors of the *Chanson de Roland* and the *Poema del Cid*."[43] Lewis sets the Calormene world in the South of his imaginary world, with Narnia in the North, but the East/West contrasts of Said, in terms of its allusions and its literary sources, are clearly those upon which Lewis drew.

We read about a Calormene meal that contained "lobsters, and salad, and snipe stuffed with almonds and truffles, and a complicated dish made of chicken livers and rice and nuts, and [...] cool melons and gooseberry fools and mulberry fools [... and ...] the sort of wine that is called 'white' though it is really yellow" (HB 75; ch. 5). The operative word here is "complicated"; as we have seen, simple, homely food is what Lewis prefers and values. It may even be that we should read, for the word "complicated," the word "worldly," and for the word "simple," the word "monastic." Exemplifying Calormene's lure, Shasta, while escaping from Tashbaan, the great city of the Calormenes, climbs a garden wall and steals "three oranges, a melon, a fig or two, and a pomegranate" (HB 91; ch. 6).

Finally and safely escaped to Narnia (across the great desert), Shasta and his companion Aravis, and their associated horses, meet the Hermit of the Southern Marsh, and Aravis is given "goats' milk" (HB 148; ch. 10). Shasta, having left her to safety and healing, presses on, encountering Aslan on his way. Then, fully in Narnia, he meets the native Narnians, a stag, a rabbit, and a Dwarf, who feed him, "and immediately, mixed with a sizzling sound, there came to Shasta a simply delightful smell. It was one he had never smelled in his life before, but I hope you have. It was, in fact, the smell of bacon and eggs and mushrooms all frying in a pan," Lewis rhapsodizes, combining the elements of "simple" and "delightful" in a perfect encapsulation of my thesis. Furthermore, "here's porridge—and here's a jug of cream—and here's a spoon," and finally, "the coffeepot and the hot milk, and the toast" (HB 173; ch. 12*)*. In other words, food like the food at home, the food of one's happiest memories of childhood. Narnia, after all, is Lewis's picture of Paradise.

This theme of food in Paradise becomes explicit in *The Magician's Nephew*, when the apple becomes its primary symbol, despite the fact that it does not appear in the Genesis depiction. Polly and Digory, who like Lewis are children of Edwardian England, have repaired to "the cave," their private hidey-hole in the attic, for "a few apples" and "a quiet bottle of ginger-beer" (MN 8; ch. 1). In extreme contrast to this, Uncle Andrew "grope[d] in his wardrobe for a bottle and a wineglass […] and poured himself out a glassful of some nasty, grown-up drink" which is, obviously, not wine (MN 81; ch. 6).

In relation to this contrast between youth and being "grown-up," "[a] lady called with some grapes for Digory's Mother," but finds the situation too dire for earthly comfort; "I am afraid it would need fruit from the land of youth to help her now" (MN 92; ch. 7). The central mechanism of the plot is set in place with this sentence; Digory will, at the climax of the novel, bring back fruit from the land of youth, Narnia, absolutely new-made, in the first hours of its creation. Uncle Andrew, on the other hand, pours and drinks "a second glass" (MN 82; ch. 6); and then asks for another "small glass of brandy" (MN 97; ch. 7). As we have seen, asking for a second helping of a specific pleasure or gift is a sign of spiritual imperfection or weakness in Lewis's symbolic system.

After the Creation of Narnia by Aslan, Digory asks the divine Lion, "please, will you give me some magic fruit of this country to make Mother well?" (MN 146; ch. 11). Aslan sends him to "the Western wild" and bids him to "Pluck an apple from that tree and bring it to me" (MN 155; ch. 12). The apple is so important to the theme of *The Magician's Nephew* that only one other food makes a significant, if brief, appearance: "toffees," which form a sort of waybread or manna for the children as they make the trip to the West; after its remains are thrown away, it is found growing, by the divine energy of the creation situation, into a tree from the supernaturally fertile earth, giving forth toffee-like fruits, a delicate example of Lewis's concept of miracle.

Finally, in the central scene of the novel, Digory sees a tree full of "great silver apples" (MN 172; ch. 13). "'Take of my fruit for others,' said Digory to himself. 'Well, that's what I'm going to do. It means I mustn't eat any myself, I suppose'" (MN 171; ch. 13). Before discussing the outcome of this event, I will explore the meaning of the apple in this context. The word "apple" is very obviously based here upon the story of Adam and Eve in Eden, though the word actually used in the King James Bible as well as in the Tanakh is "tree."[44] "Of every tree of the garden thou mayest freely eat; But of the tree of the knowledge of good and evil, thou shall not eat of it" (Genesis 2.16-17). It is Eve who first uses the word "fruit," again, without mention of apples, telling the serpent that "of the fruit of that tree which is in the midst of the Garden, God hath said, Ye shall not eat of it" (Genesis 3.3). When the serpent tells her otherwise, Eve and Adam indeed eat "the fruit thereof" (Genesis 3.6). The Tanakh, in a recent translation of the Hebrew Scriptures, says that when Eve "saw that the tree was desirable as a source of wisdom, " (Genesis 3.6/Tanakh 6) The King James version says it was "a tree to be desired to make one wise" (Genesis 3.6). Phyllis Tribble (1978) says of this scene: "The serpent and the woman discuss theology."[45] Unfortunately Eve loses the argument, accepts the serpent's interpretation, and indeed gains the promised knowledge of good and evil, along with her husband Adam; clearly, arguing about theology is not always a good thing.

The Genesis narrative is certainly one of the intended allusions in *The Magician's Nephew*, where Digory has already broken a rule by ringing the bell in the land of Charn and hence awakened the Witch Jadis, who has followed the children into Narnia. We must, in asking what Lewis actually does with this symbolic structure, consider the full resonance and range of "apple" (not simply and biblically, "fruit") as a concept, because this range is implicit in the word "apple" and is, as I think, fully invoked. Waverly Root (1980) says that the apple is a member of Rosaceae, "which includes the queen of all flowers, the rose, and the king of all fruits, the apple."[46] This is, clearly, the language Lewis is speaking in *The Magician's Nephew*. Many, many fruits have been called apples, from the akee to the tomato; apples are said to have originated in southeastern Europe or southwestern Asia; they were already in use in Europe (Switzerland) during the Neolithic. As a tree acclimated to winter, the apple is widely adaptable. Its cultivation was known from Anatolia to Egypt, Greece, Etruria, and Rome between 6500 BC and AD 23-24. In Greek mythology we read of the "golden apples of the Hesperides [...] given to Hera as a wedding present when she married Zeus";[47] another apple, the apple of discord, caused the Trojan War when Paris judged between the three goddesses and chose Aphrodite; at least, "apple" is the word used in European tradition.[48] Both these stories associate the apple with loss and probably contributed to the extra-biblical tradition that the fruit of Eden was an apple.

In *The Magician's Nephew*, however, the apple is good (when used with permission), especially for healing; this aspect of apple tradition derives, most directly for Lewis, perhaps, from the story of Avalon in *Le Morte D'Arthur*, the Island of Apples, to which King Arthur was taken, by barge, after having returned his sword Excalibur to the water: "even fast by the bank hove a little barge with many fair ladies in it." These ladies take the King away "into the Vale of Avilion to heal me of my grievous wound," says Arthur. According to many interpreters, the word "Avilion" or "Avalon" means "Isle of apples."[49] According to *The Arthurian Encylopedia* (1986), Geoffrey of

Monmouth's "'apple' etymology is probably right, the apple being paradisal or magical fruit like those of the Hesperides, or of Celtic otherworld regions portrayed elsewhere."[50] The point is that whatever the actual historical documents may or may not say, the apple in *The Magician's Nephew* carries these symbolic references.

When Satan, in Milton's *Paradise Lost*, makes his long flight to Eden—"That spot to which I point is Paradise" (Bk III, line 33), he approaches the "verdurous walls of Paradise up sprung,"

> And higher than that Wall a circling row
> Of goodliest trees loaden with fairest Fruit,
> Blossoms and fruits at once of golden hue
> Appeared, with gay enameled colors mixed
> (Bk IV, lines 146-49)

Perhaps Lewis's association of the apples of Narnia's paradise with goodness are expressed by calling them "great silver apples" instead of golden apples. Fulfilling the command of Aslan, Digory "picked an apple, and put it in the breast pocket of his Norfolk jacket. But he couldn't help looking at it and smelling it [...]" (MN 172; ch. 13). Upon inhaling its fragrance, "a terrible thirst and hunger came over him" (MN 172; ch. 13), recalling Jill's thirst in *The Silver Chair*. Then he sees the witch, who, like Milton's Satan, is an unwanted guest in the garden: "She was just throwing away the core of an apple which she had eaten. The juice was darker than you would expect and had made a horrid stain round her mouth" (MN 174; ch. 13). Defiantly, she tells Digory that "It is the apple of youth, the apple of life" (MN 175; ch. 13), and commands that he use his "magic" to return to earth to give it to his Mother immediately. She then suggests they leave his companion Polly behind into the bargain. Aided by Polly, he escapes, resisting the temptation as he had not been able to do in Charn.

Returning to Aslan, he says, "I've brought you the apple you wanted, sir" (MN 179; ch. 13). "'Well done'; said Aslan," (MN 180; ch. 14) giving him the reply the Master gave in the Parable of the Servants (Matthew 25.21; Luke 19.17). Then, because this very young servant has "hungered and thirsted and wept" for it—as Jesus hungered in the wilderness (Matthew 4.2; Luke 24.2), cried from the cross, "I thirst" (John 19.28), and wept over the death of Lazarus (John 11.35)—Digory is told to "Sow the seed of the Tree that is to be the protector of Narnia" (MN 180; ch. 14); he obeys and the tree soon springs up. At last, Aslan tells him "Go. Pluck an apple from the Tree," and sends him home to his dying mother:

> The brightness of the Apple threw strange lights on the ceiling [...] And the smell of the Apple of Youth was as if there was a window in that room that opened on Heaven." (MN 197; ch. 15)

Taking this luminous and fragrant "Apple" in his hand, "He peeled it and cut it up and gave it to her piece by piece" (MN 197; ch. 15). And she is healed. Later, he buries "the core of the Apple in the back garden" (MN 198; ch. 15), where it grows and bears "apples more beautiful than any others in England, [...] though not fully magical" (MN 201; ch. 15). The wood of this tree is later used to make the wardrobe through which the Pevensie children first enter Narnia in *The Lion, the Witch and the Wardrobe*. This motif reminds one that Lewis and his brother Warren solemnly buried their childhood toys in the backyard of their Belfast home after their father's death; perhaps these beloved items, too, came up again in Aslan's country.

The life-giving apple of Narnia is thus the equivalent of the Eucharist bread and water, giving abundant and everlasting life, whether whole, cut up in pieces, or juiced, fresh or fermented. It is also the food of knowledge which brings death if wrongly taken, or wisdom and life if rightly taken. A very different mood pertains, however, in *The Last Battle*, as the ape, Shift, who has pulled a lionskin from Caldron Pool, sends the donkey Puzzle to get "oranges or bananas" (LB 10; ch. 1), reminding one of the oranges Shasta stole from a garden in Tashbaan, as well as the usual tastes of our anthropoid relatives. Meanwhile, the last king of Narnia orders "a bowl of wine" from the Centaur Roonwit (LB 18; ch. 2), suggesting—at the very least—a more kingly form of nourishment. Then, after the King is captured, the Mice bring him "a little wooden cup," again, of wine (LB 43; ch. 4). He is also provided with cheese, oatcakes, and fresh butter, all proper Narnian food, as we have already seen. While he waits, still bound but now refreshed, the "Friends of Narnia"—at home on Earth—have "just finished their meal," which has included wine (LB 50; ch. 4). The reiteration of "wine" in the context of

Narnia's King and his kingdom's friends suggests the binding together of the Narnian and Earthly communities in one communion.

The theme of food for travel also reappears, as the King, having called upon the Friends of Narnia, finds them coming from England to Narnia. Eustace Scrubb brings with him "two hard-boiled egg sandwiches, and two cheese sandwiches, and two with some kind of paste in them" (LB 56; ch. 5). Assembled, the rescuers share "hard biscuit" (like the food eaten on a ship, as in *The Voyage of the Dawn Treader*) which they eat after boiling it into "a kind of porridge" (LN 65; ch. 5). Later, having been rescued by these Friends, the King finds himself among the Dwarfs, who serve him "a capital stew" (LB 87; ch. 7), presumably containing the meat of a non-talking form of game. When Aslan, comes to rescue the last inhabitants of Narnia, he creates a feast for the Dwarfs: "pies and tongues and pigeons and trifles and ices," like the food on Aslan's table, suggesting that there need be no more sojourning in the wilderness, and "a goblet of good wine" (LB 168; ch. 13), having saved the best of it until now. But these ungrateful guests think they are eating "hay," "old turnip," and "raw cabbage leaf," and are drinking "dirty water" (LB 168; ch. 13). As with the meal first mentioned in *Out of the Silent Planet*, to them this good food is garbage. Lewis borrowed the motif itself from George MacDonald's masterpiece, *The Princess and the Goblin* (1872), where Curdie cannot see Irene's divine Grandmother, and instead sees only "musty straw, and a withered apple, and a ray of sunlight coming through a hole in the middle of the roof."[51]

When the last King of Narnia, along with many of his subjects and the Friends, at last enters a stable set up for the false Aslan concocted by the Ape Shift, it, like the stable of Bethlehem and Narnia itself, turns out to be set on the outskirts of Heaven. As the children look about, they see that "Not far away from them rose a grove of trees, thickly leaved, but under every leaf there peeped out the gold or faint yellow or purple or glowing red of fruits such as no one has seen in our world" (LB 156; ch. 13). When they are truly in Heaven, they find there are groves of these trees "whose leaves looked like silver and their fruit like gold" (LB 202; ch. 16).

Honey Cakes and Red Wine

Lewis's final fantasy novel, *Till We Have Faces* (1956), stands by itself. It contains explicit references to ritual sacrifice and ritual meals, in a plot set in a minor kingdom in ancient times—Glome, where the goddess Ungit is worshipped.[52] The contrast between bread and wine and other foods is set forth by Batta, the nurse of the heroine and future Queen of Glome, Orual: "You'll have hard cheese instead of honey cakes then and skim milk instead of red wine" (TWF 5; ch. 1), she says, in anticipation of the King's remarriage.

In describing the worship of Ungit, Orual mentions "pigeons' blood [...] sacrificed men [...] burnt fat [...] and wine and stale incense" (TWF 11; ch. 1) in a passage which includes allusions to the worship of Canaan, of the Temple of Israel, and, with its wine and talk of sacrifice, includes prefigurations of Christian worship. "Honeycakes" (TWF 33; ch. 3), appropriately for a eucharistic motif, as offerings, reappear as they will throughout the novel; the use of honey in what is otherwise a cake made of water and flour, reminds us that Ungit is a goddess like Aphrodite, to whom honey was sacred. Wine, too, recurs, but often only as it must in a novel set east of the Mediterranean. Orual finds her father, the King of Glome, "holding a cup of wine to my lips" (TWF 57; ch. 6), after he has beaten her into unconsciousness. In this context, a "beefsteak" is recommended "for your face" (TWF 62; ch. 6). Even so, animal flesh is also explicitly sacrificed. Items mentioned as "food for the gods" (TWF 79; ch. 8), prove to be slaughtered offerings.

When, at the climax of the book, Orual finds her sister Psyche, who has been lost through sacrifice, Psyche (having survived the process) gives Orual "the little cool, dark berries of the Mountain, in a green leaf" (TWF 104; ch. 10), as if they were noble and lordly food; at least, this is what Orual says—she is writing the book and records events from her own perspective. Again, with the words, "After the banquet, the wine," Psyche gives Orual water to drink, asking afterwards, "Have you ever tasted a nobler wine?" (TWF 104; ch. 10). Orual, of course, sees only water in her cup. Of all the eucharistic motifs in all the novels, this may be the most potent and most poignant, when an unbeliever sees only "a little round, thin, cold, tasteless wafer"[53] with a sip of watered wine of some lesser vintage, and does not recognize in them the Body and Blood of Christ. "You mean you saw no cup?" Psyche asks, amazed. "Tasted no wine?" (TWF 119; ch. 11). Like Curdie in *The Princess and the Goblin* (1872), and the Dwarfs in *The Last Battle*, Orual refuses to be taken in.

As the novel draws to its close, the eucharistic elements become more and more explicit and intense. A contrast is drawn between revisionist efforts to make the Glomish state religion accord with "one of those small peaceful gods who are content with flowers and fruit for sacrifice" (TWF 240; ch. 21) in contrast to the "pouring of wine and pouring of blood" (TWF 269; II, ch. 2) to Ungit, who, as a black stone, has "a face such as you might see in a loaf" (TWF 270; II, ch. 2)—a phrase used specifically, I think, to remind the reader of bread.

Finally, in what, after the clearly expressed imagery of *The Magician's Nephew*, may be the most resonant image in the whole of *Till We Have Faces*, Orual cries out: "to expect further utterance [from the gods] is like asking for an apple from a tree that fruited the day the world was made" (TWF 280; II, ch. 2). With this profound symbol, which both begins and ends the Bible, and which Lewis has placed in the last two books of the Narnian Chronicles, describing both the beginning (*The Magician's Nephew*) and the end (*The Last Battle*) of Narnia, we come to the heart of the matter. We can, Lewis is saying, ask for that apple; and the answer will be "yes." It is the apple both of Knowledge and of Life, a food which, like the Holy Communion elements of bread and wine, will give, both physically and supernaturally, symbolically and in all reality, life abundant and life everlasting. This, at the very least, is what Lewis is trying to tell us.

Whether or not this is true—and we are free to see the berries instead of bread, and springwater instead of wine (or bread instead of God's Body and wine instead of God's Blood)—this is what Lewis not only believed and taught, but, throughout his life after his return to Christianity, lived. If what he says in his books is true, he is living it still.

Conclusion

C.S. Lewis's eleven fantasy novels contain two interlocking patterns created from the symbolic structure of eucharistic symbolism, and from the symbolism of food and drink and that of eating and drinking derived from it. One is the symbol of the fruit of the tree of the beginning (Genesis) and the end (Revelation) of creation, which bracket the Bible. The other is the eucharistic pattern, which is presented in four forms:

1) food eaten on the way, which may be called the *Exodus* situation;
2) food eaten while waiting, which may be called the Melchizedek situation;
3) food eaten in celebration, reiterating the Christmas and Easter cycles reflected in the weekly Sunday celebrations, which may be called the Aslan's Table situation; and
4) food eaten in order to meet Jesus, found in all of the above eucharistic paradigms, which may be called the Breakfast of the Lamb situation.

All six of these patterns—the bracketing fruit trees of Genesis and Revelation, and the four aspects of the Eucharist symbolically suggested in the Narnian Chronicles, are interwoven in various ways in the full sequence of the eleven novels.

I. The Food of the Beginning: the Genesis situation

The two great trees of Eden, the Tree of Life and the Tree of Knowledge, described in Genesis, are echoed in the great tree of silver apples at the center of the mountaintop garden which grows in the newly created Narnia. Such a tree is always the same tree, whether at beginning or end (Eden is Paradise, and Paradise is Heaven) because the first and last things occur outside of time. This is why the edenic apple of Narnia is able to heal Digory's dying mother as well as grow into a tree which will be present after the end of Narnia, where it reappears in Aslan's Country.

II. The Food of the End: The Revelation Situation

In *The Last Battle*, there is "a smooth green hill" surmounted by green walls; "above the wall rose the branches of trees, whose leaves were like silver and their fruit like gold" (LB 202; ch. 16). This phrase closely resembles the account in Revelation of the tree of life, "and the leaves of the tree were for the healing of nations" (Revelation 22.2). As noted above, Orual, in the final novel, *Till We Have Faces*, refers to this tree, which is a tree not only of beginning and end, but of eternity.

III. The Exodus Situation

The four eucharistic situations contained within the bracketing situation created by the great symbolic apple trees all refer to food. In the Exodus situation, the symbolism is that of travel, of the unleavened bread prepared in haste as the Exodus begins; of the manna eaten in the wilderness; of the Seder which celebrates these events of the Last Supper where Jesus breaks the bread and says, "This is my body," and lifts the cup and says, "This is my blood."

The many meals eaten in haste in the Space Trilogy embody this theme; eating and drinking in a situation of interplanetary travel in *Out of the Silent Planet*, the marvelous food which nourishes and revives Ransom in *Perelandra*, and the many picnics, fortuitous and fortunate (along with their diabolical opposites) in *That Hideous Strength*. Again, as the Narnian Chronicles open with *The Lion, the Witch and the Wardrobe*, and many times through the seven novels of the series, a situation of food taken for a journey arises, as with Mrs. Beaver's quick preparations, or of food miraculously provided, as in the perfect high tea given by Father Christmas. As God provides manna in the wilderness, so Bacchus provides wine in Narnia in *Prince Caspian*; this is the image of human life, as a journey from birth to death, and to what may lie beyond.

Finally, in *Till We Have Faces*, the central crisis of the novel occurs when Psyche offers her sister Orual the hospitality of food and drink—bread and wine—and Orual rejects it as berries and springwater. Perhaps the most touching aspect of this crucial moment is that, after all, fresh berries and pure water are themselves profound miracles; as Lewis says, all ground is holy, and every bush a burning bush.

IV. The Melchizedek Situation

Food eaten while waiting presents the point of view of the stationary person, suggesting the stability of position promised in the vows of the various Benedictine orders, and reflected in the situation of the anchorite, such as Julian of Norwich, whose cell was enclosed in the walls of a church. "Melchizedek, King of Salem," we read in Genesis 14.18, "brought forth bread and wine" as Abram (not yet

Abraham) passed through his country while returning from battle. Lewis writes in *That Hideous Strength*, that Ransom, after having been wounded in battle against the Un-man in Perelandra, eats only bread and wine; and of the Magician in *The Voyage of the Dawn Treader* who "drank only wine and ate only bread" (VDT 176; ch. 11).

These eremetical motifs of bread and wine as the sacred food of the solitary, or indeed, of the Company whose leader dines alone like the King in *Curdie*, is probably associated, in Lewis's personal life, with the Eucharist as a "private communion"; that is, communion given to an isolated person, often in a case of injury or illness. In a passage from one of his letters, which has, I think, sometimes been misunderstood, he wrote, "yes, private communions (I shared many during Joy's last days) are extraordinarily moving. I am in danger of preferring them to those in church."[54] The last sentence in that comment has suggested to some that Lewis disliked church communion because he disliked hymns, or for some other personal reason, but in this letter he writes as one who is himself an invalid, to a frequently invalided correspondent, about his invalided wife. Private communion is taken to the homes or hospitals where the communicated person is confined. It is certainly true that the experience of private communion is extraordinarily powerful, as the elements come directly into one's hospital room or home, like the descending planetary powers in *That Hideous Strength*, but most of those who have had this experience would gladly return to church for communion as soon as possible afterwards.

V. Aslan's Table: the Festival situation

All three categories of Lewis's fantasy novels—Trilogy, Chronicles, and *Till We Have Faces*, contain ceremonial banquets where the food is elaborate and the manners are formal. Although the Last Supper, and the Seder upon which it is modeled, center upon the Bread and the Wine, there is more to the Seder than matzoh and bitter herbs and wine; a splendid array of additional dishes, all ritually free of leaven, are offered and enjoyed. The Eucharist, on this model, is not always simple and monastic. Indeed, the Eucharist is intended to assuage, Lewis seems to suggest in *Perelandra*, "a new kind of hunger and thirst" and to give "a totally new genus of pleasures." And as the Trilogy ends, a moment of supreme satisfaction is expressed, just before Ransom's return to Perelandra, when "Dinner was over at St. Anne's" (THS 365; ch. 17). In *The Lion, the Witch and the Wardrobe*, Father Christmas presents a Christmas feast to the members of the merry party. In *The Voyage of the Dawn Treader*, Aslan's table suggests an elaborate Easter feast. During the yearly round of Festival communions there are two that, in actual practice, are central foci: Christmas and Easter, which celebrate respectively the birth of Christ and his Resurrection.

These examples of the banquet or festival situation, the form of elaborate ceremony associated with Aslan's Table, occurs throughout the Caspian cycle of the Narnian chronicles. In *Prince Caspian*, we read of "wheaten cakes," "nectarines, pomegranates, pears, grapes, strawberries, raspberries" (PC 211; ch. 15), fare that accords with the medieval custom of "a last course of fruit [...] and other small delicacies, [which ...] would appear to have been part of the normal routine."[55] In *The Voyage of the Dawn Treader* we encounter Aslan's Table itself: "a long table laid with a rich crimson cloth" (VDT 207; ch. 13), which seems to offer "a promise of all happiness" (VDT 208; ch. 13), of the sort experienced by "courtly folk" in the middle ages, who enjoyed "a fortnight of intermittent feasting, and to enjoy the colourful, scented delights of [courtly...] cuisine," during the Christmas season.[56] *The Silver Chair* offers two dystopic and ironic feasts, the "autumn feast" where the giants had expected to offer children and Marsh-wiggle as part of the repast, and the food served by Rilian while suffering his magically-imposed delusions. But it also contains the delightful and true feast of the land of Bism, whose blameless gnomes eat rubies and drink diamonds.

In medieval thought, according to Madeleine P. Cosman (1976), "supernatural food," as Aslan's Table must be said to be, "good is associated with divine eating. God sups with the righteous, and miraculously feeds the devoted. [What happens ...] in the Christian sacrament allows the consuming of Godliness. The altar—*mensa domini*—the Lord's Table—is table for God's feast."[57] She adds that "Medieval food and ceremony could be most artful expressions of God's plenty [...] because food potentially was expression of a human being's [...] most holy nature."[58] Those who have enjoyed the elaborate ceremonialism of the Anglican festival Eucharist associated with

Christmas, Epiphany, Easter, and Pentecost, will recognize the combination of celebration and fulfillment in these joyous banquets of the spirit, these festive participations in the bounty of Aslan's Table.

VI. The Breakfast of the Lamb: The Encounter Situation

Perhaps the most poignant eucharistic reference of all is the Breakfast of the Lamb, with its imagery of the Resurrection appearance of Jesus by the shores of Galilee, as mentioned in John 21.13, with its hint of the Loaves and Fishes: "Jesus then cometh, and taketh bread, and giveth them, and fish likewise." In the first half of the church year, which begins in early December with Advent, and continues through Christmas, Epiphany, Lent, to Easter, concluding in Pentecost with the coming of the Holy Spirit, the mood alternates between solemn and joyous. During an equally long sequence from Trinity Sunday to the Sunday Next Before Advent (Christ the King), six months of consistent encounter with Jesus occur, containing neither the highs nor lows of the first half, but instead a simple, regular, supportive, nourishing encounter. For this half of the year, the Breakfast of the Lamb, based on the post-resurrection encounter with the risen Christ, who tells Peter to "Feed my sheep," a form of marching orders like the ones Aslan is inclined to give to the children and other characters he encounters, is an exact image.

In the various anti-communions of the eleven novels there is no sense of relationship: nobody truly meets, nobody celebrates, nobody communicates, nobody gives, nobody receives, nobody heals, nobody waits in patience, nobody is recognized, nobody obeys, nobody worships, nobody provides, and nobody shares. In the many symbolic Eucharists of Lewis's fantasies, on the other hand, from first to last, in traveling, in waiting, in celebrating, and in meeting, the incarnational relationship between the Creator and created is repeatedly made manifest.

Notes

[1] Cited from "Lewis Papers: Memories of the Lewis Family, 1850–1930," Walter Hooper, *C.S. Lewis, A Companion and Guide* (London: HarperCollins, 1996) 691.

Notes

[2] Margaret Visser, *The Rituals of Dinner* (Toronto, ON: HarperCollins, 1992) 36.
[3] Visser 36.
[4] C.S. Lewis, *All My Road Before Me*, ed. Walter Hooper (London: HarperCollins, 1991) 42.
[5] C.S. Lewis, *All My Road Before Me* 59.
[6] Cited in "Lewis on Communion," *The Lewis Legacy* (Winter 1997): 3.
[7] C.S. Lewis, *Letters to Malcolm: Chiefly on Prayer* (1963; New York: Harcourt, 2002) 102.
[8] C.S. Lewis, *Miracles: A Preliminary Study* (1947; London: HarperCollins, 2001) 95.
[9] C.S. Lewis, *Miracles* 221. Lewis's emphasis.
[10] C.S. Lewis, *Miracles* 221.
[11] C.S. Lewis, *Miracles* 222.
[12] Janine Goffar, *C.S. Lewis Index: Rumours From the Sculptor's Shop* (Riverside, CA: La Sierra UP, 1995) 106.
[13] C.S. Lewis, *Miracles* 222.
[14] C.S. Lewis, *Miracles* 222.
[15] C.S. Lewis, *Transposition and other Addresses* (London: Geoffrey Bles, 1949) 10-11.
[16] *The Letters of C.S. Lewis*, ed. W.H. Lewis (London: Geoffrey Bles, 1966) 224.
[17] C.S. Lewis, *A Grief Observed* (London: Faber and Faber, 1961) 51.
[18] C.S. Lewis, *Letters to Malcolm* 101.
[19] C.S. Lewis, *Letters to Malcolm* 9.
[20] C.S. Lewis, *Letters to Malcolm* 103.
[21] Nancy-Lou Patterson, "Ransoming the Wasteland: Arthurian Themes in C.S. Lewis's Trilogy Part I," *The Lamp-Post of the Southern California C.S. Lewis Society* 8.2-3 (November 1984): 25.
[22] Margaret Fulton, *Encyclopedia of Food and Cooking* (London: B. Mitchell, 1984) 373.
[23] George MacDonald, *The Princess and Curdie* (1883; Gutenberg ebook #709) ch. 21.
[24] MacDonald, *The Princess and Curdie* ch. 22.

Notes

[25] C.S. Lewis, *Mere Christianity* (1952; HarperSanFrancisco, 2001) 64.

[26] Homer, *The Odyssey,* trans. W.H.D. Rouse (1937; New York: New American Library, 1960) 229.

[27] Homer, *The Odyssey* 330.

[28] Doris T. Myers, "The Compleat Anglican: Spiritual Style in the Chronicles of Narnia," *Anglican Theological Review* 66.2 (April 1984): 153.

[29] Myers 153.

[30] 1 have discussed the symbolism of this tea in "Artist's Statement on This Month's Cover," *The Lamp-Post of the Southern California C.S. Lewis Society* 8.4 (December 1994): 4. For the propriety of the presence of Father Christmas in Narnia, see my essay, "'Always Winter and Never Christmas': Symbols of Time in Lewis's Chronicles of Narnia," *Mythlore* 18.1 (Autumn 1991): 10-14. [Editor's note: This essay is available in *Ransoming the Waste Land Volume II.*]

[31] For the symbolism of "The Merry Party," see my "Artist's Statement about the Cover: The Merry Party," *The Lamp-Post of the Southern California C.S. Lewis Society* 19.4 (Winter 1995-96): 4-6.

[32] Richard Sturch, "Common Themes Among the Inklings," *Charles Williams: A Celebration*, ed. Brian Horne (Leominster, UK: Gracewing, 1995) 155.

[33] Hooper, *C.S. Lewis, A Companion and Guide* 413.

[34] Hooper, *C.S. Lewis, A Companion and Guide* 411.

[35] C.S. Lewis, *Letters to Children*, eds. Lyle W. Dorsett and Marjorie Lamp Mead (1985; New York: Touchstone, 1995) 44-45.

[36] C.S. Lewis, *Surprised by Joy: The Shape of My Early Life* (1955; New York: Harcourt, Brace, Jovanovich, 1966) 113.

[37] Euripides, *The Bacchae,* trans. Donald Sutherland (Lincoln, NE: Nebraska UP, 1968) 20.

[38] Euripides 20.

[39] Myers 153.

[40] Myers 153.

[41] Myers 153.

[42] I have discussed this stream in my essay "'Halfe Like a Serpent': The Green Witch in *The Silver Chair*," *Mythlore* 11.2 (Autumn 1984):

Notes

37-47. [This essay is included in *Ransoming the Waste Land Volume II*.]

[43] Edward W. Said, *Orientalism* (1978; New York: Vintage Books, 1994) 63.

[44] In point of fact, the word "fruit" first appears in Genesis 1:11—"and God said, Let the earth bring forth [...] the fruit tree yielding fruit after his kind." The Tanakh renders this as "fruit trees of every kind on earth that bear fruit with the seed in it."

[45] Phyllis Trible, *God and the Rhetoric of Sexuality* (Philadelphia, PA: Fortress Press, 1978) 109.

[46] Waverly Root, *Food* (New York: Simon and Schuster, 1980) 7.

[47] Root 9.

[48] Root 10.

[49] Sir. Thomas Malory, *Le Morte D'Arthur*, vol. II (Harmondsworth, UK: Penguin, 1969) 517 Book XXI, Ch. 5.

[50] Morris J. Lacy, ed., *The Arthurian Encyclopedia* (New York: Peter Bedwick Books, 1986) 33.

[51] George MacDonald, *The Princess and the Goblin* (1872; Gutenberg ebook #709) ch. 22.

[52] See my essay, "The Holy House of Ungit," *Mythlore* 21.4 (Winter 1997): 4-15.

[53] C.S. Lewis, *A Grief Observed* 51.

[54] C.S. Lewis, *Letters to an American Lady*, ed. Clyde S. Kilby (1967; Grand Rapids, MI: William B. Eerdmans, 1971) 115.

[55] Constance J. Hieatt and Sharon Butler, *Pleyn Delit: Medieval Cooking for Modem Cooks* (Toronto, ON: University of Toronto Press, 1976) xi-xii.

[56] Maggie Black, *The Medieval Cookbook* (New York: Thames and Hudson, 1992) 112.

[57] Madeleine Pelner Cosman, *Fabulous Feasts: Medieval Cookery and Ceremony* (New York: George Brazillier, 1976) 113.

[58] Cosman 123.

A Hierarchy of Beings

That is what people are like who come back from the stars. Or at least from Perelandra. Paradise is still going on there.

——C.S. Lewis, *That Hideous Strength*

Nancy-Lou Patterson. "Bacchus and his Wild Girls." First reproduced in *Mythlore* 18.1 (Autumn 1991). Further reproduction prohibited.

5. "The Host of Heaven": Astrological and Other Images of Divinity

"I wouldn't have felt very safe with Bacchus and all his wild girls if we'd met them without Aslan."

"I should think not," said Lucy.

——C.S. Lewis, *Prince Caspian*

Patterson explores the role of planetary symbolism in C.S. Lewis's fiction, considering the importance of classical, medieval, and Renaissance astrology to it and making comparisons between historical traditions and with the characters in the novels. The opening section is historical. The second is dedicated primarily to planetary symbols in the Space Trilogy in conjunction with Lewis's statements on the subject in The Discarded Image *and in his later novels. The third takes up the same subject in the Chronicles of Narnia and the fourth is about* Till We Have Faces. *Lewis's representation of a hierarchy of persons is echoed in his hierarchy of realities, particularly in the Narnian Mountains of Aslan; Patterson discusses both hierarchies, as Lewis does, in terms of archetypes. She concludes by noting Lewis's emphasis on the feminine aspects of God, a subject she takes up again in "Guardici Ben" and "Archetypes of the Feminine."*

Patterson also discusses the relationship of the White Witch to the Snow Queen and Father Christmas, which is considered here, in her paper "'Always Winter and Never Christmas': Symbols of Time in C.S. Lewis's Chronicles of Narnia." She turns to the subject of astrological symbolism in Lewis's fiction again in "'Halfe Like a Serpent': The Green Witch in The Silver Chair.*" Both of these papers are available in* Ransoming the Waste Land Volume II.

An earlier version of this paper was published as "The Host of Heaven: Astrological and Other Images of Divinity in the Fantasies of C.S. Lewis, Part I" in Mythlore *7.3 (Autumn 1980): 19-29, and "Part II," which addresses the Chronicles of Narnia and* Till We Have Faces, *in* Mythlore *7.4 (Winter 1981): 13-21. Part I of the original "Host of Heaven" was revised by Patterson for a proposed anthology of papers about Lewis's fiction.*

"Medieval thinkers," C.S. Lewis wrote in *The Discarded Image* (1964), "attributed life and even intelligence to one privileged class of objects (the stars) which we hold to be inorganic."[1] This attitude may be contrasted with the one most in favor today, expressed in the following conversation from *The Voyage of the Dawn Treader*:

> "In our world," said Eustace, "a star is a huge ball of flaming gas."
>
> "Even in your world, my son, that is not what a star is but only what it is made of." (VDT 226; ch.14)

However, in his fiction Lewis also drew extensively on the medieval idea of planetary intelligences, even while adapting them to a Copernican system.

Astronomy and Astrology

In the medieval world there were only five planets, as we define planets, but with the sun and moon there were seven: Moon, Mercury, Venus, Sun, Mars, Jupiter, and Saturn. Each rolled majestically about the central Earth—in the Ptolemaic system—on transparent globes revolving one within the other. Outside of these was the *Stellatum*[2] where the fixed stars dwelt, and outside of that was the *Primum Mobile*. Of the exact position of Earth in this model, Lewis says, "The earth is really the centre, really the lowest place; movement to it from whatever direction is a downward movement."[3] In his pithiest expression of this model he says, "The Medieval Model is vertiginous."[4]

The life attributed to the stars by medieval thinkers came from their origins: "planets [...] had, after all, been the hardiest of the pagan gods," as Lewis says,[5] but "They were planets as well as gods."[6] As planets, they exercised an effect, called technically an "influence," on the Earth and its inhabitants. This effect is precisely the subject matter of astrology. Lewis explains, "Astrology is not specifically medieval. The Middle Ages inherited it from antiquity and bequeathed it to the Renaissance."[7] Its basic principle was not in doubt. "Orthodox theologians could accept the theory that the planets had an effect on events and on psychology, and, much more, on plants and animals."[8] The church fought against it, however, specifically objecting to

1) the "practice of astrologically grounded predictions";
2) "astrological determinism. The doctrine of influences carried so far as to exclude free will";[9] and
3) "the worship of planets."[10]

The origin of these proscriptions is of course the Bible, where again and again God's people were called to account for having "worshipped all the host of heaven" (II Kings 17.16 and 21.3). Jeremiah had complained of his people: "they have burned incense unto all the host of heaven, and have poured out drink offerings unto other gods (Jeremiah 19.13). In Deuteronomy God explains his ways to Moses: "Ye saw no manner of similitude on the day that the LORD spake unto you in Horeb out of the midst of the fire" (Deuteronomy 4.15). He has not shown himself in visible form, God says, "lest thou lift thine eyes unto heaven, and when thou seest the sun, and the moon, and the stars, even all the host of heaven, shouldst be driven to worship them, and serve them" (Deuteronomy 4.19).

The most attractive members of the heavenly host besides the Sun and Moon were those whose graceful dance assumed so elaborate a pattern: the planets. Franz Cumont, in his classic work *Astrology and Religion Among the Greeks and Romans* (1912), gives the history of planetary association most succinctly by saying that "the names of the planets which we employ today, are an English translation of a Latin translation of a Greek translation of a Babylonian nomenclature."[11] Lewis added to this sequence their names in Old Solar. I am referring to his wonderful inventions in the Trilogy, especially as they make their appearance in *That Hideous Strength*: Viritrilbia (Mercury), Perelandra (Venus), Malacandra (Mars), Thulcandra (Earth), Glund (Saturn), Lurga (Jupiter), Arbol (the Sun), and Sulva (the Moon). His descriptions of these powerful beings are superb evocations of traditional imagery combined with his own visionary genius. I will trace the history of the system he has used and then give his descriptive passages together with the traditions upon which he has drawn, to demonstrate the splendors he has distilled.

Originally the Greeks called Venus "Herald of the Dawn," Mercury the "Twinkling Star," Mars the "Fiery Star," Jupiter the "Luminous Star," and Saturn the "Brilliant Star." After the fourth century, "the planets became the stars of Hermes, Aphrodite, Ares, Zeus, [and] Kronos," which are the names of Greek gods and goddesses, because "in Babylonia these same planets were dedicated respectively to Nebo, Ishtar, Nergal, Marduk, and Ninib."[12] Astrology, however, was not imported along with these designations.[13] Eudoxus of Cnidos expressed the Greek view of astrology, which had been invented in its Western form in Mesopotamia: "No credence should be given to the Chaldeans, who predict and mark out the life of every man according to the day of his nativity."[14] After the conquest of Persia by Alexander, however, matters changed: politics "drew Hellenism towards star-worship,"[15] as Near Eastern culture came into fashion.

It was the establishment of an accurate chronology in 747 BC that had enabled the Babylonians to pass from "empirical observations, intended chiefly to indicate omens"[16] to something more nearly approaching "scientific astronomy." They recognized "seven principal stars"[17] of which five were distinguished as planets: the Moon, the Sun, Jupiter, Venus, Saturn, Mercury, and Mars (as this group was known to medieval writers). This list has a hierarchical rather than an astronomical order: "Jupiter, or Marduk, is put at the head of the five planets, because Marduk is the principal god of Babylon."[18] Cumont remarks that it is "The peculiar distinction of the Chaldeans that they made *religion* profit by these new conceptions."[19]

Paleolithic people were able to keep accurate records of lunar phases by carving tally marks in bone;[20] some authorities believe that the builders of Stonehenge constructed an observatory capable of predicting both lunar and solar movements.[21] With their long history of astronomical observations and their lunisolar calendar, the Chaldeans could predict a wide range of celestial phenomena, and since these elegant patterns traced on the pristine sky were to them the doings of high divinities, it became possible to predict the ways of gods to men and women. Jupiter was the foremost god, Marduk. Venus was Ishtar, that lady whose very name means "Star." Saturn was Ninib, Mercury was Nebo, and Mars was Nergal, the god of war. "This astral religion," as Cumont calls it, had become established in the sixth century BC during the second Babylonian Empire, and one of its primary features was the concept of Necessity, for the divine stars demonstrably repeated themselves in an endless and fixed pattern. Upon this basis, all divinities came to include an element derived from this star sign in the cuneiform versions of their names. The god An (Anu), whose name means "Above," was the Polar Star and was represented pictographically by a star.[22]

Although this "sidereal cult" was foreign to the Greeks and Romans, so that Aristophanes remarked that "barbarians" sacrificed to Sun and Moon while Greeks addressed personal divinities, "the common people" regarded the stars as living beings. It was thus "a shock to popular belief" when Anaxagorus, like Eustace, declared the stars to be "merely bodies in a state of incandescence."[23] Plato called him an atheist for this rash statement and declared the stars to be "visible gods which He [the supreme Being] animates with his own life."[24] In all this there is clear borrowing from Mesopotamian sources quite early in the development of Greek culture: they "owed to the observatories of Mesopotamia [...] the ecliptic, the signs of the zodiac, and the majority of the planets," and "to this first influx of positive knowledge corresponds a first introduction into the Greek system of the mystic ideas which the Orientals attached to them."[25]

This occurred during the Orientalizing Period when the ports of Ionia were opened to influences from Asia,[26] resulting in a great influx of artistic motifs, such as the winged beings, the various metamorphs including the gryphon and the dragon, and vegetal motifs including the palmette. The end result of these trends was that ancient Chaldean astrology, already present in Greek culture, and given new impetus in Hellenistic times, became concentrated in "a pantheistic Sun-worship," and was raised to the level of "official religion of the Roman empire."[27] In Cumont's words, "the common creed of all pagans came to be a scientific pantheism, in which the infinite power of the divinity that pervaded the universe was revealed by all the elements of nature."[28] I suspect that this faith is held by many of the religious people of our own day, whatever name they give their beliefs.

Such was the hardiness of these conceptualizations that they were passed into medieval and Renaissance symbolism, from which Lewis extracted them, and on into the present day. Jean Seznec, in his great monograph *The Survival of the Pagan Gods* (1953) argues that the ideas and interpretations of the world of the ancients survived because they were integrated into mythology. These interpretations included numerous categories; the one that concerns us here he calls "The Physical Tradition," which declared, as he flatly states, that "The heavenly bodies are gods."[29] His description of this apprehension in "the last centuries of paganism" accords well with the role they play in Lewis's fantasies: "The stars are alive: they have a recognized appearance, a sex, a character, which their names alone suffice to evoke."[30] It was this final identification of planets with gods, Seznec says, that assured the gods of survival. He calls this a piece of good luck for the Olympians, a "providential shelter" which arranged matters so that "though [...] dethroned on earth, they are still masters of the celestial spheres."[31] It was in this role that they passed into Christianity despite initial hostility: Seznec refers to St. Paul, who reproached the Galatians for observing "days and months and times and years" (Galatians 4.9–10). Among the survivals were the names of the days of the week and the adoption of the sun's birthday as Christ's nativity.[32] The physical world of the early church was that of Hellenism; this world continued to exist into the Renaissance.

Seznec outlines the evolution of astrology in the middle ages: until the twelfth century the focus was Byzantine. The Crusades brought Europe "the Greek texts with their Arab commentaries, in Latin translations for the most part made by Jews."[33] This eclectic mélange resulted in "an extraordinary increase in the prestige of astrology."[34] An adjunct of this development was the increase in the practice of magic: the *Ghaya* (in Arabic) which became the *Picatrix* (in Latin) was frankly "a treatise on the practice of magic,"[35] and included prayers like the following evocation of Saturn, which will be familiar to readers of *That Hideous Strength*: "O Master Saturn: Thou, the Cold, the Sterile, the Mournful, the Pernicious [...] the Sage and Solitary [...] the old and cunning."[36] This work shows "the accent and even the very terms of a Greek astrological prayer to Kronos."[37]

One of the major elements in the physical tradition was the association of planets with aspects of human life: both physiology and psychology. Seznec states that "the Renaissance saw no contradiction between astrology and science; rather the dominion of the heavenly bodies over all earthly things was viewed by some as the natural law par excellence, the law which assures the regularity of phenomena."[38] Even in the sixteenth century, he says, "astrology continued to keep alive the veneration for the gods which it had served as shelter since classical times"[39] Indeed, some astrological elements may be seen in the words of a hymn by Bishop Thomas Ken, written in 1692, and recently sung at an Anglican church service:

By influence of the light divine
Let thy own light to others shine;
Reflect all heaven's propitious rays
In ardent love and cheerful praise.[40]

In this verse, astrological elements revealed in the words "influence" and "propitious" serve as a metaphor for God's direct and divine role in human affairs.

Two factors in twentieth-century thought have most assisted modern astrologists in adapting their art to their era. One is the newly developing science of periodicity in the physical world: the case is cogently (and wittily) argued by J.A. West and J.G. Toonder in *The Case for Astrology* (1970).[41] The other is Jung's sympathetic treatment of astrological insights in his psychology.[42] I have thus chosen Jeff Mayo, whose writings particularly take account of Jungian interpretation, as a resource for contemporary astrological thought. I base this choice on the suggestion of Stephanie K. Walker, B.A., B.L.S., D.F.Astrol.S., who has been Mayo's student and my consultant in astrological matters related to my research for this paper. In *Astrology* (1964) Mayo calls the Planets "Life-Principles"[43] and says they symbolize "basic human functions"[44] and are "focal points of unconscious energies."[45] He discusses the planets (ten, including the sun, moon, and the planets unknown to the ancients), through a series of brief formulae: those that are relevant here include:

Sun:	Principle of self-integration.
Moon:	Principle of rhythms, through instinct–assimilation, reflections.
Mercury:	Communicative principle through mental and nervous co-ordination, transmission.
Venus:	Uniting principle through sympathy, evolution, feeling.
Mars:	Principle of activity through enterprise, self-assertion, energetic understanding.
Saturn:	Formative principle through restriction, discipline, rigidity.[46]

Mayo is at pains in his *The Planets and Human Behavior* (1972) to disavow the "*personification* of the planets," pointing out that "to the uninformed or skeptics this method of interpretation only continues to depict astrology as [...] full of mysticism and black magic." He states flatly, "The planets are not the prime creators of the human form and psyche. The origins of the human race are likely to be most deeply rooted in the origins of the planet Earth."[47]

The Space Trilogy and *The Discarded Image*

Having traced the historical development of these ideas, I now turn to Lewis's two treatments of planetary symbols in the Trilogy side by side with his discussion of them in his expository study, *The Discarded Image*, along with an outline of the mythological motifs and divine personalities with which they are associated. I shall begin with the Sun. Lewis says of it (or him) in *The Discarded Image*, "Sol produces the noblest metal, gold, and is the eye and mind of the whole universe. He makes men wise and liberal and his sphere is the Heaven of theologians and philosophers [...] Sol produces fortunate events."[48] This is the medieval model. But listen to Lewis's description of the Sun's light as viewed from outer space in *Out of the Silent Planet*:

> The light was paler than any light of comparable intensity that he had ever seen; it was not pure white but the palest of all imaginable golds, and it cast shadows as sharp as a floodlight. The heat, utterly free from moisture [...] produced no tendency to drowsiness: rather, intense alacrity. (OSP 30; ch. 4)

Ransom, the witness of these wonders, comments on this new apprehension:

> "I always thought space was dark and cold," he remarked vaguely.
>
> "Forgotten the sun?" said Weston contemptuously. (OSP 31; ch. 4)

They are traveling through the Fields of Arbol, as the solar system is called in the primordial tongue, Old Solar. When Ransom arrives on Malacandra and learns this language, he is enabled to communicate with the guardian of the planet, Malacandra himself: as is explained in *That Hideous Strength*, "Even the Oyéresu aren't exactly angels in the same sense as our guardian angels are. Technically they are Intelligences" (THS 282; ch. 13).

In creating his Sun, Lewis drew on the "astrological notion" that, as Cumont puts it, "The starry heaven is the principal seat of the divine energy and light which are spread throughout the world."[49] This concept is expressed in the opening lines of *Il Paradiso*, in which Dante wrote,

> *La gloria di colue che tutto muove*
> *Per l'universo penetra e risplende*

Dorothy L. Sayers and Barbara Reynolds translate this:

> The glory of Him who moves all things soe'er
> Impenetrates the universe, and bright
> The splendour burns [...][50]

This is the light bathing the Fields of Arbol. For the medieval mind, Lewis writes, "The Sun illuminates the whole universe."[51] He explains: "they had no notion that earth's air magnifies and diffuses light; for them night was only the cone of earth's shadow." Lewis could not be aware when he wrote this or any of the above passages on the light of Sun that modern poets' fears of the darkness of space (against which, perhaps, he wrote) were also to be disproved when real space-travelers showed it to be, precisely as he described it, bathed in light.

In contrast with this benign solar imagery, the Moon fares less well. In *That Hideous Strength*, Ransom answers Merlin's testing question as to "the usages of Sulva" (THS 276; ch. 13).

> Sulva is she whom mortals call the Moon. She walks in the lowest sphere [...] Half of her orb is turned towards us and shares our curse. Her other half looks to Deep Heaven; happy would be he who could cross that frontier and see the fields on her further side. (THS 270; ch. 13)

In physical reality, as we now know, the far side of the moon is deeply pitted by asteroids. In the symbolism of *That Hideous Strength*, while the far side is inhabitable, its inhabitants are sterile: among the Sulvans, "the womb is barren and the marriages cold [...] real flesh will not please them [...] children they fabricate by vile arts (THS 271; ch. 13).

In *The Discarded Image*, Lewis describes the moon in medieval thought: "At Luna we cross in our descent the great frontier [...] from aether to air, from 'heaven' to 'nature,' from the realm of gods (or angels) to that of daemons, from the realm of necessity to that of contingence, from the incorruptible to the corruptible."[52] It is this medieval concept of a frontier at the orbit of the Moon that Lewis has used as a basis for his Silent Planet myth. His portrayal of the medieval Moon emphasizes its negative elements: "Her metal is silver. In men she produces wandering," either as "travellers" or as "'wandering of the wits.'" I cannot help but recall Lewis's autobiographical reference to the moon in the light of this malignant portrait: in *Surprised by Joy*, he wrote of his terrible childhood school which he nicknamed Belsen that "I feared for my soul; especially on certain blazing moonlit nights in that curtainless dormitory."[53]

Antecedents of Sun and Moon mythology may be traced to ancient Mesopotomia. There, Shamash (the Sun) was admitted to the world each morning by a pair of scorpion-men in the role of door-keepers. Shamash was in particular the god of justice, but like the Greek sun-god Apollo, he also ruled over divination.[54] It was he who rose "with healing in his wings" after each night's journey through the underworld.[55] A seal shows the sun god gleaming radiantly on the eastern horizon between two lion-surmounted posts.[56] For the Greeks, Apollo was a god of the sun, but the Sun was a divinity in itself as well: Helios, who drove the solar chariot across the sky. Apollo's epithets, "brilliant," "fair," and "of the golden locks," emphasize his solar association.[57] He shot his arrows of light and was at the same time healer and lord of divination and of music. He passed whole into the Roman pantheon without losing his name, unlike certain other of the Olympians.

In Christianity, much of this solar imagery has been transferred to Christ, from the day of Sol Invictus, the Unconquerable Sun, celebrated at the Winter Solstice and now the date of the Feast of the Nativity of Jesus, to the use of dawn imagery—"O Orient"—to symbolize his role. There is even an early Christian depiction of the Sun's charioteer as a metaphoric figure of Christ. Lewis was to incorporate these solar associations, especially the ancient Mesopotamian association of the Sun with the lion, in his depiction of Aslan in the Narnian Chronicles. In the Trilogy he emphasizes the concept of divine light, as it is used in the Surge, Illuminare, the anthem familiar to Anglicans from the *Book of Common Prayer* and derived from Isaiah 60.1:

> Arise, shine, for thy light is come, and the glory of
> the LORD is risen upon thee.

For, behold, the darkness shall cover the earth, and
gross darkness the people.
But the LORD shall rise upon thee, and his glory shall
be seen upon thee.

In Mesopotamia, Sin/Moon was chief of the astral trio of divinities:[58] Ishtar and Shamash were his children. He was conceived as an old man with a beard of lapis-lazuli who rode majestically across the night in the barque of the crescent moon.[59] In another conception the Moon was his silvery crown: Mesopotamian crowns were surmounted with horns and the crescent Moon was conceived as being horned.

In contrast to this masculine moon, for the Greeks Selene (the Moon) was the sister of Helios (the Sun), and she illuminated the night with her golden crown.[60] Her most famous love was for Endymion, a youth of extraordinary beauty who had been granted eternal youth by Zeus on condition that he remain forever asleep. Selene watched over him through the eternal round of nights, unable to consummate her love. This virginal motif is expanded in the Greek association of the moon with Artemis, who was the goddess of the chase and of forests: she is symbolized by the she-bear. Her close association with Apollo (she was his sister) made her also a light goddess. Thus she wears the crescent on her brow and bears a lance.

It is the militant virginity of Artemis, the huntress, associated sometimes with the Amazons, that has perhaps been chosen by Lewis, who makes the moon not the model of triumphant chastity but of malignant sterility; as we have seen, the moon was not a benign entity to him. To the Romans, Artemis became associated with Diana, an Italic deity who was a goddess of light, mountains, and woods.[61] It was she whose temple on Lake Nemi was to spark the writing of the pioneer work on mythology, Frazer's *The Golden Bough*.

In Christianity, the Moon is associated with the Blessed Virgin Mary because of its long association with goddesses in general and with virgin goddesses in particular. Mary is frequently depicted as standing on the moon for this reason: the association of Mary with this attribute of the Moon goddess received a remarkable impetus when the apparition of Our Lady of Guadalupe became popular in Mexico, where a Moon goddess had been worshipped in aboriginal times. This benign association does not appear in the Trilogy, with one possible exception which I will discuss in a later chapter.

The Earth of Lewis's Space Trilogy is called Thulcandra by the Oyarsa of Malacandra (Mars). That being tells Ransom, as a voyager who has come out of the silent planet, Earth, "We know nothing since the day when the Bent One sank out of heaven into the air of your world, wounded in the very light of his light" (OSP 157; ch. 18). This reference to light is based on the tradition that Satan was once Lucifer, the brightest of all the stars. In *Perelandra*, Earth's planetary ruler is described as "that supreme and original evil whom in Mars they call The Bent One" (PER 96; ch. 9). The Bent One is, of course, Satan, whose fall from heaven is detailed in *The Divine Comedy* and *Paradise Lost*. In St. Luke 10.18, Jesus says "I beheld Satan as lightning fall from heaven."

Despite its evil reputation and the interplanetary silence to which it has been submitted, Earth is portrayed with aching tenderness as Ransom remembers his native planet in *Out of the Silent Planet*: "Wild, animal thirst for life, mixed with homesick longing for the free airs and the sights and smells of earth—for grass and meat and beer and tea and the human voice—awoke in him" (OSP 191; ch. 21). Describing Ransom's return, Lewis builds image on image: "'Oh God,' he sobbed. 'Oh God!' It's *rain*.' He was on Earth." The returnee paused, "drinking great draughts of air," and when he "slipped in mud, blessed the smell of it." Even in the "pitch-black night under torrential rain," he welcomed "the smell of the field about him—a patch of his native planet where grass grew, where cows moved, where presently he would come to hedges and a gate" (OSP 194; ch. 21). It was through a gate in a hedge that he first fell upon his adventure; now they welcome him back into his own world.

This same sense of bucolic intimacy and nostalgia recurs in *That Hideous Strength* when Merlin, newly awakened, speaks of his relationship with "these fields and I, this wood and I" (THS 284; ch. 13); a place of "mould, gravel, wet leaves, weedy water," where "he listened continually to a murmur of evasive sounds: rustling of mice and stouts, thumping progressions of frogs, the small shock of falling hazel nuts, creaking of branches, runnels trickling, the very growing of grass" (THS 285; ch. 13). The magician has begun to conjure with Earth: Ransom smells "that sweet heaviness, like the smell of hawthorn" (THS 285; ch. 13). He abjures the magus: "Whatever of spirit may still linger in the earth [...] You shall not speak a word to it. You shall not lift your little finger to call it up. [...] It is in this age utterly unlawful" (THS 286; ch. 13).

The position of Earth in Western mythology shares the curious ambivalence of this jewel-like planet ruled by a fallen archon. For the Babylonians, the great gods divided the Universe in a manner resembling the demythologized world of Genesis 1.6-10. Three related deities were Anu (Sky), Enlil (Earth), and Ea (Waters).[62] Enlil (Earth) had been "Lord of the Air" in Sumer and Nippur. Earthly rulers were his vicars. His early consort was Ninhursag, "Lady Mountain," who was the Earth itself. Enlil ruled Earth as "the executive of Anu."[63] Anu was "the aloof heavens, personifying the majesty of Kingship," while Enlil, "The violent storm-wind [personified] its executive power."[64] For the Mesopotamians, according to one text, "Kingship descended from heaven."[65]

This orderly arrangement is in total contradiction to the creation story in Hesiod's poem, the *Theogony*, which recounts Greek mythology in a systematic form while reflecting the popular beliefs of the eighth century before Christ. In the beginning, Gaea (Earth) emerged from Chaos, followed by Eros through whom all things were made. Among many other births was that of Uranus, the starry sky, while a mating between sister Earth (Gaea) and brother Sky (Uranus) produced the twelve Titans. The story progresses bloodily; its details belong under the section on Cronos/Saturn below. Gaea's role in Greek mythology was minor; while Earth to the Romans was Tellus Mater (hence the term "Tellurian" for earthly things): she was a goddess of fecundity, so that both marriages and fertility came under her sway.

The bloody conflict between generations of divinities, Titans and Olympians, suggested in the *Theogony*, does have a parallel in the Babylonian creation story, which is entitled the *Enuma Elish*, named for its opening words, "When above." In the tale told in its fragmentary tablets, discovered in the ruins of the library of Ashurbanipal, 668–ca. 630 BC, the creator, Marduk, personified by the planet Jupiter and the high god of Babylon, triumphs over Tiamat, the female Sea, and organizes the universe from her slain body, making both heaven and earth from her torn corpse.[66] Tiamat is to be understood as a watery chaos, an enemy to be conquered in order that the dry land may appear: the *Enuma Elish* calls Marduk "the wisest of [the gods]" [sic] (Tablet III, line 113) and says, "his countenance shone exceedingly, [lik]e the day" [sic] (Tablet VI, line 56).[67] In this light-related form,

> He created stations for the great gods;
> The stars their likeness(es) … he set up. (Tablet V)[68]

Thus, he himself "installed the stars" which were the images of the gods, and regulated their courses.

This divinity, Marduk/Jupiter, appears in *That Hideous Strength* when the planetary intelligences are called down to Earth by Ransom and Merlin. I have mentioned him first because the Babylonians did so, though he appears in his medieval position in the novel: "It seemed to each that the room was filled with kings and queens, that the wildness of their dance expressed heroic energy" (THS 323; ch. 15), Lewis writes. At the approach of Jupiter, "Kingship and power and festal pomp and courtesy shot from him as sparks fly from an anvil." The company sensed "bells […] trumpets […] banners," for "This was great Glund-Oyarsa, King of Kings, through whom the joy of creation principally blows across these fields of Arbol, known to men in old times as Jove […]" (THS 323-24; ch. 15).

Zeus, as the Greeks called this divinity, is named for the sky and the light of day. He is represented in classical art as a mature man of grave demeanor with scythe and thunderbolt in hand. This thunderbolt bears a notable resemblance to the Tibetan *Dorje*, which is also a thunderbolt. His head is crowned with oak-leaves; oak is related mythologically to thunderstorms, and an eagle is at his feet.[69] In his Roman form he is called Jupiter; both names—Zeus and Jupiter—are derived from the same root, the Indo-European *di* or *div*, "celestial light,"[70] from which we have our word "divine," and from which is derived the Greek word *Theos*, "deity," or, in plain words, God.

Jupiter was the god of all celestial phenomena: light, thunder, rain, and finally, of the Roman Empire itself. Lewis's term "Jove" is a reminder that the character of this celestial creator god has affinities for Christians—in this role only, needless to say—with Jehovah or Yahweh, that is, with God the Father. But, of course, all these beings represent aspects of God's activity; they are agents, servants, made, like us, in his image.

Lewis wrote of Jupiter in *The Discarded Image*:

> Jupiter, the King, produces in the earth, rather disappointingly, tin [...] The character he produces in men [... is] very imperfectly expressed by the word "jovial," [...] The jovial character is cheerful, festive, yet temperate, tranquil, magnanimous. When this planet dominates we may expect halcyon days and prosperity.[71]

This benign deity of medieval thought is far removed from the gleaming Creator of Babylon, and even farther from that God who answers by fire, who showed himself to Moses in the burning bush, taking care, understandably as we now see, not to show any "manner of similitude." Many a medieval and even Renaissance depiction of God the Father has, nevertheless, drawn upon this dignified divinity, not least the Creator-Father on the Sistine Chapel ceiling, that white-haired and lordly personage who extends his forefinger to the recumbent Adam in Michelangelo's best-known work.

Lewis's Saturn precedes Jupiter in both *That Hideous Strength* and *The Discarded Image*. The treatment of Saturn is perhaps the most evocative portion of the sequence in Chapter 15 "The Descent of the Gods." The nearer planets, in this scene, have already arrived. Now, "These would be mightier energies: ancient *eldila*, steersman of giant worlds which have never from the beginning been subdued to the sweet humiliations of organic life" (THS 322; ch. 15). There is an impression of "stiff grass, hen-roosts, dark places in the middle of woods, graves," of "the Earth gripped, suffocated, in airless cold, the black sky" full of the "utter and final blackness of nonentity from which Nature knows no return" (THS 322; ch. 15). This is "Saturn, whose name in the heavens is Lurga." Lewis says "His spirit lay upon the house, or even on the whole Earth, with a cold pressure such as might flatten the very orb of Tellus to a wafer." His is the "lead-like burden" of "a mountain of centuries," characterized by "unendurable cold" (THS 323; ch. 15).

When I first read this passage (I knew nothing at the time of astrology), I was particularly struck by the reference to stiff grass and hen-roosts, with which from my childhood in Southern Illinois I *was* familiar. The passage begins with these familiar but chilling images, which echo John Keats's poem *The Eve of St. Agnes*:

> Ah, bitter chill it was!
> The owl, for all his feathers was a-cold;
> The hare limp'd trembling through the frozen grass […]

It then proceeds to evocations of intolerable emptiness, pressure, and sterility. In *The Discarded Image* Lewis expands the medieval view of Saturn from which his stupendous portrait is drawn:

> In the earth his influence produces lead; in men, the melancholy complexion; in history, disastrous events. […] He is connected with sickness and old age. Our traditional picture of Father Time with the scythe is derived from pictures of Saturn.[72]

A somewhat comic version of this forbidding figure is to be seen in newspaper cartoons each year in North America at New Year's Eve, when the old and departing year is traditionally depicted in this guise.

In Babylon, Ninib (Saturn) was worshipped at Lagash as Ninhursag or Ninurta, and was a god of fields and canals as well as hunter and warrior.[73] His baleful emblem was a lioness-headed eagle. Saturn was also an agricultural god to the Romans, and his season, which begins December 17, was a cycle of rural festivals lasting until December 23: the Saturnalia, remnants of which still cling to our Christmas–New Year's cycle. He was represented with a sickle in one hand as well as a spray of wheat in the other: in the midwinter celebrations of Ukrainians, still practiced in North America, a sheaf of wheat, hailed as *Didukh* or "the old man," is brought into the house and propped up in a place of honour. Stiff grass and hen-roosts are explained here, but what of the intolerable pressures, the hints of annihilation?

In the *Theogony* we come to the source: to the Greeks, Saturn was Cronus. He was one of the twelve Titans born to Gaea (Earth) by her brother Uranus (Sky). In this awful story Cronus conspired with his mother to use her attribute—the sickle, representing the harvest of earth's bounty—to castrate his father. The parental genitals, thrown into the sea, raised a foam from which Aphrodite was born. The Titans were a divine race and by this ultimate Freudian act, Cronus became their chief; in his turn he became a terrible father who devoured his own children. His attribute has become the scythe, for he is, as Lewis says, the counterpart of Father Time.

Only when Zeus was born did one of Cronus's children escape, for Zeus's mother hid him (at Uranus and Gaea's advice) in a cavern on Crete, where his grandmother, Gaea the Earth goddess, gave him to the care of the nymphs of Mount Ida. Zeus grew up to overthrow Cronus in his turn, as well as the other Titans, aided by the other young gods of the Olympian pantheon: Cronus was imprisoned beneath the earth.[74]

This combination of motifs appears in Lewis's Narnian Chronicles in *The Silver Chair*, the children have found their way into the Narnian Underworld:

> here, filling almost the whole length of [a smaller cave], lay an enormous man, fast asleep. He was far bigger than any of the giants, and his face was not like a giant's, but noble and beautiful. His breast rose and fell gently under the snowy beard that covered him to the waist. (SC 146; ch. 10)

When Puddleglum enquires about this figure, the Warden of Underland replies, "That is old Father Time, who was once a King in Overland […] They say he will wake at the end of the world" (SC 146; ch. 10). And indeed, in *The Last Battle*, Aslan summons Father Time and "the great giant raised a horn to his mouth […] they heard the sound of the horn: high and terrible, yet of a strange deadly beauty." The immediate result of this act is that "the sky became full of shooting stars" (LB 172; ch. 14) (see below). Finally, at Aslan's word, "The giant threw his horn into the sea. Then he stretched out one arm—very black it looked, and thousands of miles long—across the sky till his hand reached the Sun […] And instantly there was total darkness" (LB 180; ch. 14). This is that "utter and final blackness of nonentity" (THS 322; ch. 15) which Lewis first evoked in *That Hideous Strength*.

The first of the planets to appear in "The Descent of the Gods," however, is Mercury or Viritrilbia, as he is called in *That Hideous Strength*. It is he who appropriately heralds the arrival of the gods on Earth:

> Now of a sudden they all began talking loudly at once, each, not contentiously but delightedly, interrupting the others. A

stranger coming into the kitchen would have thought they were drunk […] (THS 318; ch. 15)

The allusion to Pentecost is no accident: "These men are full of new wine" (Acts 2.13) was the response of some hearers when the Spirit-filled apostles began to "speak with other tongues" (Acts 2.4) so "that every man heard them speak in his own language (Acts 2.6). The doom of Belbury is to be the confusion of tongues, and this enspiriting freedom of speech in St. Anne's-on-the-Hill is the first note of the coming triumph of the planetary rulers over the microbes who have been infesting the Earth.

There are "plays upon thoughts, paradoxes, fancies, anecdotes, theories laughingly advanced"; while upstairs, "a rod of coloured light, whose colour no man can name or picture, darted between them" (THS 318-19; ch. 15). At the approach of Viritrilbia, "needle-pointed desires, brisk merriments, lynx-eyed thoughts" dart among them, "For the lord of Meaning himself, the herald, the messenger, the slayer of Argus, was with them: the angel that spins nearest the sun, Viritrilbia, who men call Mercury and Thoth" (THS 319; ch. 15). Lewis described this deity in *The Discarded Image*: "Mercury produces quicksilver, Dante gives his sphere to beneficent men of action […] he is the patron of profit […] the man born from under Mercury will be 'studious' and 'in writinge curious' […] 'Skilled eagerness' or 'bright alacrity' is the best I can do."[75]

These elements are found in Mercury from his first appearance in Babylon, when as Nergal or Nabu, he was the son of Marduk, and it was his task to engrave his father's decrees upon sacred tablets. Intellectual activity was thus under his protection. His attribute was the serpent-headed dragon.[76] As Hermes, he was *psychopompus*, the shepherd of souls, to the Greeks, as well as the messenger of Zeus. With his winged heels and hat (the *petasus*) and his caduceus, the winged staff entwined with serpents, he traversed the universe from end to end and from depth to height. Among his benevolent acts was the rescue of Dionysus when his mother, Semele, was destroyed by the fire in which the fecundating Zeus had visited her. We shall hear more of Dionysus below. To the practical-minded Romans Mercury was related to merchandise and trade: Plautus in the *Amphytrion* refers in particular to his role as messenger.[77]

In *That Hideous Strength*, Ransom explains these various beings to Jane:

> There is no Oyarsa in Heaven who has not got his representative on Earth. And there is no world where you could not meet a little unfallen partner of our own black Archon, a kind of other self. That is why there was an Italian Saturn as well as a Heavenly one, and a Cretan Jove as well as an Olympian. It was these earthly wraiths of the high intelligences that men met in old times when they reported that they had seen the gods. (THS 313; ch. 14)

In the context of *That Hideous Strength*, the Greek and Roman divinities are manifestations of the great archetypes who are really the steersmen and steerswomen of the planets. The novel is a fantasy, and its truths are embodied in fantastic ways. But they are still truths. The archetypal images which are part of the human psyche—and of which the cosmos itself is in a sense a projection or model—lie behind these endlessly reiterated images as they appear and reappear in the various cultures we have described. Even the "black Archon" can be read as an image of the Jungian Shadow. All these beings represent aspects and powers which lie within the human personality.

The great divinities who escort the earth are, respectively, male (Mars) and female (Venus) and they appear with vivid clarity in the sky because they are so near. Lewis gives them by far the most attention, for *Out of the Silent Planet* is set on Mars and *Perelandra* on Venus. Perhaps that is why he treats them so briefly in *The Discarded Image*, where he says, "Mars makes iron. He gives men the martial temperament […] He causes wars. His sphere, in Dante, is the Heaven of martyrs."[78] And "In beneficence Venus stands second only to Jupiter […] Her metal is copper […] In mortals she produces beauty and amorousness; in history, fortunate events."[79] Thus the medieval model: the mythological sources are mixed in the importance they grant to these beings.

For the Mesopotamians Nergal/Mars was the god of destruction and war, and he became the husband of Ereshkigal, Queen of the Underworld, thus becoming lord of the dead as well.[80] Ishtar/Venus, "goddess of the Morn and goddess of the Evening"—clearly the morning and evening star—was both a war goddess and a goddess of love. It was she who descended into the underworld and escaped again, divesting and investing herself of her splendid attire in the process. I cannot help but think of her (as well as of Our Lady) in association with the passage in the Song of Solomon 6.10: "Who is she that looketh forth as the morning, fair as the moon, clear as the sun, and terrible as an army with banners?"

The Greek Ishtar/Astarte was a fertility goddess, Aphrodite. Traditionally, her son was her primeval precursor, Eros, who was also the youngest of the gods. He was the husband of Psyche ("soul") and it is her myth, taken from *The Golden Ass of Apuleius*, that Lewis tells in *Till We Have Faces*. The Roman Venus was a goddess of spring, very minor in her original form. Mars, "the most Roman of all the Gods,"[81] was the father of Romulus and Remus, founders of Rome, and a god of agriculture as well as of war.

Together these deities play for Lewis the roles of archetypal male and female: he had been deeply moved by Coventry Patmore's writings on love, marriage, and the religious dimensions of human sexuality (1968). In "*Aurea Dicta*" XIII Patmore wrote: "Lovers put out the candles and draw the curtains, when they wish to see the god and the goddess."[82] That Lewis wrote with a knowledge of this passage is suggested by Jane's visionary perception of Arthur and Camilla Denniston, an ideal young married couple. To her they look "as if the god and goddess in them burned through their bodies and through their clothes and shone before her in a young double-natured nakedness of rose-red spirit that overcame her" (THS 320; ch. 15). I would suggest, in the last simile, a touch of Charles Williams's sensibility. He too wrote extensively of the sensual element in divine love. The particular theme of Patmore's that moved Lewis most deeply I shall refer to below in my discussion of Lewis's Venus, but as he begins with Mars—in *Out of the Silent Planet*—I shall discuss him (one cannot say "it") first.

The novel's highest moment occurs when the Oyarsa of Malacandra arrives in person: we share Ransom's perception of him:

> Every visible creature in the grove had risen to its feet and was standing, more hushed than ever, with its head bowed; and Ransom saw (if it could be called seeing) that Oyarsa was coming up between long lines of sculptured stones. Partly he knew it from the faces of the Malacandrians as their lord

> passed them; partly he saw—he could not deny that he saw—Oyarsa himself. He never could say what it was like. The merest whisper of light—no, less than that, the smallest diminution of shadow—was travelling along the uneven surface of the groundweed; or rather some difference in the look of the ground, too slight to be named in the language of the five senses, moved slowly towards him. Like a silence spreading over a room full of people, like an infinitesimal coolness on a sultry day, like a passing memory of some long-forgotten sound or scent, like all that is stillest and smallest and most hard to seize in nature, Oyarsa passed between his subjects and drew near and came to rest, not ten yards away from Ransom, in the centre of Meldilorn. Ransom felt a tingling of his blood and a prickling on his fingers as if lightning were near him; and his heart and body seemed to him to be made of water. (OSP 151; ch. 18)

Here the *mysterium tremendum* appears with the slightest of sensory signals, as in I Kings 19.11-12, when "the LORD was not in the wind … not in the earthquake; … not in the fire," but rather, in "a still small voice." Rudolf Otto (1923) discusses one of the Upanishads which "aims at making perceptible […] that before which 'all words turn back,'"[83] that, as he says, "in whose presence we must exclaim 'aaah!'"[84] The Sanskrit phrase of wonderment he translates, "'What unthing […] is this?' in the sense in which this expression is popularly used for a thing of which no one can say what it is or whence it comes, and in whose presence we have the feeling of the uncanny."[85] In Lewis's scene, he who approaches is "the Oyarsa of Malacandra, the great archon of Mars," "the Lord of Malacandra," or sometimes, simply, "Malacandra."

It was natural for Lewis (perhaps for many Christians) to depict the first divinity encountered by Ransom as male. "What is above and beyond all things is so masculine that we are all feminine in relation to it," he writes in *That Hideous Strength* (THS 313; ch. 14). The kind of deity implied in such an utterance may well be related to the figure of Mars. Lewis speaks of an importunate, jealous being, present indeed in wind, earthquake, and fire (as on Sinai): "the masculine itself: the loud, irruptive, possessive thing—the gold lion, the bearded bull—which breaks through hedges and scatters the little kingdom of your primness" (THS 312; ch. 14) as Ransom says to Jane. It is thus that Aslan—"the gold lion"—behaves in the last scene of *The Silver Chair*, when Jill and Eustace (who began the book crouching for cover behind a laurel hedge) return to triumph over their tormenters after Aslan knocks down the wall of Experiment House. Thus too, Jesus, rid the Temple of "thieves" with a whip of cords.

This explicitly martial mood is clearly expressed in Malacandra's approach to the upper chamber in *That Hideous Strength*: "Merlin saw in memory the wintry grass on Badon Hill, the long banner of the Virgin fluttering above the heavy British-Roman cataphracts, the yellow-haired barbarians" (THS 321; ch. 15). There are impressions of "fires […] blood […] eagles […] sky." Then, "They felt themselves taking their places in the ordered rhythm of the universe, side by side with the punctual seasons and patterned atoms and obeying Seraphim" (THS 322; ch. 15). Thus "Ransom knew, as a man knows when he touches iron, the clear, taut splendour of that celestial spirit which now flashed between them: vigilant Malacandra, captain of a cold orb, whom men call Mars and Mavors, and Tyr who put his hand in the wolf-mouth" (THS 322; ch. 15).

But to know the male is not to know the completeness of the divine. In the great epiphany at the end of *Perelandra*, the god and goddess attempt to show themselves. Their usual appearance is "The very faint light—the almost imperceptible alterations in the visual field—which betokens an *eldil*" (PER 169; ch. 16). Now, however, they appear as pillars, flames, "talons and beaks," snow, cubes, heptagons, wheels (as in Ezekiel)—and at last:

> […] suddenly two human figures stood before him on the opposite side of the lake.
>
> They were taller than the *sorns*, the giants whom he had met in Mars. They were perhaps thirty feet high. They were burning white like white-hot iron. (PER 170; ch. 16)

Lewis says of the divine pair: "their long and sparkling hair stood out straight behind them as if in a great wind" (PER 170; ch. 16), and adds, "a flush of diverse colours began at about the shoulders and streamed up the necks and flickered over face and head and stood out around the head like plumage or a halo" (PER 170; ch. 16). This image perhaps owes something to David Lindsay's *A Voyage to Arcturus*

(1920), which Lewis much admired; Lindsay wrote of the woman on the planet Tormance, Joiwind:

> Her skin was not of a dead, opaque colour, like that of an earth beauty, but was opalescent; its hue was continually changing, with every thought and emotion, but none of these tints was vivid—all were delicate, half-toned, and poetic.[86]

As with Maskull's inability to describe the special colors—hale and ulfire—shed upon Tormance by its double suns, Ransom "could in a sense remember these colours [...] but that he cannot by any effort call up a visual image of them nor give them any name" (PER 170; ch. 16).

Before Ransom's amazed vision, "The Oyarsa of Mars shone with cold and morning colours, a little metallic—pure, hard, and bracing. The Oyarsa of Venus glowed with a warm splendour, full of the suggestion of teeming vegetable life." The faces "were as 'primitive,' as unnatural [...] as those of archaic statues from Aegina," bearing an expression of absolute "charity"—"Pure, spiritual, intellectual love shot from their faces like barbed lightning." Although their naked bodies "were free from any sexual characteristics, either primary or secondary," they were clearly "Masculine and Feminine" (PER 171; ch. 16).

In this passage, masculine and feminine are presented as coequal and divine. The vision takes place on Perelandra, where the manifestation can be, as it were, celestial. On Earth, which is the setting of *That Hideous Strength*, "there is a terrestrial as well as a celestial Venus" (THS 314; ch. 14). Thus the goddess appears in two forms, just as C.G. Jung said that "the Mother Archetype" does, as both "the loving and the terrible mother."[87] Jane encounters her in a bedroom at St. Anne's House:

> A flame-coloured robe, in which her hands were hidden, covered this person from the feet to where it rose behind her neck in a kind of high ruff-like collar, but in front it was so low or open it exposed her large breasts. Her skin was darkish and Southern and glowing, almost the colour of honey. Some such dress Jane had seen worn by a Minoan priestess on a vase from old Cnossos. The head, poised motionless on the muscular pillar of her neck, stared straight at Jane. It was a red-

cheeked, wet-lipped face, with black eyes—almost the eyes of a cow—and an enigmatic expression. (THS 301; ch. 14)

Jane notes that "there was an almost ogreish glee in the face" (THS 301; ch. 14), like the glee of the Hindu goddess Kali in her necklace of skulls, or the Mesopotamian Anath hip-deep in the blood of battle. And she is not alone: "fat dwarfs in red caps with tassels on them, chubby, gnome-like little men, quite insufferably familiar, frivolous and irrepressible," make a shambles of the bed as Jane watches helplessly. These "gnomes" are earth-spirits, the nature spirits of the physical earth, derived from a medieval system in which fire, water, air, and earth have each a race of natural spirits native to their particular element.

"The strange woman had a torch in her hand" (THS 302, ch. 14), the passage continues. In Proverbs, "a strange woman" (6.24) is, frankly, "a whorish woman" (6.26 and 2.16). The Solomonic speaker admonished his "son" in verse 5.35: "the lips of a strange woman drop as a honeycomb, and her mouth is smoother than oil: But her end is bitter as wormwood, sharp as a two-edged sword. Her feet go down to death; her steps take hold on hell." The words of these passages may not be describing an ordinary woman of the streets, but a temple prostitute, whose profession was thus, to the writer, doubly abominable. The goddess served by these devotees had indeed gone down to death, for it was Ishtar who had descended to the Underworld and returned, according to the Mesopotamian myth. The motif recurs in Revelation, where for the early church, the city of Rome was perceived as the Whore of Babylon, where the saints were condemned to death in the arena.

Christian readers may find their perceptions of this passage colored by biblical concepts of the Strange Woman and the Whore of Babylon; Lewis gives a compassionate portrait of this cult in *Till We Have Faces* where the goddess in her chthonic form is called Ungit. "In the furthest recess of her house where she sits it is so dark that you cannot see her well, but in summer enough light may come down from the smoke-holes in the roof to show her a little. She is a black stone without head or hands or a face, and a very strong goddess" (TWF 4; ch. 1). The lack of face and hands reiterates the description in *That Hideous Strength*—"her hands were hidden"—reminding us of the Venus of Willendorf and other Paleolithic sculptures which are both handless and faceless.

Ungit has her servitors; Orual, the Queen of Glome whose memoirs are recorded in *Till We Have Faces*, recalls,

> I had seen their kind before, but only by torchlight in the house of Ungit. They looked strange under the sun, with their gilt paps and their huge flaxen wigs and their faces painted till they looked like wooden masks. (TWF 42; ch. 4)

The torchlight of Ungit's house will have burned with the light and smoke of the torch in the hand of the earthly Venus. Orual continues: "The girls stood stiffly at each side of [the Priest's] chair, their meaningless eyes looking always straight ahead out of the mask of their painting. The smell of old age, and the smell of the oils and essences they put on those girls, and the Ungit smell filled the room. It became very holy" (TWF 43; ch. 4). It is part of the point of *Till We Have Faces* that Ungit's house really *was* holy; that a religion which is too "thin" to include physical reality is not "thick" enough to satisfy the needs of a full human existence. For Lewis, Christianity was a "thick" religion, for which even the earthly elements of Ungit's cult were a necessary preparation.

When Jane appeals to Ransom to explain the presence of "that Huge Woman" (THS 313; ch. 14), he tells her "I have long known that this house is deeply under her influence. There is even copper in the soil. Also—the earth Venus will be specially active here at present. For it is tonight that her heavenly archetype will really descend" (THS 314; ch. 14). That sublime event brings Venus into the presence of the watchers, as with the others, by a gradually increasing crescendo of imagery.

"How warm it was [...] to-night the smell of logs seemed more than ordinarily sweet" (THS 319; ch. 15). There was "a smell of burning cedar or of incense," of "nard and cassia's balmy smells and all Arabia breathing from a box" (THS 319; ch. 15). This is the same odor, perhaps, as that which wafted from Ungit's girls. In using these olfactory motifs, Lewis drew upon the sense which is of all the most nostalgic, the most fundamental.

The descending archetype, like the earthly goddess, has her masculine attendants: "not the gross and ridiculous dwarfs [...] but grave and ardent spirits, bright winged, their boyish shapes smooth and slender like ivory rods" (THS 320; ch. 15). These are derived from *erotes*, pretty flying boy spirits which are often depicted on Greek pottery. The olfactory motif continues too: there is a "ponderous fragrance of night-scented flowers, sticky gums, groves that drop odours, and with cool savour of midnight fruit" (THS 320; ch. 15). Ransom, of course, is remembering the sensory delights of Perelandra as the goddess descends, bringing her redolant atmosphere with her.

Finally, the goddess herself, in her full selfhood—as "the consuming fire"—is present:

> It was fiery, sharp, bright and ruthless, ready to kill, ready to die, outspeeding light: it was Charity [...] the translunary virtue, fallen upon them direct from the Third Heaven [...] They were blinded, scorched, deafened. They thought it would burn their bones. [...] So Perelandra, triumphant among planets, whom men call Venus, came [...] (THS 320; ch. 15)

This lady is that goddess who, with the god, is seen by lovers who "put out the candles and draw the curtains" What is more, to continue the passage from Coventry Patmore: "in the higher Communion, the night of thought is the light of perception."[88]

It is this light which shines in this lady's hand, for she is the Holy Wisdom of Proverbs and, the Sophia of Wisdom in the Apocrypha: God's own feminine self. Patmore wrote in "Homo": "The external man and woman are each of the projected simulacrum of the latent half of the other,"[89] and, more specifically, "The woman is the man's 'glory,' and she naturally delights in the praises which are assurances that she is fulfilling her function."[90] Patmore explained, "You may see the disc of Divinity quite clearly through the smoked glass of humanity, but no otherwise" [sic].[91] These concepts are the source of the passage which Jane finds in a book at St. Anne's Manor:

> The beauty of the female is the root of joy to the female as well as to the male, and it is no accident that the goddess of Love is older and stronger than the god. (THS 60; ch. 3)

Lewis wrote to Owen Barfield on June 10, 1930, about one of Patmore's books:

> I have just finished the *Angel in the House*. Amazing poet! [...] What particularly impressed me was his taking [...] the Lilithian desire to be admired, and making it his chief point—the lover is primarily the mechanism by wh. the woman's beauty apprehends itself. [...] Venus is a female deity, *not* "because men invented the mythology," but because she is.[92]

Her femininity is thus as necessary to her divinity as Malacandra's was to his.

Each of the three novels of the Trilogy culminates in an epiphany: *Out of the Silent Planet* with the coming of Oyarsa who is Malacandra (Mars); *Perelandra* with a manifestation of Malacandra and Perelandra (Venus) together; and in *That Hideous Strength* it is all High Heaven who are called down by Merlin and Ransom upon the heads of their enemies. In his abbreviated version of that novel, Lewis excised a number of mythological motifs, but this pivotal chapter he left substantially intact, for it presents the full mythological structure of the Trilogy.

The stupendous sequence of images in *That Hideous Strength* is, in total, an invocation of the planetary intelligences as aspects of the human personality when humanity is considered relative to the image of the God who created them. It is one of Lewis's most breathtaking and audacious achievements, and these richly sensual images adorn the structure of his narrative with a splendor worthy of their medieval prototypes; indeed, of the divinities the pre-Christian world bequeathed to us.

The Chronicles of Narnia: The Mountains of Aslan

The world of the Space Trilogy is, granting the elements of science fiction and of the matter of Britain conflated within it, our world. As such it is not by any means a "secondary creation." Narnia too is something of a contingent universe, but in a different sense. In *That Hideous Strength*, Dr. Dimble tells Camilla that "something we may call Britain is always haunted by something we may call Logres" (THS 367; ch. 17). There is for every people, Ransom adds, "its own haunter" (THS 368; ch. 17). The archetypes are always present, just "the other side of the invisible wall" (THS 367; ch. 17). Something of that dependency exists for Narnia as well: she is created in the presence of human onlookers; humans also witness her end. Her corrupter is a witch from the dead world of Charn but she has been brought to Narnia by human agency. And it is for the sake of a human traitor that Aslan intervenes, is killed, and is resurrected. What is more, Narnia, like Britain, is but a "shadow or a copy of the real Narnia," as Digory explains to Peter in *The Last Battle*. There is an archetypal Narnia just as there is an archetypal Britain. "It's all in Plato, all in Plato," Digory exclaims. And in the very last chapter of the Narnian Chronicles, "Farewell to Shadow-Lands," we learn that all lands, physical or fictional, primary or secondary, are part of Aslan's country. Mr. Tumnus explains:

> That country and this country—all the *real* countries—are only spurs jutting out from the great mountains of Aslan. (LB 209; ch. 16)

Many elements of Narnian life reveal these affinities, but there are certain differences. Lewis has taken care to provide Narnia with its own astrology. In *Prince Caspian*, Dr. Cornelius, Prince Caspian's new tutor, tells him: "To-night I am going to give you a lesson in Astronomy. At dead of night two noble planets, Tarva and Alambil, will pass within one degree of each other. Such a conjunction has not occurred for two hundred years" (PC 48; ch. 4). The boy and his teacher observe this splendid sight from a tower, watching as the planets "hung rather low in the southern sky, almost as bright as two little moons and very close together" (PC 49; ch. 4). Dr. Cornelius explains this event to Caspian: "The great lords of the upper sky know the steps of their dance [...] Their meeting is fortunate and means some great good for the sad realm of Narnia. Tarva the Lord of Victory salutes Alambil the Lady of Peace" (PC 50; ch. 4). The tutor has called this lesson "astronomy"; in twentieth-century Britain and North America, it is called "astrology."

Not surprisingly, in a land where animals can talk and even the trees are ambulatory and inhabited by lissome intelligences, the stars themselves are alive. We meet the first of them in *The Voyage of the Dawn Treader*: he is the magician Coriakin. Lucy, the seeress of Narnia, "saw coming toward them an old man, barefoot, dressed in a red robe. His white hair was crowned with a chaplet of oak leaves, his beard fell to his girdle, and he supported himself with a curiously carved staff" (VDT 173; ch. 11). This being, we learn later, is a star who "might have shone for thousands of years more in the southern winter sky," but was condemned for some "faults a star can commit," to inhabit a small island and rule over the foolish Duffers (VDT 226; ch. 14). He does so by what he calls ruefully, "this rough magic" (VDT 174; ch. 11)—a term from *The Tempest*, whose magical ruler Prospero is thus invoked. Lewis remarks of Coriakin, "the Magician himself drank only wine and ate only bread" (VDT 176; ch. 11)—as did Princess Irene's father in George Macdonald's *The Princess and Curdie* (1883) another invocation by Lewis of a white-haired patriarch. Aslan himself says, "Many stars will grow old and come to take their rest in islands" (VDT 174; ch. 11).

But the stars in Narnia, or at least their progeny, are not always old. Toward the end of his journey in *The Voyage of the Dawn Treader*, Prince Caspian meets his future bride, the daughter of the star Ramandu:

> Now they could see that it was a tall girl, dressed in a single garment of clear blue which left her arms bare. She was bareheaded and her yellow hair hung down her back. And when they looked at her they thought they had never before known what beauty meant. (VDT 214; ch. 13)

She carried "a tall candle set in a silver candle-stick," the flame of which burned "straight and still." Presently we meet Ramandu himself:

> there came a figure as tall and straight as the girl's but not so slender. It carried no light but light seemed to come from it. As it came nearer, Lucy saw that it was like an old man. His silver beard came down to his bare feet in front and his silver hair hung down to his heels behind and his robe appeared to be made from the fleece of silver sheep. He looked so mild and grave that once more all the travelers rose to their feet and stood in silence. (VDT 221; ch. 14)

This "Old Man" tells them, "I was a long way above the air [...] the days when I was a star had ceased long before any of you knew this world, and all the constellations have changed" (VDT 225; ch. 14). He is, as Edmund, says, "a *retired* star," or as he adds, "a star at rest" (VDT 226; ch. 14). It is he who gently chides Eustace that a ball of flaming gas is "not what a star is but what it is made of." One day, he says, "when I have become as young as the child that was born yesterday, then I shall take my rising again (for we are at earth's eastern rim) and once more tread the great dance" (VDT 226; ch. 14).

I have wondered if perhaps there is a third descended star in Narnia—the Hermit of the Southern March. Lewis describes him in *The Horse and His Boy*: "In the middle of the gateway stood a tall man dressed, down to his bare feet, in a robe colored like autumn leaves, leaning on a straight staff. His beard fell almost to his knees." At any rate, there is one more scene in the Narnian Chronicles in which the Narnian stars appear; in *The Last Battle*, when Father Time, at Aslan's bidding, winds his horn, and "immediately the sky became full of shooting stars" (LB 172; ch. 14). This "rain of stars" continues until the sky is empty, for "All the stars were falling: Aslan had called them home" (LB 173; ch. 14).

Lewis explains:

> stars in that world are not the great flaming globes they are in ours. They are people [...] So now they found showers of glittering people, all with long hair like burning silver and spears like white-hot metal, rushing down on them out of the black air, swifter than falling stones. (LB 173; ch. 14)

These stars, like the animals and trees of Narnia, are indigenes. But there are other beings present, both benign and malign, including divinities. Some of these are patterned more closely than the Narnian stars, after Tellurian models. Some are even frankly visitors from our world, but in accordance with my treatment of these images as parts of a continuum, I will speak of the less earthly first. There is in Narnia an Anti-Aslan, the god Tash.

> In the shadow of the trees on the far side of the clearing something was moving [...] it was gray and you could see things through it. But the deathly smell ["Is there a dead bird somewhere about?" LB 90; ch. 7] was not the smell of smoke [...] It was roughly the shape of a man but it had the head of a bird; some bird of prey with a cruel, curved beak. It had four arms [...] and its fingers—all twenty of them—were curved like its beak and had long, pointed, bird-like claws instead of nails. It

floated on the grass instead of walking, and the grass seemed to wither beneath it. (LB 92; ch. 8)

Aslan, the divine Lion, is opposed by another form of animal being; as the lion is in origin a Mesopotamian image, so Tash seems modeled after the metamorphic entities of Mesopotamia, often depicted as attendant genii of the Tree of Life in their art. One of the most moving moments in the Narnian Chronicles occurs in *The Last Battle* when Emeth, the pious young Calormere (his name is the Hebrew word for "truth") meets Aslan; Emeth tells the story himself, describing how all his life he has served Tash, but upon seeing the Lion, he knows immediately to whom his true service is due. Aslan, he reports, said to him, "Child, all the service thou hast done to Tash, I account as service to me." Emeth continues:

> But I said also (for the truth constrained me), Yet [sic] I have been seeking Tash all my days. Beloved, said the Glorious One, unless thy desire had been for me thou wouldst not have sought so long and so truly. For all find what they truly seek. (LB 189; ch. 15)

This element in Lewis's understanding of the relationship of Christ—for Aslan is He—to all other religion seems to me one of his most important contributions to the faith he served all *his* days. And it is his exquisite courtesy in this matter which inspired me to write the present essay, one I would dedicate to Gracia Fay Ellwood, who first suggested to me that a Christian might learn from astrology as well as from other religions some truths about God. Perhaps it is only in the company of Aslan, however, that these aspects of the creation may be confronted in safety; hence my epigraph.

I have referred above to Phyllis Ackerman's interesting essay, "Stars and Stories." Her most intriguing association is that of Dionysus with a star motif. Plutarch, she writes, called him "the Night Sun"; Pindar, "the pure star"; and in *Antigone* Sophocles called him "the leader of the fire-breathing stars."[93] The phrase "the leader" was a Babylonian usage for Sirius, the brightest star in the northern heavens and especially noticeable (on the horizon) at the vintage season. And, Ackerman says, "'the stars aflame with fire' of which Dionysus as Sirius was Leader were the Pleiades."[94] She describes a second-century Gnostic version of the familiar Matthew 1.2 Epiphany narrative in which "there appeared to them an angel in the form of that star." The star in this case was, she says, Sirius, and "the Mazdean angel of that star, Tishtriya, was himself in direct charge of leading the magi to see and shower the infant Jesus with gifts—a mission befitting Tishtriya, a beneficent deity."[95] The Epiphany is the oldest feast of the birth of Christ, and celebrates the coming of the Magi (a title used for the astrologers of ancient Persia) by the leading of a star. This star, Ackerman is saying, was associated with Dionysus (Bacchus), acting as a herald for the coming of Christ.

In *Prince Caspian*, Aslan returns to the Narnia he has created and redeemed, a second time. As the children who have summoned his aid stand watching, "Low down in the East, Aravir, the morning star of Narnia, gleamed like a little moon. Aslan, who seemed larger than before, lifted his head, shook his mane, and roared (PC 156; ch. 11). In response, all Narnia wakens, and in their midst, Lucy sees that

> One was a youth, dressed only in a fawn-skin, with vine-leaves wreathed in his curly hair. His face would have been almost too pretty for a boy's, if it had not looked so extremely wild. You felt, as Edmund said when he saw him a few days later, "There's a chap who might do anything—absolutely anything." He seemed to have a great many names—Bromios, Bassareus, and the Ram were three of them. There were a lot of girls with him, as wild as he [...] And everybody was laughing: and everybody was shouting out, "Euan, euan, eu-oi-oi-oi." (PC 157; ch. 11)

"Bromios" means "The Thunderer."[96] Many of the details of Lewis's description of Bacchus probably come from the *Bacchae* of Euripedes:

> Joyful on the mountains—
> When from the rushing dancing throng
> Sinks he to the ground,
> With his holy fawnskin round him,
> Pursuing blood, slaughter of goats,
> Joy of raw flesh devoured,
> Pressing on to the mountains of Phrygia, Lydia,
> And the leader is Bromios!
> Euoi!

> And the ground is flowing with milk, flowing
> with wine,
> With the nectar of bees [...][97]

On the conclusion of Lewis's sequence, after a mad romp with the Lion and his companions including these, Susan confides in Lucy:

> "The boy with the wild face is Bacchus and the old one on the donkey is Silenus [...]"
>
> "Yes, of course. But I say, Lu—"
>
> "What?"
>
> "I wouldn't have felt very safe with Bacchus and all his wild girls if we'd met them without Aslan."
>
> "I should think not." (PC 160; ch. 11)

E.R. Dodds in his *The Greeks and the Irrational* (1951) makes Dionysus (whom the Romans called Bacchus) thus patron of *telestic* or ritual madness. By the wild dancing and repairing to mountain fastnesses, his followers found a ritual outlet for the "infectious irrational impulses."[98] He gave them the freedom to stop being themselves: "There must have been a time when the maenads or thyriads or [Bacchae] really became [...] wild women whose personality has been temporarily replaced by another." Still, one cannot know if these acts took place in Euripides's time, Dodds writes in 1951—which was before the resurgence of interest in altered states of consciousness made us more likely to expect ecstatic behavior.[99]

Dodds compares the maenadic behavioral traits with those known to anthropology from many cultures and finds them characteristic of ecstatic behavior: drumming, head-tossing, baby-stealing, immunity to pain, snake-handling, and the tearing to pieces and eating raw of a wild animal. As Dodds says, "if you want to be like god you must eat god [...] And you must eat him quick and raw [...] for 'the blood is the life.'"[100] The latter phrase appears as a motif in *Dracula*, uttered by the madman (not Dracula) who tries to increase his life by consuming other lives, beginning with flies and spiders. Dodds says of the god, "He may appear in many forms, vegetable, bestial, human, and he is eaten in many forms."[101] He makes the final suggestion that there once existed "a more potent [...] form of this sacrament [...] the rending, and [...] the eating, of God in the shape of man."[102] As Edmund says, "There's a chap who might do anything—absolutely anything" (PC 157; ch. 11). The God who gives, not another's body and blood to be eaten, but his own, is he who greets the Pevensie children in the last chapter of *The Last Battle*, when "He no longer looked to them like a lion."

The calling of Narnia's people by Aslan arouses more than Bacchus/Dionysus and his maenads: there are "certain other people" as well. In *The Discarded Image*, Lewis quotes Martianus Capella's "dancing companies of *Longaevi* who haunt woods, glades and groves, and lakes and springs and brooks; whose names are Pans, Fauns, […] Satyrs, Silvans, Nymphs."[103] The first Narnian we meet in all the Chronicles is, of course, Tumnus: anybody who does not remember Lewis's enchanting description of him, which culminates in the laconic ascertain, "he was a faun," has not yet read *The Lion, the Witch and the Wardrobe*, and is advised to do so at once, for the passage is unforgettable.

The Chronicles of Narnia are filled with longaevi, and it is not part of my study to examine them in detail, except to say that they come from the same world that gave us Dionysus/Bacchus. A famous frieze, "The Retinue of Dionysus" (or "The Triumph of Bacchus"), on a sarcophagus in the National Museum, Naples, shows us exactly the scene described in *Prince Caspian*, including Silenus transported on a donkey: satyrs, fauns, centaurs, maenads, erotes, and the Lord Dionysus himself, depicted as a beautiful youth lounging in his car.

Clearly the tree spirits, river deities, nymphs, and fauns are nature spirits, and Aslan has created them along with Narnia. In *The Magician's Nephew* we read his creative words "Narnia, Narnia, Narnia, awake. Love. Think. Speak. Be walking trees. Be talking beasts. Be divine waters" (MN 126; ch. 9). And within moments of this primal event, "Out of the trees wild people stepped forth, gods and goddesses of the wood; with them came Fauns and Satyrs and Dwarfs. Out of the river rose the river god and his Naiad daughters" (MN 127; ch. 10). On Trajan's column in Rome, a river god lifts up his bearded head to see a group of Roman soldiers sack a city: how much the more, then, should a river god rise up to see the triumph of Aslan!

In addition to these beings from the cultures of Greece and Rome, the dwarfs and giants of Narnia are modeled after Norse mythology. H.R. Ellis Davidson in her *Gods and Myths of Northern*

Europe (1964) gives the tales concerning these beings which were preserved by the Christian writer Snorri in the *Prose Edda*, of the primal earth giant, the frost-giants, the dwarfs "who bred in the earth like maggots,"[104] and the various affairs of "The Giants and the Dwarfs,"[105] to which she devotes a whole section. I am glossing over these catalogs of beings as if my readers will recognize fauns, centaurs, giants, and dwarfs by the mere mention of them. This recognition is part of my own life because as a child I both studied Classical and Norse mythology, and read the myths for my own pleasure. If children no longer do this, they can still know these beings personally, because they have their life in the Narnian Chronicles. Lewis said of himself that he was the last of the Old Western Men, and that is nowhere more true than in this!

Silenus, a part of the retinue of Dionysus in Greek thought, just as Lewis shows him, is a "cheerful drunkard" who has been the tutor of the god.[106] His name comes from the Sileni, rural divinities from Phyrgia, who personified rivers and springs.[107] Satyrs are forest spirits who combine in their appearance the monkey and the goat: Hesiod remarked on their sensuality and cheer.[108] Satyrs are "the peculiar attendants of Dionysus," Guthrie says;[109] they come from a past already deep in Classical times. They may derive aetiologically from warrior dance rites of extreme antiquity. There are whirling male dancers painted on the walls of the earliest Neolithic Anatolian villages, wearing spotted leopard skins (and Dionysus often rides a leopard in art). Pan, the god of the flocks, is also a part-man, part-goat being, a phallic divinity of the shepherd's world.[110] The same physical appearance is shared by the fauns, who were associated in Roman thought with Faunus, a god of field and pasture (conflated with the Greek Pan). Fauns are half-man, half-goat too: their upper bodies are human (except for goatish horns), but their lower bodies are those of goats, shaggy limbs, cleft hooves and all. In Roman tradition, Faunus had taught humankind to plant crops and breed stock.[111] The faun Tumnus, described by Lewis, figures as the psychopomp or escort into the world of Narnia for Lucy in *The Lion, The Witch, and The Wardrobe*. He may derive his name in part from the shape-changing Roman god Vertumnus (the Latin word *vertere* means "to change"), who was an associate of Silvanus, a forest god often confused with, and hence associated with, Faunus (Roman) and Pan (Greek).[112] Centaurs, part-man and part-horse, were given their "definitive appearance" in the time of Phidias, when they were carved in this form on the frieze of the Parthenon; it is this shape that Lewis gives to them.[113] Nymphs, in ancient Greece, were feminine beings associated with natural objects.[114] Oreads were mountain nymphs, Meliae and Dryads were tree nymphs, Naiads were fresh water nymphs, and Nereids were sea nymphs. They were indeed long-livers: there is a fragment of Hesiod that suggests their length of days adds up to one hundred thousand years. The life of a Dryad was "bound up with her tree," and trees are indeed the longest-living things.[115]

Jacob Grimm in his *Teutonic Mythology* (1883) made the interesting comment that "Man's body holds a medium between those of the giant and the elf."[116] The dwarf is even smaller than the elf, and is always old, being "a greybeard in the seventh" year of his life.[117] The dwarf is a figure of Indo-European mythology, appearing in Sanskrit texts as well as those of the North: the same is true of the giant, for the titans of Greek thought were giants. But the particular form of dwarf and giant used by Lewis is that of Norse myth. Of giants, Grimm says, "By so much of bodily size and strength as man surpasses the [...] dwarf, he falls short of the giant; on the other hand, the race of [...] dwarfs has a livelier intellect and subtle sense than that of men, and in these points again the giant falls far below mankind."[118] Lewis uses these traits for his giants, such that they are notoriously stupid, but divided between good-hearted and evil-hearted; and his dwarfs, which in *The Last Battle* are too lively-minded for their own good, sticking to their own opinions to the point of refusing to go into Aslan's country when Narnia's end is come.

In contrast with beings from the essentially benign catalogue of Martianus Capella—the *Longaevi*—Lewis has also written of beings like those in the passages he quotes in *The Discarded Image* from Milton's *Comus*: "Blue meager Hag [...] unlaid ghost—/ [...] goblin or swart Faery"[119]; from *Beowulf*, *ylfe* ["—ogres and elves and evil shade—/as also giants"],[120] and from Reginald Scott, "spirits, witches, urchins, elves, hags, fairies, satyrs, pans, faunes, sylens, tritons, centaurs, dwarfs, giants, nymphes, Incubus, Robin Good Fellow."[121] One thinks of the "dull, gray voice" (PC 166; ch. 12) which belonged to a "Wer-Wolf" (PC 161; ch. 12) which was summoned, along with a Hag, by the dwarf Nikabrik in *Prince Caspian*: all three—dwarf included—are dispatched by the end of the chapter "Sorcery and Sudden Vengeance."

Lewis gives for the *longaevi*, which include, in addition to the beings already mentioned, the "High Fairies," four medieval explanations:

1) "that they are a third rational species distinct from angels and men,"[122]
2) "that they are angels, but a special class of angels who have been [...] 'demoted' [rather like Coriakin]";[123]
3) "That they are dead";[124] and
4) in an answer extracted under torture, "That they are fallen angels; in other words, devils."[125]

The result of the last was that "A churchyard or brimstone smell came to hang about [...] them" and the High Fairies were "expelled by a darkening of superstition."[126] Lewis for his part has illuminated again these lovely peoples, and has given to Arbol's fields, *eldila* (angels), *hrossa*, *sorns*, *pfifltriggi*, Perelandrians (Tor and Tinidril), and humankind, while making Narnia home to animals, *longaevi*, and stars.

A world in which animals speak, trees walk, and everything is inhabited by or is a manifestation of spirit, is a shamanistic world. I have already quoted E.C. Dodds on elements of the irrational in Greek religion. E.A.S. Butterworth, in his *Some Traces of the Pre-Olympian World in Greek Literature and Myth* (1966) has pointed out striking elements of shamanic cosmology underlying the later rationalizations of Olympian religion. It is not part of my intention to delve deeply into the question of what Greek religion "really" or "originally" was—readers will have seen that I have relied on the most public, developed, received versions of Greek mythology, for these are the versions handed down through medieval and Renaissance periods to the era of Lewis and ourselves. Nevertheless, Lewis has seized upon precisely the aspects of Greek (and Norse) world view that are oldest, most primitive, most—in the literal sense of the word—pagan, which means "country person"—*paganus*. As Lucy said, "when trees dance, it must be a very, very country dance indeed" (PC 138; ch. 10). Lewis wrote that "Christians and Pagans had much more in common with each other than either has with a post-Christian. The gap between those who worship different gods is not so wide as that between those who worship and those who do not."[127] The kind of pagan Lewis had in mind he embodied in Emeth, the follower of Truth. Something of this thought may also be seen in Patmore's aphorism in "Knowledge and Science."

> The Pagan who simply believed in the myth of Jupiter, Alcmena, and Hercules, much more he who had been initiated into the unspeakable names of Bacchus and Persephone, knew more of living Christian doctrine than any "Christian" who refuses to call Mary the "Mother of God."[128]

Lewis's expression of this idea is characteristically more eirenic.

Lewis summarized the Narnian universe in his introduction to D.E. Harding's *Hierarchy of Heaven and Earth* (1952):

> At the outset, the universe appears packed with will, intelligence, life and positive qualities; every tree is a nymph and every planet a god. Man himself is akin to the gods. The advance of knowledge gradually empties this rich and genial universe: first of its gods, then of its colours, smells, sounds and tastes, finally of solidity itself as solidity was originally imagined.[129]

Lewis has made it his task to restore these traits to their original position, having concluded perhaps, that he must make his readers good Pagans before he could make them good Christians.

One last figure from our world makes a brief appearance in Narnia, and an examination of his role there (and of his origins here), suggests the rightness of what some readers reportedly regard as an intrusion. "He was a huge man in a bright red robe (bright as hollyberries) with a hood that had fur inside and a great white beard that fell like a foamy waterfall over his chest" (LWW 106; ch. 10). This figure, based on the British Father Christmas rather than the North American Santa Claus, "was so big and so glad, and so real, that they all became quite still. They felt very glad, but also solemn." He gives presents to the Pevensie children and their guides: a repaired dam to the Beavers, a shield and sword to Peter, a bow and quiver and an ivory horn to Susan, a bottle of cordial "of the juice of one of the fireflowers that grow in the mountains of the sun" (LWW 109; ch. 10) and a new dagger to Lucy. "Then he cried out 'Merry Christmas!

Long live the true King!' and cracked his whip, and he and the reindeer and the sledge and all were out of sight" (LWW 109; ch. 10).

The reindeer provide a significant clue as to the role of Father Christmas in *The Lion, The Witch, and The Wardrobe*. Lewis tells us that his reindeer "were far bigger than the Witch's reindeer, and they were not white but brown." The Lion, it seems is not the direct opponent of the Witch; rather, Father Christmas, like her an invader from another world, is her antagonist and opposite. His weapons will figure in all that humans (or Narnians) can do to oppose her. Her ultimate defeat is at the hands of one who does not do battle at all.

Readers may compare Lewis's Father Christmas with that of J.R.R. Tolkien in *The Father Christmas Letters* (1976), for more light on the conventional figure of British "popular culture" c. 1920-30. A famous work of folklore originally published in 1912 describes this figure as "a sort of incarnation of Christmas [rather] than a saint with a day of his own."[130] Most pregnantly for the appearance of Father Christmas in Narnia, Clement Miles (1912/1976) suggests, "In England there are signs that supernatural visitors were formerly looked for during the Twelve Days [between Christmas and Epiphany—December 25 and January 6].[131] This sacral period, which surrounds the supremely transitional moment when the sun's power ceases to wane and begins to wax, is fraught with peculiar dangers, such as the possibility that the dead might return or devils break in. Christmastime is the popular season for telling ghost stories in England. Benign happenings, too, are associated with Christmas Eve, the beginning of this season: especially appropriate to Narnia is the tradition "that on Christmas Eve animals have the power of speech."[132]

Saturn, patron of the *Saturnalia*—the ancient Roman festival of the Winter Solstice which gave many of its customs to Christmas—is, as we have seen, *Time*, and Father Christmas comes to Narnia to prepare the Sons of Adam and Daughters of Eve—that is, human beings from Earth—for the advent of Aslan. The White Witch is an alien from Charn, as we learn in *The Magician's Nephew*. Aslan, however, returns to his own Creation. Father Christmas is thus the appropriate Elijah/St. John the Baptist to this apocalyptic event, for he appears to human (English) children. He is no more alien than the White Witch and forms a foil to her; *he* is the anti-witch, not Aslan. The Witch is thus no Anti-Aslan but a visitant brought to Narnia by human agency. Lewis's audacious capacity to baptize the gods is as active in the Father Christmas sequence as anywhere.

There is more, it appears, to the character of Father Christmas than the saintly or seasonal: William Sansom (1968) calls him "half St. Nicholas and half an ancient Yule god."[133] He asks, "Who else ever went in and out by the chimney? Early hearth-gods and gods of the yule-log."[134] Pursuing this theme, he muses, "there has always been a varying male yule-figure […] often a Silenus, sometimes a hoary old man, his head often wreathed in mistletoe and holly, his gown varying in colour, white, red, green, or fustian brown."[135] He concludes—by a dazzling syncretic leap—that "this old man of Christmas is a later impersonation of Saturn—who ate his own children […] allied to the Carthaginian Baal-Hammon, a ram-horned god to whom children were sacrificed. […] The devil of course was also Beelzebub, Baal (Lord) of the Flies."[136] The European Santa Claus figures are accompanied by beings that are often hairy and horned who transport his punitive switches and (shades of human sacrifice) ashes. In fact, we are here at a point rather earlier than Babylon: horns and hair take us back to the shamanic universe. Joan Vastokas (1973/1974), an eminent authority on Canadian Native art, writes:

> Another component of contemporary Christmas folklore, probably having shamanistic roots, is Santa Claus himself. Like a shaman, he descends to earth from the sky through the smoke-hole (chimney) after a magical flight through the air, assisted by his guardian and helping spirits, the reindeer. Reindeer, moreover, are animals of the sub-Arctic tundra, where Eurasian shamanism and the sacred birch trees once flourished and where reindeer were important shamanistic guardians. These northern origins are, in fact, retained in current folklore, for Santa's abode is in the north where, within shamanistic ideology, shamans are born.[137]

The relationship of this complex of ideas, not only to Tolkien's *jeu d'esprit* for his children, with his letters from the North Pole, but to Lewis's Narnia with its theme of Northernness, is left to the reader to ponder.

Lewis's vivid description of Father Christmas's reindeer is matched by one of those belonging to the White Witch: "The reindeer were about the size of Shetland ponies and their hair was so white that even the snow hardly looked white compared with them; their branching horns were gilded and shone like something on fire when the sunshine caught them. Their harness was of scarlet leather and covered with bells" (LWW 31; ch. 3). The lady these marvelous beasts accompany and transport, owes a great deal to a story with a number of elements of northern shamanism in it, including a Lappish sorceress. The White Witch of Narnia closely resembles the Snow Queen of Hans Christian Andersen's masterpiece. Lewis says of the White Witch's coming "there swept into sight a sledge drawn by two reindeer" (LWW 30; ch. 3), and Edmund sees that "in the middle of the sledge sat [...] a great lady [...] She also was covered in white fur up to her throat" (LWW 31; ch. 3). Lewis's description of her is striking:

> Her face was white—not merely pale, but white like snow or paper or icing sugar, except for her very red mouth. It was a beautiful face in other respects, but proud and cold and stern. (LWW 31; ch. 3)

In another place, Lucy explains the White Witch's role: "she has made a magic so it is always winter in Narnia—always winter, but it never gets to Christmas" (LWW 42; ch. 4). With the arrival of Father Christmas, the light (Aslan) is heralded, and after him, the Spring arrives, in a sequence of heartbreaking beauty.

The parallels between Lewis's description of the White Witch and Andersen's of the Snow Queen are striking. In Kay's first vision of her, she appears to him in a snowflake: "She was pretty and delicate, but she was of ice, blinding, dazzling ice; yet she was alive. Her eyes gazed out like two bright stars, but there was no rest or quietness in them."[138] After the magic bits of glass enter his eye and heart, he cares only for snowflakes seen through a magnifying glass, rather like Eustace. Presently, "a large sledge came by; it was painted white all over, and in it was someone wrapped in a shaggy white fur and wearing a shaggy white cap."[139] As Kay looks, "the person who was driving in it rose. The fur and the cap were all of snow: it was a lady, tall and slender, shining white—the Snow Queen."[140] It is the pure maiden Gerda who rescues Kay from the Snow Queen's grip, and, as they leave her palace of ice together, Spring begins. Readers who know this story in its entirety, rather than from abbreviated or animated versions, will be aware of the Christian elements in it, and will not be surprised at the apposite nature of Lewis's use of it as a source.

Till We Have Faces: The God of Love

Lewis's masterpiece, *Till We Have Faces*, has been analyzed by a number of distinguished writers, and I have already mentioned some of its elements, especially his Ungit/Venus. My paper has been devoted to Lewis's use of mythological beings, especially the planetary deities and their associates. I shall discuss only one figure from this novel, the character of Cupid, who is Eros, the son of Aphrodite/Venus. This divinity is described in Lewis's source, the story within a story in *The Golden Ass of Apuleius*, as "her winged son Eros, alias Cupid, that very wicked boy, with neither manners nor respect for the decencies."[141] When Psyche's father offers her up for her "dreadful wedding"[142] she "was left alone weeping and trembling at the very top of the hill, until a friendly west wind suddenly sprang up."[143] The wind bears her to a beautiful valley where in wandering she comes upon a palace, the description of which causes the reader to agree that it is "too wonderfully built to be the work of anyone but a god."[144] Ensconced within, she eventually hears "the whisper of her unknown husband," who makes her his wife.[145] Her happiness is to be spoiled by her jealous sisters, and she begs her husband to let her have sight of him: she only knows him by her tactile sense: "these fragrant curls dangling all around your head; these cheeks as tender and smooth as my own; this breast which gives out such extraordinary heat."[146] Finally her sister's goading drives her to the fateful act: by the light of a forbidden lamp she sees her husband with her own eyes: "there lay the gentlest and sweetest of all wild creatures, Cupid himself, the beautiful Love-God."[147]

> [...] she stared at Cupid's divine beauty; his golden hair, washed in nectar and still scented with it, thick curls straying over white neck and flushed cheeks and falling prettily entangled on either side of his head—hair so bright that the flame of the lamp winked in the radiant light reflected from it. At his shoulders grew soft wings of the purest white, and though they were at rest, the tender down fringing the feathers quivered naughtily all the time. The rest of his body was so smooth and beautiful that Venus could never have been ashamed to ac-

> knowledge him as her son. At the foot of the bed lay this great god's bow, quiver and arrows.[148]

Considering the sensual riches of these passages, Lewis has wisely refrained from direct description of the god. His novel is a book for grown-ups; I suspect he may have thought—or at least hoped—that his readers might have been familiar with Apuleius. At any rate, he begins his evocation of the "god of the Grey Mountain" to whom Psyche is to be sacrificed, with the approach of the "West-wind"—as I read the novel, the God of the Grey Mountain and West-wind are in fact the same personage. Like Apuleius's "wicked boy," Lewis's West-wind is a merry, rough god" (TWF 112; ch. 10). His appearance is described by Psyche to her sister Orual:

> "The wind got wilder and wilder. It seemed to be lifting me off the ground so that, if it hadn't been for the iron round my waist, I'd have been blown right away, up in the air. And then—at last—for a moment—I saw him."
>
> "Saw whom?"
>
> "The West-wind."
>
> "*Saw* it?"
>
> "Not it; him. The god of the wind: West-wind himself."
>
> "Were you awake, Psyche?"
>
> "Oh, it was no dream. One can't dream things like that. He was in human shape. But you couldn't mistake him for a man. Oh, Sister, you'd understand if you'd seen. How can I make you understand?" (TWF 110; ch. 10)

The Biblical word for spirit is *ruach*: S.G.F. Brandon (1969) says of it, "the Hebrews also had the word *ruach*, usually translated 'spirit,' to describe the outstanding mental and physical energy that characterized such men as Elijah."[149] This is that wind that bloweth where it listeth (John 3.8). Mary's apparitions at Lourdes were presaged by a wind: "Suddenly [...] Bernadette heard, as she put it, 'a sound of wind as though it were blowing up for a storm'" and "The wild rose and the branches [...] 'were shaking to and fro, below the topmost opening, but all around there was no movement. ... In the opening a moment later I saw a girl in white.'"[150] And of course, the "rushing, mighty wind" (Acts 2.2) of Pentecost heralds the coming of the Holy Spirit. In the Old Testament, "The LORD hath his way in the whirlwind and in the storm and the clouds are the dust of his feet" (Nahum 1.3). Lewis's Psyche says, "And he took me [...] in his beautiful arms which seemed to burn me (though the burning didn't hurt)" just as Apuleius's Cupid presses Psyche to his breast of "extraordinary heat" (TWF 112; ch. 10).

Jung reminds us that "In Thebes the chief god Khnum, in his cosmogonic aspect, represented the wind-breath, from which the 'spirit [*pneuma*] of God moving over the waters' was later developed,"[151] and describes Indra (a Hindu divinity) as the "psychopomp who delivers souls to the wind, to the generating pneuma, the individual and universal *prana* (life-breath), to save them from 'repeated death.'"[152] In Psyche's case the West-wind is indeed a psychopomp, for it is Psyche (soul) herself who is borne up in his arms. The magical heat and the magical flight are alike elements of shamanic experience, as is the experience of Orual who descends to the Pillar Room "of living rock" where she is stripped, like Ishtar, of her veil, and understands her identification with the goddess, called Ungit in Lewis's novel.

A propos of the heat, the burning of the "beautiful arms" of West-wind, and the "extraordinary heat" of Cupid's breast, Mircea Eliade (1958) tells us, "many primitives think of the magicoreligious power as 'burning,' and express it by terms meaning heat, burn, very hot."[153] He adds, "In modern India, the Mohammedans believe that a man in communication with God becomes 'burning hot.'"[154] As Elijah says in I Kings 18.24, "the God that answereth by fire, let him be God." As to magic flight and descent, Eliade states, "on the plane of primitive religions ecstasy signifies the soul's flight to Heaven [...] or, finally, its descent to the subterranean world, among the dead."[155] He continues, in describing shamanic initiation in particular, "in many regions the candidate is believed to visit the sky," while "other initiations involve a descent to the realm of the dead; for example, the future medicine man [...] is transported underground." [156] Psyche, in *Till We Have Faces*, functions as a healer, the characteristic shamanic role.

In Orual's case, Lewis writes of her identification with Ungit, "Ungit in each must bear Ungit's son" (TWF 301; II ch. 2). At the end of her revelatory ordeal, Orual perceives that "The most dreadful, the most beautiful, the only dread and beauty there is was coming" (TWF 307; II ch. 2) for the god is coming into his house. At this point, Orual finds that she also is Psyche (TWF 308; II ch. 2). In the Eleusinian mysteries at the highest moment, the hierophant announced, "She who is Magnificent has given birth to a sacred child, Brimo." In this case, Earth has borne Wheat, for the god was exhibited as a "Ripe ear of grain,"[157] in a manner similar to the lifting up in Christian rites, of the sacred Host. Indeed, in the Eleusinian mysteries the physical mystery of earth and grain is an image of the spiritual mystery of divinity and humanity. It is almost possible to say that in *Till We Have Faces*, God is known first in a female form as Ungit: "Ungit in each must bear Ungit's son." Jung says "certain early Christian sects gave a maternal significance to the Holy Ghost," adding, "It is not without reason that the dove of Aphrodite is the symbol of the Holy Ghost."[158]

This beautiful idea is given vivid expression in an important essay which outlines the maternal imagery of God in the Bible: "God reveals himself to us in the Bible as not only like a father, and like a husband, but also like a mother—even, by implication, a virgin mother, for God is One and the sole Source of all."[159] God is seen as a maternal bird, as a rock, a tree, the sea, a womb, a watering spring: all motifs of the mother goddess. When God is our mother, we are her sons: Sons of God, whether male or female. Ungit's divine son is in this sense "the god," who is "the only dread and beauty there is." No wonder Lewis refrains from describing him precisely, for "God is love" (I John 4.8) and this god of love *is* God, of whom Moses said, "the LORD thy God is a consuming fire" (Deuteronomy 4.24), who, manifesting himself on the mountainside, burns but does not consume.

Compared to these audacities, the inclusion of planetary divinities as parts of the universe seems almost commonplace, Christ as a sun-lion, almost a platitude. The gods are aspects of God's Creation, but *this* God *is* God. The divine pair of Mars and Venus in the Space Trilogy are here replaced by the divine Mother and her divine Son, who is the God "so masculine that we are all feminine" to him, and thus, like Psyche, his brides.

Notes

[1] C.S. Lewis, *The Discarded Image: An Introduction to Medieval and Renaissance Literature* (Cambridge: Cambridge UP, 1964) 93.
[2] C.S. Lewis, *The Discarded Image* 96.
[3] C.S. Lewis, *The Discarded Image* 98.
[4] C.S. Lewis, *The Discarded Image* 98.
[5] C.S. Lewis, *The Discarded Image* 104.
[6] C.S. Lewis, *The Discarded Image* 105.
[7] C.S. Lewis, *The Discarded Image* 103.
[8] C.S. Lewis, *The Discarded Image* 103.
[9] C.S. Lewis, *The Discarded Image* 103.
[10] C.S. Lewis, *The Discarded Image* 104.
[11] Franz Cumont, *Astrology and Religion Among the Greeks and Romans* (New York: Dover, 1912) 46.
[12] Cumont 27.
[13] Cumont 30.
[14] Cumont 31.
[15] Cumont 32.
[16] Cumont 6.
[17] Cumont 7.
[18] Cumont 8.
[19] Cumont 10.
[20] See Alexander Marshack, *The Roots of Civilization* (New York: McGraw-Hill, 1972).
[21] See G.S. Hawkins, *Stonehenge Decoded* (New York: Dell Publishing, 1966).
[22] Phyllis Ackerman, "Stars and Stories," *Myth and Mythmaking*, ed. Henry A. Murray (Boston, MA: Beacon Press, 1968) 93.
[23] Cumont 22.
[24] Cumont 23.
[25] Cumont 25.
[26] Cumont 26.
[27] Cumont 56.
[28] Cumont 56.
[29] Jean Seznec, *The Survival of the Pagan Gods* (1953; Princeton, NJ: Bollingen, 1972) 37.
[30] Seznec 41.

Notes

[31] Seznec 42.
[32] Seznec 43.
[33] Seznec 52.
[34] Seznec 52.
[35] Seznec 53.
[36] Seznec 53.
[37] Seznec 53-54.
[38] Seznec 59.
[39] Seznec 62.
[40] Editor's note: This hymn is available at various websites. See, for example, "Morning Hymn" at *Christian Classics Ethereal Library* <http://www.ccel.org/ccel/palgrave/sacredsong.h177.html>.
[41] J.A. West and J.G. Toonder, *The Case for Astrology* (New York: Coward-McCann, 1970) 170-92.
[42] See C.G. Jung, *Synchronicity* (Princeton, NJ: Bollingen, 1952) passim.
[43] Jeff Mayo, *Astrology* (London: St. Paul's House, 1964) 17.
[44] Mayo, *Astrology* 43.
[45] Mayo, *Astrology* 19.
[46] Mayo, *Astrology* 21.
[47] Jeff Mayo, *The Planets and Human Behavior* (London: L.N. Fowler, 1972) 25.
[48] Lewis, *The Discarded Image* 106.
[49] Cumont 64.
[50] Dante Alighieri, *The Divine Comedy, Cantica III Paradise*, trans. Dorothy L. Sayers and Barbara Reynolds (Harmondsworth, UK: Penguin, 1962) 53.
[51] C.S. Lewis, *The Discarded Image* 111.
[52] C.S. Lewis, *The Discarded Image* 108.
[53] C.S. Lewis, *Surprised by Joy* (1955; Harcourt, Brace, Jovanovich, 1966) 34.
[54] *Larousse Encyclopaedia of Mythology* (New York: Prometheus Press, 1959) 56; new edition (Putnam, 1968) 57-58. [Editor's note: The 1968 Putnam edition was the closest to the 1959 Prometheus edition used by Patterson that was available for source checking. Since structural editing seems to have resulted in some wide

Notes

variations in page references, as well as alterations in the material itself, references to both volumes are given here.]

[55] John Gray, *Near Eastern Mythology* (London: Hamlyn, 1969). The quotation is from Malachi 4.2.

[56] Alexander Heidel, *The Babylonian Genesis*, second edition (1951; Chicago, IL: University of Chicago Press, 1963) 44.

[57] *Larousse* (1959) 120; (1968) 113.

[58] *Larousse* (1959) 56; (1968) 57.

[59] Lapis-lazuli is a blue stone, so the concept of the "blue moon" was already known.

[60] *Larousse* (1959) 162; (1968) 143.

[61] *Larousse* (1959) 223; (1968) 120-23.

[62] Gray, *Near Eastern Mythology* 52-53. See also Samuel Noah Kramer, *Mythologies of the Ancient World* (Garden City, NY: Anchor Books, 1961) 96.

[63] Gray, *Near Eastern Mythology* 17.

[64] Henri Frankfort, *Kingship and the Gods* (Chicago, IL: University of Chicago Press, 1948) 231.

[65] Frankfort 237.

[66] *Larousse* (1959) 50; (1968) 56-57.

[67] Heidel 35, 48.

[68] Heidel 44.

[69] *Larousse* (1959) 103, 105; (1968) 98.

[70] *Larousse* (1959) 216; (1968) 203

[71] C.S. Lewis, *The Discarded Image* 105-106.

[72] C.S. Lewis, *The Discarded Image* 105.

[73] *Larousse* (1959) 58; (1968) 60.

[74] *Larousse* (1959) 89-96; (1968) 98-106.

[75] Lewis, *The Discarded Image* 107-108.

[76] *Larousse* (1959) 63; (1968) 63.

[77] *Larousse* (1959) 220; (1968) 207.

[78] C.S. Lewis, *The Discarded Image* 106.

[79] C.S. Lewis, *The Discarded Image* 107.

[80] *Larousse* (1959) 64; (1968) 64, 98.

[81] *Larousse* (1959) 214; (1968) 202.

Notes

[82] Coventry Patmore, "*Aurea Dicta*," The *Rod, the Root, and the Flower* (New York: Books for Libraries Press, 1968) ch. XIII.
[83] Rudolf Otto, *The Idea of the Holy* (New York: Oxford UP, 1923) 191.
[84] Otto 192.
[85] Otto 192.
[86] David Lindsay, *A Voyage to Arcturus* (1920; New York: Ballantine, 1968) 46.
[87] C.G. Jung, *The Archetypes and the Collective Unconscious* (Princeton, NJ: Bollingen, 1959) 82.
[88] Patmore, "*Aurea Dicta*" ch. XIII.
[89] Patmore, "Homo," *The Rod, the Root, and the Flower* ch. I.
[90] Patmore, "*Aurea Dicta*" ch. CXXXIII.
[91] Patmore, "*Aurea Dicta*" ch. CL.
[92] When I wrote about this passage in "Anti-Babels: Images of the Divine Centre in *That Hideous Strength*," *Mythcon II Proceedings* (Los Angeles: The Mythopoeic Society, 1972) 6-11, I was unable, as was Walter Hooper to whom I appealed for help, to find the source of this passage as an exact quote. Joe R. Christopher, however, suggested Coventry Patmore as the source of its idea, reminding me of the letter cited. [Editor's note: Patterson does not give a source for the letter she refers to, however, it is available in *The Collected Letters of C.S. Lewis, Volume I: Family Letters, 1905–1931*, ed. Walter Hooper (New York: HarperCollins, 2004) 904.]
[93] Ackerman 96.
[94] Ackerman 97.
[95] Ackerman 100.
[96] W.K.C. Guthrie, *The Greeks and Their Gods* (Boston, MA: Beacon Press, 1950) 150.
[97] Guthrie 152.
[98] E.R. Dodds, *The Greeks and the Irrational* (Berkeley, CA: University of California Press, 1951) 76.
[99] Dodds 271.
[100] Dodds 277.
[101] Dodds 277.
[102] Dodds 278.

Notes

[103] C.S. Lewis, *The Discarded Image* 122.
[104] H.R. Ellis Davidson, *Gods and Myths of Northern Europe* (Harmondsworth, UK: Penguin, 1964) 28.
[105] Davidson 39-44.
[106] Larousse (1959) 182; (1968) 161.
[107] Larousse (1959) 183; (1968) 161.
[108] Larousse (1959) 182; (1968) 161.
[109] Guthrie 155.
[110] Larousse (1959) 183; (1968) 161.
[111] Larousse (1959) 220; (1968) 207-209?
[112] Larousse (1968) 210. [Editor's note: This citation has been added.]
[113] Larousse (1959) 184; (1968) 161.
[114] John Pinsent, *Greek Mythology* (London: Hamlyn, 1969) 43.
[115] Pinsent 43.
[116] Jacob Grimm, *Teutonic Mythology*, vol. II (1883; Gloucester, Mass.: Peter Smith, 1976) 449.
[117] Grimm 448.
[118] Grimm 518.
[119] C.S. Lewis, *The Discarded Image* 123.
[120] C.S. Lewis, *The Discarded Image* 124; see *Beowulf*, trans. Michael Alexander (Harmondsworth, UK: Penguin, 1973) 54.
[121] C.S. Lewis, *The Discarded Image* 125; see Reginald Scott, *The Discoverie of Witchcraft* (1584), (London, 1886) 122.
[122] C.S. Lewis, *The Discarded Image* 134.
[123] C.S. Lewis, *The Discarded Image* 135.
[124] C.S. Lewis, *The Discarded Image* 136.
[125] C.S. Lewis, *The Discarded Image* 137.
[126] C.S. Lewis, *The Discarded Image* 138.
[127] C.S. Lewis, "De Descriptione Temporum," *Selected Literary Essays*, ed. Walter Hooper (Cambridge: Cambridge UP, 1969) 5.
[128] Patmore, "Knowledge and Science," *The Rod, The Root, and The Flower* ch. XXVII.
[129] C.S. Lewis, *A Mind Awake*, ed. Clyde S. Kilby (London: Bles, 1968) 219.
[130] Clement C. Miles, *Christmas Customs and Traditions* (1912; New York: Dover, 1976) 220.

Notes

[131] Miles 240.

[132] Miles 233.

[133] William Sansom, *A Book of Christmas* (Toronto, ON: McGraw-Hill, 1968) 100.

[134] Sansom 103.

[135] Sansom 104.

[136] Sansom 104.

[137] Joan M. Vastokas, "The Shamanistic Tree of Life," *artscanada* (Dec. 1973/Jan. 1974) 149.

[138] Hans Christian Andersen, *The Snow Queen*, ch. Story the Second (Gutenberg ebook # 442).

[139] Andersen, *The Snow Queen*, ch. Story the Second.

[140] Andersen, *The Snow Queen*, ch. Story the Second.

[141] *The Golden Ass of Apuleius*, trans. Robert Graves (Farrar, Straus and Young, 1951; New York: Farrar, Straus and Giroux, 2009) 98. [Editor's note: the page citations have been converted to the more recent edition.]

[142] *The Golden Ass of Apuleius* 100.

[143] *The Golden Ass of Apuleius* 101-102.

[144] *The Golden Ass of Apuleius* 102.

[145] *The Golden Ass of Apuleius* 104.

[146] *The Golden Ass of Apuleius* 112.

[147] *The Golden Ass of Apuleius* 117.

[148] *The Golden Ass of Apuleius* 117-18.

[149] S.G.F. Brandon, *Religion in Ancient History* (London: George Allen and Unwin, 1969, 1973) 79.

[150] Leonard Von Matt and Francis Trochu, *St. Bernadette* (London: Longmans Green and Co., 1957) 18.

[151] C.G. Jung, *Symbols of Transformation* (Princeton, NJ: Bollingen, 1956) 240 note.

[152] Jung, *Symbols of Transformation* 422.

[153] Mircea Eliade, *Rites and Symbols of Initiation* (New York: Harper Torchbooks, 1958) 85.

[154] Eliade, *Rites and Symbols of Initiation* 86.

[155] Eliade, *Rites and Symbols of Initiation* 95.

[156] Eliade, *Rites and Symbols of Initiation* 99.

Notes

[157] Eliade, *Rites and Symbols of Initiation* 111.

[158] Jung, *Symbols of Transformation* 138.

[159] Gracia Fay Ellwood, "Both God's and Mary's Son," *Queen of All Hearts* (January-February 1976): 15.

6. "This Equivocal Being": The Un-Man in *Perelandra*

> No reference to the Devil or devils is included in any Christian Creeds, and it is quite possible to be a Christian without believing in them.
>
> —C.S. Lewis, "Answers to Questions on Christianity"

Patterson shows how C.S. Lewis uses archetypal motifs to represent evil in Perelandra. *Beginning with the battle waged between the protagonist and the Un-man, she demonstrates parallels with similar scenes in the Bible and such literary classics as* Beowulf *and* Paradise Lost, *including the diabolic, violence, underwater descent, and over-water and under-water pursuits. She further elucidates Lewis's use of personal experience as recounted in his autobiographical works in the characterization of the Un-man, specifically those summed up in the motifs of the corpse, the schoolboy, war, and madness. Patterson's interlocutors include Colin Manlove (1992) on Christian fantasy, Mark Hobart (1985) on enquiries into the nature of evil as an exercise in "snark" hunting, and David C. Downing (1992) on "transrational truths."*

This paper was first published in The Lamp-Post of the Southern California C. S. Lewis Society *19.3 (Fall 1995): 4-15; and 19.4 (Winter 1995-1996): 7-19. It is Patterson's sixth paper on the representation of evil in Lewis's fiction. "This Equivocal Being" is included here as an important contribution to Patterson's study of the dynamic relationships between individuals in Lewis's fictional hierarchy of being.*

With the character of the Un-man in *Perelandra,* C.S. Lewis reached the climax, or perhaps the nadir, of his sequence of symbolic depictions of evil in his Christian fantasies. J.I.M. Stewart (1992) has pungently expressed the latter viewpoint (that it represents the nadir) in his ironic summary of the plot of *Perelandra*: "Satan has possessed himself of the body of an atheistic scientist, Weston, in order to prosecute his temptation of the Lady. Happily, Ransom manages to bash in the face of this equivocal being with a stone and hurl him into a lake of fire. So all is well on Perelandra."[1] In considering this intense scenario, Kath Filmer (1993) remarks, with some accuracy,

"Well might readers enquire what personal fear of evil, what personal psychological agenda, would lead Lewis to create such a monstrosity?"[2] The monstrosity in question is precisely the equivocal being of Stewart's summary, the character of the Un-man in *Perelandra.* Taking Filmer's rhetorical questions seriously, I shall attempt to account for this particular portrayal of evil by referring both to the broad catalogue of symbolism based in the 800-year-old tradition of Christian fantasy, and to the specific motifs indeed derived from Lewis's "personal fear of evil" and "personal psychological agenda"; that is, from the life experiences that formed him, as we are all formed, into the man and hence the artist he became.

The Un-Man

Colin Manlove (1992) has remarked that "The Un-man itself is no hideous or melodramatic devil, but the devil in the body of a middle-aged Cambridge scientist."[3] At least since graduating, few of us have found middle-aged academics frightening, so the equivocality and/or monstrosity must lie elsewhere. Webster's Dictionary defines the equivocal as "having two or more significations," and the monstrous as "deviating greatly from the natural form or character." The horror lies in the dual presence, and most particularly, dual voices, of a middle-aged Cambridge scientist and the devil. This special form of duality, equivocality, and monstrosity, is based directly upon the passages depicting demonic possession in the Gospels.

Jesus encounters "the devil" (Matthew 4.1), "the tempter" (Matthew 4.3), and "Satan" (Matthew 4.10) in person in the episode usually called "The Temptation in the Wilderness." But he meets "demons" (Matthew 8.31) who are inhabiting possessed humans even more frequently, and in these cases, there are two voices: one, the voice of the possessed (a human) and the other, the voice of the possessor(s) (demon[s]). The best-known episode of this kind is probably the one usually called "The Gadarene Swine," which ends when the demons, at their own request, leave their human host and enter a herd of swine. Perhaps the most potent and explicit of these Gospel accounts is the earliest, that of Mark, where "a man out of the tombs with an unclean spirit met him" (Mark 5.2): "Night and day he was always howling and bruising himself with stones. When he saw Jesus he ran and bowed down before him, and he shouted at the top of his voice, 'What have you to do with me, Jesus, Son of the Most High God? I adjure you by God, do not torment me'" (Mark 5.5-7). Here it is the man who speaks, but when Jesus asks him "What is your name?" he answers, "My name is Legion, for we are many" (Mark 5.9). Now we hear directly from the man's resident tormentors: "the unclean spirits begged him, 'Send us into the swine; let us enter them'" (Mark 5.12). In Matthew, thought to postdate Mark, we hear first the voices of the "two demoniacs" (Matthew 8.29). "They" shout at Jesus, "What have you to do with us, Son of God? Have you come here to torment us before the time?" (Matthew 8.29). These questions are followed by the voices of "the demons" themselves: "If you cast us out, send us into the herd of swine" (Matthew 8.31). Characteristically, in the accounts of Jesus's encounters with possessed persons, the demons possessing them recognize him by name as the Son of God and obey his commands to leave their human hosts. Such obedience is not evident in the encounter between Ransom and the Un-man.

These biblical passages clearly form the direct prototypes for Lewis's depiction of the Un-man, whose double voice, sometimes arguably that of the human Weston, and sometimes clearly demonic, makes him both equivocal and monstrous, because he not only speaks with two voices, but combines identities that should not be combined. Before addressing Lewis's use of this motif in *Perelandra*, I must identify the meaning of such biblical motifs, and any Christian motifs, in fantasy. Manlove points out that "whatever truth a fantasy may contain, it is only an image of the real."[4] He devotes an entire volume, *Christian Fantasy,* to tracing the genre from 1200 to the present, examining in individual chapters the *Quest del Saint Graal,* Dante's *Commedia*, *Pearl,* Spenser's *The Faerie Queene,* Marlowe's *Dr. Faustus,* Milton's *Paradise Lost,* Bunyan's *The Pilgrims Progress,* Swedenborg, Blake, George MacDonald, Charles Kingsley, Charles Williams, and C.S. Lewis. He summarizes their meaning in a variety of fantastic settings, thus: "The Christian rhythm, embodied in Christ, is that the way to gain is through loss, the way to the light through darkness, at least for fallen man."[5] It is this "way" that Ransom follows in his pursuit of the Un-man.

The Cambridge scientist Weston first appears in *Perelandra* in what Ransom, having already traveled with Weston to Malacandra (Mars) as a captive in *Out of the Silent Planet,* recognizes to be a spaceship. The Lady of Perelandra, however, calls this vehicle "the thing that fell out of Deep Heaven this morning (PER 70; ch. 6). The "thing" has brought "Professor Weston," "the great physicist," to "the sinless waters of Perelandra" (PER 70; ch. 6). When the two men meet at the end of the chapter, Ransom notes of Weston that "his face had something about it which seemed subtly unfamiliar" (PER 73; ch. 6), though the change is not described, and the physicist seems to be the same domineering and truculent fellow as before. He greets Ransom with a challenge: "May I ask you, Dr Ransom, what is the meaning of this?" (PER 73; ch. 6). The narrator, Lewis himself, purportedly recounting the story as told to him by Ransom, notes the "massive egoism" and "authoritative vulgarity" of the man, which readers of *Out of the Silent Planet* will immediately recognize.

But there *has* been a change, one of a spiritual nature, as Weston tells Ransom,

> To spread spirituality, not to spread the human race, is henceforth my mission [...] I worked first for myself; then for science, then for humanity; but now at last for Spirit itself I might say, borrowing language which will be more familiar to you, the Holy Spirit. (PER 78; ch. 7)

Ransom questions this identification, and asks the following theological question about the purported Spirit: "is it in any sense at all personal—is it alive?" (PER 79; ch. 7). He asks this because the Holy Spirit, by definition (in terms Ransom could understand), is both a Person (one of the Three in the Holy Trinity), and a mode of contact with the one living God. At this, Weston suddenly adopts "a gangster's or a schoolboy's whisper [...] so unlike his usual orotund lecturing style that Ransom for a moment felt a sensation almost of disgust" (PER 79; ch. 7), and confides, in a manner evidently both confidential and indecent, "I'm being guided" (PER 80; ch. 7). As the argument between the two men continues over several pages, Weston reveals that his guide is in fact the devil, and to Ransom's horror, he takes his final step beyond that of a servant or tool, to that of identification:

> Do you see, you timid, scruple-mongering fool? I *am* the Universe. I, Weston, am your God and your Devil. I call that Force into me completely ... (PER 82; ch. 7)

Thus in the space of two chapters the identification of Weston and his diabolical master is gradually and fully cemented. From this point on, the old bombastic character of Weston begins to change: "Something which was and was not Weston was talking" (PER 91; ch. 8)—a state of being that Ransom explicitly feels as a "monstrosity." By the next morning, he discovers Weston at work mindlessly destroying a series of colorful Perelandrian frogs: "The face which he raised from torturing the frog had that terrible power which the face of a corpse sometimes has of simply rebuffing every conceivable human attitude one can adopt towards it" (PER 95; ch. 9). Ransom realizes clearly now "that Weston's body was kept, walking and undecaying, in Perelandra by some wholly different kind of life, and that Weston himself was gone" (PER 95; ch. 9). Here a second motif of great power for Lewis, that of the "corpse," has been introduced in the strongest possible terms.

Lewis includes a third motif, that of war: in responding to his battle with this terrible being, he recalls that "men in war or sickness are surprised to find how much can be borne [... what is feared ...] happens and we find ourselves neither mad nor dead, still held to the task" (PER 96; ch. 9). This passage, apparently a simple gloss on the situation, also contains a reference to a fourth motif *very* personal to Lewis, that of madness. By the end of the ninth chapter, Ransom has arrived at a name for this dreadful adversary: "the thing he had to deal with—the managed corpse, the bogey, the Un-man" (PER 105; ch. 9). With this identifying name, the characterization of Weston as the Un-man is complete, and it combines four elements most emotionally resonant to Lewis: the corpse, the schoolboy, war, and madness (in this case, identified with demonic possession, the biblical depiction of madness). The chapter concludes with a sequence during which the Un-man endlessly repeats its human antagonist's name:

> "Ransom," it said.
> "Well?" said Ransom.
> "Nothing," said the Un-man. (PER 105; ch. 9)

The "union" in the Un-man "of malice with something nearly childish" is compared by the narrator Lewis with the "petty, indefatigable nagging as of a nasty little boy at a preparatory school" (PER 106; ch. 9). As there are seventeen chapters in the novel, this full recognition in the ninth chapter of the Un-man as corpse, demon, possessed person, and malignant child forms the central pivot of the narrative.

The Battle

These effects, so skillfully managed, do not depend entirely on frightening motifs, however; it is Lewis's complex orchestration of contrasting moods that gives *Perelandra* its evocative power. In the first two chapters of the book, we are clearly warned of dangers to come, when the narrator—C. S. Lewis as a character in his own story—himself suffers a demonic attack. Following this ominous beginning, Chapters 3, 4, and 5 create a paradisal atmosphere as Ransom explores the watery planet Perelandra (Venus), so voluptuous and aesthetic that it alone may account for the fact that *Perelandra* is often cited by readers as their favorite of all that Lewis wrote. This mood of dreamy loveliness, comparable, perhaps, to life in the womb, prepares us for the shock of Weston's arrival. Chapters 7 through 10—four chapters—detail the attempted temptation of the lady by the Un-man.

Various writers have noted that Lewis, with his characteristic referentiality, includes numerous elements from earlier literary fantasies in his depiction of what follows—the five chapters (11 through 15) from Ransom's recognition of a call to arms to Ransom's final encomium to his fallen foe. Among those sources often cited are *Beowulf* and *Paradise Lost*; the three motifs most often discerned as arising from these sources are the diabolic, the use of violence, and the underwater descent. None of these motifs are, of course, original to *Beowulf* or to *Paradise Lost.*

A characteristic analysis of such sources, such as Darlene Logan's (1982), compares the battle strategy of *Perelandra* with that of *Beowulf* with reference to such common features as the villain as outcast, the evenly matched combatants, the hero's righteous anger toward the villain, the weaponless hero, and the passage through the sea to complete the combat.[6] A note of ambivalence on the one hand, and opposition on the other, is nicely struck in this characterization; while the antagonists are approximately matched in age, profession, and strength, and are alike unarmed, they are operating according to differing premises.[7] In noting similarities between *Perelandra* and *Paradise Lost*, Frank S. Kaster (1993) quotes Lewis to make clear how mismatched the antagonists must be; Ransom "had full opportunity to learn the falsity of the maxim that the Prince of Darkness is a gentleman."[8] Kaster notes of Lewis that "Milton's tempter seems to have shaped his own Senior Devil, Screwtape, as well as Un-man Weston in *Perelandra*."[9] The antagonists are mismatched because the Un-man is, in his own words, "guided" by a "Spirit," and it is clear that the Spirit can become villainous, perverted, and irrational, as in the examples of the witch Jadis in Lewis's *The Lion, the Witch and the Wardrobe* and *The Magician's Nephew,* Weston in *Perelandra*, and the severed head of Alcasan in *That Hideous Strength.*[10] Of course the spirit can also be pure and reasonable, as we are to understand Maleldil to be in Perelandra where Ransom receives his call to combat.

Ambivalence and opposition can also appear in cases of violence in a positive sense; Patricia Alice McKenzie (1974) points out that violence "functions both as an identifying characteristic of evil and as an instrument for the chastisement of evil."[11] I discuss this fundamental opposition (as well as my own ambivalence about it) in my section on Lewis's concepts and experiences of war, below, but there is no doubt that his depiction of the epic conflict between Ransom and the Un-man owes something to *Beowulf,* as well as to other sources which Lewis himself expressly cites or to which he makes allusions in *Perelandra,* such as *The Battle of Maldon,* from which Ransom finds himself "shouting a line" in Chapter 12.

Beowulf provides the model for the over-water and underwater pursuits of the Un-man by Ransom in *Perelandra,* almost certainly as a deliberate strategy of allusion by Lewis. Beowulf and Breca race across the sea for five nights and days (a pursuit comparable to the five chapters in *Perelandra* devoted to the combat between Ransom and Weston):

> Thus stroke for stroke we stitched the ocean
> five nights and days, drawn apart then
> by cold storm on the cauldron of waters[12]

And in the fight in the Mere between Beowulf and Grendel's Mother, the Water-hag, we see a source for the descent into the underwater world and the motif of unarmed conflict, already cited above, as Beowulf flings aside his sword:

[…] his own strength would suffice him,
the might of his hands. A man must act so
when he means in a fight to frame himself
a long-lasting glory; it is not life he thinks of.[13]

With these comparisons and allusions in mind, we can now turn to the story as Lewis wrote it, or at least as I propose to read it. In Chapter 11, which I shall designate Day 1, Ransom becomes aware of the presence of Maleldil, and knows of himself that however much he may try not to know it, he is "Maleldil's representative as the Un-man was the representative of Hell" (PER 120; ch. 11). It would be hard to make the situation any more explicit than this; Maleldil is, in Lewis's Trilogy, God. Gradually, then, Ransom becomes aware that "he would certainly try to kill the Un-man tomorrow" (PER 127; ch. 11). Not everybody will agree that there is a direct logical (not to say moral) progression from one of these realizations to the other; I discuss this matter, too, in my section on war.

In Chapter 12 (Day 2), when "tomorrow" comes, Ransom awakens, and, after a search, finds the Un-man plucking and strangling a helpless bird. Ransom is aroused to action by this pathetic and atrocious spectacle: "Some memory of boxing at his preparatory school must have awaked, for he found he had delivered a straight left with all his might to the Un-man's jaw" (PER 129; ch. 12). Here is an explicit reference to the schoolboy's life, also to be discussed below; Lewis had personally observed the torture of his fellow schoolboys by an insane schoolmaster, and the language he uses to express those experiences contains not only the memory of fear, but of rage. It is as the physical conflict is thus initiated, "one middle-aged scholar against another" that Ransom finds himself "shouting a line out of *The Battle of Maldon*" (PER 131-32; ch. 12). The two scholars chase one another, and like Beowulf and Breca, they enter the sea. Here each mounts a fish (PER 133; ch. 12), which, unlike "the fishes of the deep" in *Beowulf*, are aroused to aid the two seafarers rather than to "unfriendliness."

Chapter 13 (Day 3) begins as darkness falls upon the Perelandrian sea; on they race until daylight, and through the day; this time Ransom confronts the remnants of Weston in what to me is the most terrifying and heartrending episode in the book, probably because it is taken directly from Lewis's own life, as we shall see, so that he could endow it with an unbearable verisimilitude. Weston begs Ransom for help, and describes the "thin little rind of what we call life, put on for show, and then—the *real* universe for ever and ever" (PER 143; ch. 13). Weston is saying that the "*real* universe" is Hell and that human consciousness ("life") is only its rind. This dreadful view of reality is clearly based upon "the pathetic Doc [who] anticipates the Un-man of *Perelandra*," who is "Mrs. Moore's brother [...] the man to whom Lewis referred in his autobiography as having lost his mind," just as James Como (1991) says.[14] After this poignant and pathetic interview, Ransom exclaims, "What the devil are you doing?"—Lewis never uses such language lightly or without a specific plot intention—and his "Enemy" grasps his legs and bears him down into the depths. The interview, if that is what it was, with Weston, is over.

Finally, in Chapter 14 (Day 4), Ransom comes to himself in a cave, where he waits, and, in a perfect rhapsody of allusion such as I suppose only Lewis would so unabashedly and delightedly indulge, setting forth for all his future interpreters an agenda not only challenging but positively pugnacious, recites "all that he could remember of the *Iliad,* the *Odyssey,* the *Æneid,* the *Chanson de Roland, Paradise Lost,* the *Kalevala,* [and] the *Hunting of the Snark*" (PER 148; ch. 14). Take that in the eye, all you source-hunters, he seems to be saying, joyously throwing down the gauntlet to all who come after him! Following this outburst, the Un-man follows Ransom into the cave, and there Ransom smashes his face in, just as Stewart says, and shoves him into "the sea of fire: and then that was the end of it" (PER 156; ch. 14).

On Day 5 (Chapter 15), which I call a day because Lewis calls this sequence a "long Sabbath" (PER 159; ch. 15); that is, a day of great but indeterminate length, like the days on which God worked upon Creation; indeed, like the day upon which God rested from these efforts, Ransom makes his way to the cavern's mouth and there is tended "by the planet Venus herself" during that "long sabbath" (PER 159; ch. 15). I have wondered if in this setting, at once paradise—"a winding and wooded valley" (PER 159; ch. 15)—and the world at the end of the birth canal when the child is taken into the arms of its mother, implies that Ransom, making his way out of the cavern into a place where he can as it were suckle upon the breast of the goddess, has in some way died and been reborn. In any event, as "Day by day

[…] he came to know more of the place" (PER 160; ch. 15), he carves onto the cliff from which he has emerged a memorial to "EDWARD ROLLES WESTON […] FIRST OF THE TELLURIANS [WHO] TRAVELLED THROUGH DEEP HEAVEN TO MALACANDRA AND TO PERELANDRA WHERE HE GAVE UP HIS WILL AND REASON TO THE BENT ELDIL" (PER 161; ch. 15). Does all this mean that Ransom has indeed and appropriately killed the Un-man as "Maleldil's representative? One must first ask if he has indeed killed Weston. On this question Lord Feverstone (Devine, Weston's companion in *Out of the Silent Planet*) tells Mark Studdock that Weston was murdered, and that "The murderer is a respectable Cambridge don with weak eyes, a game leg, and a fair beard." And, says Feverstone, Weston was murdered "For being on our side" (THS 39; ch. 2). But we know better than to believe Lord Feverstone on any subject!

Many blows are recorded in *Perelandra,* but none prevent the battered body of Ransom's foe from continuing to serve as the devil's vehicle; indeed, some passages suggest, through their references to the image of the corpse, that Weston is already dead and merely kept moving by his infernal occupant. Finally, Ransom throws the body (dead or alive; we are not sure) into the fire, where it is presumably rendered unusable for the demon, and—as none of the living knows the fate of the dead—perhaps even then, saved from Hell by the intervention of Maleldil through this cleansing action of the aptly named Ransom. This final, therapeutic act by Ransom, in causing the body to be burned, may be interpreted as some sort of expiation or exorcism which will free not only the body but the soul.

As for the demon; what becomes of him, or perhaps I should say, it? In *The Five Gospels,* the translators give authentic status to the passage from Luke 10.24, offering one of the Bible's most potent depictions of demonic behavior in the form of a parable told by Jesus: "When an unclean spirit leaves a person, it wanders through waterless places in search of a resting place. When it doesn't find one, it says, 'I will go back to the house I left.'"[15] One recalls that for that person to whom the unclean spirit returns, the last state is worse than the first! Anyway, if the situation described in the parable is true, then, in terms of Lewis's fantasy, the "unclean spirit" inhabiting Weston would have been unable to find the "home" it had left because Weston's body was consumed in the lake of fire, admittedly with Ransom's help in hurling it there.

A major premise of the Trilogy is that the devil has only been able to break the quarantine confining demons to Tellus (Earth) ever since the Fallen Angels fell, because Weston has traveled to Malacandra by space ship. There is a suggestion here that, having breached the law in such matters, Weston's body appropriately forms the vehicle by which the devil in his turn now travels to Perelandra, to attempt the corruption of a new and unfallen race. One may suppose that a devil who on such a mission becomes unbodied—evicted by the burning to bits of his vehicle, Weston—must cease to function in the dimension where he/it loses this physical toehold, and returns to whatever dimension angelic beings (including fallen angels) characteristically occupy; in the case of the devil, Hell suggests itself. Lewis is silent upon the fate of this particular demon.

But it is the case that in *That Hideous Strength,* the returned space traveler Ransom finds that demons are on Earth busily occupying not only the head of the dead criminal Alcasan, but the highest level of leadership among the N.I.C.E., including most particularly Wither and Frost, who like Weston have surrendered their will and their reason to their diabolical masters. One notes that in these cases, as well as in the cases of their final initiates, Straik and Filostrato, death comes by, or is followed by fire, as is not the case for the others of the eight characters who die (including Lord Feverstone). What befalls any of them afterwards is as invisible to us as is the ultimate fate of Weston.

Weston, Wither, and Frost have made themselves vehicles, puppets, automata, of the devil. This is not the case with Ransom, who as Maleldil's representative is sent, seemingly quite on his own, to do battle with the devil and win. There is even a suggestion, as I said above, that he has been so close to death that his recovery is in some way a rebirth; he emerges with a renewed body, gifted in many ways far beyond his previous capacities, albeit wounded in the heel, not with the triumphant wounds of Christ, but with a continually bleeding foot subject to flashes of pain, only at last to be healed in Avalon—Perelandra—where Paradise is still going on. His way has indeed led him by the end of the Trilogy "to gain through loss, the way to the light through darkness," as Manlove says it must.[16]

I turn now to the four sources of these images in the life of Lewis himself, in order to discuss, as Filmer suggests, "what personal fear of evil, what personal psychological agenda," lies behind this extraordinarily potent narrative which has aroused such intense responses. Before undertaking to discuss Lewis's use of his own life experiences, however, I must defend my method by saying what I do *not* intend to do. I do not intend to show that he worked out of unconscious phobias. All that I discuss, I learned from his own writings, all of which, including the diaries, were written for readers beyond himself. He chose to record these experiences so they would be read, including the diary which he says himself that he read to a select audience. What I *do* intend to do is show how he made use of those of his experiences that would clarify and intensify his writing because of their potency and familiarity to women and men (and for those experiences reserved to men, met vicariously through contact with these men, by women) of his era: childhood bereavement and consequent contact with the corpse; the brutalities of a schoolboy's life; trench warfare; and encountered madness. Clearly he expected readers to whom these elements would be not only recognizable, but profoundly significant. From his own experiences then, he drew powerful images that not only make *Perelandra* unforgettable, whether they move, horrify, or infuriate his readers, but also perfectly recognizable. He had indeed hit upon motifs of enormous emotional power, and he used them skillfully, some would say ruthlessly.

The Corpse

Because there is good reason to think that my four motifs have been drawn from Lewis's own life, and that these are the very ones that have most resonated with, and hence horrified or offended readers, evidently in an equally personal way, I examine these in the order in which they occurred in Lewis's life. Lewis, who produced not one but three autobiographical works, first the allegory *The Pilgrim's Regress* (1933); followed by the second and, I think, the more successful of his two attempts to depict the events between his birth and his conversion, *Surprised by Joy* (1955); and then, his matchless meditation upon bereavement, A *Grief Observed* (1961), gives a very striking description of his childhood.

"My childhood, at all events, was not in the least other-worldly," he declares— "it lives in my memory mainly as a period of humdrum, prosaic happiness.[17] And then, in a swift and telling reversal, he adds:

> To this general happiness there was one exception […] the terror of certain dreams. […] [I]t still seems to me odd that petted and guarded childhood should so often have in it a window opening on what is hardly less than Hell.[18]

He then explains that "My bad dreams were of two kinds, those about spectres and those about insects. [… And] to this day I would rather meet a ghost than a tarantula."[19] This phobic vision accounts for the otherwise inexplicable, even distracting appearance in Perelandra's cavern, of a train of grotesque insects following the reappearance of the Un-man there. I assume they are intended to suggest the "Hell" to which Lewis alluded in the passage cited above; certainly the parallels are almost exact.

He writes in *Surprised by Joy* of "a certain detestable picture in one of my nursery books [… of …] a midget child […] threatened […] by a stag-beetle much larger than himself," which could be made to "open and shut like pincers; snip-snap—snip-snap—I can see it while I write." And he blames his *mother* for having "allowed this abomination into the nursery"![20] In *Perelandra* this figure appears as a "thing […] in three parts […] a huge, many-legged, quivering deformity, standing just behind the Un-man" (PER 154; ch. 14). Readers may recall that at one point in *The Screwtape Letters,* Uncle Screwtape momentarily metamorphoses into a centipede. This material is clearly phobic—surely there is nothing, in reason, to justify calling a stag-beetle an "abomination" or a three part insect (admittedly very large) a "deformity." But as a person who will both stamp on a centipede and carry on a chatty conversation with a grey house-spider, I suspect that this phobia is shared by many who read *Perelandra*, and that Lewis (even while unable to rid himself of his phobia against insects) knew it would be. In any event after Ransom has killed the Un-Man, "All that he had felt from childhood about insects […] died that moment" (PER 155; ch. 14). And later in his "subterranean journey" (PER 157; ch. 15) Ransom sees "four of the great earth-beetles […] drawing behind them a flat car" bearing "a mantled form," and concludes "Assuredly the inside of this world was not for man" (PER 157; ch. 15). I cite this motif as a direct proof that Lewis included autobiographical motifs in his writing.

Here is what Lewis says about the specific subject of "the corpse" in *Surprised by Joy*:

> I was taken into the bedroom where my mother lay dead; as they said, "to see her," in reality, as I at once knew, "to see it." There was nothing that a grown-up would call disfigurement—except for that total disfigurement which is death itself. [...] To this day I do not know what they mean when they call dead bodies beautiful. The ugliest man alive is an angel of beauty compared with the loveliest of the dead.[21]

My own mother had a similar experience, lifted up, at the age of three, to see her dead mother's body; she suffered as long as she lived from a certain moaning, shuddering nightmare which I could hear from my bed and that only my father (whom she met at fourteen and married at eighteen) could calm. As for myself, I did not (would not) see my mother's body, nor that of my eldest daughter, after they died. Instead, I first encountered that clear evidence of perfect absence when I visited the body of an elderly Carmelite nun. She wasn't ugly; she wasn't frightening; but, also, she wasn't, absolutely wasn't, *there*.

Lewis returns to the subject of the corpse in *Surprised By Joy* as he gives the few glimpses he allows of his experiences in the trenches of France in World War I: "Familiarity both with the very old and the very recent dead confirmed that view of corpses which had formed the moment I saw my dead mother."[22] Obviously these intense remarks about wartime corpses are based in part on his response to his own mother's body as a nine-year-old child. When he refers to "the managed corpse" (PER 105; ch. 9) of the Un-man as "the bogy," he is basing the horror of this "body [...] kept, walking and undecaying [...] by some wholly different kind of life" (PER 95; ch. 9) upon his childhood experience of his mother's corpse, reaffirmed when he encountered corpses on the battlefield. He expresses this horror and its autobiographical basis most tellingly in the following unforgettable passage, already cited in part above:

> He saw a man who was certainly Weston [...] But the terror was that he was also unrecognisable. He did not look like a

> sick man: but he looked very like a dead one. The face which he raised from torturing the frog had that terrible power which the face of a corpse sometimes has of simply rebuffing every conceivable human attitude one can adopt toward it. (PER 95; ch. 9)

This was the horror Lewis had experienced upon seeing his dead mother: "What could you say—what appeal or threat could have any meaning—to *that*?" (PER 95; ch. 9). That, mind you; not "him" or—most pathetically—"her."

The monstrosity of the mangled corpse goes beyond the operation of the dead body by infernal means, beyond the combination of what ought to be motionless made indecently active, as in so many horrid depictions of that subject, from the late medieval Dance of Death to the animate corpses which appear so frequently in films. The monstrosity arises most terribly, most unendurably, from the recognition that the person one has known, loved (or, as with Weston, cordially disliked), is, irrevocably, *absent.* The corpse utterly abandoned by all that gave it identity beyond mere semblance is an absolute refutation of all living experience; as Lewis concludes in *Surprised by Joy,* "simply rebuffing every conceivable human attitude."

The Schoolboy

Janice Witherspoon Neuleib refers to the motif of "schoolboy nastiness" in her discussion of "The Concept of Evil in the Fiction of C.S. Lewis" (1974), and as I have already attempted to show above, it is, as David C. Downing (1992) says, true that "terms such as *nurse, boy,* and *moonlight,*"[23] used to potent effect in recreating his boyhood in *Surprised by Joy,* offer aid "in interpreting recurring images in the trilogy by giving readers a more exact sense of their emotional association for Lewis."[24] Further, Downing proposes the antithesis: "Childhood vs boyhood."[25] For Lewis, he says, "*childhood* referred to the years from his birth [...] until he was nine, the year his mother died and he was sent off to [...] school." [26] This period was associated with "simplicity, self-forgetfulness, imagination, and wonder."[27] Interestingly, when Downing says that *Surprised by Joy* "illuminates the master motifs of the Ransom stories," he includes in these motifs "the recovery of childhood."[28] The recovery of childhood forms the antithesis of what for Lewis is the generally pejorative term, *boy.* One notes that Mark Studdock's salvation in *That Hideous Strength* begins its expression when, expelled from the N.I.C.E. by Merlin with a slap on the back, and finding his way towards St. Anne's Manor where his wife awaits him, he discovers "a serial children's story which he had begun to read as a child but abandoned because his tenth birthday came when he was half way through it and he was ashamed to read it after that. Now, he chased it from volume to volume till he had finished it. It was good" (THS 358; ch. 17). Lewis here *means* "good," in all its senses.

As we have seen, the transitional moment from childhood to boyhood began, indeed, occurred, when Lewis gazed upon the corpse of his mother. His "boyhood," spent in minor, cruel, and worldly schools in England (as opposed to Ireland), continued well into Lewis's young adulthood, as he created a new home with an "adopted mother" (Mrs. Jane Moore) which he carefully hid (one can easily see why) from the bereaved father who paid for it, all unknowing. Here Lewis continued his attempts to return to a childhood situation until his conversion, which may explain why, soon after, he began to spend all his working days in his college living quarters and the homelife he describes so lovingly in *All My Road Before Me* was placed firmly at a distance and confined to weekends as he, at last, became a man instead of a boy.

Lewis's associations of *schoolboy* with all that is not good—evil might be too strong a word—include not only unpleasant boyish behaviors, but the genuine horrors of "public school" life. I will refer in the next section to Lewis's descriptions of war: little befell him in battle that surpassed his experiences at school. Witness this portion of his list of "the kinds of adversity" a soldier undergoes in war: "pain," "ill lodging," "cold," "toil, humiliation, injustice and arbitrary rule," separation "from all you love," and "close quarters with uncongenial companions."[29] These elements appear not only in *Surprised by Joy* (as I shall show below), but in a genuinely terrifying little essay, "My First School," which describes "The bellowing and grimacing old man with his cane, his threats, and his ogreish facetiousness, the inky walls, the stinking shed which served both as a latrine and as a store for our play boxes."[30] These grotesque, even obscene details are exactly those of the *Inferno* of Dante. In *Surprised by Joy,* Lewis entitled his chapter on the same school, "Concentration Camp," and gave its name as "Belsen." Nobody who has read it will ever forget his description of the child who, made to run the length of the classroom after each stroke of the cane, produced, "toward the end of the torture [...] a noise quite unlike a human utterance. That peculiar croaking or rattling cry, that, and the gray faces of all the other boys, and their deathlike stillness, are among the memories I could willingly dispense with."[31]

In 1924, in his diary posthumously published as *All My Road Before Me,* Lewis tells the story from another angle: he and his brother visit several sites near Wynyard (Belsen), and he meditates:

> if we could only have seen as far as this out of the hell of Wynyard. I felt a half comic, half savage pleasure [...] to think that by the mere laws of life we had completely won and Oldy [his sadistic schoolmaster] had completely lost. For here were we with our stomachs full of sandwiches sitting in the sun and wind, while he had been in hell these ten years.[32]

As in so many of these young man's jottings, in this delicious enjoyment of youth over age (its temporary nature all unsuspected), we sniff that other sense of "schoolboy," that ignoble quality Lewis intended when he gave Weston a "schoolboy's whisper" and caused Ransom to feel in its presence "a sensation almost of disgust" (PER 79; ch. 7). It is to the schoolboy in this sense that Lewis compares the Un-man, as he describes the next to last encounter of Ransom with Weston, before he finally undertakes combat:

> What chilled and almost cowed him was the union of malice with something nearly childish. For [...] blasphemy, for a whole battery of horrors, he was in some sort prepared: but hardly for this petty, indefatigable nagging as of a nasty little boy at a preparatory school. (PER 106; ch. 9)

The motif of the schoolboy first appears in the Trilogy in *Out of the Silent Planet,* when Ransom first encounters Weston—who greets him, prophetically, by saying "May I ask [...] who the devil you may be and what you are doing here?" (OSP 8; ch. 1)—and Devine, who reappears in *That Hideous Strength,* as the egregious Lord Feverstone. These two—Devine and Ransom—greet each other in an elaborate exchange of mutual recognition, and shake hands "with the rather laboured cordiality which is traditional in such meetings. In actual fact Ransom had disliked Devine at school as much as anyone he could remember" (OSP 9; ch. 1). Within a few paragraphs we have been treated to several displays of Devine's style, including his imitation of "the noise of a cork being drawn from a bottle—Ransom remembered it had been one of Devine's tricks at school" (OSP 11; ch. 1). It is with the contents of this bottle that Devine is about to drug Ransom and kidnap him to serve as a human sacrifice on Malacandra (Mars). The behavior of Devine is reflected in Lewis's description of how his relations with both his brother and his father deteriorated when Lewis was at Malvern (Wyvern), his second school in England, and he notes certain "savagely underlined" passages in his "father's copy of *The Lanchester Tradition"*—"They are passages about a certain glazed insolence, an elaborate heartless flippancy" in this story of a "reforming Headmaster."[33] But the behavior of Weston, as he deteriorates under the guidance of his demonic infester, reaches lower than this, to the ignoble archetype of whatever a boy may become at his worst.

The Narnian Chronicles include at least three examples of evil done by schoolboys: in *The Lion, the Witch and the Wardrobe,* the boy Edmund is actually "a traitor," ready to turn his sisters and brother over to the White Witch in order to eat more of the addictive Turkish Delight with which she has tempted him. The insufferable Eustace (the unpleasant schoolboy in the mind of God, as it were) in *The Voyage of the Dawn Treader* gorges on water that is supposed to be saved and shared with everyone on shipboard. And in *The Magician's Nephew,* Digory Kirke (the boy who grows up to be Professor Kirke in *The Lion, the Witch and the Wardrobe*) is responsible for reawakening Jadis, who is to become the White Witch of Narnia, and whose first act is to introduce a note of contradiction into the newly created Narnia's Paradise garden.

Lewis often said that in his efforts to understand sin, he had only to look within, and *All My Road Before Me* displays a series of small sins—lies he told his father, the casual use of racist and misogynist epithets, little blasphemies ("the uncomfortable sacrament"),[34] and the smug, cozy, us-against-the world relationship he shared with his "mother," in a series of diary entries explicitly intended for her eyes. The motif of the schoolboy—with all its load of affect—remains minor, however, compared to the open element of war, to which I shall now turn.

War

The wars in which Lewis participated were both experienced by him as righteous wars, wars seen as conflicts of good against evil, World War I and World War II. In the first, he served and was wounded as a soldier; in the second he shared his home with children sent away from the reach of bombers, and, among other things, wrote, lectured, and broadcast about Christianity at the request of various branches of the government (the Church of England being a state church). *Perelandra* can best be understood, I suspect, as a war novel, a work published in 1943 in the depth of the second World War, comparable to many works (including films such as *In Which We Serve*) which were produced in that atmosphere perhaps best expressed and remembered in the wartime speeches of Sir Winston Churchill.

Many members of a younger generation (than mine as well as than his) who are only familiar with, or at least have read most about, Vietnam or any of the many other smaller but no less ignoble wars produced by the delusions of the Cold War, will not be able to remember, perhaps not even be able to imagine, the point of view that Lewis expresses. A glimpse of it, in retrospect, may have been afforded by the remembrances of the fiftieth anniversary of D-Day, in progress when I prepared this present essay. Lewis enlisted in 1917 and was "drafted into a Cadet Battalion," being commissioned a Second Lieutenant in the Somerset Light Infantry; he remarks laconically, "I arrived in the front line trenches on my nineteenth birthday (November 1917), saw most of my service in the villages before Arras […] and was wounded at Mr. Bernenchon, near Lillers, in April 1918."[35]

He tells, succinctly, of the discomforts of war; like the veterans of World War II who filled my university classrooms when I was a student (I married one of them), of whom those who had been in combat spoke least about their war, Lewis is brief. "Through the winter," he says, "weariness and water were our chief enemies. I have gone to sleep marching and woken again and found myself marching still. One walked in the trenches in thigh gum boots with water above the knee."[36] Elsewhere, he says frankly, "All that we fear from all kinds of adversity, severally, is collected together in the life of a soldier on active service."[37] In the characteristically slim first volume of poetry he published in 1919, *Spirits in Bondage,* he writes in "French Nocturne (Monchy-Le-Preux),"

> […] speech of fellow-brutes that once were men
> Our throats can bark for slaughter: cannot sing.[38]

As he records, Lewis was wounded. He describes "the moment, just after I had been hit, when I found […] that I was not breathing and concluded that this was death." He continues, tellingly, "I had proved that there was a fully conscious 'I' whose connections with the 'me' of introspection were loose and transitory."[39] This brush with death, and his observations of the newly and long dead, cited above, resulted in the poem "Death in Battle," where the voice of the dying soldier speaks:

> Sorely pressed have I been
> And driven and hurt beyond bearing this summer day,

and concludes, in the poem's unexpected (for those who do not know Lewis's preoccupations) conclusion:

> Ah, to be ever alone,
> In the flowery valleys among the mountains and silent wastes untrod,
> In the dewy upland places, in the garden of God,
> This would atone!"[40]

Strikingly, this exactly predicts the sublime experience of Ransom as he recovers in the paradisal valley on Perelandra, in a sequence which cumulates in the supernal vision of the Great Dance so beloved by readers of *Perelandra.*

Lewis regarded military service in World War I the way Ransom regards the task of killing the Un-man in *Perelandra,* as a necessary, terrible, and appropriate duty. He says in his essay "Why I Am Not a Pacifist" that he is not a pacifist because the "voice of almost all humanity,"[41] with the exception of "certain dominical utterances,"[42] agree in opposing pacifism. These dominical utterances, that is, the words of Jesus, are accompanied in the case of that speaker by the act of offering himself, without resistance, to torture, humiliation, and death at the hands of Roman soldiers. He was called to die but not to kill. It seems presumptuous to disagree with "the voice of almost all humanity" but it is not impossible to imagine a Christian (or otherwise) here and there who might take those "dominical utterances," and that example, seriously.

Lewis points out that the soldier's life includes "pain and death" along with a whole catalog of disagreeable experiences cited above, in short: "every evil except dishonour and final perdition" while "Pacifism threatens you with almost nothing,"[43] except, one assumes, dishonor and final perdition. Certainly pacifism offers dishonor in this world; George Orwell, some of whose works Lewis admired, said that "Pacifism is objectively pro-fascist."[44] Whether it offers "final perdition"—I think of certain Quakers and Mennonites whom I have known over the years—I am not so sure.

As we might expect, Lewis includes the schoolboy Eustace as one of the least two pacifists he portrays in his fantasies. Having swung Reepicheep by his tail in *The Voyage of the Dawn Treader,* Eustace is challenged to a duel by the aggrieved mouse (who, you may recall, is very proud of this appendage), and replies, "I'm a pacifist. I don't believe in fighting" (VDT 35; ch. 2). I made a note on this page, having acquired the book in 1956, stating that "a pacifist would never pull anyone's tail." Lewis's idea of a pacifist is also embodied in Fairy Hardcastle, head of the secret police of the N.I.C.E. in *That Hideous Strength,* one of the evil characters dispatched during the "Banquet at Belbury," where she is, appropriately, eaten by a tiger. Lewis says of her:

> She had been at different times, a suffragette, a pacifist, and a British Fascist. She had been man-handled by the police and imprisoned. (HST 67; ch. 3)

Fairy Hardcastle is Lewis's example of a pacifist who suffers dishonor and perdition.

Regarding dishonor (though not, I should think, perdition), Dorothy Day, a passionate Roman Catholic who spent her life aiding the homeless in the Bowery, acknowledged that

> Lots of Catholics were angry at us when we maintained our pacifism, with agony, during the Second World War. Lots of Catholics were angry when we weren't running to build bomb

> shelters in the 1950s, when we protested the madness of bomb shelters in a nuclear age, the madness of war in *any* age.[45]

Dorothy Day went to prison twice for her beliefs: once, like Fairy Hardcastle, for participating in a suffragist demonstration, and once for refusing to enter a bomb shelter during a mock air-raid many years later.

Regarding the matter of dominical utterances, Jacques Ellul (1988) says of Christianity that "The central text is the saying of Jesus: 'I am the truth.'" The truth, Ellul adds, "is not doctrine [...] the truth is a person."[46] Forced belief, he reminds us, has led to the conquest and destruction of peoples, the depredations of the inquisition (not to say the pogroms, the Holocaust, and the McCarthy era); it also leads to the situation, still occurring in the last decade of the twentieth century, where, as Ellul says, "When two nations went to war, each was sure that God was on its side."[47]

The specific dominical utterance quoted by Lewis in regard to pacifism is found in Matthew 5.39 and Luke 6.29. In the Sermon on the Mount, Matthew's summary of Jesus's teaching, Jesus says, "I say to you, Do not resist an evildoer. But if anyone strikes you on the right cheek, turn the other also." In Luke, Jesus says, "If anyone strikes you on the cheek, offer the other also" (both NRSV). Interestingly, the so-called "Jesus Seminar" has declared these utterances to be indeed an authentic record of what Jesus actually and historically said.[48] The editors also give this status to the saying of Jesus in Luke 10.18, "I was watching Satan fall like lightning from heaven," which is of some relevance here.

The dominical utterance about turning the other cheek is related to four usages of this image in the Hebrew Bible: a passage in both 1 Kings 22.24 and 2 Chronicles 18.23, which describe the prophet Micaiah being slapped because he gives a prediction from God that his interlocutor does not want to hear; Job 16.10, where the long-suffering victim of Satan (the "Adversary" or "accuser") laments that "they have struck me insolently on the cheek"; and Psalms 3.7, where the psalmist calls on God to "strike all my enemies on the cheek," in a reversal of the previously mentioned situations, to which Lewis in part replied in *Reflection on the Psalms,* when he said that "the spirit of hatred [...] strikes us in the face is like the heat from a furnace mouth"[49] in the so-called "cursing psalms." As regards schoolboys and soldiers, among others, Lewis points out feelingly, and probably from personal experiences both as causer and recipient of hatred in situations of power: "Let all of us who have never been school prefects, N.C.O.s, schoolmasters, matrons of hospitals, prison wardens, or even magistrates, give hearty thanks for it."[50]

Despite all this, the matter of pacifism is perfectly clear to Lewis; Ransom engages in direct physical combat with the body of Weston, fists, nails, "bone against bone" (PER 130; ch. 12), and all, and experiences "The energy of hating, never before felt without some guilt" (PER 132; ch. 12). Here Lewis uses the figure of a boy in what he clearly intends as a positive context: "As a boy with an axe rejoices on finding a tree, or a boy with a box of coloured chalks rejoices on finding a pile of perfectly white paper, so he rejoiced in the perfect congruity between his emotion and its object" (PER 132; ch. 12). I am not surprised that readers have become queasy upon reading, after this passage that "His hands taught him terrible things" (PER 132; ch. 12), having to do with breaking ribs and cracking jawbone. Happily, at this point the sea-race begins and the grappling combatants are separated.

It is important to remember that this is a fantasy, that the fight is symbolic. But the presence of a human body, realistically described, gives the impression that it is Weston, not his demonic guide, who suffers, that even if we are to assume that all this damage is inflicted on a corpse rather than on a living man, if this is indeed the case, such an insult to a dead body is in itself indecent and unacceptable. The plot suggests that it is the destruction of the body that is required—hence the lake of fire—but this scene of combat is separated from that scene of quick dissolution by the passage in *Perelandra* that I found most horrifying when I first read it, the confrontation between Ransom and, perhaps, the momentary presence of Weston's personality as the two conclude their race on their fishy mounts across the Perelandrian seas. For an understanding of this powerful sequence I turn to the fourth and last of my sources in Lewis's personal life.

Madness

At the moment in *Perelandra* that seems most precisely to be based on Lewis's personal experience, Ransom is quoted by name: "'Ransom,' it said again in a broken voice, 'for God's sake speak to me'" (PER 140; ch. 13). As I have suggested elsewhere, Lewis never permitted a character to evoke either God or the devil without a reason. "But are you really Weston?" asks Ransom, with reasonable suspicion, and the speaker, "on the verge of tears," answers "Who else should I be?" (PER 141; ch. 13). Who else, indeed! In reply to the tearful speaker's cries, Ransom urges him to "Buck up, Weston. It's only death, all said and done. We should have to die some day, you know" (PER 141; ch. 13). To this, Weston retorts that what comes after death may be—indeed, is worse—"What do *you* know about death?" And here Weston reiterates the themes so potent to Lewis: the child and the corpse:

> A little child that creeps upstairs when nobody's looking and very slowly turns the handle to take one peep into the room where its grandmother's dead body is laid out—and then runs away and has bad dreams. […] [T]hat child knows something about the universe which all science and all religion is trying to hide. (PER 142; ch. 13)

Then, referring to the *Odyssey* (and to a motif repeated in the *Æneid*), Weston declares: "Homer—knew that *all* the dead have sunk down into the inner darkness […] All witless, all twittering, gibbering, decaying" (PER 143; ch. 13).

Finally, in his last desperate attempt to gain Ransom's sympathy—or perhaps in the demon's last attempt to deflect Ransom from his mission, Weston tells of a dream he has had, of being "nicely laid out," dead, and of being confronted by "a tramp, you know, only it was himself not his clothes that was coming to pieces" who tells him: "I began like that. We all did. Just wait and see what you come down to in the end" (PER 144; ch. 13). Ransom calls out to his companion: "Say a child's prayer if you can't say a man's. Repent your sins. Take my hand. There are hundreds of mere boys on Earth facing death this moment. We'll do very well" (PER 146; ch. 13). But it is too late: as Ransom cries, "What the devil are you doing?" the Un-man pulls him down into the depths, and Weston's chance, if it was a chance, appears to have passed. This long sequence of Weston's presence begins with Weston's invocation of God, and ends with Ransom's invocation of the devil. Strikingly, in his last appeal to Weston to repent and call upon God, he includes a mention of children and boys; obviously, to him, suggesting their commonality, at least, as having been both.

Now for the potent autobiographical element in this scene of confrontation between the two men, the last in which Ransom and Weston address one another as fellow humans: Lewis wrote in *Surprised by Joy:*

> it had been my chance to spend fourteen days, and most of the fourteen nights as well, in close contact with a man who was going mad. He was a man whom I dearly loved, and well he deserved love. And now I helped to hold him while he kicked and wallowed on the floor, screaming out that devils were tearing him and that he was that moment falling down into Hell.[51]

Lewis, despite the man's protestations that this madness stemmed from an early bout of syphilis (as it probably did), notes that the man "had flirted with Theosophy, Yoga, Spiritualism, Psychoanalysis, what not?" and that "For some months after that nightmare fortnight, the words 'ordinary' and 'humdrum' summed up everything that appeared to me most desirable."[52] One recalls that childhood, for Lewis—that period before the death of his mother—was characterized by "humdrum, prosaic happiness."

A full account of this nightmare fortnight appears in *All My Road Before Me;* the episode occurred in 1923, when Lewis was 25 years old, having survived his war, returned to Oxford, and taken up housekeeping with a deceased fellow soldier's mother, Mrs. Moore. The sufferer was "the Doc," her brother, Dr. Robert Askins, a government medical officer to whom she had fled from her husband, who she nicknamed "the Beast."[53] The subject takes up many pages in the diary but a few excerpts will reveal the source of Lewis's convincing portrait of the possessed Weston: "After lunch he began raving […] explained that he was haunted by horrible blasphemous and obscene thoughts […] told Mary and D that he was doomed—lunacy and death."[54] Soon he suffered "another frightful fit—rolling on the floor and shrieking that he was damned forever and ever […] I noticed how exactly he reproduces what Faustus says in Marlowe."[55] How apposite that *Dr. Faustus* by Marlowe is one of the Christian fantasies listed and discussed by Manlove!

Lewis writes poignantly, "I found the worst thing I had to contend with was a sort of horrible sympathy with Doc's yellings and grovellings—a cursed feeling that I could quite easily do it myself."[56] To my ear, this describes exactly the mood of Ransom in his last efforts to sympathize with, while keeping up his guard against, the raving Weston. And this sympathy continues in Lewis's encounter with the Doc: "Even between the attacks he never rallies now; a frightful expression of misery and lethargy has settled on his face [...] For painfulness I think this beats anything I've ever seen in my life."[57] Lewis confesses that "The sight of these attacks has almost changed my deep rooted conviction that no mental pain can equal bad physical pain."[58] This is the statement of a man who had been wounded in battle, a man who still carried shrapnel in his body. Only a year previously he had noted in the same diary, on 15 April, 1922, "It was this day four years ago I was wounded at Mt. Bemchenon."[59] On this occasion the reminder had come from Mrs. Moore, but another day he is reminded by his own body: "Worried today by shooting pains in my left armpit near the old wound."[60]

Lewis's experiences of struggling physically to control the physical and verbal evidence of madness, as the desperate paretic cried for his help, as it were, from Hell, obviously made a deep impression. All of the elements I have cited as sources in his personal life for the depiction of the Un-man occurred while he was young—from age nine to age 25 (1907–1923), and the last of these, the madness of the "Doc," took place while Lewis was still an undergraduate, in that "fourth year at Oxford during which I read English so as to get a second string to my bow";[61] that is, during a last, extra year, when he added additional subjects to this knowledge so as to have as wide as possible a range of subjects which he might be hired to teach.

He had three years to go before, "going up Headington Hill on the top of a bus," he made his "wholly free" choice. He says, "I chose to open, I unbuckle, to loosen the rein."[62] Weston, we remember, is also offered a chance—his last chance, perhaps, to call on God for help, to loosen the rein he had himself invited the devil to cast upon him; we do not know if, in his heart, Weston at that last moment before his demonic occupant snatched back, or tightened its grip, upon those reins, opened himself to God, but we do know, according to the Creeds that Christ himself descended into Hell to harrow it. As Lewis, for his part, let go of the constraints of his atheism, his Adversary (God) "only said ... 'I am,'"[63] which is the answer God gave to Moses from the Burning Bush. It is also the answer Jesus, always recognized by the demons who salute him from the mouths of demoniacs, as "Son of God," give by ironic reversal when his captors ask him, "are you the Son of God?" (Matthew 26.63) and he replies, "You say that I am" (Luke 22.70).

In his efforts to help Mrs. Moore's brother, Lewis, the young atheist, could not advise him to "say a child's prayer." He could only talk to him about "being a man and not afraid of the bogeys." Ransom, however, is a Christian, as was Lewis when he wrote *Perelandra,* and Ransom's pleas, at the end of his final interview, perhaps, with the "man" (as opposed to the Un-man), Weston, tells him, not only to pray, but to repent of his sins. We do not learn, in the end, whether he does. But we may imagine, if we believe the Creeds, that maybe, just maybe, his true and only and most powerful "Adversary," Maleldil the Younger, followed Weston to Hell and rescued him, even there.

Conclusion

I suggested above that Lewis may have been thumbing his nose at future commentators when he gave his list of Ransom's remembered readings, not least because he concludes that list with *The Hunting of the Snark* by Lewis Carroll. Interestingly, a very telling essay on evil by Mark Hobart (1985) uses this potent poem to say that "Enquiring into the nature of evil is a little like the Hunting of the Snark."[64] In exploring this thesis (it *is* his thesis) he summarizes a point of view which reminds us that Lewis caused his *alter ego,* Professor Kirke, to say, "It's all in Plato":

> Socrates [...] held the intellectualist stance that no one would willingly stray from *agathón,* the good, except out of ignorance. His disciple Plato, by contrast, shifted his ideas to see good and evil, *kakón,* not as value judgements so much as hypostatized realities [...] objects potentially willed by the soul [...] In a few strokes good and evil become real, dual and either moral or comic.[65]

It is this Platonic, or, in Christian terms, Neo-platonic view of reality, that Lewis uses in creating his images of both good and evil in *Perelandra.*

Hobart, for his part, turns as many anthropologists do, to Clifford Geertz (1973), for the following explanation of why and how concepts of evil arise in human culture:

> The strange opacity of certain empirical events, the dumb senselessness of intense or inexorable pain, and the enigmatic unaccountability of gross iniquity all raise the uncomfortable suspicion that perhaps the world [...] has no genuine order at all [...] And the religious response to this suspicion is in each case the same: the formulation, by means of symbols, of an image of such a genuine order of the world which will account for, and even celebrate, the perceived ambiguities, puzzles, and paradoxes in human experience.[66]

For my essay, the watchword in Hobart's summary of Greek thought is the phrase, "potentially willed by the soul," for that is what Ransom sees Weston as doing; and in Geertz's meditation upon what Lewis once called "the problem of pain," the phrase is "by means of symbols." In *Perelandra,* Lewis uses the symbol of the Un-man, who is ambiguity personified, and opposes to him Ransom, the earnest, fallible, and in the end, good man, who is, by his name, a representative of that other combination of a spiritual being and a man, the Incarnate God.

In 1926, before his conversion, Lewis had a conversation with a skeptical fellow don who remarked favorably on "the evidence for the historicity of the Gospels,"[67] saying of Frazer's notion of the Dying God, "It almost looks as if it had really happened once."[68] As Downing observes, Lewis found that the "Greek myths, Nordic sagas, and Irish legends"[69] he had loved as a youth were fully and finally validated as precursors of the revelation he would soon acknowledge to be true. For Lewis, in Downing's potent words, "They became reservoirs of transrational truths."[70]

C.S. Lewis has made a significant addition to the sum of such transrational truths as they appear to us embodied in works of Christian fantasy, which always draw from those two great reservoirs of transrational truth in Western culture: Christian and Jewish mythology, that body of symbolic utterance which has outlived, and indeed, *will* outlive, all the best efforts of scholars to find what they hope may be the "true" core of reality within. Heaven and Hell are part of these myths, infinitely resonant embodiments of states of being which can be embodied in no other way, at least while we live and see through the glass darkly. As archetypes, they have their parallels in the mythology of the supernal and the infernal in most of the world's other religions, as the many writings Ransom meditates upon make clear. These transrational truths are always the point of everything Lewis wrote. ... As to whether the devil actually exists, as such, he believed people can be Christians without making up their minds; "I do believe such beings exist," he wrote, "but that is my own affair."[71]

Notes

[1] J.I.M. Stewart, "Floating Islands," *Critical Essays on* C.S. *Lewis.* George Watson, ed. (Aldershot: Scolar Press, 1992) 264.

[2] Kath Filmer, *The Fiction of C.S. Lewis: Mask and Mirror* (New York: St. Martin's Press, 1993) 33.

[3] Colin Manlove, *Christian Fantasy from 1200 to the Present* (Notre Dame, IN: Notre Dame UP, 1992) 249.

[4] Manlove 5.

[5] Manlove 67.

[6] Darlene Logan, "Battle Strategy in *Perelandra*: *Beowulf* Revisited," *Mythlore* 9.3 #33 (1982): 19, 21.

[7] See Lowenberg's paraphrase of Bettie Jo Knight's PhD dissertation from Oklahoma State University (1983), "Paradise Retained: *Perelandra* as an Epic," noting that she cites "Ransom's fists and teeth as his weapons," the same weapons as those of the Un-man. Knight also discusses the "descent into the underworld" in *Perelandra*. Susan Lowenberg, *C.S. Lewis, A Reference Guide, 1972-1988* (New York: G.K. Hall, 1993) 183.

[8] Frank S. Kaster, "C.S. Lewis's John Milton: Influences, Presence, and Beyond," *CSL: The Bulletin of the New York C.S. Lewis Society* 24.9-10 (July/August 1993): 4.

[9] Kaster 4.

[10] Charlotte Spivak, "Images of Spirit in the Fiction of Clive Staples Lewis," *Mythlore* 14.2 (1987): 35-37.

Notes

[11] Patricia Alice McKenzie, "The Last Battle: Violence and Theology in the Novels of C.S. Lewis," PhD dissertation, University of Florida (1974); quoted in Lowenberg 41.

[12] *Beowulf*, trans. Michael Alexander (Harmondsworth, UK: Penguin, 1973) 68.

[13] *Beowulf* 99.

[14] James Como, "Spirit in Bondage," rev. of *All My Road Before Me, 1991, CSL: The Bulletin of the New York C.S. Lewis Society* 22.8 (June 1991): 4.

[15] Robert W. Funk, Ray W. Hoover, and the Jesus Seminar, *The Five Gospels: The Search for the Authentic Words of Jesus* (New York: Macmillan, 1993) 330. This interesting enterprise includes not only Matthew, Mark, Luke, and John, but also The Gospel of Thomas.

[16] Manlove 67.

[17] C.S. Lewis, *Surprised by Joy: The Shape of My Early Life* (1955; Harcourt, Brace, Jovanovich, 1966) 8.

[18] C.S. Lewis, *Surprised by Joy* 8.

[19] C.S. Lewis, *Surprised by Joy* 8.

[20] C.S. Lewis, *Surprised by Joy* 9.

[21] C.S. Lewis, *Surprised by Joy* 20.

[22] C.S. Lewis, *Surprised by Joy* 195.

[23] David C. Downing, *Planets in Peril: A Study of C.S. Lewis's Ransom Trilogy* (Amherst, MA: University of Massachusetts Press, 1992) 33.

[24] Downing 33.

[25] Downing 13.

[26] Downing 14.

[27] Downing 15.

[28] Downing 32-33.

[29] C.S. Lewis, "Why I Am Not a Pacifist," *Timeless at Heart* (London: Collins, Fount, 1987) 64.

[30] C.S. Lewis, "My First School," *Present Concerns* (London: Collins, Fount, 1986) 25.

[31] C.S. Lewis, *Surprised by Joy* 17.

[32] C.S. Lewis, *All My Road Before Me* 343.

[33] C.S. Lewis, *Surprised by Joy* 127.

Notes

[34] C.S. Lewis, *All My Road Before Me* 179.
[35] C.S. Lewis, *Surprised by Joy* 188.
[36] C.S. Lewis, *Surprised by Joy* 195.
[37] C.S. Lewis, "Why I Am Not a Pacifist" 64.
[38] C.S. Lewis, *Spirits in Bondage* (New York: Harcourt, 1984) 4.
[39] C.S. Lewis, *Surprised by Joy* 197.
[40] C.S. Lewis, *Spirits in Bondage* 74.
[41] C.S. Lewis, "Why I Am Not a Pacifist" 65.
[42] C.S. Lewis, "Why I Am Not a Pacifist" 61.
[43] Lewis, "Why I Am Not a Pacifist" 65.
[44] Quoted in Michael Coren, "A Different Light on George Woodcock," *The Globe and Mail,* Toronto, ON, Monday May 23, 1994, C-2.
[45] Dorothy Day quoted in Robert Coles, *Dorothy Day: A Radical Devotion* (Boston, MA: Da Capo Press, 1989) 83.
[46] Jacques Ellul, *Anarchy and Christianity* (Grand Rapids, MI: Eerdmans, 1988) 26.
[47] Ellul 30.
[48] Funk 143, 144, 294.
[49] C.S. Lewis, *Reflections on the Psalms* (London: Geoffrey Bles, 1958) 20.
[50] C.S. Lewis, *Reflections on the Psalms* 25.
[51] C.S. Lewis, *Surprised by Joy* 202-203.
[52] C.S. Lewis, *Surprised by Joy* 203.
[53] C.S. Lewis, *All My Road Before Me* 3.
[54] C.S. Lewis, *All My Road Before Me* 202.
[55] C.S. Lewis, *All My Road Before Me* 202.
[56] C.S. Lewis, *All My Road Before Me* 202-203.
[57] C.S. Lewis, *All My Road Before Me* 211-12.
[58] C.S. Lewis, *All My Road Before Me* 212.
[59] C.S. Lewis, *All My Road Before Me* 20.
[60] C.S. Lewis, *All My Road Before Me* 29-30.
[61] C.S. Lewis, *Surprised by Joy* 212.
[62] C.S. Lewis, *Surprised by Joy* 224.
[63] C.S. Lewis, *Surprised by Joy* 227.

Notes

[64] Mark Hobart, "Is God Evil?" *The Anthropology of Evil* (Oxford: Blackwell, 1985) 165.
[65] Hobart 166.
[66] Clifford Geertz, "Religion as a Cultural System," *The Interpretation of Culture (*New York: Basic, 1973) 107-108.
[67] C.S. Lewis, *Surprised By Joy* 223-24. This account is also cited by Downing 31.
[68] C.S. Lewis, *Surprised by Joy* 224.
[69] Downing 31.
[70] Downing 31.
[71] See epigraph. C.S. Lewis, "Answers to Questions on Christianity" (1944), *God in the Dock: Essays on Theology and Ethics*, ed. Walter Hooper (Grand Rapids, MI: Eerdmans, 1970) 56.

7. "Some Kind of Company" in *That Hideous Strength*

> "You keep talking of *We* and *Us*. Are you some kind of company?"
>
> "Yes. You may call it a company."
>
> ——C.S. Lewis, *That Hideous Strength*

Patterson analyzes the "good" or "saved" characters of the St. Anne's Company: Elwin Ransom, Andrew MacPhee, Dr. Grace Ironwood, Cecil and Margaret Dimble, Arthur and Camilla Denniston, Mr. Bultitude and the other household animals, Ivy Maggs, Jane Studdock, Merlin, Tom Maggs, and finally Mark Studdock. In the section on the animals, she notes their place in Lewis's hierarchy of beings and the role of Old Solar as a language connecting them to it. In her conclusion, she speculates on the significance of Ransom's tripartite role as Fisher King, Director, and Pendragon and on the characters who might take up those roles in the future beyond the novel's closing.

This paper was previously published as "'Some Kind of Company': The Sacred Community in That Hideous Strength*" in the* Proceedings of the Sixteenth Annual Convention of the Mythopoeic Society *(Wheaton, Illinois: Mythcon XVI, 1985): 247-70, and reprinted in* Mythlore *13.1 (Autumn 1986): 8-19. It was revised by Patterson for a proposed anthology of papers about Lewis's fiction.*

C.S. Lewis wrote his *Preface to Paradise Lost* (1942) partly to defend Milton against the charge that Satan is its most interesting character. He was well aware of the problems presented by evil characters in literature, and tried to overcome them by turning the story of Satan inside out in *The Screwtape Letters* so that the devil would present a humorous spectacle from that topsy-turvey point of view. In *That Hideous Strength* he created his most elaborate portrait of evil in the occupants of Belbury, headquarters of the N.I.C.E. A reading of his novel that deals solely with the evil characters produces a sense of awful claustrophobia, like St. Teresa of Avila's vision of hell as a little niche in a brick wall built just her size. This paper, however, is a reading of *That Hideous Strength* dealing exclusively with the good or at least saved characters.

Lewis made nearly all of these characters members, early or late, of the household—the "Company"—at St. Anne's Manor. Belbury and St. Anne's Manor constitute the most profound polarities: Belbury is a cluster with a dead or bodiless head, in which there is no allegiance, no loyalty, no brother or sisterhood, no principle of coherence, and in the end, no center. St. Anne's is, in absolute contrast, what? The collection of differing, even ill-fitted parts to create a coherent whole is a figure for the body, in which each part differs and is meaningless on its own, but is indispensable to the whole. Margaret Hannay has given an excellent description of the Company in her study *C.S. Lewis* (1981): she states that it succeeds by "Ranging an odd assortment of professors, housewives, gardeners, and *eldila* with Merlin against a seemingly omnipotent fascist bureaucracy," so that "the powerless, helped by divine power, against all expectations overcome their oppressors."[1] Clearly, this Company is like the Fellowship of the Ring in Tolkien's great work *The Lord of the Rings*, with its elf, dwarf, wizard, hobbit, and human members ranged against the awesome power of Sauron; and like the Company of Logres in Charles Williams's Arthurian poem cycle, *Taliessin Through Logres* (1938) and *The Region of Summer Stars* (1944).[2] Some writers have further suggested that the Inklings, the group of friends which included C.S. Lewis, Charles Williams, and J.R.R. Tolkien among others, were something of a Company, though the members themselves (perhaps from modesty) seem to have denied this.

When Jane Studdock is first made aware of the actual nature of the Company at St. Anne's, a young woman whom she admires, Camilla Denniston, calls it "Our little household, or company, or society, or whatever you like to call it" (THS 111; ch. 5). Grace Ironwood tells Jane of her former maid Ivy Maggs that "She is one of our company" (THS 137; ch. 7). The Director of the Company, Elwin Ransom, asks Jane "to become one of our army" (THS 142; ch. 7), and says of Merlin, "He *is* a member of the organisation" (THS 277; ch. 13).

What is the purpose of this Company, household, society, army, organization? Andrew MacPhee, the gardener of St. Anne's Manor, puts the question plainly: "I'd be greatly obliged if anyone would tell me what we *have* done—always apart from feeding the pigs and raising some very decent vegetables" (THS 368; ch. 17). The reply comes from Ransom: "You have done what was required of you," a paraphrase of the words of the returning master to his servants in the Parable of the Talents, told by Jesus in Matthew 25.21: "Well done, good and faithful servant: thou has been faithful over a few things, I will make thee ruler over many things: enter thou into the joy of thy lord."

Membership in the Company comes by free will, and yet is preordained; and it has a leader. Arthur Denniston clarifies: "[Ransom] was told that a company would in fact collect round him and he was to be its Head" (THS 112; ch. 5). It is this title "Head," which makes the role of Ransom and of his Company clear. An analysis of its membership, and the relations between them, suggests that they represent a paradigm of the Body of Christ. In describing the Church in Ephesians 4.4, St. Paul explains to his hearers: "There is one body, and one spirit, even as ye are called in one hope of your calling." And in Ephesians 4.11-13, he continues:

> And he gave some apostles, and some, prophets; and some evangelists; and some pastors and teachers; For the perfecting of the saints, for the work of the ministry, for the edifying of the body of Christ: Till we all come in the unity of the faith, and of the knowledge of the Son of God, unto a perfect man, unto the measure of the stature of the fullness of Christ.

Of this body, Jesus "is the head, *even* Christ: From whom the whole body [is] fitly joined together and compacted by that which every joint supplieth" (Ephesians 4.15-16).

Finally, the number of the Company is twelve, the same as the number of apostles. Its true head, then, is Maleldil the Younger (the name used in this fantasy for the Second Person of the Holy Trinity), not Ransom; and in the Company at St. Anne's there is no Judas, but only a potential traitor—Mark Studdock—who is saved in the end. These twelve persons are discussed here one at a time in the order of their adherence to the Company.

Elwin Ransom

Well known to the readers of the first two volumes of Lewis's Trilogy, where he occupies the center of the narrative on every page, Elwin Ransom plays a much different role in *That Hideous Strength.* Here, he is still at the center, but this time the action is viewed not from his point of view but from that, alternately, of Mark and Jane Studdock. His importance is only very gradually revealed to Jane, and Mark never meets him at all. The first reference to him defines his role precisely, though Jane (to whom the speaker presents the idea) cannot understand it when it is first revealed: "Our little household, or company, or society, or whatever you like to call it is run by a Mr Fisher-King" (THS 111; ch. 5). Nobody is to know, just yet, that Mr. Fisher-King is Elwin Ransom. Hints are given, of course; some may guess the riddle: "He is a great traveller but now an invalid. He got a wound in his foot, on his last journey, which won't heal" (THS 112; ch. 5). At this point, readers of *Perelandra* may well prick up their ears, for Ransom acquired a wound in the heel in combat with the Un-man, the body of the scientist Weston in a state of diabolical possession. At the end of the novel we read that "Ransom looked down and saw that his heel was still bleeding. 'Yes,' he said, 'it is where the evil one bit me'" (PER 189; ch. 17).

The speaker who is describing Mr. Fisher-King to Jane continues with what for the initiated reader is a second clue: "He had a married sister in India, a Mrs Fisher-King" (THS 112; ch. 5). Readers with very perfect memories might be expected to recall that in *Out of the Silent Planet* Ransom innocently revealed to his would-be kidnappers (Weston and an odious former schoolmate, Devine) that he has no living relatives near enough to note his absence, "Only a married sister in India" (OSP 14; ch. 2).

Jane finally meets Mr. Fisher-King face-to-face about a third of the way through the novel: "On a sofa before her, with one foot bandaged as if he had a wound, lay what appeared to be a boy, twenty years old" (THS 139; ch. 7). He is "so strong" that "Now it was manifest that the grip of those hands would be inescapable, and imagination suggested that those arms and shoulders could support the whole house" (THS 139; ch. 7). In a word, he is like the Sun, which holds the solar system in its orbiting tracks. He is the "chief," the "Head," the centralizing force around which the action of the novel revolves. This solar imagery suits the title of "Director," which is used for Ransom as soon as Jane meets him. MacPhee, in a later passage, comments on this title:

> "I don't just remember how you came to be called Director: but from that title and from one or two other indica-

> tions a man would have thought you behaved more like the leader of an organisation than the host at a house-party." (THS 195; ch. 9)

Ransom agrees. "It is, no doubt, an organisation: but we are not the organisers" (THS 196; ch. 9). As an image of kingship, Merlin ends on his knees in recognition of the Director's rank in the scene of their confrontation: "I am the Pendragon," Ransom tells him, and in response, combining metaphors of earth and sea, "as though a mountain sank like a wave, [Merlin] sank on one knee" (THS 271; ch. 13). We are accorded a final portrait when we see "Ransom crowned," before he is translated to Perelandra.

Andrew MacPhee and Dr. Grace Ironwood

The primary members of the household are Ransom—Mr. Fisher-King—the householder who has purchased this fine old manor with monies inherited from his sister for the purpose of assembling a Company to await the outbreak of danger foretold by the Sura, his sister's spiritual director. In his house Ransom has two attendants. One is the gardener: there is a very large garden, one well beyond the care of an invalid. Was MacPhee the gardener of the former owners? Ransom says of him, "He's one of my oldest friends" (THS 181; ch. 9). Perhaps as a friend of Ransom's youth, he is now provided with a comfortable sinecure. Certainly MacPhee is modeled on Lewis's beloved tutor Kirkpatrick, who spent his spare time and old age in his garden.

And because Ransom is now an invalid, he also requires the services of a doctor. This is Grace Ironwood, clearly defined as, and performing the tasks of, a doctor. Her origins are obscure—some mystery or tragedy lies in her past—and one may ask why she is a resident in the house. A doctor who is the personal physician of a very wealthy person is not impossible, but her relationship with Ransom may go beyond that. Perhaps we are to assume she was a previous acquaintance of Ransom's, recruited when his need befell him. She seems to have been based on Lewis's friendship with Janie McNeill, to whom *That Hideous Strength* is dedicated. In any event these necessary attendants are primary: they, with Ransom, form the three-personed nucleus of the Company.

The first glimpse we have of Dr. Grace Ironwood is through Jane's praeternatural foresight:

> She saw Miss Ironwood, dressed all in black, sitting with her hands folded on her knees and then someone leading her into Miss Ironwood's presence and saying "She's come," and leaving her there. (THS 43; ch. 2)

The accuracy of her vision is proved some pages later, when

> The hands which were folded on her knees were very big and boney though they did not suggest coarseness, and even when seated Miss Ironwood was extremely tall. Everything about her was big—the nose, the unsmiling lips, and the grey eyes. She was perhaps nearer sixty than fifty. (THS 61; ch. 3)

It is very much a picture of a dreaded interview with a headmistress or even a mother superior. There is everything here of the female hierophant: the Isis-like posture, the stern visage, and most of all, the powerful hands. When Jane returns to St. Anne's Manor for the third time, it is to stay. She has been tortured by the secret police of the N.I.C.E., and now has reached St. Anne's as a place of refuge and healing. Here at last we see "Miss Ironwood" in her healer's role: "She examined and dressed the burns, which were not serious" (THS 160; ch. 8).

Later, there is a discussion in the Blue Room (Ransom's chamber), in which each member of the Company gives the reason each has joined it:

> Grace Ironwood looked up with a set expression on her face, which had grown rather pale. "Do you wish …?" she began.
>
> The Director laid his hand on her arm. "No," he said, "No. There is no need for all these stories to be told." (THS 195; ch. 9)

Something secret lies in her past, which none but the Director may know. Has he rescued her in someway? Has she, too, fled from some evil or danger? All we learn, finally, of her background is that she is indeed a doctor: Dimble speaks of her as "The doctor who dressed the burns" which Jane has received.

In our last glimpse of Dr. Ironwood, we see her as the equal of Ransom: they are seated, "Ransom crowned, at the right of the hearth; Grace Ironwood, in black and silver, opposite him" (THS 365; ch. 17). When all the Company have been dismissed by Ransom, Dr. Ironwood and the Dennistons remain: we may presume that they will see him depart for the Third Heaven and remain to perpetuate the Company. The new and operative word in the last description of Grace Ironwood is "silver." We already know that Ransom is associated with gold: she in her silver is his counterpart and opposite, her Moon in balance to his Sun.

From the first moment he is mentioned, we are aware of Andrew MacPhee's role as gardener at St. Anne's Manor: Lewis describes him as Jane first sees him at the scullery door: "a tall grizzle-headed man, who wore gum boots and seemed to have just come from the garden, was drying his hands" (THS 163; ch. 8). These gardener's hands. like the healer's hands of Dr. Ironwood, are given special attention: "His own hand was very large and coarse in texture, and he had a shrewd hard-featured face" (THS 163; ch. 8). The honesty and expressiveness of the hands of these close attendants of Ransom constitute a motif which is probably derived from George MacDonald's *The Princess and Curdie* (1883), a book mentioned in *That Hideous Strength*: Curdie is granted by the goddess-like Queen Irene the power to discover, when grasping anyone's hand, what sort, of person or animal is present within.

MacPhee's identification as an Ulsterman, which is reiterated, has not excited much comment. Lewis, so long a resident in England, was an Ulsterman too, proud of and attached to his home and identity. Likely to have been teased for his brogue as a schoolboy, he longed for the green hills of his homeland and regarded the trip to England by way of Liverpool as a repeated *via dolorosa*. It is this motif which appears in Jane's next encounter with MacPhee, when he describes the travels between the worlds of the Director and sets forth the "interplanetary" situation. In conclusion he offers his personal and distinctive point of view that it all may be a fantasy: "If anything wants Andrew MacPhee to believe in its existence, I'll be obliged if it will present itself in full daylight" (THS 190; ch. 9). When Jane, startled by this acerbic touch of skepticism, calls upon him to show loyalty, he "suddenly looked up with a hundred covenanters in his eyes" (THS

191; ch. 9). If ever Lewis showed a specific love and loyalty to his own roots it was here!

The relationship between Ransom and his two fundamental companions is summarized in his remark, made as MacPhee and Dr. Ironwood fall to arguing:

> "If you two quarrel much more," said the Director, "I think I'll make you marry one another." (THS 197; ch. 9)

It is a joke, of course; coercion against the grain is no part of Ransom's role. But the note of authority is there, and the relationship of these two highly developed individuals to one another exists through him.

Cecil and Margaret Dimble

The next to join the Company were presumably the Dimbles: Cecil and Margaret, of whom we hear early on in the novel that

> Cecil Dimble, a Fellow of Northumberland, had been Jane's tutor for her last years as a student, and Mrs Dimble (one tended to call her Mother Dimble) had been a kind of unofficial aunt to all the girls of her year. (THS 27; ch. 1)

I think it likely that Ransom sought out Cecil Dimble and perhaps even settled at St. Anne's where he could be near this fellow academic, with whom, as it eventuates, he shares a profound interest in the "true" meaning (within the context of this fantasy) of Arthurian legend.

Dr. Cecil Dimble appears from time to time in the action of the story. Conferences at St. Anne's frequently involve the whole group, who talk over their plans and fears in evident equality. In a significant scene the Company discusses Jane's dream of seeing the Head of the N.I.C.E., who is, literally, a head, the severed head of the criminal Alcasan. Dimble's response is recorded:

> "Then this filthy abomination." said Dr Dimble, "is real—not only a dream." His face was white and his expression strained. (THS 193; ch. 9)

Dimble is not a man with Dr. Ironwood's iron control or MacPhee's skeptical reserve. As an effective communicator, he is passionate, expressively visaged, and committed to serve an ideal.

The closest we come to the interior of Dr. Dimble's personality is in his confrontation with Mark. Mark demands to know where his wife has gone and Dimble hotly informs him that she has been tortured by the N.I.C.E. Mark's blustering response pierces Dimble's armor (which as we have seen already, is not very thick): "Dimble's conscience had for years accused him of a lack of charity towards Studdock" (THS 216; ch 10). When Dimble recovers himself he offers Mark a chance to leave the N.I.C.E.—he extends to him "a way back into the human family"—with risk, no security, just "a place on the right side" (THS 220; ch. 10). In this offer Lewis encapsulates the essential meaning of the Company. The people who join it have a place on the right side. That place may be difficult, perilous, frustrating, insecure. But, in the end, there is no other. It is not surprising that Mark is unable, when the matter is put so badly, to accept. But the offer of salvation has been held out to him.

The role of Dimble, as well as Denniston, in the Company is clarified when the gods indeed descend upon the Manor and it is Mercury who most affects these two men, "as they had stood, one on each side of the fireplace, in a gay intellectual duel" (THS 318; ch. 14). Dimble, as communicator and intellectual, is both learned and empassioned. Under the influence of her own most appropriate planet, Venus, Jane the seer has a vision of the Dimbles in her turn: they are "like ripe fields in August, serene and golden with the tranquility of fulfilled desire" (THS 319; ch. 15). In the final scene, just before Ransom's departure, the Dimbles are the first to be dismissed: "He laid his hands on their heads: Cecil gave his arm to his wife and they went" (THS 375; ch. 17). The old scholar's wisdom is no longer required. He and his wife can depart in peace.

The Dimbles are very much a couple, but each of them is also a considerable person in his and her own right. James Patrick (1985) has suggested that "The childless Professor and Mrs. Dimble who kept a Christian salon across the river from the college [...] are surely drawn from Clement and Eleanor Webb, whose hospitality at Holywell Ford was recalled by guests."[3] Like her husband, Margaret Dimble is close to Jane, of whom we catch an early glimpse as Mrs. Dimble sees her; the passage gives us as much about Mrs. Dimble's forthright nature as about Jane:

> She had been particularly fond of Jane with that kind of affection which a humorous, easy natured and childless woman sometimes feels for a girl whom she thinks pretty and rather absurd. (THS 27; ch. 1)

As a consequence, perhaps, of this affectionate attitude, when Mrs. Dimble needs help, it is Jane with whom she asks to be allowed to stay. When she arrives she reports that Dr. Dimble has gone to stay at his college because they have been turned out of their house! It is through her eyes, not Jane's, that we see the beginning of the terrible destruction of which the N.I.C.E. is capable. But there is hope: "Cecil and I are to go out to the Manor at St. Anne's" (THS 74; ch. 4). "We have to be there so much at present," she explains. She and her husband have been regular visitors and now they will become residents.

We meet Mother Dimble again at St. Anne's Manor in the great kitchen there: "The comfortable form of Mrs Dimble [...] was seated in a kitchen chair [...] engaged in preparing vegetables" (THS 163; ch. 8). As we have seen, vegetables, like other products of a garden, are signs of goodness in this novel. In addition, the adjective "comfortable" has a special resonance for Anglicans, and thus likely for Lewis, because the Holy Spirit is called "the Comforter," and the Order for Holy Communion in the *Book of Common Prayer* presaged the Consecration with the beautiful if archaic saying: "Hear what comfortable words our Saviour Christ saith unto all that truly turn to him."

Lewis does not mean this character merely to represent a comfortable, motherly housewife. He gives her a powerful scene of her own. Again, she and Jane are alone. They have been sent to "the Lodge" to prepare it as a marriage chamber for Jane's former part-time domestic servant, Ivy Maggs, who now lives at St. Anne's too, awaiting her husband's release from prison. Jane is surprised at the zest with which the earthly task of preparing the bed for these renewed nuptials is taken up by her companion: "Mother Dimble, for all her nineteenth-century propriety, or perhaps because of it, struck her this afternoon as being herself an archaic person" (THS 298; ch. 14). Margaret Dimble and her husband are warmly satisfied lovers. She knows more of nuptial pleasure than Jane does. Lewis reinforces this idea with a poignant descriptive sentence:

> The frost had ended and it was one of those days of almost piercingly sweet mildness which sometimes occur in the very beginning of winter. (THS 299; ch. 14)

This is a perfect figure for the relationship of the Dimbles. Lewis has prepared this passage as a revelation for Jane of the inherent dignity of the feminine role which she has heretofore rejected. He has chosen images of profound power to make his point.

Arthur and Camilla Denniston

Although I have suggested that Cecil and Margaret Dimble became members of the Company before them, it is obvious that Arthur Denniston and his wife were forced from their home and repaired there too. It would seem that Denniston was recruited by Dimble and that he married Camilla just before taking up residence at St. Anne's.

We learn of Arthur when a senior colleague, Curry, tells Mark that "Denniston was your chief rival" (THS 17; ch. 1) for the fellowship at Bracton College which Mark now holds: here we are told plainly, were we able to recognize the clue, that Lord Feverstone (formerly Dick Devine), to be revealed as a major architect of the N.I.C.E., has personally recruited Mark, and for some reason other than academic ability, to his Bracton appointment. Mark does not learn until well on into the novel that his chief qualification for this appointment was his marriage to Jane.

Curry gabbles unheedingly on about Arthur—"A brilliant man [...] but he seems to have gone quite off the rails [...] with all his Distributivism and what not. They tell me he's likely to end up in a monastery" (THS 17; ch. 1). And so, in a sense, he does, for St. Anne's Manor is very like a religious community: a large house with a large garden and a wall, containing a group of people who share the household tasks from the most humble to the most lofty and are gathered under obedience to a superior and in mutual loyalty to a sacred central authority higher still, who has by some means or other called them all together.

The Dennistons try to explain their present allegiance while they make their attempt to recruit Jane: "We don't belong to Grace Ironwood. She and we both belong to someone else" (THS 111; ch. 5). This someone is Elwin Ransom. Jane's response to their approach is mixed, for despite her strong desire not to become entangled, she feels a strong attraction to the couple: "Jane saw at once that both the Dennistons were the sort of people she liked" (THS 110; ch. 5). Lewis seems to suggest here and elsewhere that they are also the sort of people Jane and her husband might have *been*, had she married someone else. She and even Mark—were intended to be this sort of people. Exactly what sort of people are these? They are people who are capable of making, with wisdom and accuracy in their decision to do so, an absolute commitment.

We may speculate that Denniston and his wife originally joined the household, in fact, to be employed; that Arthur, having failed to win a fellowship, first went to St. Anne's to work as a resident research assistant. He may, like the young George MacDonald, have gone to the great old country house to put its library in order. The narrator only states that "Dimble and [Ransom] and the Dennistons shared between them a knowledge of Arthurian Britain which orthodox scholarship will probably not reach for some centuries" (THS 197; ch. 9). This is a central tenet of the fantasy. And, in such a great house, a wife might join her husband in the apartments provided for him. What precisely was Camilla's task is not made clear but at the least she acts as receptionist for Dr. Ironwood.

Arthur Denniston and his wife Camilla are, along with Grace Ironwood, the only people who remain with Ransom as he readies for his departure. As Jane's Venus-inspired vision indicates, Camilla is an essential element in this picture. In *That Hideous Strength* we meet and hear of Camilla for the first time when: "the door opened and Jane found herself facing a tall woman of about her own age" (THS 59; ch. 3). Here Camilla is the guardian of the door in the wall of St. Anne's. She is also a mirror image, like and yet not like, of Jane. Camilla is very much committed to Arthur Denniston, as Jane is not to Mark, and to St. Anne's, as Jane very much fears to become. After questioning Jane and learning that she comes from Dr. Dimble, Camilla admits her, carefully locking the door, and goes ahead of her along the garden path, where walkers can only proceed one at a time. She is familiar with its labyrinthine way, and leads Jane as easily through this great image of conditional access as if she were Ariadne in the palace of Minos.

Inside the equally labyrinthine house, Camilla leaves Jane to wait, and when she reappears,

> Jane now conceived for her that almost passionate admiration which women, more often than is supposed, feel for other women whose beauty is not of their own type. (THS 61; ch. 3)

I cannot guess how Lewis came to know of this capacity of women so to admire one another but it is quite true in my own experience. Lewis thought that this was the way women ought to perceive themselves through the eyes of others.

In contemplating the magnificent garden sequence which introduces Jane (and the reader) to the Manor at St. Anne's for the very first time, it is easy to overlook the fact that Camilla accompanies and indeed leads Jane through it. She is its natural denizen, that Lady in the Garden, whether Eve, or Venus, or Mary, who is almost ubiquitously present in paradisaical symbolism. When MacPhee has opened Jane's eyes to the interplanetary dimensions of their situation, Camilla enters, and "Jane seized her friend's hand." Together the two young women go out into a cold starry night and climb "to the very summit of the garden." There they see the Moon as "the huntress, the untameable virgin" (THS 191; ch. 9). In this one case, the Moon becomes a benign instead of a malign symbol.

In a later scene, when Jane returns from the fulfillment of her visionary task to find the household fast asleep through the magical intervention of the newly-awakened Merlin, she sees that Camilla is "curled up in an attitude which was full of grace, like that of an animal accustomed to sleep anywhere" (THS 274; ch. 13). This reference to natural grace, beauty which requires no artifice, is Lewis's characteristic mode of describing Camilla, but his use of the exceedingly resonant phrase "full of grace"—elsewhere associated with the angelic salutation as the opening phrase of the rosary: "Hail Mary, full of grace"—cannot be accidental. Camilla, the married woman, retains the purity, the spiritual virginity, which Jane in her own marriage has feared to lose.

There are four married couples and a male and female celibate pair whom Ransom jokingly threatens with marriage. The sexual balance is perfect except for one final and essential pairing: Ransom and Merlin. It is notable that Ransom, so obviously heterosexual in Jane's response to her first meeting with him, has no female attachments. Despite the many identifications of this character, because he is a philologist, with Tolkien, and the plot structure which makes Lewis a narrator-character in the framing of the action, I very much suspect that Ransom is an idealized version of Lewis himself. Here we have a Lewis who is truly celibate, truly free of female entanglements, truly able to enjoy that perfect male friendship. Ransom and Merlin meet as equals, and turn their gaze by mutual assent not, after testing and salutation, toward one another, but toward the celestial powers they have met to invoke. It is here that the Company truly resembles the Inklings.

The Household Animals

The human characters so far discussed are the members of the Company when the novel opens. But there are other personages present in the household when Jane makes her three visits who are clearly part of the Company too. These are the animals: Pinch the cat, Baron Corvo the Jackdaw, an assembly of un-named mice, and the bear, Mr. Bultitude. Lewis uses the animals to demonstrate several ideas: that hierarchy encourages rather than prevents collaboration and companionship, that humankind raises animals by means of domestication to a new level of being, and that at the animal level the "ancient unities" proposed by Owen Barfield function completely, just as they did in human consciousness in the earliest periods of development. But the presence of the animals as full members of the household is in itself a powerful symbol: in this Company the continuum of being extends from angels to humans to animals, with humanity in the middle.[4] This is the classical Christian view of the world, and Lewis gives it a vivid portrayal in his fantasy, where such matters are properly made explicit.

The first of the animals to be seen in *That Hideous Strength* is the cat, Pinch: Jane is just about to be summoned to meet the Director for the first time when

> A very large cat which Jane had not noticed before jumped up and occupied the chair which Ivy Maggs had just vacated. (THS 138; ch. 7)

This is a very natural feline gesture and one which Lewis, who was something of a cat-lover, must have observed from real life, but the cat's appearance with Ivy is significant, and so is its appearance just before Jane's encounter with the Director. There is a striking sequence during which Dr. Dimble, about to go in search of Merlin, practices his greeting in Old Solar, the original tongue of the Solar System, which is spoken by the *eldila* and the *Oyéresu*. This is the language which, having learned to speak it, Ransom is able to use to communicate with the three native species of Malacandra, the warm-blooded, water-loving *hrossa*, the gigantic, birdlike *seroni*, and the froglike *pfifltriggi*. At the sound of it, "even the bird, and the bear, and the cat, were still, staring at the speaker" (THS 225; ch. 10). If they understand any language at all in Lewis's cosmos, it is this.

His view, borrowed from his friend Owen Barfield, also includes the original oneness of meaning and physical being, which, as with the primary language, is the oldest mode of consciousness. These ideas are not, of course, specifically or even fundamentally Christian. They are speculative, and what better place than in speculative fiction—that is to say, science fiction—to try them out?

The second animal to appear in the novel is the jackdaw, whimsically named Baron Corvo, which of course means "crow," and is the pseudonym of Frederick William Rolfe (1860–1930), the writer whose novel, *Hadrian VII* (1904) was something of a sensation.[5] Its use is a whimsey of Lewis's or perhaps of Ransom's. We first see Baron Corvo when Jane is ushered for the first time into Ransom's chamber: "On one of the long window sills a tame jackdaw was walking up and down" (THS 139; ch. 7). He is part of the setting, and an element which Lewis had enjoyed in private life: he wrote in his letters a charming description of such a bird, and he was to make a jackdaw a feature of the Narnian creation scene in *The Magican's Nephew*.

Perhaps because of Lewis's special delight in jackdaws, he gives him a little scene in the festival of fecundity that ends the novel: "What's the matter with that jackdaw?' said Dr Dimble" (THS 374; ch. 17). And his wife replies:

> "Another love affair," said Mrs Dimble. "It sounds as if Jack had found a Jill." (THS 374; ch. 17)

With this, the loving couple are dismissed from the narrative.

It is Ransom himself who introduces Jane to the mice. These are exquisitely described as "dainty quadrupeds, almost, when they sat up, like tiny kangaroos, with sensitive kid-gloved forepaws and transparent ears" (THS 147; ch. 7). Lewis seems to be reflecting a personal delight in these charming observations, or perhaps suggesting a new understanding on the part of Jane. Ransom explains, as these guests consume the crumbs of his simple meal, that "obedience and rule are more like a dance than a drill—specially between man and woman where the roles are always changing" (THS 147; ch. 7). The mice wish to eat, the Director wishes to dispose of the crumbs; each has a need which the other is empowered to fulfill. This whimsical demonstration of so great a meaning as the reciprocity of marriage, in which, surely, one partner is not a mouse while the other is a man, has probably blunted the force of this central teaching of Lewis's, and allowed readers to misinterpret his concepts of obedience.

Like the jackdaw, the mice make a final appearance in the general nuptials at the end of the novel when their scufflings and squeakings are heard by Ransom.

> "It's my friends behind the wainscot," he said. "There are revels there too—
>
> *So geht es Snützepützhäusel*
> *Da singen und tanzen die Mäusel*! (THS 376; ch. 17)

"So goes it in Snützepützhäusel house: The singing and dancing of mice." This whimsical refrain, from an "eighteenth century German folksong, depicts a "topsy-turvey world" where snails bark and table and chairs get drunk,[6] well befitting the reversal of summer and winter with which the novel concludes.

Lewis portrayed one animal in *That Hideous Strength* who is truly a major character and who plays a truly significant role in the narrative. This is the bear Mr. Bultitude. His name comes from the father who inadvertently changes places with his schoolboy son in the comic novel *Vice Versa* by Fredrick Anatey (1856–1934), a work which Lewis enjoyed. He and his brother so nicknamed a favorite bear of theirs at the Whipsnade Zoo.[7] The use of literary allusion is probably intended to parallel the use of Baron Corvo as the name of the jackdaw, in a household heavily populated by academics.

Mrs. Maggs introduces Mr. Bultitude to Jane by speaking of him after she awakens for the first time as a resident of St. Anne's Manor. Jane soon discovers him in the bathroom:

> Inside, sitting up on its hunkers beside the bath and occupying most of the room, was a great, snuffly, wheezy, beady-eyed, loose-skinned, gor-bellied brown bear. (THS 161; ch. 8)

Presently Jane again finds Mr. Bultitude, "this time on his hind legs, meditatively boxing a punching-ball." The association of bear with boxing recurs in *The Horse and His Boy*, in which Corin Thunderfist boxes the Lapsed Bear of Stormness into becoming a "reformed character" (HB 224; ch. 14).

Bears formed a staple ingredient in the finely-spun edges of Lewisian fantasy: Bultitude himself is pronounced to be one of the Seven Bears of Logres, an invention which is not elaborated in the text but which suggests a long line of Logrean bears, one great, one snuffy, one wheezy, one beady-eyed, one loose-skinned, one gor-bellied, and now, Bultitude himself, the quintessentially brown bear of this latest incarnation of Logres.

The novel is within about a hundred pages of its conclusion when this bear begins his development into a full participant in affairs rather than an onlooker or resident symbol. After "a very agreeable morning investigating the turnips" (THS 304; ch. 14), he "approached the garden wall"—one thinks of the wall of the Garden of Eden—in search of "endless green lands [...] and hives innumerable, and bees the size of sparrows" (THS 304; ch. 14)—one thinks of the bees in Beorn's garden in *The Hobbit*—and of "someone stickier, sweeter, more yellow than honey itself"—suggesting a "pre-Adamite" apprehension of a God whose judgments are in the words of the Old Testament, "sweeter also than honey and the honeycomb" (Psalms 19.10).

Now Mr. Bultitude goes over the wall and directly into the path of two men in a van from the N.I.C.E. who are searching for a bear which has escaped from the laboratory menagerie. They render him unconscious and muttering "Christ" at appropriate intervals, drive off toward Belbury with their quarry. The bear wakens in the animal cages of Belbury. Presently, Merlin releases him, along with the rest of the animals and the human prisoners:

> He laid his hand on its head and whispered in its ear and its dark mind was filled with excitement as though some

long forbidden and forgotten pleasure were suddenly held out to it. (THS 348; ch. 16)

We do not see the bear again until he is sighted by a doomed resident of Belbury,

> A huge bear, rising to its hind legs as he came in sight of it, had met him in the doorway—its mouth open, its eyes flaming, its fore-paws spread out as if for an embrace. (THS 353; ch. 16)

At this point every shred of domestication drops away and we see Mr. Bultitude as in reality a bear always is, a wild, untamed, and totally unabashed force of nature.

His dreadful task accomplished, the bear returns home. But he is not alone: Ivy reports "a strange bear; another one" who is refreshing herself in the kitchen. She "is the future Mrs Bultitude," Ransom says calmly, and after laying his hands on her head and blessing her, he sends the couple away to their nuptials: "Take her, Bultitude. But not in the house" (THS 375; ch. 17).

Ivy Maggs

In the first chapter of *That Hideous Strength*, we learn that Jane has "a woman who comes in twice a week." This reference implies that Ivy Maggs has at least four other days free to work. From the familiarity with which she is regarded both by Mrs. Dimble and at the Manor, we might further assume that she spent two days a week at each of these other households. It is thus not surprising that when the Dimbles and she are turned out of their homes simultaneously, they repair together to St. Anne's for refuge.

It is Mrs. Dimble who tells Jane that "You've lost Ivy Maggs." Presumably Ivy has called her senior female employer, either to beg assistance or to inform her that she cannot come to work, perhaps both. And, Mrs. Dimble adds, "She's gone out to St. Anne's." The meeting of Ivy's three apparent employers seems fated and her role as a nexus in their meeting more than casual, though she does not know it. It is Ivy who best deals with Mr. Bultitude, and indeed, with MacPhee, both of whom she treats with amiable bullying. The bear responds only to his master, to Ivy, and to Merlin. Mrs. Maggs's presence in that august Company suggests that she is a considerable personage. It is not for nothing that Lewis compares her to a "pert fairy" and a "dapper elf," taking these terms from Milton's *Comus*.

When Jane comes to St. Anne's for the third and final time, exhausted and in pain, she is "received by a woman in pyjamas and an overcoat who turned out to be Mrs Maggs" (THS 156; ch. 7). Ivy has risen in the night at the sound of knocking, thrown on an overcoat, and answered the door. In the morning, "Mrs Maggs came in and lit the fire and brought the breakfast" (THS 160; ch. 8). These are the actions of a trained domestic servant, from bringing Ransom his meal to lighting the fire and bringing Jane her breakfast. Ivy here serves Jane in her own professional way, just as Grace Ironwood is to do a moment later when "She examined and dressed the burns" (THS 160; ch. 8). Although the housework at St. Anne's is shared, certain tasks (serving, healing, gardening) seem to be delegated to those most expert in their practice.

It is for Ivy that Jane and Mother Dimble prepare the Lodge as a marriage chamber, or as Jane, not quite reformed, thinks: "Ivy Maggs and her jail-bird husband" (THS 298; ch. 14). Jane cannot yet accept that even she, like the Dimbles and Ivy, is "one of the Director's charities" (THS 165; ch. 8). Ivy and Jane are parallels in all but station. Ivy is, however, Jane's spiritual superior in her forgiving acceptance of her husband's weaknesses. Her fundamental decency and loyalty are part of her identity as a person who is often referred to by the phrase "the salt of the earth."

It is in this role, a preserver of what is traditional and permanent, that the bear intuitively sees her as being like one of the "little deities of wood and water." The narrator says that "much of Ivy's conversation was the expression not of thought but of feeling" (THS 305; ch. 14). As a person who is herself intuitively in tune with the fundamental moral law, which—in Lewis' view—controls the universe, Ivy is in a stronger moral position at this moment than Jane.

Jane Studdock

The first descriptive passage Lewis gives of Jane has to do with her clothing: "She liked her clothes to be rather severe and in colours that were really good on serious aesthetic grounds" (THS 26; ch. 1). Jane, we learn, does not really know herself. Mrs. Dimble thinks her "Pretty and slightly absurd," not at all the sort of person who should wear severe clothing in seriously aesthetic colors. Jane "still believed that if she got out of all her notebooks and editions and really sat down to the job"—of "her own career as a scholar"—"she could force herself back into her lost enthusiasm for the subject" (THS 12; ch. 1). She has had six months of almost perfect isolation from her husband, a period in which a person with a true scholarly vocation would have been on well on with the task. But she has done nothing. And now she is troubled with dreams.

Jane is neither ill-educated nor of inferior intellect—Lewis does not mean *that* when he says that she is "not perhaps a very original thinker" (THS 12; ch. 1). Rather, she is profoundly intuitive: she *sees*, not only in dreams, but in intuitions and even in visions, what is hidden from conscious thought. The truths she sees are not original with her: how could they be? But they are true. In her own way she is as gifted in prophetic powers as Merlin: apparently, at least for the purpose of this fantasy, the use of these gifts, is licit and even necessary.

When the Dennistons press her to join their Company, but request that she ask Mark's permission before doing so, they touch upon her deepest fear, the fear that has kept her from being able to offer a full welcome to Mark even after marriage. At the very hour of her conversion—which takes place in the garden—she wonders: what if everybody who ever "had infuriatingly found her sweet and fresh when she wanted them to find her also interesting and important" (THS 315; ch. 14) were right? But at that moment she encounters God, and understands herself to be "a made thing, made to please Another and in Him to please all others" (THS 316; ch. 14). Lewis thought that in God's presence, everyone was "feminine." This is why his central character, Jane, whose conversion is a watershed in his novel, is a woman.

Jane is one of those dismissed by Ransom before his departure: "Your husband is waiting for you in the lodge. It was your own marriage chamber that you prepared" (THS 377; ch. 17). And in the final scene of the novel we see her: "And now she was half way to the lodge, and thought of Mark and of all his sufferings" (THS 380; ch. 17). It is the first time in all the novel that she has thought, really thought, about Mark in such a way. He had hoped, after all, to find much of the acceptance he sought so desperately and unrewardedly at

Belbury, in her, and now he will. "Obviously it was high time she went in" (THS 380; ch. 17).

Merlin

The most important subject of Jane's dreams has been Merlin, or as he is called here by his formal Latin name, *Merlinus Ambrosius*. The passage introducing the site of his hidden burial chamber is reserved for the narrator, but the buried Merlin himself first appears in a dream of Jane's. In the first direct description of Merlin in the novel, he is wearing the garb of a tramp whose encampment he has encountered, having emerged naked from his tomb as is appropriate to a new birth from the "parachronic state" in which he has so long lain. Merlin rides on ahead of his seekers to the very portal of St. Anne's, and, admitted through the scullery door by its guardian MacPhee, he bursts into the midst of the Company, brought, as it were, by the wind.

Lewis's description of the Magus is as a force of nature:

> his great mass stood as if it had been planted like a tree [...] and the voice, too, was such as one might imagine to be the voice of a tree, large and slow and patient, drawn up through roots and clay and gravel from the depths of the Earth. (THS 269; ch. 13)

There is a touch of Treebeard here. Merlin is—like MacPhee and Ivy—profoundly in touch with the earth.

The searchers now return, to find the household cast into sleep, and to see Ransom and Merlin together: "there they were, the pair of them [...] The man who had been dug up out of the earth and the man who had been in outer space" (THS 275; ch. 13). Jane's horror is echoed by MacPhee, who phrases aloud what all the Company fear:

> "It gives me little pleasure, I assure you, to see yourself dressed up like something out of a pantomime and standing hand in glove with that yogi, or shaman, or priest, or whatever he is." (THS 276; ch. 13)

Lewis, in referring to Merlin explicitly as a shaman, must have been well aware that the two contrasted figures in red and blue, "the man who had been dug up out of the earth and the man who had been in outer space," exactly embody the shamanic two-fold path to the immanent powers below the level of consciousness, and to the transcendent powers above the level of consciousness. Bringing these forces together in Merlin and Ransom creates the psychic energy, the supernatural force capable of resisting and in the end destroying the demonic outbreak of the N.I.C.E.

In response to protestations voiced by MacPhee, Ransom declares: "He *is* a member of the organisation, and I must command you all to accept him" (THS 277; ch. 13). Merlin has proved to be friendly not to the N.I.C.E. but to the Company. Dr. Dimble explains the situation to his wife: Merlin, he says, "is the last vestige of an old order in which matter and spirit were, from our modern point of view, confused" (THS 282; ch. 13). He will thus be able to act as a receptacle to collect and then direct the spiritual forces poured upon him by the planetary intelligences when, through the breach in the quarantine between devil-occupied earth and the rest of the cosmos, which was opened by the scientist Weston's space ship, they descend from Deep Heaven to Thulcandra.

Merlin, like Ransom, MacPhee, and Grace Ironwood, has significant hands:

> The druid sat in a chair facing [Ransom], his legs uncrossed, his pale large hands motionless on his knees, looking to modern eyes like an old conventional carving of a king. (THS 283; ch. 13)

The hands of the magician (or druid, or shaman), the hands of the king (Ransom, the Pendragon), the hands of the healer, and the hands of the gardener are all alike in their licit, natural, good, and even holy operations. When the hour has come, Merlin "received the power into him" (THS 324; ch. 15) and "He looked different next day [...] No one doubted that his final severance from the body was near." Merlin has lain in an enchanted state, suspended from death, for centuries before the awakening. His departure, the severance of body from spirit, is long overdue.

It is Merlin who saves the three captives at Belbury: Mr. Bultitude, Tom Maggs, and Mark Studdock. Soon after, Edgestow goes up in a great holocaust and is buried under a wave of earth, the fundamental medium of Merlin's magical art. The character of Merlin is as complete a figure of fantasy as could be imagined, almost as fantastic as the apotheosized Ransom, whose place he takes as the focusing lens of divine power. Lewis has surrounded these two figures with very finely drawn portraits of natural people who are in the act of surpassing themselves.

Tom Maggs

As we have seen, Ivy and Jane are doublets in their plight as deserted women. We now turn to the first of the two deserted husbands. The story of Tom Maggs is soon told, but it is related relatively late in *That Hideous Strength*, and by Ivy herself:

> Mr Maggs had stolen some money from the laundry that he worked for. He had done this before he met Ivy and at a time when he had got into bad company. (THS 299; ch. 14)

Ivy tells this story straight forwardly and without apology. As she says herself, "I always say, you can't expect to know everything about a boy till you're married, not really" (THS 299; ch. 14).

A little later there is terrible news. Grace Ironwood brings it to the Director:

> "Ivy is back, sir," she said. "I think you'd better see her. No; she's alone. She never saw her husband. The sentence is over but they haven't released him. He's been sent to Belbury for remedial treatment. (THS 314; ch. 14)

In Ivy's agony we come closer than at any other moment of the novel to the full horror of the N.I.C.E. and all that it stands for.

When Merlin releases the bear, along with the other animals, he also releases Tom Maggs, along with the other human prisoners. To Tom he hands a note for Ivy: "come as quick as you can to the Manor at St. Anne's" (THS 348; ch. 16). And in due course he arrives; Ransom willingly provides for them: "Mother Dimble has put you both in the little room half way up the stairs" (THS 375; ch. 17). They are not "upstairs," perhaps, but neither are they ever to be entirely "downstairs" again. And Ransom sends Ivy to her husband with his own kiss: "Don't cry. You are a good woman. Go and heal this man" (THS 376; ch. 17).

Mark Studdock

It is important to remember, in discussing Mark Studdock and his relationship to his wife, Jane, that he becomes one of the saved characters. Ransom sends Jane back to him, but he is a changed, or at least changing man. It is notable that Lewis gives almost nothing in the way of description of Mark. Jane is described as she appears to Mark: his "eyes rested on her with indolent, early morning pleasure" (THS 44; ch. 2) as she brushes her hair. But of him, we learn only his inward and humiliated version following a quarrel:

> The upshot of it was that Mark gave himself a very bad cut while shaving (and saw, at once, a picture of himself talking to the all-important Wither with a great blob of cotton-wool on his upper lip). (THS 45; ch. 2)

And indeed, the only direct portrait we get of Mark confirms his fears:

> On his way up the wide staircase Mark caught sight of himself and his companion in a mirror. [...] The blob of cotton wool on Mark's upper lip had been blown awry during the journey, so that it looked like one half of a fiercely up-turned moustache. (THS 50; ch. 3)

He is going up a very wide staircase indeed, rising at the diabolical N.I.C.E. where it were better not to rise, and the "false moustache" is a vivid figure for the falsity of his position in such a place. We do not really "see" Mark until more than halfway through the novel, when "For one moment, the first for many years, [he] saw himself exactly as a man like Dimble saw him" (THS 216; ch. 10). This moment is probably the beginning of Mark's salvation, though he resists the old scholar's offer to come to St. Anne's.

When Mark is by his own free choice, saved, the cold-hearted tempter Frost prepares to conclude the ritual initiation to which he has been submitting Mark. The final task of the ordeal is to desecrate a crucifix. For the first time, Mark refuses. He says to Frost, "It's all bloody nonsense, and I'm damned if I do any such thing" (THS 334; ch. 15). These words are absolutely, literally true. The N.I.C.E. is about to become a "bloody nonsense"—a bloody mass of people who can speak nothing but nonsense—and Mark would indeed have been damned if he had done what Frost wanted him to do. From this moment, by his refusal, Mark is, unknown to himself, a member of the Company.

Merlin finds Mark unconscious and awakens him with "water dashed in his face"—like a rough baptism—Mark and Merlin go "out under the stars, bitter cold and two o'clock in the morning, Sirius bitter green, a few flakes of dry snow beginning to fall" (THS 349; ch. 16). In ancient Egypt, Sirius was the herald of the flood of the life-giving Nile. In twentieth-century England, its brilliant form is a characteristic element of a winter night. For Mark, it makes a cold but long-needed awakening.

Finally, as Mark makes his way toward St. Anne's and the Company, he reflects that "He was going to be admitted only out of kindness, because Jane had been fool enough to marry him" (THS 358; ch. 17). Of course, he had been admitted to Belbury for the same reason, though not out of kindness! While he is at this nadir of humility, Mark, like Jane, encounters Venus. "He looked up and perceived a great lady standing by a doorway in a wall" (THS 380; ch. 17). This great doorkeeper-goddess now admits Mark to his true marriage chamber, saved, shriven, baptized, and ready for his proper nuptials.

Conclusion

In conclusion, let us consider Lewis's use of a treble role and a treble name-change for Ransom in *That Hideous Strength*. When Jane is first told of his existence he is called "Mr Fisher-King." The title means something very specific: that the owner and chief resident of St. Anne's Manor is a wounded leader whose environs are threatened with ruin, decay, sterility, and death. In consequence, this is the first title we hear, the title which predicts the direction and main action of the plot in the novel in which the symbolism of the Waste Land, present throughout the Trilogy, reaches its logical florescence.

As Jane draws nearer and is ushered into the presence of this man, a new title springs into being and replaces the first. This is the title of Director. Here is a very twentieth-century term and it has a specific meaning too. Ransom is the Director of the Company. In some way he is in charge, and he does indeed make plans, issue directives, and send forth those under his direction. In this role his suffering and helplessness do not interfere; a Director does not act—he or she directs. Indeed, in the climactic moment when the supernatural beings descend, it is not he who is filled with their power and ultimately consumed, but Merlin; we may therefore conclude that Ransom's role and position as Fisher King cannot be handed on directly to another holder because it is a singular visitation upon himself which he has not invited and cannot escape. However, the Directorate of the Company of St. Anne's Manor can continue to function with a new incumbent: I nominate Grace Ironwood for this position. In the cool, ongoing aftermath, she will be the silver reflection of the former, golden wielder of that directorial power in an hour of great need. But there is likely to be need again someday, and there may be any number of Directors of this quiet Company, awaiting that hour's return.

Which brings me to Ransom's third title, that of Pendragon. It is at this point that critics have become most restless. Not one Arthurian title, but two! Surely this is overkill, gratuitous excess! But I think it was done deliberately and effectively and points to a third theme in the story, that Ransom is the inheritor of the crown of the secret kingdom of Logres, which has continued since the days of Arthur during the rise of mere Britain. Ransom thus has a third title to pass, the title of Pendragon. Merlin's condemnation of Jane and Mark for failing to produce a child who would—the reader is forced to conclude—have been a Pendragon who would have become public, open, known, and somehow triumphant, reveals what the Pendragon could, at some point, be. But this does not come to pass. Therefore, we must assume that when Ransom departs, there will be yet another private, secret, unknown Pendragon to take his place.

Lewis has given a powerful hint of this inheritor in the name of Arthur Denniston. Camilla remains with Arthur in the Blue Room of the Director to await his departure to Venus. I can easily imagine her as a full partner of the next Pendragon and probably the mother of the next after that, taking Jane's place in that role. Ransom has said to her: "We in this house are all that is left of Logres. You carry its future in your body" (THS 225; ch. 10).

My point is that, in the expanded historical context proposed by the novel, the Director of the Company of St. Anne's and the Pendragon need not be and perhaps had been for one time only combined in a single personage, the unique interplanetary traveler, Ransom. As Fisher King he is to be transported to Aphallon on Perelandra, there to await whatever Melchizidec and Arthur and their like await. As Director he may be replaced by Grace Ironwood, ever Ransom's equal and co-worker. And as Pendragon he may pass on that title and role to a married man who with his wife will rule in secret, worthily and well.

And what of Jane and Mark? By fulfilling, late and reluctantly, at least one of the roles assigned to each—she to act as seer for the Company, and he (very belatedly) to join her as consort and protector—they are on the "right" side and have thus entered into salvation. She has allowed herself to be taken into the Company, and he has at last joined the true inner ring he has always sought. Will they remain in the Company as it continues its watchful role in the quiet country house? Lewis doesn't tell us, but I know what I would do!

Notes

[1] Margaret Hannay, *C.S. Lewis* (New York: Frederick Ungar, 1981) 105.

[2] Charles Williams, *The Arthurian Poems of Charles Williams* (Cambridge: D.S. Brewer, 1982) Part 2, 36.

[3] James Patrick, *The Magdalene Metaphysicals: Idealism and Orthodoxy at Oxford, 1901–1945* (Macon, GA: Mercer UP, 1985) 45.

[4] For a discussion of the angelic planetary intelligences, see Nancy-Lou Patterson, "The Host of Heaven: Astrological and other Images of Divinity in the Fantasies of C.S. Lewis," Part I, "The Fields of Arbol," *Mythlore* 7.3 (Autumn, 1980): 19-25. [Editor's Note: "The Host of Heaven" is included in this volume 93-144.]

[5] "In His Own Image," Peter Luke, Hadrian Vll (Haymarket: Theatre Royal, 1969) no pagination. This theatrical programme was lent to me by Professor Walter Martin and Partricia Martin, whose aid is gratefully acknowledged.

[6] Otto Bockel, *Handbuch des Deutschen Volksliedes* (1908; Hildesheim, Germany: Georg Olms Verlagsbuchhandlung, 1967) 339. The translation and resource materials for the interpretation of this folksong were provided by Professor Gisela Brude-Firnau (Department of Germanic and Slavic Languages, University of Waterloo), who remembers singing it as a child. To her, heartfelt thanks!

Notes

[7] Martha Sammons, *A Guide Through C.S. Lewis's Space Trilogy* (Westchester, IL: Cornerstone Books, 1980) 150.

8. "Banquet at Belbury": The Company of the Damned

This is the hour of pride and power,
Talon and tush and claw.

——Rudyard Kipling, *The Jungle Book*

Patterson defends the violent banquet scene in That Hideous Strength *from its numerous critics by arguing that the novel is, as C.S. Lewis himself claimed, a fairy tale or romance. Drawing on Northrop Frye's theorization of the night world in the romance, particularly the frisson of the "cannibal" feast, she compares the effectiveness of the banquet at which the members of the N.I.C.E. are killed by the animals with scenes from such classics as Euripides's* The Bacchae, *Lewis Carroll's* Through the Looking Glass, *Rudyard Kipling's* The Jungle Book, *and others. She also identifies some of Lewis's methods of demonstrating the effects of evil, including the characterization of the banquet attendees in relation to the fates that befall them.*

Patterson expands her discussion of the banquet scene to a detailed analysis of food symbolism in Lewis's fiction in "Miraculous Bread ... Miraculous Wine."

This paper was previously published as "'Banquet at Belbury': Festival and Horror in That Hideous Strength" *in* Mythlore *8.3 (Autumn 1981): 7-14, 42. Patterson identified it as the first of her seven papers on the representation of evil in C.S. Lewis's fiction. She revised it for a proposed anthology of papers about Lewis's fiction.*

In twenty-five pages, comprising much of the last part of *That Hideous Strength*, C.S. Lewis describes the destruction of the National Institute of Coordinated Experiments: many people die through the agencies of fire, water, earthquake, and wild beasts. In particular, Lewis describes the deaths of eight people, all of whom are central figures in the development of the N.I.C.E. Not everybody associated with the N.I.C.E. dies: Mark Studdock, who is a central figure in the book, for example, survives. Lewis has called his novel "a modern fairy tale for grownups," and like every proper romance, it ends with nuptials—of the very animals who have killed some of the people and with Mark restored to Jane's arms. Another survivor is Curry, about whom Jared Lobdell (1971-72) has written an article with a self-explanatory title: "Petty Curry: Salvation by a Taste for Tripe and Onions."[1] A number of other people whose names we learn—Cosser, Stone, Capt. O'Hara, Wilkins, Winter, Gould, Kitty, Daisy, and Joe—either die without mention or escape without comment. And there are deaths which take place earlier in the novel, some caused by the N.I.C.E.—Compton and Mary Prescott—(THS 217; ch. 10) and, in particular, the scientist William Hingest (THS 79, 81; ch. 5), murdered for having attempted to leave the service of the N.I.C.E., and the murderer Alcasan, whose execution provides his head to Professor Frost as Jane sees in the revelatory dream which begins the novel (THS 12; ch. 1).

Writing in a tone of outrage, Diana Waggoner (1978) describes the deaths of those who, named or unnamed, do not escape the destruction:

> In *That Hideous Strength* […] the characters are mere caricatures of both the good qualities he [Lewis] approved and the bad ones he abhorred. All his prejudices—against science, against journalism, against vivisection, against sociology—are laid on to the villains, who are eventually dispatched in one of the most savage scenes in modern literature, in which a horde of maddened wild animals invades a dinner party.[2]

Numerous writers have condemned and defended Lewis's positions regarding science, journalism, vivisection, and sociology: it is my intention here to explain and perhaps account for his "savage […] dinner party." The sequence, discussed in detail below, may be summarized as follows: at a banquet at Belbury, the headquarters of the N.I.C.E., pandemonium (literally, in the end) breaks out when the after-dinner speaker begins to utter nonsense syllables. The author of the disaster is Merlin, who, having been sought by the N.I.C.E. in hopes that he will aid them, becomes their nemesis. He has cast a "doom of gibberish" (THS 345; ch. 16) upon the them, just as God had caused the builders of the Tower of Babel—the "Gate of God"—to fail in their attempts to storm heaven, by descending to "confuse their language" (Genesis 11.19 RSV). When the confusion at Belbury has already caused rioting and even death, Merlin frees the animals kept by the N.I.C.E. for vivisection and experiment. The beasts kill many of the banqueters. Some of the leaders of the N.I.C.E. escape, but they fall upon and kill one another, or commit suicide. The final escapee, under the influence of Merlin, heads into the last center of catastrophe, in which the town of Edgestow is destroyed.

The N.I.C.E. is brought to its end by the activities of Merlin, by its members' own hands, by avenging animals, and by the outraged Earth; but the sense of horror expressed by Waggoner is centered upon the banquet, rather than upon the subsequent events, and the language used by Lewis does indeed evoke horror, of a very special kind. There are two especially potent passages in which food and tragedy are combined which are, interestingly, followed by additional passages in which food is combined with comedy. At the banquet, Lewis says, the elephant was "continuously trampling like a girl treading grapes, heavily and soon wetly trampling in a pash of blood and bones, of flesh, wine, fruit, and sodden table-cloth" (THS 346; ch. 16). As the killing continues, "food and filth, spoiled luxury and mangled men, each more hideous by reason of the other" (THS 349; ch. 16), are contrasted deliberately and horrifyingly. Again, when Mr. Bultitude, having killed his man at Belbury, continues his feast at St. Anne's with a she-bear guest, who, Ivy Maggs reports, has "eaten up all what was left of the goose and half the ham and all the junket and now it's lying along the table [...] wriggling from one dish to another and a breaking all the crockery," while Bultitude is dancing in victory—"and he's put one foot into the plum pudding already and he's got his head all mixed up in the string of onions" (THS 373; ch. 17).

This latter, comedic scene, as well as the scene of destruction, has more than a few elements in common with the nightmare dinner party in Lewis Carroll's *Through the Looking Glass*:

> [...] some of them put their glasses upon their heads like extinguishers, and drank all that trickled down their faces—others upset the decanters, and drank the wine as it ran off the edges of the table—and three of them (who looked like kangaroos) scrambled into the dish of roast mutton, and began eagerly lapping up the gravy [...][3]

The passage continues—"already several of the guests were lying down in the dishes"[4] and concludes, "one good pull, and plates, dishes, guests, and candles came crashing down together in a heap on the floor."[5]

There is something not only funny but vaguely ominous in these passages, which becomes explicit in the following exchange:

> "You look a little shy: let me introduce you to that leg of mutton," said the Red Queen. "Alice—Mutton; Mutton—Alice."[6]

Alice, "not knowing whether to be frightened or amused,"[7] offers the Queen a slice of mutton.

> "Certainly not," the Red Queen said, very decidedly: "It isn't etiquette to cut any one you've been introduced to."[8]

The scenario is repeated, and though Alice declines to be introduced to the next course, a plum-pudding, the Queen growls the introductions anyway and commands the pudding to be brought back. Conquering her shyness under the circumstances, Alice cuts a slice for the Queen.

> "What impertinence!" said the Pudding. I wonder how you'd take it, if I were to cut a slice out of *you*, you creature!"[9]

As if referring to these passages, Northrop Frye writes in *The Secular Scripture* (1976), his recent study of romance, "At the bottom of the night world we find the cannibal feast." He continues that "the image which causes that *frisson* [is] the identifying of human and animal natures in a world where animals are food for man."[10]

The elements to which Waggoner objects are present in *That Hideous Strength* precisely because it is a romance. Lewis wrote of it, "I have called this a fairy-tale in the hopes that no one who dislikes fantasy may be misled by the first two chapters into reading further, and then complaining" (THS Preface 7). Waggoner, of course, read on, and complained mightily, not only of the terrifying climax, but of the characterizations which lead up to it. But as Northrop Frye says:

> The characterization of romance is really a feature of its mental landscape. Its heroes and villains exist primarily to symbolize a contrast between two worlds, one above the level of ordinary experience, and one below it. There is, first a world associated with happiness, security, and peace; the emphasis is often thrown on childhood or on an "innocent" or

> pre-genital period of youth, and the images are those of spring and summer, flowers and sunshine.[11]

This description strongly suggests St. Anne's, especially as the weather grows preternaturally warm at the end of the novel, though Lewis, who was no Freudian, imagined a paradise in which the genital period of wedded adulthood was happily and licitly present. Belbury, too, seems to be exactly described by Frye:

> The other is a world of exciting adventures, but adventures which involve separation, loneliness, humiliation, pain, and the threat of more pain. I shall call this world the demonic or night world.[12]

Mark's experiences at Belbury follow just such a path. The whole structure of *That Hideous Strength* involves continuous movements from St. Anne's to Belbury and back, just as Frye says it should be in a romance: "Because of the powerful polarizing tendency in romance, we are usually carried directly from one [world] to the other."[13]

The ceremonial dinner interrupted and finally ravaged is appropriate here: Frye writes, "Most of what goes on in the night world is cruelty and horror, yet what is essential is not cruelty as such but the presence of some kind of ritual."[14] In this case, that ritual is an elaborate formal dinner. Frye adds a second essential: "the kind of chaos and disorder that is contrasted with the courtly occasion"[15] is especially reflected in "the reducing of humanized beings to something subintelligent and *subarticulate*."[16] Precisely: the guests at Belbury are first reduced to the "sub-articulate," and then destroyed by the speechless beasts.

The contrast of festival and horror is, in fact, a very old element in literature and human culture. In discussing the dual nature of Dionysus's actions in *The Bacchae* of Euripides, Donald Sutherland (1968) speaks of "his kindliness and his deadliness," and observes that "it corresponds to the double and unarguable nature of experience in the world, *its pleasurable or festive elements and its horrible or catastrophic elements*, which are not distributed very well according to what we think is human merit."[17] In *That Hideous Strength*, this distribution is rectified.

In *The Bacchae*, the young ruler Pentheus defies the beautiful god Dionysus. He is persuaded by that god to disguise himself as a woman in order to learn what rites the women carry out on the mountain tops: his own mother tears him to pieces, only learning when her frenzy passes that she has not killed a lion, but her own son. The contrast and juxtaposition of festival and horror have never been more fiercely drawn: "the fresh blood of the slain goat and the ecstasy / of the raw feast we go racing to win," the women cry. "And the ground is flowing with white milk and flowing with red / wine and flowing with nectar of bees."[18] Thus his Maenads describe the scene of Dionysus's revels. But when Pentheus goes there, "His body lies dispersed, one part below / the rugged cliffs, another among the leafage of the deep woods […] / His mother somehow got into her hands / his battered head […]"[19] Thus Pentheus, bemused by Dionysus as the residents and guests of Belbury are bemused by Merlin, himself becomes the main course of the feast.

In *That Hideous Strength*, the animals have been imprisoned and subjected to cruel experiments. Early in his stay at Belbury, Mark takes a walk on the grounds:

> This time he wandered round to the back parts of the house […] Here he was surprised by a stable-like smell and a medley of growls, grunts, and whimpers—all the signs, in fact, of a considerable zoo. (THS 100; ch. 5)

He recognizes this as part of "an immense programme of vivisection, freed at last from Red Tape" In his previous meditations upon this aspect of the Institute's program he "had thought vaguely of rats, rabbits, and an occasional dog." But,

> The confused noises from within suggested something very different. As he stood there a loud melancholy howl arose and then, as if it had set the key, all manner of trumpetings, brayings, screams, laughter even, which shuddered and protested for a moment and then, died away into mutterings and whines. (THS 100; ch. 5)

Mark is not moved—he "had no scruples about vivisection. What the noise meant to him was the greatness and grandiosity of this whole undertaking […] thousands of pounds' worth of living animality, which the Institute could afford to cut up like paper on the mere off-chance of some interesting discovery" (THS 100; ch. 5).

In Lewis's novel, these offences against animals are avenged by the animals themselves. Indeed, hunting culture myths frequently tell of disasters brought upon humankind by offenses against the etiquette required between animal and human, as in the Nishga (Tsimshian) myth from coastal British Columbia, which describes a lava flow brought down into the Nass valley by children who tormented a salmon. I saw the lava field myself: the Nishga live mainly on freshly-caught salmon even today. Hunting culture myths tend to cluster around a problem with two phases: first, both humans and animals are children of the Earth. Second, human killing of animals is thus fratricide. The solution to this dilemma lies in the formula: "We live in harmony with the animals: they give themselves to us so that we can live."[20] In this ancient system, sin lies in humans offending animals (or the lord of the animals) so that this self-giving ceases and humans starve.

A particularly telling appearance of the ideas involved in this complex is found in the Kwakiutl myth of Elxabae (also from British Columbia). He goes as a guest to the table of Grizzly (a bear), only to find that he is the main course, a motif which appears in Lewis's *The Silver Chair*, where the children naively visit man-eating giants. With great irony, all the etiquette of a man about to eat an animal is practiced by Grizzly before eating Elxabae. After being eaten, Elxabae is restored to life, and "being twice-born [he] is now a man of power." By dying as animals do (for food), the hero becomes a powerful food-provider. These hunting-culture themes tell in animal terms what in Neolithic culture became the Corn-god myth, which finds its ultimate expression—and, Christians believe, historic fulfillment—in the concept of a God who, in Jesus, dies and rises again, forever after to give His own body and blood as the meat and drink of eternal life to all who believe in Him. We are dealing here with motifs of the utmost antiquity, and the utmost sacrality.

I don't think *That Hideous Strength* is precisely *about* the etiquette of animal/human relationships, but, as with the two novels which precede it, and with the Narnian Chronicles, that motif figures as part of Lewis's whole preoccupation with the role of humankind in nature. Lewis did not disapprove of the domestication of animals, nor was he a vegetarian. He thought, in common with much of conservative or traditional humankind the world over, that humans have a right to eat animals as well as plants. He also thought that this required responsible behavior on the part of the humans, rather in line with Old Testament views: a swift, clean kill, no killing without the necessity of eating the prey, and a due exercise of responsibility in the case of animals domesticated and kept, whether for companionship, burden-bearing, or food. He *was* opposed to vivisection, which he interpreted as the infliction of pain upon helpless animals. I am not ready to argue this matter entirely from his point of view, but he was thinking of the needless pain inflicted upon animals to test their reaction, as when rats are subjected to electric shock. This kind of thing *might* be seen as related to the experiments carried out on living people by Nazi doctors, or the experiments on American blacks early in the century, in which men were allowed to die of syphilis when the cure was known. Humans *do* behave abominably, both to animals and to humans. There is little fantasy in the ideas and practices of the N.I.C.E., and the things Lewis feared had come and have come to pass again and again.

Four years before Lewis was born, Rudyard Kipling wrote his children's masterpiece, *The Jungle Book* (1894). The animals Lewis describes in *That Hideous Strength*, to which he refers as "pantomime animals" (THS Preface 7), bear a strong resemblance to that Victorian work, just as the fatal dinner party resembles the one attended by Alice. *The Jungle Book* begins with the poem which has furnished my epigraph:

> This is the hour of pride and power,
> Talon and tush and claw.
> Oh, hear the call!—Good hunting all
> That keep the Jungle Law!

The Jungle Law required, among other things, that animals greet one another with the salutation, "We be of one blood, ye and I." Mowgli, the wolf-suckled child, makes himself kin to the animal world, and all the stories in *The Jungle Book* deal at least in part with animal-human relationships. One may compare Lewis's descriptions of his animals with those of Kipling.

Lewis describes "The beasts [...] Merlin sent to the dining room, maddened with his voice and touch" (THS 348; ch. 16). In the order of their arrival, they are: tiger, wolf, snake, gorilla, elephant, and bear. Each of these has a parallel in Kipling: Shere Khan, Father and Mother Wolf, Kaa, the Bandar-log, Kala Nag, and Baloo. In *That Hideous Strength*, the tiger first appears as "a gleam of black and tawny" (THS 345; ch. 16). Then, "He [Mark] saw the hideous head, the cat's snarl of the mouth, the flaming eyes" (THS 345; ch. 16). In similar words, Kipling wrote, "Shere Khan's great square head and shoulders were thrust into the entrance,"[21] and the mother wolf faced "the blazing eyes of Shere Khan."[22]

After the tiger, the wolf appears at Belbury as "a glimpse of something smaller and greyer [...] It ran along the table, its tail between its legs, slavering" (THS 346; ch. 16). In *The Jungle Book*, a mated pair of wolves are described: of Father Wolf, Kipling writes

> [...] if you had been watching, you would have seen the most wonderful thing in the world—the wolf checked in mid-spring [...] he shot straight up into the air [...] landing almost where he left ground.
>
> "Man!" he snapped. "A man's cub. Look!"[23]

When Shere Khan threatens the baby, "Mother Wolf [...] sprang forward, her eyes, like two green moons in the darkness [...]"[24]

The wolf is followed into Belbury's dining-room by a snake: "Something else had darted between his feet. Mark saw it streak across the floor and enter the scrum and wake that mass of interlocked terror into new and frantic convulsions" (THS 346; ch. 16). Kipling's parallel is the great python Kaa:

> They found him stretched out on a warm ledge in the afternoon sun [...] darting his big blunt-nosed head along the ground, and twisting the thirty feet of his body into fantastic knots and curves, and licking his lips as he thought of his dinner to come.[25]

After the snake, a gorilla appears at the devastated table: "As if in imitation a great gorilla leaped on the table where Jules [the director of the N.I.C.E., just killed] had sat and began drumming on its chest. Then, with a roar, it jumped down into the crowd" (THS 346; ch. 16). Lewis had seen the film *King Kong*, and remarked upon it in one of his letters. The motif of imitation as a simian trait appears in Kipling's description of the monkey band who captures Mowgli:

> One of the monkeys made a speech and told his companions that Mowgli's capture marked a new thing in the history of the Bandar-log, for Mowgli was going to show them how to weave sticks and canes together as a protection against rain and cold [...] [T]he monkeys tried to imitate; but in a very few minutes they lost interest [...][26]

The climactic animal arrival in *That Hideous Strength* is that of the elephant, whose approach is heralded by a great pounding at the door. Then,

> Out of the darkness there came a grey snaky something. [...] After that, monstrous, improbable, the huge shape of the elephant thrust its way into the room: its eyes enigmatic, its ears standing stiffly out like the devil's wings [...] (THS 346; ch. 16)

The elephant kills both by catching up people in his trunk and trampling them beneath his feet. These elements are present in Kipling's stories too:

> There was nothing in the way of fighting that Kala Nag, the old wise Black Snake [the elephant's name] did not know, for he had stood up in his time to the charge of the wounded tiger, and, curling his soft trunk to be out of harm's way, had knocked the springing brute sideways in mid-air [...] and knocked him over, [...] kneeling upon him with his huge knees [...][27]

Just as the elephants' dancing-ground is seen by little Toomai, a child who rides on Kala Nag's back in *The Jungle Book*, the dance of the mating elephants is seen by the residents of St. Anne's in the final chapter of *That Hideous Strength*, when nuptials of both animals and humans conclude the novel.

The last animal to make a kill in *That Hideous Strength* is the only one of the avenging beasts to have a name: Mr. Bultitude. His appearance, as he is first encountered by Jane—as a "great, snuffly, wheezy, beady-eyed, loose-skinned, gor-bellied brown bear" (THS 161; ch. 8)—is paralleled in *The Jungle Book* by Mowgli's teacher, Baloo: "The big, serious, old brown bear."[28] Bultitude's benign behavior at St. Anne's is in contrast with his actions at Belbury:

> Down the long, empty passages [...] it padded [...] Saliva dripped from its mouth and it was beginning to growl. It was thinking of warm, salt tastes, of the pleasant resistances of bone, of things to crunch and lick and worry. (THS 348; ch. 16)

Baloo, too, is capable of battle: coming to the rescue of Mowgli, who has been carried off by the Bandar-log, "he threw himself squarely on his haunches, and, spreading out his fore-paws, hugged as many as he could hold."[29]

The animals in these passages—whether from Lewis or Kipling—go about their awesome tasks of violence with a ceremonial dignity and splendor which precisely matches the romantic prescription of festival and horror. Grace Ironwood says of the elephants at St. Anne's: "how ceremonial they are. It is like a minuet of giants. They are not like the other animals. They are a sort of good daemons" (THS 377; ch. 17). And Ransom, the Director of St. Anne's, replies, "They are not common beasts" (THS 377; ch. 17). The animals of *That Hideous Strength* are playing a symbolic role, like those depicted inhabiting Perelandra, whether in the world above ordinary experience, where they resemble the heraldic beasts of courtly display, or in the night world below, where they are magnificent avengers with blazing eyes and irresistible power.

Thus far I have concentrated on the elements of Belbury's destruction which most impressed Waggoner: the "horde of maddened wild animals" which "invades a dinner party." In them the identification of human and animal natures truly causes the *frisson* to which Northrop Frye refers, for these animals come not from a zoo but from the unconscious mind of the reader. In them the "cannibal feast" is most horrifyingly presented. Nevertheless, the novel contains a number of scenes of killing in which humans kill humans.

In order to understand the meaning of all these deaths, it is necessary to examine them as they actually occur in the narrative. In the order of their deaths, the dead are: Horace Jules, Director of the N.I.C.E., killed by Fairy Hardcastle; Fairy Hardcastle, killed by a tiger; Steele, killed by an elephant; Filostrato, killed by Straik and Wither; the Rev. Mr. Straik, killed by Wither; Deputy Director Wither, killed by Mr. Bultitude the bear; Professor Frost, killed by his own hand; and Lord Feverstone, killed by the Earth herself. I shall give the passages in which these deaths occur below, and couple each one with Lewis's description of the dead as he or she first appears.

The order of appearance of these characters is partially the reverse of the order of their deaths: I include below all those whose deaths we witness. They are: Alcasan, seen in Jane's dream (THS 12; ch. 1); Frost, seen by Jane in the same vision (THS 13; ch. 1 and 124; ch. 6); Lord Feverstone (Dick Devine), who is first mentioned by Curry (THS 16; ch. 1) and then appears before Mark (THS 22; ch. 1); Wither, to whom Lord Feverstone sends Mark (THS 41; ch. 2), and whom Mark then meets (THS 50; ch. 3); Jules, who is mentioned in almost the same breath (THS 41; ch. 2) by Lord Feverstone, but who actually appears just in time for the fateful banquet; William Hingest, who meets Mark, and is then murdered (witnessed by Jane in a dream) (THS 75; ch. 4) and discovered dead (THS 79; ch. 4); Steele, who meets Mark (THS 56; ch. 3); Filostrato, also introduced to Mark; Fairy Hardcastle, mentioned to Mark by Filostrato and then introduced to him (THS 59; ch. 3); and the Rev. Mr. Straik, also met by Mark (THS 76; ch. 4). All of these characters first appear when met by Mark or, more rarely, seen in a dream by Jane: Mark witnesses the deaths of those killed by animals, and Jane witnesses the deaths of those killed before the Belbury banquet. All the rest die for the reader alone.

What is the meaning of all these deaths? They are arranged, as is characteristic of a romance, so that in each case the distribution of festival and catastrophe—so poorly arranged in our world—is rectified to accord with justice. Whether or not it accords with mercy is another matter.

At the Belbury banquet, the first to die is the after-dinner speaker, Jules, whose gabbling incoherence (caused by Merlin) has begun a riot. He is shot by the policewoman, Fairy Hardcastle. She has been told via an unintelligible note, to do something. In response, she has locked the door to the room and fought her way to the head table. "There came an ear-splitting noise and after that, at last, a few seconds of dead silence. Mark noticed that Jules had been killed: only secondly, that Miss Hardcastle had shot him" (THS 344; ch. 16). Horace Jules, Director of the N.I.C.E., is described by Lewis: "He was a very little man, whose legs were so short that he had unkindly been compared to a duck. He had a turned-up nose and a face in which some original *bonhomie* had been much interfered with by years of good living and conceit" (THS 335; ch. 5). Feverstone had said of him to Mark—"You don't imagine that little mascot has anything to say to what really goes on?" (THS 42; ch. 2). But Jules has "insisted on regarding himself not as a figure-head but as the real director of the Institute" (THS 334; ch. 15). As after-dinner speaker on the occasion of a great banquet at Belbury, he is the first to undergo the doom of gibberish, and the first to die. His position as first in prominence in the N.I.C.E. is thus ironically fulfilled.

Almost immediately afterwards, his murderer, Fairy Hardcastle, dies, killed by a tiger which has entered the room from "another door, the one used by the servants" (THS 345; ch. 16). This death is directly witnessed by Mark:

> He saw the hideous head, the cat's snarl of the mouth, the flaming eyes. [...] Then the tiger had disappeared again. Something fat and white and bloodied was down among the feet of the scrummers. Mark could not recognise it at first, for the face, from where he stood, was upside down, and the grimaces disguised it until it was quite dead. Then he recognised Fairy Hardcastle. (THS 345; ch. 16)

The dead woman had first appeared before Mark when he found himself in "the stoker's or carter's hand-grip of a big woman in a black, short-skirted uniform" (THS 59; ch. 3). She is the only woman included among the dead whose names we learn. "Despite a bust that would have done credit to a Victorian barmaid, she was rather thickly built than fat and her iron-grey hair was cropped short. Her face was square, stern and pale, and her voice deep" (THS 59; ch. 3). She wears poorly-applied lipstick and chews a cheroot. Mark finds her "rankly, even insolently, sexed and at the same time wholly unattractive" (THS 67; ch. 3). She is the head of "the police side of the Institute," charged with "all sanitary cases—a category which ranged from vaccination to charges of unnatural vice" (THS 67; ch. 3). It is she who tortures Jane by burning her with a lighted cheroot in an effort to find out where she had traveled (in actual fact to St. Anne's) (THS 153; ch. 7). She has already caused the death of Hingest, and has, as we have seen, coolly shot Jules. As a murderer and torturer she is executed by a tiger, her counterpart, as "man-eater," in the animal kingdom.

Following her death, many more die, as a wolf, a snake, a gorilla, and other animals enter. Then the elephant breaks in, killing Steele. "Mark saw distinctly how it swooped down, curled itself round a man—Steele, he thought, but everyone looked different now—and lifted him bodily high off the floor" (THS 346; ch. 16). The passage continues, in an echo of Kipling's Kala Nag: "It stood for a second with Steele writhing in the curl of its trunk and then dashed him to the floor" (THS 346; ch. 16). Steele is head of the Sociology Department of the N.I.C.E. As first seen by Mark, "He was a tall, unsmiling man with that kind of face which, though long and horse-like, has nevertheless rather thick and pouting lips" (THS 56; ch. 3). Mark is presented to him as a sociologist for his department by the ill-fated Hingest. Steele contemptuously rebuffs Mark and he is rescued from embarrassment by Filostrato (THS 57; ch. 3). Later on, Mark learns that he is, after all, to be in Steele's department (THS 82; ch. 4). Steele is described to Mark by Cosser (Steele's assistant) as "rather a dangerous man" (THS 83; ch. 4). Mark's first task is to arrange the destruction of Cure Hardy, an ancient and exquisite village (THS 83; ch. 4), but again Steele frustrates him. "I know nothing about your position" (THS 93; ch. 5). Mark then learns that his *real* job will be to arrange the public rehabilitation of the criminal Alcasan (THS 96; ch. 5): Fairy Hardcastle gives him this news. In attempting to clarify his position with Wither he learns that he has lost his original post at Bracton College (THS 103; ch. 5), even though he had hoped to keep it until he could find out for sure if he is to be retained by the N.I.C.E. In this helpless position, he accepts a small stipend with the diabolical Institute, and is told by Wither to make himself useful (THS 116; ch. 6). "Elasticity" is what is required. Mark, finally a part of the N.I.C.E., as he has so much wished to be, finds that his first official task is to help engineer a riot. "He enjoyed it even more when he heard Steele and Cosser talking about it in a way which showed that they did not even know how it had been engineered" (THS 166; ch. 8). Steele has been tossed aside by the Inner Ring of the N.I.C.E. In the end, he is tossed aside to his death by the elephant in the same way that he has been prepared to toss Mark (and no doubt others).

Aroused by the smell of killings and by a newly released female bear, Mr. Bultitude (with the whispered words of Merlin in his ear) sets out. Nearly everyone has been killed in the dining room by one or another of the animals, but not all, for Wither has already left the room, as have Straik and Filostrato. Straik and Wither drag the hapless Filostrato toward the room where the Head of the decapitated criminal, Alcasan, which has become the mouthpiece for a Dark *Eldil* or Macrobe, true leader of the N.I.C.E., is kept "alive" by tubes. They stand naked before it, and it calls them to "Adore!" (THS 351; ch. 16). Filostrato's escorts then decapitate him in a device he himself has designed. "His last thought was that he had underestimated the terror" (THS 352; ch. 16).

Filostrato, "the great physiologist" (THS 58; ch. 3), is described as Mark first meets him: "His dark, smooth face and black hair were unmistakable, and so was the foreign accent" (THS 58; ch. 3). "He was fat to that degree which is comic on the stage, but the effect was not funny in real life" (THS 58; ch. 3). For him, the "*real* work" of the N.I.C.E. is to preserve "the existence of the human race" (THS 58; ch. 3). To do this he is quite willing to engineer disturbances: "this is how things have to be managed" (THS 126; ch. 6). His ideal is "the civilised tree" (THS 169; ch. 8), made of metal: indeed, he wants to "*clean* the planet" (THS 169; ch. 8) of all organic life. And if that cannot be, at least all "stallions and bulls" must be rendered "geldings and oxen." But the sterile Moon remains his ideal (THS 170; ch. 8). For him, the future is enshrined in the Head of Alcasan, to whom he presents Mark: Jane sees her husband in a dream, accompanied by "a great fat man" (THS 179; ch. 9). Filostrato's end is to be sacrificed to that which he has adored, beheaded by two of his closest associates (THS 351; ch. 16) and thus submitted to an ultimate form of castration and separation from the flesh.

Almost immediately, another sacrifice is called for; Straik is then killed by Wither: "Straik reached the ante-room, slipped in Filostrato's blood. Wither slashed repeatedly with his knife. He had not strength to cut through the neck, but he had killed the man" (THS 352; ch. 16). Straik has been a clergyman, viewed by Mark in "the threadbare clothes and clumsy boots, the frayed clerical collar, the dark, lean, tragic face, gashed and ill-shaved and seamed, and the bitter sincerity of his manner" (THS 76; ch. 4). Straik expects the Kingdom of God to be realized "in this world." He sees science, through the N.I.C.E., as the instrument of this realization. To him the head of Alcasan has undergone resurrection, "The real life everlasting" (THS 78; ch. 4). In the end he adores this monstrous resurrected being, and becomes its final sacrifice, when Wither kills him.

Wither is then killed by Mr. Bultitude. "A huge bear, rising to its hind legs as he came in sight of it, had met him in the doorway—its mouth open, its eyes flaming, its fore-paws spread out as if for an embrace" (THS 353; ch. 16). He dies from a bear-hug, as Baloo's monkey enemies had been killed in *The Jungle Book*. Deputy Director John Wither of the N.I.C.E. enters the novel when Lord Feverstone remarks, "Let me run you across tomorrow to see John Wither" (THS 41; ch. 2). In fact, Feverstone has been recruiting Mark with talk of "biochemical conditioning in the end and direct manipulation of the brain" (THS 40; ch. 2), and has said, "You are what we need: a trained sociologist with a radically realistic outlook, not afraid of responsibility." He is telling Mark the truth about the kinds of tasks he will be asked to perform but concealing from him the secret desire of the N.I.C.E. to obtain Jane, Mark's wife. "Also," Feverstone continues, "a sociologist who can write" (THS 41; ch. 2).

When Mark meets him, "Wither was a white-haired old man with a courtly manner. His face was clean-shaven and very large indeed, with watery blue eyes and something rather vague and chaotic about it" (THS 50; ch. 3). Mark does not succeed in learning from Wither precisely what job he has been hired to do. Indeed, he fears that "a perfectly direct question would [be ...] a crudity which might suddenly exclude him from the warm and almost drugged atmosphere of vague, yet heavily important, confidence in which he was gradually being enfolded" (THS 52; ch. 3). This atmosphere resembles that created by the Green Witch in *The Silver Chair*, which was only dispelled by the crudity of the smell of burnt Marsh-wiggle!

Wither is one of the central figures of the N.I.C.E. and has almost entirely abandoned any hold on reality. He and Frost are in direct contact with the diabolical and true masters of the Institute. Indeed, he has so far lost contact with his body that his image is often seen pottering about, vaguely humming in unexpected places "a tall, stooped, shuffling, creaking figure" (THS 210; ch. 10). Lewis remarks of him, "it may [...] be that souls who have lost the intellectual good do indeed receive in return [...] the vain privilege of thus reproducing themselves in many places as wraiths" (THS 210; ch. 10). It is from Wither that Mark finally learns what the N.I.C.E. wants of him

> [H]ere his face suddenly changed. The widely opened mouth looked all at once like the mouth of some enraged animal: what had been the senile vagueness of the eyes became an absence of all specifically human expression. "And bring the girl. Do you understand? Get your wife." (THS 209; ch. 10)

Wither, who has killed Filostrato and Straik, now meets his own fate. He, whose "widely opened mouth" had frightened Mark, falls prey to the great bear Bultitude, who greets him with "its mouth open" (THS 209; ch. 10).

Feverstone, meanwhile, gets furthest away of all those who had been in the dining room at Belbury. He heads toward Edgestow. He had watched "the whole massacre, his eyes bright, something like a smile on his face" (THS 353; ch. 16). Frost, on the other hand, finds Straik, Wither, and Filostrato dead in the chambers of the Head. After this discovery, he retires to the "Objective Room" where he had been carrying out his initiation of Mark. There, he locks himself in, and pushes the key through a speaking tube into the passage. Then he "poured out the petrol and threw a lighted match" (THS 355; ch. 16). As he dies, he realizes "that souls and personal responsibility existed." Then, "with one supreme effort he flung himself back into his illusion. In that attitude eternity overtook him as sunrise in old tales overtakes trolls and turns them into unchangeable stone" (THS 356; ch. 16).

Frost first appears in Jane's dream: "He was a good-looking man in his rather cold way, but he wore pince-nez, and these kept catching the light so as to make his eyes invisible. This, combined with the almost unnatural perfection of his teeth, somehow gave Jane a disagreeable impression" (THS 13; ch. 1). Mark, too, in his turn is puzzled by "the silent man with the pince-nez and the pointed beard" (THS 124; ch. 6), whose presence in the inner circle of the N.I.C.E. he does not understand. When Mark returns to the N.I.C.E. after a last attempt to disentangle himself, during which he has actually tried to bring Jane there, he sees "a man in a grey suit whose pince-nez as he glanced toward Mark and towards the light, became opaque windows concealing his eyes" (THS 245; ch. 11). Here again are "the pointed beard, the extreme whiteness of forehead, the regularity of features, and the bright Arctic smile" (THS 245; ch. 11).

Frost is to be Mark's novice-master as he is initiated into the innermost ring of the N.I.C.E. He introduces him to the Objective Room, and to the fact that Alcasan's head has not really been kept alive by science, but is "used by a different mind" (THS 253; ch. 12); in fact, by "*macrobes*" who are "outside the whole world of our subjective emotions" (THS 255; ch. 12). This precisely describes the fate which awaits Frost, for he has become "a mere spectator" of his own actions, which is why we always see him from the brightly-reflecting outside (since he is *all* outside): "His flashing pince-nez and pointed beard looked into the room of the Head itself" (THS 355; ch. 16). Dying, "He became able to know (and simultaneously refused the knowledge) that he had been wrong from the beginning" (THS 356; ch. 16). As he draws back from this terrible realization, his body perishes. As for his soul, the very name Frost, and the reference to the Arctic, suggest that he is headed for the icy sea of Dante's nethermost Inferno.

In his excellent study, *Narnia Explored* (1979), Paul A. Karkainen includes an interesting note on Wither and Frost, both of whom were directly under the control of the Head of the N.I.C.E. He writes:

> The hag and wer-wolf [of *Prince Caspian*] are reminiscent of the characters of Mr. Wither and Dr. Frost in *That Hideous Strength*. It was Lewis's idea that evil shatters things—breaks them up into their separated components—and that evil tends to take one character trait and exaggerate it to the exclusion of all else.[30]

This exaggeration of traits through the operation of evil is what Lewis was trying to show in the effects which Waggoner calls "mere caricatures," but which the great critic Frye might describe as "feature[s] of its mental landscape."[31] Karkainen aptly summarizes these characterizations: "Mr. Wither and the hag represent one tendency of evil. The tendency toward vapid nothingness." On the other hand, "Dr. Frost and the wer-wolf are alike in their ruthless coldness and in their direct, unrelenting approach to pursuing their evil desires."[32] As we saw, the vague Wither meets dissolution by being devoured; the "Arctic" coldness of Frost is consumed in self-ignited flames.

As all this chaos ensues, Lord Feverstone, congratulating himself on his escape, passes the traffic pouring out of Edgestow. All its residents have become inspired to leave it through a variety of intuitions and premonitions, but he rushes toward it. "It was about four o'clock that Feverstone found himself flung on his face. That was the first shock." More earth tremors follow. Then, "The temperature began to rise." The snow melts, fog rises, there is another shock. Gradually he finds himself descending, until an "earth wave" overtakes him: "His mouth and hair and nostrils were full of earth. [...] Then the whole wave of earth rose, arched, trembled, and with all its weight and noise poured down on him" (THS 365; ch. 17).

Feverstone is first presented through the sound of his loud voice: "Lord Feverstone—Dick Devine as he used to be" (THS 16; ch.1), Curry calls him, speaking to Mark, and signaling to the reader of *Out of the Silent Planet* that the unpleasant former schoolmate of Elwin Ransom has very much risen in the world. Expanding upon his theme, Curry informs Mark, "He got you your Fellowship" (THS 16; ch. 1). Some time after Mark has digested this disconcerting news, Feverstone's presence is heard: "Then came a new voice from quite a different part of the Soler. Lord Feverstone had risen" (THS 22; ch. 1). He "inquired icily" after a matter of college politics. A little later still, "Lord Feverstone sprang to his feet, folded his arms, and looking straight at the old man said in a very loud, clear voice" (THS 26; ch. 1) something brutally insulting.

Lewis gives us long passages of Feverstone's loud, bright, sharp-edged conversation. But we do not *see* him until nearly sixty pages into the novel, when Mark catches sight of Feverstone and himself in a mirror: "Feverstone looked, as always, master of his clothes, his face, and of the whole situation" (THS 50; ch. 3). This is exactly what Mark would like to be—hence the shared mirror—but never, probably to his soul's salvation, succeeds in becoming.

Lord Feverstone, whom "Ransom had disliked [...] at school as much as anyone he could remember" (OSP 9; ch. 1) is the first N.I.C.E. member Mark meets in the *That Hideous Strength*, and the last to die. He becomes Mark's patron and patronizer: "Man has got to take charge of Man," he opines. "That means, remember, that some men have got to take charge of the rest" (THS 40; ch. 2). This is the nub of the evil embodied in the N.I.C.E., and this is why the very Earth rises up against Lord Feverstone. Weston, the visionary scientist, dies on Perelandra (Venus) and is buried with dignity in the Third Heaven, to which Ransom is himself to return; but Devine (Lord Feverstone), the perfect worldling, dies on, and indeed, *in* the Earth (Thulcandra), with nothing but the vanished Edgestow to mark his grave, the last of Ransom's adversaries to perish.

Notes

[1] Jared Lobdell "Petty Curry: Salvation by a taste for Tripe and Onions," *Orcrist* 6 (Winter, 1971-1972): 11-13.

[2] Diana Waggoner, *The Hills of Faraway—A Guide to Fantasy* (New York: Atheneum, 1978) 34.

[3] Lewis Carroll, *Alice's Adventures in Wonderland and Through the Looking Glass* (1865; Harmondsworth, UK: Puffin Books, 1975) 336.

[4] Carroll 337.

[5] Carroll 338.

[6] Carroll 332.

[7] Carroll 333.

[8] Carroll 335.

[9] Carroll 334.

[10] Northrop Frye, *The Secular Scripture* (Cambridge, MA: Harvard UP, 1976) 118.

[11] Frye 53.

[12] Frye 53.

[13] Frye 53.

[14] Frye 113.

[15] Frye 116.

[16] Frye 116. My italics.

[17] Donald Sutherland, *The Bacchae of Euripides* (Lincoln: University of Nebraska Press, 1968) 123, my italics.

[18] Sutherland 8.

[19] Sutherland 53.

[20] S. Freud, quoted in Susan Reid, "The Kwakiutl Man Eater," *Anthropologica* XXI.2 (1979): 252.

Notes

[21] Rudyard Kipling, *The Jungle Book* (1894; New York: Grosset and Dunlop, 1950) 8.
[22] Kipling 9.
[23] Kipling 7.
[24] Kipling 9.
[25] Kipling 55.
[26] Kipling 64.
[27] Kipling 183.
[28] Kipling 39.
[29] Kipling 70.
[30] Paul A. Karkainen, *Narnia Explored* (Old Tappan, NJ: Fleming H. Revell Co., 1979) 53.
[31] See Frye 53.
[32] Karkainen 53.

The Unfathomable Feminine Principle

Nature sets before us for our delight
the unfathomable feminine principle.
—C.S. Lewis, *Arthurian Torso*

Nancy-Lou Patterson. "Jane and Mark." First reproduced on the back cover of *Mythlore* 12.3 (Spring 1986). Further reproduction prohibited.

9. "Guardaci Ben": The Visionary Woman in *That Hideous Strength* and the Chronicles of Narnia

"*Guardaci ben: ben sem, ben sem Beatrice*" ("Look on us well; we are indeed, we are Beatrice")

——*The Divine Comedy of Dante Alighieri*

Patterson analyzes C.S. Lewis's two principal female seers, Jane in That Hideous Strength *and Lucy in the Chronicles of Narnia, relative to the Jungian terms anima and animus, shadow, and the four functions of personality: thinking, sensation, intuition, and feeling, drawing on C.G. Jung, and Jungian scholars such as Irene Claremont de Castillejo, M. Esther Harding, Emma Jung, and Erich Neumann as interlocutors. Her discussion is supported by comparisons with such mythological characters as Demeter, Inanna, and Psyche, as well as literary classics, such as Frances Hodgson Burnett's* The Secret Garden *(1911), Bram Stoker's* Dracula *(1897), and Lewis's own* Till We Have Faces. *The incorporation of Jill Pole of* The Silver Chair *and* The Last Battle, *Aravis of* The Horse and His Boy, *and Polly of* The Magician's Nephew *punctuates the importance of insightful female characters as heroines in Lewis's fiction. Patterson's concluding observation is that Lewis's fictional visionary women are characterized in ways consistent with Kabbalistic mysticism.*

Patterson returns to the subject of the seeress in "'Halfe Like a Serpent': The Green Witch in The Silver Chair*" available in* Ransoming the Waste Land Volume II.

This paper was previously published in Mythlore *in 6.3 (Summer; 1979): 6-10 and 6.4 (Autumn 1979): 20-24. "Guardaci Ben" is included here as an important part of Patterson's larger considerations of C.S. Lewis's hierarchy of beings and representation of women in his fiction.*

In a pivotal chapter entitled "Breaking Point" of his memoir, *Blind Ambition*, John Dean tells of traveling to Camp David, where he decides he must tell President Nixon that the Watergate affair can destroy him. In this decision, Dean's wife, "Mo," plays a significant role. There is a symbolic event presaging this development:

Now our White House driver announced that he was lost. The main road to Camp David was closed for repairs, and Mo was giving him advice, based on instincts, about which back road was the right one to a place she had never been. My thoughts settling back into reality, I suggested that the driver use his radio to ask for directions. But he was embarrassed to be lost and didn't want to admit it on the radio. Mo might be right, he thought. In fact she was, and we soon arrived, were checked through and shown our cabin.[1]

In his conversation with his wife after he tries to settle down to write a report "that says everything is okay and no one in the White House has any problems,"[2] Maureen says:

> "That's not true, though is it?"
> "No, it's not."
> "Then, John, you shouldn't write that report. That's not very smart."
> She was right, but her innocence annoyed me.[3]

In this passage, Maureen Dean, whose translucent beauty and transfixed gaze made her an excellent target upon which her husband could, to put it in Jungian terms, project his anima, expresses to him what until this point he has been unable to admit even to himself.

A woman who plays this visionary role, becoming, as Jung said, "a source of information about things for which a man has no eyes," is described by Irene Claremont de Castillejo in *Knowing Woman* (1974), as the fourth of four types (the other three are the maternal, the hetaira, and the amazon):

> [...] here we have par excellence the woman whose principal role is that of mediator.
> She is permeated by the unconscious of another person and makes it visible by living it [...] I have known women who were working in a group to dream dreams which seemed unmistakably to be messages to the group as a whole.[4]

Such a woman may be, as John Dean described his wife to be, quite "unconscious" of her role; or she may be fully aware of it. M. Esther Harding, in *The Way of All Women* (1933), describes this conscious visionary woman:

> Certain women [...] who have advanced beyond the sophisticated stage are yet particularly well fitted for this role of *femme inspiratrice* on account of their own contact with the deeper things within them. Such a woman can lead a man whom she loves into touch with the hidden truths of life because of the reality of her own inner experience [...] Such a woman is in a different category from one who is nothing but anima, for she gives of herself and is not playing a role in which her unconscious motive is to hold the man. She is a "redeemed" anima woman—redeemed, that is, from the hold of her own biological instincts, on the one hand, and from self-seeking and egotistic motives, on the other.[5]

The visionary woman, in both her conscious and unconscious role, appears in many works of fantasy, and is vividly evoked in the fantasy novels of C.S. Lewis.

That Hideous Strength

The visionary woman is a seer, and Lewis based his fantasies on seeing. "Everything began with images," he wrote, "a faun carrying an umbrella, a queen on a sledge, a magnificent lion."[6] And again:

> [...] in a certain sense, I have never exactly "made" a story. With me the process is much more like bird-watching than like either talking or building. I see pictures.[7]

In exactly this manner, *That Hideous Strength* begins with Jane Studdock idly thumbing a newspaper and seeing "a picture on the back page" (THS 12; ch. 1). And, "The moment she saw the picture she remembered her dream." The dream is described: "She had begun by dreaming simply of a face" (THS 12; ch. 1). It is not, in fact, an ordinary dream, but a vision of something happening in another place: visual and auditory elements are combined. Then, "At this point the dream abandoned all pretence to realism and became ordinary nightmare" (THS 13; ch. 1). Jane tries to justify the experience in rational terms but fails, and, vaguely disquieted, abandons the attempt and leaves her isolated flat. On the neighborhood high street she meets Mrs. Dimble, whom she accompanies home to lunch. There, with Professor Dimble, the conversation turns speculative and even metaphysical, and Jane responds by fainting. Returning to consciousness,

"Jane attempted to excuse her absurd behaviour by telling the story of her dream" (THS 30; ch. 1). She suggests jestingly that they "can both start psycho-analyzing me now," but to her surprise they take her perfectly seriously. When she returns home she is still uneasy, and telephones the Dimbles for help, at which point they give her the name of Grace Ironwood as one whom she ought to visit concerning the matter. This, after a quarrel with her husband Mark, she does.

While Mark is being drawn into contact with the malignant National Institute of Co-ordinated Experiments (known by its ironic acronym as the N.I.C.E.) which is taking over his college and much of the countryside in a kind of diabolical infection of which Jane's dream is to prove a significant symptom, Jane visits St. Anne's-on-the-Hill. "'I've let myself in for it now,' thought Jane, 'I shall have to tell this woman that dream and she'll ask all sorts of questions'" (THS 60; ch. 3). Her interview with Grace Ironwood is indeed extremely disagreeable, for again, she is taken seriously. "The reason you cannot be cured is that you are not ill," the woman tells Jane. It emerges that Jane, nee Tudor, is a descendant of visionary stock: "Your ancestor gave a full and, on the whole, correct account of the battle [...] But he was not at it. He was in York at the time." He had dreamed of the battle, for, Miss Ironwood says, "Vision—the power of dreaming realities—is sometimes hereditary" (THS 63; ch. 3). Jane, in fact, has been sent by the Dimbles to St. Anne's-on-the-Hill to give information by means of her visionary gift.

She resists, but in the end her dreams force her back to "the company"—"I saw them killing a man" (THS 75; ch. 4), she tells Mrs. Dimble. "Windows into huge, dark landscapes were opening on every side and she was powerless to shut them" (THS 81; ch. 4). She is, as Arthur Denniston tells her, "a seer: a person with second sight" (THS 112; ch. 5), and as Camilla Denniston says, "You are our secret service, our eyes" (THS 113; ch. 5).

Jane's dreams are vividly described in the novel, and are animus-centered: that is, they are focused on the image of a dominant, compelling male figure or figures. Emma Jung (1957) wrote of a woman experiencing dreams of this type:

> I would conclude from the presence of a powerful animus figure [...] that the person in question gives too little attention to her own masculine-intellectual logos tendency, and has either

> developed and applied it insufficiently or not in the right way. Perhaps this sounds paradoxical because, from the outside, it appears as if it were the feminine principle which is not sufficiently taken into account, since the behavior of such women seems on the surface to be too masculine and suggests a lack of femininity.[8]

This is precisely Jane's problem; she is an educated woman who, as a wife, has abandoned her intellectual pursuits and now feels restless and frustrated. Emma Jung says, almost as if describing Jane:

> To busy ourselves simply in an intellectual or objectively masculine way seems insufficient, as can be seen in many women who have completed a course of study and practice a hitherto masculine, intellectual calling, but who, nonetheless, have never come to terms with the animus problem.[9]

Lewis opened *That Hideous Strength* by sketching with a few deft strokes the predicament of Jane Studdock:

> She had always intended to continue her own career as a scholar after she was married: that was one of the reasons they were to have no children [...] She still believed that if she got out all her notebooks and editions and really sat down to the job, she could force herself back into her lost enthusiasm for the subject. But before she did so—perhaps in order to put off the moment of beginning—she turned over a newspaper which was lying on the table and glanced at a picture on the back page. (THS 12; ch.1)

Thus Lewis has described Jane's problem as a prefix to beginning his narration of her visionary experiences, for this phrase launches them with the "picture on the back page." The rest of the book describes Jane's resolution of her problem, by a means which Emma Jung may be seen to summarize:

> What is really necessary is that feminine intellectuality, logos in the woman, should be so fitted into the nature and life of the woman that a harmonious cooperation between the feminine and masculine factors ensues [...][10]

But the end of the book is far away when Jane begins to dream. Her very first dream is of "a foreign-looking face, bearded and rather yellow, with a hooked nose," and "a rather good-looking man with a pointed grey beard" (THS 12; ch. 1). Emma Jung wrote of the animus: "for women the animus appears either as a plurality of men, as a group of fathers, a council, a court, or some other gathering of wise men"[11] and "this figure can come on the scene [...] as sage, judge, artist, aviator, mechanic, and so on. Not infrequently it appears as a 'stranger.'"[12] When Jane's dream of the foreign-looking man (stranger) and the good-looking man turns to "ordinary nightmare" she sees "a head with a flowing white beard all covered with earth. It belonged to [...] a sort of ancient British, druidical sort of man" (THS 13; ch. 1). These figures are later explained as apparitions of the murderer, Alcasan; an official of the N.I.C.E., Frost; and the ancient magus, Merlin. But their occurrence in her dream marks them as animus images; as Emma Jung says, "In dreams or phantasies, the animus appears chiefly in the figure of a real man."[13]

Jane has "one recurrent dream" in which "someone who had apparently drawn a chair up to the bedside and then sat down to watch" (THS 121; ch. 6). He looks "like a doctor," as befits an animus figure. It is the man she has already seen: "the pince-nez, the well-chiselled, rather white features, the little pointed beard." All three of the figures so far described are bearded, a motif of masculine identity which is probably deliberate on Lewis's part: I shall refer to the bearded animus figure again below, when it appears to Lucy in a Narnian novel. The image just described—with its white features and little pointed beard—is remarkably similar to a figure in another novel, *Dracula*, where the theme of the woman who sees in a trance the threatening activities of a dangerous male figure is given especially powerful expression.

In *Dracula*, Dr. Van Helsing hypnotizes Mina Harker so that she can describe the journey being made by Count Dracula as his coffin of ancestral earth is transported (with his body inside it) by water. Dracula has the power to call Mina to him but by the same route she has access to him. She assists not only in a hypnotic trance but by the use of her reason, for she works out an analysis of Dracula's plan which convinces the others and proves, ultimately, to be true; as Dr. Van Helsing exclaims: "Our dear Madam Mina is once more our teacher. Her eyes have been where we were blinded. Now we are on the track once again, and this time we may succeed."[14] Erich Neumann (1955) wrote of such a situation, "when consciousness and reason cannot [...] be drawn upon to decide a situation, the male falls back on the wisdom of the unconscious, by which the female is inspired."[15] At the end of *Dracula*, Mina Harker gives the description of Count Dracula's death:

> He was deathly pale, just like a waxen image, and the red eyes glared [...]
>
> As I looked, the eyes saw the sinking sun, and the look of hate in them turned to triumph.
>
> But, on the instant, came the sweep and flash of Jonathan's knife.[16]

This terrible visage strongly resembles the face haunting Jane Studdock's dreams.

Her climactic dream takes her into a cold, underground darkness. This time she recognizes that she is dreaming, and begins to explore. She finds the body of a large bearded man in coarse clothing: all known by touch alone. The dream ends with a visual image:

> She had a picture of someone, someone bearded but also [...] divinely young. (THS 133; ch. 6)

This positive animus figure heralds her meeting with Elwin Ransom, Director of St. Anne's:

> someone all golden and strong and warm coming with a mighty earth-shaking tread down into that black place. (THS 133; ch. 6)

It is an image reminiscent of the *Harrowing of Hell* in some medieval illumination, in which a gleaming Christ descends into Hell to release the many souls held in bondage there. Immediately following this dream Jane sees with her eyes for the first time the terrible "waxworks face" of Frost. The confrontation drives her to St. Anne's and her meeting with Ransom, the Pendragon. The passage in which Jane meets the master of St. Anne's may be analyzed for its visionary elements.

> Jane looked; and instantly her world was unmade.
>
> On a sofa before her, with one foot bandaged as if he had a wound, lay what appeared to be a boy, twenty years old.

> […] all the light in the room seemed to run towards the gold hair and the gold beard of the wounded man.
>
> Of course he was not a boy—how could she have thought so? The fresh skin on his forehead and cheeks and, above all, on his hands, had suggested the idea. But no boy could have so full a beard. And no boy could be so strong. (THS 139; ch. 7)

In this passage, Jane becomes the visionary for the reader; we see the transformed Ransom through her eyes. She thinks of Arthur, of Solomon.

> Solomon—for the first time in many years the bright solar blend of king and lover and magician which hangs about that name stole back upon her mind. For the first time in all those years she tasted the word *king* itself with all linked associations of battle, marriage, priesthood, mercy and power. (THS 140; ch. 7)

The figure of Ransom as Lewis has described him most perfectly fits the vision of Eros as Psyche unveils him in *The Golden Ass of Apuleius*. Lewis has described Eros elsewhere, in *Till We Have Faces*, as he appears to Psyche's sister (invented by Lewis), Orual. There she sees "the look of lightning, pale, dazzling" (TWF 172; ch. 15) which reveals "the beauty this face wore" (TWF 173; ch. 15). In commenting on the Psyche legend itself, Robert A. Johnson (1976) writes, in a passage suggesting the gamut of Jane's reactions to her first visit to the Pendragon Ransom:

> If one takes [the Psyche legend …] entirely as a woman's story, Eros is a woman's own interior animus who is being strengthened, healed, brought out of his boyish, trickster characteristics and made into a mature man worthy of being her mate. This is all done by her labor and by his cooperation. He in turn redeems her.[17]

And in fact, Ransom, as Eros did to Psyche, sets Jane a task. She finds him both profoundly attractive and profoundly frightening, but when he speaks, it is to tell her that "your information is so valuable" (THS 141; ch. 7). Nonetheless the conversation is discomfiting. She is told she must go back to her husband, to try to free him, by dissuasion, from his association with the N.I.C.E. Her chief discomfiture, however, comes from "that inner commentator, who had more than once during this conversation shown her her own words and wishes in such a novel light [...]" (THS 143; ch. 7). Emma Jung says of such a situation: "It [the animus] comes to us as a voice commenting on every situation in which we find ourselves [...][18] This entity as experienced by Jane may be described as her conscience or her animus. The conversation (which has a three-person element: Jane–Director–Commentator) is interrupted by the approach of an *eldil*, which Jane is able to sense but is not allowed to see.

On leaving, Jane finds that she is "so divided against herself that one might say there were three, if not four, Janes [...] (THS 147; ch. 7). These are

1) "a Jane simply receptive of the Director,"
2) a "second Jane [who] regarded the first with disgust,"
3) "The third Jane [who] was a new and unexpected visitant [...] this moral Jane [...]," and
4) "the fourth Jane, who was Jane herself and dominated all the rest [...]" (THS 148-49; ch. 7).

There is a certain correspondence between these Janes and the four functions of the personality as described by C. G. Jung. The concept may be expressed in the following diagram:

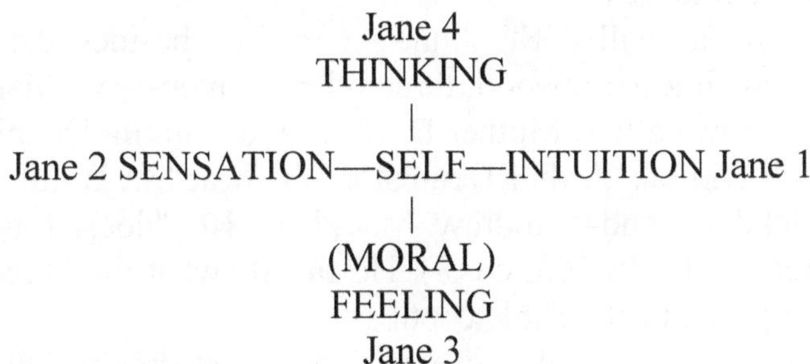

Jane has been, as an intellectual, the kind of woman whose superior function is Thinking. For this reason her inferior function is Feeling, which would probably be better called Judgment, for it has to do precisely with those moral responses which Jane discovers welling up within herself, as the voice of Jane 3, as they would be bound to do in a function unknown, that is, hitherto unconscious. The first two Janes suggest Intuition (Jane 1) whose direct response to the Director is the supreme and positive manifestation of her visionary gift which has previously shown her only negative images, and Sensation (Jane 2) whose response to Jane 1's intuitive grasp is described in such physical terms. Jane 4 is the one "in the sphere of Jove" (THS 149; ch. 7)—it was He (Jove) whose *eldil* approached the chamber—whose Joy in everything she sees is described in terms of sunlight, rabbits, an old man "sweet as a nut," music, sonnets, and buttered toast. And "her own beauty [...] expanding like a magic flower" (THS 149; ch. 7). Jane's ego has been invested in the Thinking function, and the Self, a rich compendium or unity of all four functions together, culminates in the mandalic flower image of this climactic passage.

Immediately after this sequence, Jane undergoes a terrible encounter with still another component of her psyche as Jung has outlined it: she meets her shadow in Fairy Hardcastle. The Shadow is always a member of one's own sex, and contains to a repugnant degree just those traits one least knows and/or most detests in oneself. The Fairy is an "ogress" (THS 152; ch. 7) with a lighted cheroot between her teeth. This phallic evidence of her aggressive and Amazonian nature the Fairy uses to torture Jane, without success in making her reveal where she has been. Jane escapes, having kept secret her visit to St. Anne's. This ordeal ends with her return to the manor, this time with permission to stay.

The house called St. Anne's contains, besides the Director (Ransom) and Grace Ironwood, three other women—Ivy Maggs, Mrs. (or as she is now called) Mother Dimble, and Camilla Denniston—as well as Cecil Dimble, Arthur Denniston, the bear Mr. Bultitude, some mice, a jackdaw, and—Andrew MacPhee. He "doesn't believe in [Jane's] dreams" (THS 163; ch. 8). He fulfills what the Director calls the "very important office" of sceptic.

Jane now has another dream, "the worst dream I've had yet" (THS 178; ch. 9) as she tells the Director and Grace Ironwood. She has seen the head of Alcasan kept artificially alive in the central laboratory of the N.I.C.E. Most horrible of all, she sees her husband Mark brought before the Head and formally introduced. It is MacPhee, whom the Director calls his "oldest friend" who outlines for Jane the situation of conflict between St. Anne's and Belbury, the mansion housing the N.I.C.E.

Considerably further on in the story, after failures of the N.I.C.E. to trap Jane and failures by Dr. Dimble to save Mark, Ransom states, "Last night Jane Studdock had the most important dream she's had yet" (THS 222; ch. 10). This time she has seen the entrance to the cave in which Merlin, for whom the N.I.C.E. has been searching in hopes that he will become their aid, has been hidden. Furthermore, Jane has perceived that Merlin has already wakened: "[…] there was a man in the tunnel. Of course I couldn't see him: it was pitch dark. But a great big man. Breathing heavily" (THS 223; ch. 10). All her dreams are of men; this is the man of all men that she has been sent to see, for Merlin is sought as the key to victory by the N.I.C.E. but is, in fact, to be the key for St. Anne's. The company sets out to find him.

"Jane has to go because she is the guide," says Ransom (THS 225; ch. 10). The search is full of references to vision: "'I can't see a thing,' said Jane (THS 228; ch. 11). And finally: "'There he is,' said Jane. 'Can you see him?' said Dimble. 'I haven't got your eyes'" (THS 233; ch. 11). Jane has been facing, for the first time in her life, the actual prospect of both death and the existence of God (Maleldil); that "Maleldil might be, quite simply and crudely, God" (THS 231; ch. 11). She "was trying to see death in the new light of all she had heard […]" (THS 231; ch. 11) and the "thought glowed in her mind for a second like a spark that has fallen on shavings, and then a second later, like those shavings, her whole mind was in a blaze" (THS 231; ch. 11).

Meanwhile, members of the N.I.C.E. are discussing Jane: "The authorities had access to the woman's mind for only a short time. They inspected one dream only—a most important dream, which revealed, though with some irrelevancies, an essential element in our programme" (THS 236; ch. 11). Their fears are justified, as we have seen. And she has a role to play for Mark too, as he in his turn faces the prospect of his own death. "This—this death of his—would be lucky for Jane" (THS 244; ch. 11), he thinks in his prison cell. He is reminded of his twin sister, Myrtle: "it was her large wondering eyes and naif answers to his accounts of the circle he was now moving in which had provided at each stage most of the real pleasure of his career" (THS 244; ch. 11). Myrtle has been his anima, a position into which he has subsequently attempted to fit Jane:

> And he now knew, for the first time, what he had secretly meant to do with Jane [...] she was to have been the great hostess—the secret hostess in the sense that only the very esoteric few would know who that striking-looking woman was and why it mattered so enormously to secure her good will. (THS 244; ch. 11)

The "secret hostess" seems an eminently exact way to describe the anima, and the role of a woman upon whom a man attempts to project that hidden element of his own personality. But now, with the imminence of his own death, he sees Jane in her own selfhood, in which role she can actually save him:

> She seemed to him [...] to have in herself deep wells and knee-deep meadows of happiness, rivers of freshness, enchanted gardens of leisure, which he could not enter but would have spoiled. (THS 244; ch. 11)

In this moment, Frost, whose appearance in her dreams had so frightened Jane, enters the cells, and Mark for the very first time sees him for the human monster he is.

Meanwhile the search for Merlin, led by Jane, goes on. "'Oh look! Look!' cried Jane. 'Stop him. Quick!'" (THS 251; ch. 12) And again, "'Come on. Run! Didn't you see?'" It is Merlin, who escapes them even as they see him: "with some streaming garment blown far out behind him in the wind, the great figure of a man" (THS 251; ch. 12). The search has been carried out in the pouring rain, which impedes the efforts of the searchers. But the rain has been followed by wind: "It was a good deal lighter now that the rain had stopped, but the wind had risen and was roaring about them" (THS 250; ch. 12). Both water and wind have significance for the scene of seeking. Neumann writes,

> [...] the woman is the original seeress, the lady of the wisdom-bringing waters of the depths, of the murmuring springs and fountains, for the "original utterance of seerdom is the language of water."[19]

This water has become a torrent, almost overwhelming Jane and those who follow her lead, when Merlin appears, momentarily, in the passage quoted above. His appearance is accompanied by the risen wind and he wears streaming garments: Emma Jung writes that "the woman's animus in its superhuman, divine aspect is comparable to [...] a spirit and wind-god."[20] This animus spirit is "he who, when evoked, can create by a wish"[21]—a figure like the windswept magician Merlin.

When at last Jane and the others encounter Merlin face to face he is already in the company of Ransom: to Jane, "The two robed figures looked to be two of the same sort" (THS 275; ch. 13). This observation of Lewis's reminds us of what powerful animus figures they have been in Jane's spiritual life. Merlin's response to Jane's presence is astounding:

> "Sir, you have in your house the falsest lady of any at this time alive [...] For, Sir, it was the purpose of God that she and her lord should between them have begotten a child by whom the enemies should have been put out of Logres for a thousand years." (THS 275; ch. 13)

This charge was, in C.S. Lewis's eyes, deeply serious. In his personal life, he wrote, in a terrifying letter to Sheldon Vanauken (1977), whose wife had recently died:

> [...] One Flesh must not [...] "live to itself" any more than the single individual. It was not made, any more than he, to be its Own End. It was made for God and (in Him) for its neighbours—first and foremost among them the children it ought to have produced. (The idea behind your voluntary sterility, that an experience, e.g., maternity, wh. cannot be shared shd. on that account be avoided, is surely v. unsound. For a. (forgive me) the conjugal act itself depends on opposite, reciprocal and therefore unshare-able experiences. Did you want her to feel she had a *woman* in bed with her? b. The experience of a woman denied maternity is one you *did not & could not* share with her. To be denied paternity is different, trivial in comparison.)
>
> One way or another the thing had to die. Perpetual springtime is not allowed. You were not cutting the wood of

> life according to the grain. There are various possible ways in wh. it cd. have died tho' both the parties went on living. You have been treated with a severe mercy.[22]

And from this point in the novel, Jane plays little more role in the central affairs at St. Anne's; her eyes are no longer needed. But in Mark's life she becomes ever more central. He is being made to undergo an initiation in Belbury, and Jane forms his only hold upon what, in contrast with his experiences in degradation, he now perceives as "the 'Normal.'" "It was all mixed up with Jane and fried eggs and soap and sunlight [...]" (THS 297; ch. 14). Jane, for her part, undergoes a sort of initiation herself, into the mysteries of the marriage chamber, as she and Mrs. Dimble prepare a room for Ivy Maggs and her husband.

Here Jane encounters a full-blown vision: not a dream, not a waking encounter with ordinary reality, however terrifying, but an absolute, fully conscious confrontation with an archetype. It is, quite properly, a female entity—the earthly Venus, mistress of the house. It is preceded, briefly by "the image of Mark dead, that face dead, in the middle of a pillow, that whole body rigid [...]" (THS 301; ch. 14). Then—"It was very still [...] so still that she could hear the movements of a small bird which was hopping along the path outside the window" (THS 301; ch. 14). The bird, as befits a harbinger role frequently assigned to birds, and appearing also in the Narnia stories, as will be seen below, leads Jane to a threshold, where the goddess sits. "It is ignoring me. It doesn't see me" (THS 301; ch. 14), Jane thinks. "With a great glow and a noise like fire the flame-robed woman and the malapert dwarfs had all come into the house" (THS 302; ch. 14). The room becomes alight and alive with vegetation. Lewis writes:

> It never occurred to her to think she was dreaming. People mistake dreams for visions: no one ever mistook a vision for a dream. (THS 302; ch. 14)

Jane is freed from this visitation of her (one might say for a woman, the) Shadow, by the arrival of Mother Dimble.

> "I must see the Director at once," said Jane. [...] I'd like to see the Director at once. (THS 303; ch. 14)

Mark meanwhile has been having his own encounter, with a common tramp whom the N.I.C.E. have mistaken for Merlin. Mark and the tramp build together a genuine camaraderie, the true "inner ring" for which Mark has been searching all his life.

When Jane does see the Director he assures her that her vision "was real enough" (THS 311; ch. 14). He explains:

> And you yourself ... you are a seer. You were perhaps bound to meet her. She's what you'll get if you won't have the other. (THS 311; ch. 14)

The "other" is what is represented by Mother Dimble, "a Christian wife." And to protect herself from this raw "Old Woman," Jane must become a Christian, become what is "richer, sharper, even fiercer, at every rung of the ascent" (THS 312; ch. 14). In order to serve God, she is to begin with learning to love her husband.

In going into the garden to ponder this, "at one particular corner of the gooseberry path, the change came" (THS 315; ch. 14).

> A boundary had been crossed. She had come into a world, or into a Person, or into the presence of a Person. (THS 315; ch. 14)

It is an experience beyond vision.

Immediately, the central chapter of the book begins—"The Descent of the Gods"—the complex astrological symbolism I have discussed at considerable length in another paper.[23] The divinities of the planets descend to St. Anne's Manor. Only one of them is described in terms of Jane's perception and this one is, quite properly, Venus, whose presence shows Jane the Dimbles "like ripe fields in August," and the Dennistons, so godlike "she could hardly bear to look on them" (THS 319; ch. 15). Animus figures in this holy atmosphere appear not as "the gross and ridiculous dwarfs which she had seen that afternoon, but grave and ardent spirits, bright winged, their boyish shapes smooth and slender as ivory rods" (THS 320; ch. 15).

Mark's initiation, intended to bring him into the center of the N.I.C.E., in fact brings him to Christianity. Resisting Frost for the first time intentionally, Mark refuses to desecrate a crucifix. Nonetheless he is present at the last public event of the N.I.C.E., a great dinner given in honor of the guest speaker Jules; at which the doom of tongues, followed by an invasion of animals kept for vivisection, overwhelms and destroys Belbury in its hour of triumph.

Mark alone escapes, and makes his way to St. Anne's. "He was going to see Jane: [...] In fact, he was going to see Jane in what he now felt to be her proper world" (THS 358; ch. 17). When he comes to St. Anne's he too has a vision of "a woman divinely tall, part naked, part wrapped in a flame-coloured robe" (THS 380; ch. 17). She ushers him into the doorway in the wall of the house of which she is guardian. Jane, descending the garden path to join him, has no more need of visions.

> When she came to the lodge she was surprised to see it all dark and the door shut. [...] Then she noticed the window, the bedroom window, was open. Clothes were piled on a chair inside the room so carelessly that they lay over the sill: the sleeve of a shirt—Mark's shirt—even hung over down the outside wall. And in all this damp, too. How exactly like Mark! Obviously it was high time she went in. (THS 380; ch. 17)

She has seen the Goddess, but she has gone beyond sight to recognize the presence of God. This experience has returned her to the world of ordinary reality, ready now to mediate that vision for her husband, for the vision is most hers when she shares it: "Come and look!" as Lucy says, again and again.

The Chronicles of Narnia

Lucy Pevensie is the seeress of the Narnian Chronicles, as Jane Studdock is the seeress of *That Hideous Strength.* In *The Lion, the Witch and the Wardrobe*, the first of the seven tales of Narnia, Lucy's first visit to Narnia begins inside an old wardrobe, with a sensation of touch and sound: "she noticed that there was something crunching under her feet" (LWW 8; ch. 1). Then, "she felt ["with her hand"] something soft and powdery and extremely cold." And, "rubbing against her face and hands was [...] something hard and rough" (LWW 8; ch. 1). Vision begins when she is "a step or two" across the boundary between the worlds: "And then she saw that there was a light ahead of her [...] " (LWW 8; ch. 1).

Looking back, she sees her own world: "It seemed to be still daylight there" (LWW 9; ch. 1). In the world inside the wardrobe, Narnia, it is night, but there is a light there, a lamp-post. By its mysterious (and, we learn in *The Magician's Nephew*, organic) illumination, Lucy meets her first Narnian, Tumnus the Faun. This masculine being functions as her guide, an animus figure, and leads her into the forest and to his cave, where he offers her tea, sardines, toast, honey and cake, and regales her with tales of Narnian life. "He had a strange, but pleasant little face with a short pointed beard and curly hair, and out of the hair there stuck two horns" (LWW 10; ch. 1). We have already seen the beardedness of the animus figures for Lewis. The repast Lucy shares with Mr. Tumnus—"a wonderful tea"—in his cave, is reminiscent of the pomegranate, the fruit eaten by Persephone in Hades which confined her there for half a year in the perpetual round of Winter and Summer; it had been plucked from a tree which "grew in the garden of the king of the underworld."[24] This slight suggestion of the underworld motif appears later in the series, as will be seen. The lamp-light in which Lucy's first encounter with Narnia and the Narnians is bathed, is related to a symbolic system with an Eleusinian coloring—the Eleusinian mysteries celebrated the myth of Persephone. Johnson writes of

> the light-bearing capacity of women. In the Eleusinian mysteries, the women often carry torches, which shed a peculiarly feminine kind of light. A torch softly lights up the immediate surroundings, shows the practical next step to be taken.[25]

In Lucy's return to England from Narnia, she runs from lamppost back to daylight, where she stands panting, "I'm here. I've come back" (LWW 23; ch. 2). The returned visionary meets a doubting reception and is pronounced "batty" by her brother Edmund and "silly" by her sister Susan. To prove her point she shows the doubters, along with her more tolerant brother Peter ("She's just making up a story for fun") (LWW 24-25; ch. 3) the wardrobe interior.

> Then everyone looked in and pulled the coats apart; and they all saw—Lucy herself saw—a perfectly ordinary wardrobe. (LWW 25; ch. 3)

Lucy's name means "light," and the light meant is that which is symbolized by the torches carried in the Eleusinian mysteries, the light of inspiration or visionary experience. Lucy is named after a saint who made a sacrifice of the eyes her lover had adored, in order to dedicate herself wholly to Christ. St. Lucy's symbol is a pair of eyes, and her feast, which falls in December, is associated with the light symbolism of the Winter Solstice season. In Sweden, for example, little girls or young women wearing a crown of lighted candles represent the "Lucia Bride" or "Bride of Light."

Lucy's first experience of Narnia is mediated through light. When Edmund, a few days later, stumbles into Narnia, he too "saw a light." But for him the light comes from "a pale blue sky" where the sun is "just rising, very red and clear" (LWW 29; ch. 3). His eyes show him a different being from the one encountered by Lucy: "there swept into sight a sledge drawn by two reindeer" (LWW 30; ch. 3). The image is reiterated: "The sledge was a fine sight as it came sweeping toward Edmund" (LWW 31; ch. 3). It bears the White Witch Jadis, a malignant anima or female guide for Edmund, and she sweeps him away on her sledge (she has a Dwarf attendant), offering him her own sort of feast: "a jeweled cup full of something that steamed" and "several pounds of the best Turkish Delight [...] sweet and light to the very center" (LWW 36-37; ch. 4). This food Lewis describes as frankly addictive. Later on, Edmund meets Lucy in the wood, and after their return to England, Edmund denies his vision, to Lucy's great distress.

The next visit to Narnia takes all four children through the wardrobe door, and again, as Susan says, "It's getting light—over there" (LWW 54; ch. 6). "All four children stood blinking in the daylight of a winter day" (LWW 55; ch. 6). This time they find Tumnus's cave ransacked and a notice proclaiming the rule of "Jadis, Queen of Narnia." But another guide discloses himself, to Lucy, first: "Lucy said, 'Look! There's a robin, with such a red breast. It's the first bird I've seen here'" (LWW 60; ch. 6).

The robin, of whom Lewis says, "You couldn't have found a robin with a redder breast or a brighter eye," plays a role which is typical of that attributed to birds in folklore. A similar figure is seen in a children's novel popular during Lewis's childhood, *The Secret Garden* (1911) by Frances Hodgson Burnett. In searching for a garden which has been closed for ten years, a little girl, Mary Lennox, "saw a bird with a bright red breast sitting on the topmost branch of one of [the trees of the garden]."[26] A few chapters later the robin shows her first the key and then the door to the garden which gives the book its name. The robins in Britain are brighter-breasted than the larger, somewhat rusty-breasted robins of North America.

Lucy's robin leads the Pevensies to their encounter with Mr. and Mrs. Beaver, and thus well into their Narnian adventures. The spell of endless winter which the self-proclaimed Queen-witch has cast over Narnia is to be broken by the coming of Aslan, Narnia's true Lord. He is preceded in his coming by another sledge-rider, Father Christmas, "a huge man in a bright red robe (bright as holly-berries)" (LWW 106; ch. 10). Lewis remarks, "though you see people of his sort only in Narnia, you see pictures of them [...] even in our world—the world on this side of the wardrobe door" (LWW 107; ch. 10). "But when you really see them in Narnia it is rather different" (LWW 107; ch. 10).

The coming of Aslan is experienced by three of the four Pevensie children at once (Edmund having absented himself), "and this is what they saw. They were on a green open space from which you could look down on the forest spreading as far as one could see in every direction—[...] far to the East, was something twinkling and moving" (LWW 125; ch. 12). In the midst of the field, before "a wonderful pavilion" (LWW 125; ch. 12) "Aslan stood." His companions are described in detail, "But as for Aslan himself, the Beavers and the children didn't know what to do or say when they saw him" (LWW 127; ch. 12). Most clear to them was the sight of "the great, royal, solemn, overwhelming eyes; and then they found they couldn't look at him" (LWW 127; ch. 12).

Aslan becomes the liberator of Narnia and the savior of Edmund: he gives his life in place of the boy. After the death of the Lion, Lucy and Susan lie in an exhausted calm:

> But at last Lucy noticed two other things. One was that the sky on the east side of the hill was a little less dark than it had been an hour ago. (LWW 158; ch. 15)

At the exact moment of dawn, when "The rising of the sun had made everything look so different" (LWW 161; ch. 15) they see the risen Aslan:

> There, shining in the sunrise, larger than they had seen him before, shaking his mane [...] stood Aslan himself (LWW 162; ch. 15).

The preceding material is a compendium of references to sight and to light. Lucy sees the lamp-light of Narnia and the sunlight of earth; Edmund sees the red sun of Narnian dawn; the sledge of Jadis is "a fine sight" (LWW 31; ch. 3); the Pevensie children together see Narnia getting lighter (LWW 160; ch. 15); the robin has "a brighter eye" (LWW 60; ch. 6); Father Christmas, a picture in our world, is "really" seen in Narnia; and when Aslan appears at last, the children were speechless "when they saw him" and, abashed by his "overwhelming eyes," they "couldn't look at him" (LWW 127; ch. 12). Not surprisingly, then, the culminating vision of Aslan resurrected is expressed in the same terms.

This visionary pattern recurs in *Prince Caspian*: tumbled from a railway platform into "such a woody place that branches were sticking into them [...] They all rubbed their eyes," and Peter exclaims, "I can't see a yard in all these trees" (PC 5; ch. 1). Working out of the thicket, "Everything became much brighter," and they are on the shores of the sea (PC 5; ch. 1). The first chapter contains a series of sightings by Lucy—"'Look!' said Lucy suddenly, 'What's that?'" and it proves to be a stream of fresh water (PC 9; ch. 1).

> "I say!" exclaimed Lucy, "I do believe that's an apple tree."
>
> It was. (PC 11; ch. 1)

Thus food is provided. Again.

> "And what's that?" said Lucy, pointing ahead.
> "By Jove, it's a wall," said Peter. (PC 13; ch. 1)

When the enclosure is entered, "they all blinked because the daylight became suddenly much brighter" (PC 13; ch. 1).

This introductory sequence prefigures a central moment in the book, one which concerns Lucy in particular. The first eight chapters of the novel take place on an island off the shore of Narnia, where the Dwarf Trumpkin tells the story of Prince Caspian's childhood. Chapter VIII is "How they Left the Island." Chapter IX is entitled, "What Lucy Saw."

The tired children are asleep on the Narnian mainland: all but Lucy.

> She knew that one of the best ways of getting to sleep is to stop trying, so she opened her eyes. Through a gap in the bracken and branches above she could just see a patch of water in the Creek and the sky above it. Then, with a thrill of memory, she saw again, after all those years, the bright Narnian stars. (PC 115; ch. 9)

In the moonlight, the forest begins to come to life. "Lucy's eyes began to grow accustomed to the light, and she saw the trees that were nearest her more distinctly" (PC 116; ch. 9). As in her first entry into Narnia in *The Lion, the Witch and the Wardrobe*, her vision occurs at night. Neumann writes, "over and over again we find this mantic woman connected with the symbols of caldron and cave, of night and moon."[27] Harding says that the goddess of prophecy is manifested in moonlight and rain. She points out that "The ancients knew no inner or psychological realm, to them the inner world was conceived of as the underworld, the spirit realm, the place where all spirit things dwelt." And, "Thus the Underworld Queen is mistress of all that lives in the hidden parts of the psyche, in the unconscious as we should say." This same lady, as moon goddess, is styled "Giver of Visions," Harding says.[28]

Lucy calls on the forest to waken fully, but the moment passes: "Lucy had the feeling [...] that she had just missed something." She falls asleep, waking to "a gray twilight (for the sun had not yet risen)" (PC 118; ch. 9). The children continue their journey, a hard, irritating trip. Then, suddenly:

> "Look! Look! Look!" cried Lucy.
>
> "Where? What?" asked everyone.
>
> "The Lion," said Lucy. "Aslan himself. Didn't you see?" Her face had changed completely and her eyes shone.
>
> "Do you really mean—?" began Peter.
>
> "Where did you think you saw him?" asked Susan.
>
> "Don't talk like a grown-up," said Lucy, stamping her foot. "I didn't *think* I saw him. I saw him." (PC 125; ch. 9)

This time, Edmund takes her part. But the others disagree, and Peter exercises his authority as High King, and the party goes on in spite of Lucy's vision. Needless to say, the trip goes badly and in the end many weary steps have to be retraced and the children sleep again. Again, too, Lucy is called at night.

> Lucy woke out of the deepest sleep you can imagine, with the feeling that the voice she liked best in the world had been calling her name […] She was looking straight up at the Narnian moon, which is larger than ours […]
>
> "Lucy," came the call again […] The moon was so bright that the whole forest landscape around her was almost as clear as day, though it looked wilder. (PC 137; ch. 10)

Under this superbly mantic moon, the forest indeed awakens, "And then—oh joy! For *he* was there; the huge Lion, shining white in the moonlight, with his huge black shadow underneath him" (PC 141; ch. 10). After a rapturous but admonitory greeting, Aslan sends her back to waken the others, a difficult task. She finally arouses Edmund:

> "Aslan!" said Edmund, jumping up. "Hurray! Where?"
>
> Lucy turned back to where she could see the Lion waiting, his patient eyes fixed upon her. "There," she said, pointing.
>
> "Where?" asked Edmund again.
>
> "There. There. Don't you see? Just this side of the trees."
>
> Edmund stared hard for a while and then said, "No. There's nothing there. You've got dazzled and muddled with the moonlight. One does, you know. I thought I saw something for a moment myself. It's only an optical what-do-you-call-it."
>
> "I can see him all the time," said Lucy. "He's looking straight at us."
>
> "Then why can't I see him?"
>
> "He said you mightn't be able to."
>
> "Why?"
>
> "I don't know. That's what he said."
>
> "Oh bother it all," said Edmund. "I do wish you wouldn't keep on seeing things. But I suppose we'll have to wake the others." (PC 145-46; ch. 8)

Thus aroused, and following Lucy as she heeds Aslan's direction, they make their way. One by one the others see their true guide: Edmund first, then Peter, and finally,

> "Lucy," said Susan in a very small voice.
> "Yes?" said Lucy.
> "I see him now. I'm sorry."
> "That's all right." (PC 152; ch. 11)

Lucy's visionary role continues in *The Voyage of the Dawn Treader*. She and Edmund are visiting Eustace Scrubbs, when they see "a picture of a ship" on the wall of Lucy's guest room. With a gilded prow "shaped like the head of a dragon [...] 'she is such a very Narnian ship,'" says Lucy (VDT 4-5; ch. 1)—and when Eustace questions her preference, she says

> "I like it because the ship looks as if it were really moving. And the water looks as if it were really wet. And the waves look as if they were really going up and down." (VDT 6; ch. 1)

And with that "The things in the picture were moving" (VDT 7; ch. 1) and the children are drawn into Narnia again, to the aid of a now-adult Prince Caspian. On board the Dawn Treader, as the ship proves to be, Lucy renews her old acquaintance with Reepicheep, the valiant mouse whose quest for Aslan's country forms a major element in the novel. Despite an early set-to with Eustace, Reepicheep becomes his best companion when the disagreeable boy turns into a dragon. In his altered state Eustace sees Aslan coming to him in the moonlight, and is restored to his former shape, much improved in personality. He thinks he has dreamed, but the others assure him of the reality of his experience.

Lucy is given one vision in this novel, in the Magician Coriakin's house, where, fearfully climbing to the second floor, she tiptoes along the hall past a series of doors.

> After about the sixth door she got her first real fright. For one second she felt almost certain that a wicked little bearded face had popped out of the wall and made a grimace at her. She forced herself to stop and look at it. And it was not a face at all. It was a little mirror just the size and shape of her

> own face, with hair on the top of it and a beard hanging down from it, so that when you looked in the mirror your own face fitted into the hair and beard and it looked as if they belonged to you. "I just caught my own reflection with the tail of my eye as I went past," said Lucy to herself. "That was all it was. It's quite harmless." But she didn't like the look of her own face with that hair and beard, and went on. (VDT 159-60; ch. 10)

Lewis, as narrator, remarks, "(I don't know what the Bearded Glass was for because I am not a magician.)" But one might hazard that the magician (an animus figure) and his house represent yet another revelation for Lucy, this time of her own self. The little bearded—that is, masculine—image is Lucy's perception of her own animus. She is going upstairs in a house dominated by male knowledge and power, seeking for the magician's book, by which she hopes to wield that power to make the magician and all in his house and lands become visible. At the moment, the magician is invisible: Neumann says, "The spiritual aspect of the unconscious confronts women as an invisibly stimulating, fructifying, and inspiring male spirit."[29] The Bearded Glass is an image of this disquieting intention. And Lucy does find the book. It contains a host of spells, One, "*to make beautiful her that uttereth it*" (VDT 163; ch. 10) shows Lucy pictures of herself in a state of dazzling beauty, power, and prestige—and in the midst, the face of Aslan appears in warning. "He was growling and you could see most of his teeth" (VDT 165; ch. 10). She is saved, then from the temptation to absolute power. Again, "she came to a spell which would let you know what your friends thought about you" (VDT 165; ch. 10). This time she yields, says the spell, and "as nothing happened she began looking at the pictures" (VDT 165-66; ch. 10), and of course she finds out what her friends think and is sorry at what she learns. Another spell shows her beautiful pictures "for the refreshment of the spirit" (VDT 167; ch. 10); a story "about a cup and a sword and a tree and a green hill," which we would like to be able to read ourselves. At last she finds the spell she is seeking. It is "*A Spell to make hidden things visible*" (VDT 168; ch. 10). She has sought this spell to make the invisible inhabitants of the magician's island visible again. Emma Jung points up the role the magician plays for Lucy: "For the more exacting woman, the animus figure is a man who accomplishes deeds, in the sense that he directs his power toward something of great significance."[30]

The words said, Lucy hears a sound of "soft, heavy footfalls," and turns, her face "almost as beautiful as that other Lucy in the picture" (VDT 169; ch. 10) to see "Aslan himself, The Lion, the highest of all High Kings."

> "Oh, Aslan," said she, "it was kind of you to come."
>
> "I have been here all the time," said he, "but you have just made me visible."
>
> "Aslan!" said Lucy almost a little reproachfully, "Don't make fun of me. As if anything I could do would make *you* visible!"
>
> "It did," said Aslan. "Do you think I wouldn't obey my own rules?" (VDT 169-70; ch. 10)

At the same time, the Dufflepuds have been made visible along with their master, the magician Coriakin.

The novel continues its account of the voyage, which concludes with the supernal vision, for Reepicheep, Eustace, and
Lucy have "the privilege of seeing the last things" (VDT 232; ch. 14). As usual Lucy sees the most—"'Look,' she said," and it is the sea people, so beautiful the sailors cannot be allowed to see them. Again, "'Look!' said Lucy, who was in the stern of the boat. She held up her wet arms full of white petals and broad flat leaves" (VDT 257; ch. 16) and they are in the Lily Lake, the Silver Sea. Reepicheep's coracle runs up the final wave of this ultimate sea, and Lucy and Eustace reach the shore of Aslan's country, where they see a lamb "so white on the green grass that even with their eagles' eyes they could hardly look at it" (VDT 267; ch. 16). The Lamb becomes Aslan, "scattering light from his mane" (VDT 269; ch. 16), who sends them back to England, where he has "another name," by which they are to learn to know him, for they are now too old to return to Narnia.

There are four more Narnian books, however. In *The Silver Chair*, it is Jill Pole who first sees Aslan. She has already seen the edge of a terrible cliff, over which Eustace has fallen. "Some huge, brightly colored animal" (SC 17; ch. 1) rushes to blow the falling boy safely down into Narnia. "So she turned and looked at the creature. It was a lion" (SC 18; ch. 1). Aslan sends her after Eustace to look for a series of signs which lead, when correctly recognized, to Prince Rilian, hidden in the Narnian underworld. Jill is thus made the guide for her companions, including Puddleglum the Marsh-wiggle. The underground journey is suggested in *That Hideous Strength* as Jane twice enters the souterraine or underground passage to Merlin's tomb: in *The Silver Chair*, as John D. Cox has pointed out in his sensitive essay, "Epistemological Release in *The Silver Chair*" (1977), the journey to the Underworld is the major theme.[31] In making this journey, Jill is the leader. Psyche makes the same journey in the original myth of Eros and Psyche: in *Till We Have Faces* the underground journey is described as Orual experiences it, for she too is Psyche, and she is also Ungit; Ungit is the Mother Goddess, Aphrodite/Venus, and one recalls that the Goddess Inanna visited the Underworld at the behest of her sister, its goddess/ruler, Ereshkigal, and that the Goddess Demeter's daughter, Persephone, rules there for half of every year. In fact, Persephone offers Psyche food when she travels there in her turn, and Psyche, in order to return, refuses.[32] The pomegranate was the food which, eaten by Persephone, confined her for half a year to Hades.[33]

There is a girl in *The Horse and His Boy*, Aravis, who accompanies Shasta, the novel's hero. She too becomes the guide, not because she has seen a vision, but because her horse (a mare) knows the way. Shasta and Aravis are drawn together on a moonlit night—"the moonlight, astonishingly bright, showed up everything almost as if it were broad day" (HB 28; ch. 2) by the roars of a lion who is ultimately revealed to be Aslan. We have already noted the tendency of Aslan to be manifested by moonlight. Aravis rides Hwin, a talking mare who is a native of Narnia. Hwin is humble, but wise, and she aids her humans and the stallion Bree who is Shasta's mount in disguising themselves to pass through the city of Tashbaan on the way to Narnia. Aravis is given an encounter with Aslan but it is a terrible one, for she is dealt deep scratches in recompense for a whipping she had caused her servant girl to suffer when she first started out for Narnia. Afterwards Aravis is recovering in the enclosure of the Hermit of the Southern March, when by looking into a pool he (an animus figure with a long white beard) reveals to Aravis and Hwin all that is happening to Shasta, now become Prince Cor. At the end, Aslan comes leaping into the enclosure; Hwin goes to him immediately, full of trust, and the repentant Aravis learns who has wounded her, and is forgiven.

In *The Magician's Nephew*, the girl is Polly; she is the friend of Digory, in whose house the wardrobe leading to Narnia is one day to stand. Polly finds Digory crying, and he shows her his secret play-room under the eaves of a garret. With a candle they set out to explore because it occurs to Polly that they "could get into the other houses" of the row (MN 9; ch. 1). And they do. They find a door, and "Polly's curiosity got the better of her. She blew out her candle and stepped out into the strange room" (MN 12; ch. 1): it is the room of Digory's Uncle Andrew, a would-be magician. The old man tricks them into serving as subjects for his latest experiment. And it is Polly who is sent by this maladroit animus figure into another world, or rather, into "The Wood Between the Worlds" (MN 31; ch. 3). When Digory is sent after her, they go together into Charn, where despite Polly's warnings, Digory awakens the witch Jadis, who is for him, as for Edmund in *The Lion, the Witch and the Wardrobe*, a malign anima figure. She follows the children back to England where she is more than a match for Uncle Andrew. Through the magician's fault, both pairs find their way into Narnia, along with a horse and cabby; there they witness the creation of Narnia by Aslan. In a sense the "Fall" of Narnia has already occurred, and is the result of proceeding (against warnings) by two male figures, Digory and Uncle Andrew. Aslan sends Digory and Polly flying on the newly-winged cab horse to a sacred garden, where they obtain an apple by which Digory's mother is cured of an otherwise fatal illness, and we learn how the lamp-post was planted in Narnia: it grew in the supernaturally fertile soil of its newly-created earth from a fragment the witch has brought with her from England.

In *The Last Battle* help comes to Prince Tirian from England when he sees the seven friends of Narnia—those who have been transported there at one time or another—gathered around a table: and in a moment Eustace and Jill come to his aid. Again Jill plays a role as guide—"It was Jill who set them right again: she had been an excellent Guide in England. And of course she knew her Narnian stars perfectly, having traveled so much in the wild Northern Lands" (LB 69; ch. 6).[34] She wins the admiration of Tirian for her skills. Jill leads

Tirian to the brink of a hill within sight of a stable in which the false Aslan (an ass in lion's clothing) is hiding.

> "Well done," said Tirian to Jill. She had shown him exactly what he needed to know.
>
> They got up and Tirian now took the lead.
>
> (LB 70; ch. 6)

Later in the novel, all the former child visitors to Narnia, now its everlasting Kings and Queens, reappear to Tirian. Lucy is among them. "Lucy led the way and soon they could all see the Dwarfs" (LB 164; ch. 13). The Dwarfs, unlike the seeress Lucy, are blinded. That is, they cannot, or will not, see the salvation offered them.

> "Are you blind?" said Tirian.
>
> "Ain't we all blind in the dark!" said Diggle.
>
> "But it isn't dark, you poor stupid Dwarfs," said Lucy. "Can't you see? Look up! Look round! Can't you see the sky and the trees and the flowers? Can't you see *me*?
>
> (LB 165; ch. 13)

But it is no use. Just in that moment,

> A brightness flashed behind them. All turned. Tirian turned last because he was afraid. There stood his heart's desire, huge and real, the golden Lion, Aslan himself." (LB 167; ch. 13)

Yet even Aslan cannot make the Dwarfs see what they will not.

The visionary role of Lucy is repeated in the final episode of the novel and of the Narnian Chronicles as a series:

> "I see," she said at last, thoughtfully. "I see now. This garden is like the stable. It is far bigger inside than it was outside." (LB 206; ch. 16)

And again:

> "I see," she said. "This is still Narnia [...] I see ... world within world, Narnia within Narnia ... (LB 207; ch. 16)

And finally:

> And Lucy looked this way and that and soon found that a new and beautiful thing had happened to her. Whatever she looked

> at, however far away it might be, once she had fixed her eyes steadily on it, became quite clear and close as if she were looking through a telescope." (LB 207; ch. 16)

She sees the whole of Narnia laid out and now eternally linked to Aslan's Country.

> [...] she at once cried out, "Peter! Edmund! Come and look! Come quickly." And they came and looked, for their eyes also had become like hers. (LB 208; ch. 16)

One is reminded of Beatrice, who said to Dante on the outskirts of Paradise, "*Guardaci ben: ben sem, ben sem Beatrice*" ("Look on us well; we are indeed, we are Beatrice,"[35] but who, in Paradise itself, fades from his view, leaving him to contemplate the beatific vision directly, having guided him there from afar since her first salute as a child in Florence. Lucy's companions no longer see through a glass darkly, but face to face, for they see Aslan as he is:

> And as He spoke He no longer looked to them like a lion; but the things that began to happen after that were so great and beautiful that I cannot write them (LB 210; ch. 16).

The visionary women in Lewis's fiction depend on the divine—on each narrative's equivalent for God—for their visions. Jane Studdock, the reluctant dreamer whose visions lead her to the presence of God, in her turn leads her husband Mark to salvation. Lucy, the mystical visionary; Jill, the perceptive guide; Aravis, the valiant warrior-maiden; and Polly, the befriender and companion; all these too find the ultimate source and goal of all vision in the divine character of Aslan. Lewis's conception of the visionary woman thus finds its ultimate expression in the Godhead; for him, as in Kabbalistic mysticism, the light of God—his glory, the Shekhinah—is feminine.[36]

Notes

1 John Dean, *The White House Years: Blind Ambition* (New York: Simon and Schuster, 1976) 213.
2 Dean 216.
3 Dean 216.

Notes

[4] Irene Claremont de Castillejo, *Knowing Woman: A Feminine Psychology* (New York: Putnam's Sons for the C.G. Jung Foundation for Analytical Psychology, 1973) 67.

[5] M. Esther Harding, *The Way of All Women* (New York: Harper and Row, 1970/Colophon Edition, 1975) 26.

[6] C. S. Lewis, "Sometimes Fairy Stories May Say Best What's To Be Said," *Of Other Worlds: Essays and Stories,* ed. Walter Hooper (New York: New York: Harcourt Brace Jovanovich, 1966) 36.

[7] C. S. Lewis, "On three ways of writing for children," *Of Other Worlds: Essays and Stories*, ed. Walter Hooper (New York: New York: Harcourt Brace Jovanovich, 1966) 32.

[8] Emma Jung, "On the Nature of the Animus," *Animus and Anima* (Zurich: Spring Publications, 1957/1972) 12.

[9] Emma Jung 13.

[10] Emma Jung 13.

[11] Emma Jung 27.

[12] Emma Jung 28.

[13] Emma Jung 29.

[14] Bram Stoker, *Dracula* (1897; New York: Bantam Classic, 1981) 374; ch. XXVI.

[15] Erich Neumann, *The Great Mother,* Bollingen Series XLVII (Princeton, NY: Princeton UP, 1955) 295.

[16] Stoker 398; ch. XXVII.

[17] Robert A. Johnson, *She: Understanding Feminine Psychology* (New York: Perennial Library, Harper and Row, 1977) 69.

[18] Emma Jung 20.

[19] Neumann 296.

[20] Emma Jung 17.

[21] Emma Jung 17.

[22] Sheldon Vanauken, *A Severe Mercy, With Letters by C. S. Lewis* (San Francisco, CA: Harper and Row, 1977) 209; (Bantam Edition, 1979) 211. Abbreviations in original, based upon calligraphic practices characteristic of Lewis.

[23] Nancy-Lou Patterson, "The Host of Heaven: Astrological and Other Images of Divinity in the Fantasies of C. S. Lewis," a paper read before Mythcon VIII, The annual conference of the Mythopoeic

Notes

Society, San Diego, CA, 1977. [Editor's note: see *Mythlore* 7.3 (Autumn 1980): 19-27; and 7.4 (Winter 1981): 13-21; and the paper in this volume 93-144.]

[24] C. Kerenyi, *Eleusis, Archetypal Image* of *Mother* and *Daughter* (New York: Bollingen Foundation/Pantheon Books, 1967) 134.

[25] Johnson 27.

[26] Frances Hodgson Burnett, *The Secret Garden* (1911; New York: J. B. Lippincott Co., 1938/1949) 37.

[27] Neumann 296.

[28] M. Esther Harding, *Women's Mysteries: Ancient and Modern* (Boston, MA: Shambhala Publications, 1971) 114.

[29] Neumann 294.

[30] Emma Jung 3.

[31] John D. Cox, "Epistemological Release in *The Silver Chair*," *The Longing for* a *Form,* ed. Peter J. Schakel (Kent State, OH: Kent State UP, 1977) 163.

[32] Johnson 64.

[33] Kerenyi 134.

[34] By "Guide in England" Lewis means a Girl Guide, as Girl Scouts are called in Britain (and Canada).

[35] Dante Alighieri, *The Comedy Divine of Dante Alighieri, The Florentine*, Cantica II Purgatory, trans. Dorothy L. Sayers (Harmondsworth, UK: Penguin Books, 1955) XXX: 73.

[36] Gershom G. Scholem, *Major Trends in* Jewish Mysticism (New York: Schocken Books, 1961), see especially 225-230. Scholem remarks that Kabbalism was a doctrine for and by men, lacking the women mystics such as Mechthild of Madgeburg, Juliana of Norwich, and Teresa de Jesus who are so characteristic of Christianity (37). These profound mysteries are further implied in the phrase: "In thy light shall we see light." *Psalm* 36.9, *The Book of Common* Prayer. *The Jerusalem Bible* has "by your light we see the light," and the King James version, for once, agrees with the Prayer Book.

10. "Some Women" in *That Hideous Strength*

"We are four men, some women, and a bear."

——C.S. Lewis, *That Hideous Strength*

Patterson refutes criticism of C.S. Lewis's androcentricism in That Hideous Strength *by arguing that readers have a choice in how they understand the contradictory aspects of Lewis's characterizations of women and their relationships with men. She provides a detailed analysis of the sentence "We are four men, some women, and a bear," placing it in relation to Western cultural practice in general and the Bible in particular. Her favored interlocutor is Elisabeth Schüssler Fiorenza.*

This paper was first published in Pilgrimage of the Toronto C.S. Lewis Society *1.1 (Jan. 1994) 1-7. It is included here as an extension of the discussion Patterson began in "The Host of Heaven" and "Some Kind of Company" about C.S. Lewis's representation of the hierarchy of being. More specifically, it addresses Lewis's representation of women and the feminine, also taken up by Patterson in the other papers in this section.*

In her study, *The Fiction of C.S. Lewis, Mask and Mirror* (1993), Kath Filmer, an Australian scholar, critic, writer, and journalist, devotes three chapters to attitudes toward the women in C.S. Lewis's fiction. "He gives full range to his misogyny," she writes forcefully, "in *That Hideous Strength.*"[1] She has already stated that in his writing, "There is no attempt to show women [...] who are simply intelligent and highly competent,"[2] that he equates "higher things" with "obedience to men,"[3] and that for him women are "either temptresses or goddesses."[4] In fact *That Hideous Strength* does depict intelligent and competent women; it calls for obedience in a number of situations, one of which involves not "men" in general, but husbands in particular; and, while there are no temptresses in the novel, there is indeed a goddess, Perelandra (or Venus).

Filmer's most potent indictment of Lewis is expressed in the following passage, to which my paper will be confined and dedicated:

> [...] in *That Hideous Strength*, C.S. Lewis tells readers that the Company at St. Anne's consisted of 'four men, some women, and a bear.' [...] Women do not merit a numerical record; their individuality and their contribution is diminished by the collective 'some.'[5]

The phrase "Lewis tells readers" both is and is not accurate. Of course Lewis is telling the story, and of course the whole novel says exactly what Lewis wants it to say. But the quoted line—"We are four men, some women, and a bear" (THS 289; ch. 13)—is spoken by a character in the novel, Elwin Ransom, an interplanetary-traveling Cambridge don, or as he is styled in particular, Mr. Fisher-King, the Pendragon of Logres, and the Director of the Company of St. Anne's. Merlin, who has returned from his long sleep to a mid-twentieth century Britain, where humanity is under direct diabolical attack, asks Ransom, "are we not big enough to meet them in plain battle?" It is to this question that Ransom gives his rueful reply about the number of his warriors, whom he counts as "four men, some woman, and a bear."

Margaret Hannay (1981), another and in my opinion a better feminist commentator on *That Hideous Strength*, describes the Company more accurately as "an odd assortment of professors, housewives, gardeners, and *eldila*."[6] The *eldila* are angels, in this case planetary intelligences, in other words, the armies of heaven, with whose aid the little company in fact succeeds in defeating the forces of the N.I.C.E., whose secret leaders are devils, and whose own forces are recruits mostly more, and in a few cases, less, under diabolical control. Lewis is quite explicit about the members of the N.I.C.E., as he describes eight major characters who meet defeat at the hands of Merlin, the *eldila*, certain animals who had been kept by the N.I.C.E. for vivisection, and one animal, the aforementioned "bear," who is the only member of the Company of St. Anne's to meet these adversaries in open combat.

Of those eight villains killed, seven are men, and only one is a woman, Fairy Hardcastle, a harshly and potently portrayed lesbian who is the head of the N.I.C.E. secret police. I do not defend Lewis's grotesquely stereotyped portrayal, which is unquestionably offensive, but I do call attention to her singularity. A description of the N.I.C.E. would have to list "seven men, one woman, and uncounted macrobes," Lewis's word for devils. Their behavior, vividly detailed by Lewis in the novel, is echoed in an interview by John Le Carre (1993), "It is actually only very excited, over-stimulated men on very short sleep, together with all the toys of supersecrecy and the helicopters and the special passes, that inevitably produce irrational behaviour."[7] This is the N.I.C.E. in a nutshell.

My own critical ground is based on Elisabeth Schüssler Fiorenza's study *But She Said: Feminist Practices of Biblical Interpretation* (1992). Schüssler Fiorenza describes a "theory of language" that "understands language as a tool which enables readers to negotiate and create meanings in specific contexts and situations. Consequently, it consciously asserts the interpreter's agency, subjecthood, contextuality, particularity, stance, and perspective. It does not focus, therefore, on the androcentric linguistic medium but on the practice of reading."[8] In other words, I am going to treat the text of *That Hideous Strength* the way I have always read it, over and over, since I first encountered it in the 1950s. It is my favorite book, not only by C.S. Lewis, but my favorite by any author for adults.

Schüssler Fiorenza describes succinctly the philosophical base of an androcentric—male-centered—point of view, the one that not only C.S. Lewis but nearly every other male in Western culture has been taught, and she describes the social organization that results from this intellectual structure. "In the analogical argument of Greek philosophy, the chain 'Greek–male–human' represents culture, whereas that of 'barbarian–woman–animal' represents nature."[9] Barbarians, which means nearly everybody who is not a Greek, are seen as being in opposition to Greeks, women to men, and animals to humans, in these analogical sets, which results, you will note, in the ultimate opposition of nature to culture, and the clear implication to Greeks, who thought barbarians were inferior to Greeks, women were inferior to men, and animals were inferior to humans, that nature was inferior to culture. The present devastated state of our planet can be traced directly to this point of view.

Ransom's troops, the members of the Company of St. Anne's, on the other hand, are composed of "four men, some women, and a bear"—men, women, and an animal. In fact there are a number of animals at St. Anne's, not only Mr. Bultitude the bear, but a community of mice, Pinch the cat, and Baron Corvo the raven, who are joined at the end of the novel by many of the animals who escape from the N.I.C.E. There is also an impressive collection of flowers and vegetables in the form of magnificently described gardens which fill the grounds of St. Anne's Manor. Camilla Denniston, one of the "some women" Ransom mentions, defines the Company as "this house, all of us here, and Mr Bultitude and Pinch" (THS 192; ch. 9), thus incorporating even the house into the group. MacPhee, the gardener and resident skeptic of St. Anne's, says the Director thinks "we're going to defeat a powerful conspiracy by sitting here growing winter vegetables and training performing bears" (THS 189; ch. 9), but even he calls the Company's members "colleagues," which seems to include the whole range of being, animate and, if there is such a thing, inanimate.

This brings me to the possible point Lewis was trying to make by including mineral, vegetable, animal, human, and *eldilic*: that all creation is related in an hierarchical chain which places humans "between the angels who are our elder brothers and the beasts who are our jesters, servants and playfellows" (THS 376; ch. 17). Lewis often referred to Plato, and Schüssler Fiorenza says that "Plato rearticulates the analogical argument [...] into the hierarchy of 'the great chain of being,'"[10] a concept of which Lewis was extremely fond. This pattern takes the Greek notion of sets of opposites and places them in a sequence from the least to the most, not in a set of equal links as in a real chain, and as, I should imagine, the passionate environmentalist would desire to do. For Aristotle, Schüssler Fiorenza continues, the "rhetorical model" was "the patriarchal household in which wives, children, slaves, and property were owned by and at the disposal of the freeborn Greek male head of household."[11] If you think the Greeks were the only people who thought in these terms, I call your attention to a verse from Thomas Carlyle's translation of Martin Luther's great hymn *Ein' feste Burg*, usually translated as "A Mighty Fortress":

> And though they take our life,
> Goods, honour, children, wife,
> Yet is their profit small;
> These things shall vanish all,
> The city of God remaineth, Amen.

This is Hymn 405 of the Anglican Church of Canada hymnal, and it suggests in the strongest terms that the "we" implied is men, and that their possessions, listed in descending order, are "Goods, honour, children, wife," all willingly let go in favor of their owner's even higher desire.

The situation described here is what Schüssler Fiorenza calls "the politics of submission,"[12] and there is no doubt that some passages in *That Hideous Strength* seem to come dangerously close to sounding as if that is what C.S. Lewis was recommending. According to Schüssler Fiorenza, early Christianity was an "emancipatory" movement. She speaks of "the notion of the *ekklēsia*"—the Church—"as a community of friends."[13] The contradiction of such ideas with the Greek context of expanding Christianity is, according to Schüssler Fiorenza, not just an historical phase or period but "a struggle that is still going on." What she describes as "this classical contradiction between 'the politics of patriarchal submission' and the 'equality of all citizens' surfaced in the first century C.E. with the revival of Aristotelian philosophy which was directed toward emancipatory movements"[14] including those of the early church. A major example of teachings which are opposed to the "community of friends" are "Paul's incipient patriarchal rhetoric"[15] especially in his two Letters to the Corinthians with their texts requiring women to resume the veil and to refrain from speaking and prophesying in church.

Schüssler Fiorenza proposes to read the New Testament "in terms of the 'contradiction'" between these two modes, and I find the same "contradiction" between the "politics of submission" and the "community of friends," along with the same opportunity to choose one's own reading, in the text of *That Hideous Strength*. Lewis, like the writers of the New Testament, exhibits both of these on-going elements of Christian thought. It is as if he wrote with both halves of his brain. Some observers have suggested that he had a "rational" mind that argued by logic and another "imaginative" mind that expressed itself through story and image. I don't care much for arguments based on oppositions because they tend to lead toward demonization of one of the two terms. Instead, I approach the text, and in particular the passage using the words "some women," as Schüssler Fiorenza approaches the New Testament, by reading beyond the androcentric surface which Lewis breathed in with his education, to see what inklings of the community of friends I can find.

First of all, I don't think the phrase "some women" was used either as an empty expression or as a diminution of women. Lewis is quite capable of precision in regard to the number of females in a scene when he speaks as narrator. For instance, he writes of "Dimble, who had been sitting with his face drawn, and rather white, between the white faces of the two women" (THS 225; ch. 10). Lewis has already named these women and has gone on to speak of Dimble. When he gives Ransom the phrase "some women" he is being, I think, allusive. He is probably alluding to Scripture.

The dictionary defines "some" as an adjective, and in Lewis's phrase "some women," the adjective "some" modifies the noun "women." "Some" is taken from the Old English *sum*, meaning "a certain one," derived from the Indo-European base which also produced "same." Thus, the word "some" is defined as meaning "a certain one or ones not specified," or as "of a certain unspecified ... number." In *That Hideous Strength*, the unspecified number is actually five. The interplay of "some" and "certain" suggests that the terms are interchangeable, and a look at the New Testament persuades me that Lewis's allusion is to the custom of numbering, as well as naming, the males, usually called apostles, and not numbering or, in most cases, naming (let alone identifying as apostles) the females who followed Jesus during his earthly ministry. The most potent of these passages, and the model, I think, for the Pentecostal moment when the planetary angels from "deep heaven" descend with their powers upon men and women alike at St. Anne's Manor, is the description in Acts 1.13-14 of the events just prior to the coming of the Holy Spirit upon the newly born Church:

> When they had entered the city, they went to the room upstairs where they were staying, Peter, and John, and James, and Andrew, Philip and Thomas, Bartholomew and Matthew, James son of Alpheus, and Simon the Zealot, and Judas son of James. All these were constantly devoting themselves to prayer, together with certain women, including Mary, the mother of Jesus, as well as his brothers.

This translation is from the New Revised Standard Version; the King James Version reads, "the women." Here, a very significant woman is specifically named, almost like a counterbalance to the long list of males.

On the other hand, here is Luke 24.22, "Yea, and certain women also of our company made us astonished, which were early at the sepulchre." The translation here is from the King James Version; the New Revised Standard Version gives it as "some women"! You will notice the presence in this passage of the phrase "our company." Lewis never did anything without a purpose! In fact, Luke is a symphony of variations on this theme: "And all his acquaintance, and the women that followed him from Galilee, stood afar off, beholding these things" (Luke 23.49 KJV); "and the women also, which came with him from Galilee, followed after, and beheld the sepulchre, and how his body was laid" (Luke 23.55 KJV); and finally, this time naming names, "It was Mary Magdalene, and Joanna, and Mary the mother of James, and other women that were with them, which told these things unto the apostles" (Luke 24.10 KJV).

If the Company of St. Anne is indeed a figure for the Church, is the Church portrayed by Lewis "as a community of friends" or as based upon "the politics of submission"? In order to consider this question, I will review the members of the Company. As the story opens, it involves five people: Ransom, who owns the house through a bequest from his sister; his resident doctor, Grace Ironwood; his resident gardener, Andrew MacPhee; and a young couple, Arthur and Camilla Denniston, who are sent to try to persuade Jane Studdock to join them. Of these five people, Ransom, Miss Ironwood, and MacPhee are all unmarried; the Dennistons are husband and wife. In the course of the novel they are joined by four more married couples, of whom Margaret and Cecil Dimble come first and together. Ivy Maggs comes next, to be joined by her husband Tom next to last, followed by Jane Studdock, whose husband Mark arrives last of all, and, before the arrival of these tardy husbands, the magus Merlin, who like Ransom and his two aides, is not married.

This makes a full household of twelve, four single people and four couples. At the end, the Company consists of ten people, because Ransom and Merlin have been each in their own way taken up into heaven. The final Company contains an exact gender balance of five men and five women. Whether they stay together is not made clear but there is a very strong suggestion that some—perhaps most, even all—of them will. When Filmer says "there is no attempt to show women [...] who are simply intelligent and highly competent," this is simply not true. Grace Ironwood, the doctor, is eminently in possession of these qualities, but all of the women are described as persons of significant gifts and capabilities, including Jane, the seeress. Only the two late-arriving men, Tom, a thief and released prisoner, and Mark, a near traitor, are shown to be less than competent at their chosen fields, and they both arrive at the house as successful penitents, a category of person that Jesus was willing to admit to Paradise from the cross.

The reasons for the adherence of these persons to their self-chosen Company are complex. Of the two most powerful persons, those who finally withdraw, Ransom has come because of a woman—his sister, and Merlin has come because of a man—Ransom. One woman and one man came independently, each of them through a relationship, perhaps professional, with Ransom. Two women come to St. Anne's because of their husbands: Camilla Denniston and Margaret Dimble; their husbands obviously came because of Ransom. Two men come because of their wives: Mark Studdock to Jane and Tom Maggs to Ivy. Jane came because of Grace Ironwood, and Ivy, through some connection to the other characters: she was Jane's "daily" or part-time housekeeper and I think she may also have worked for the Dimbles. Jane, Ivy, and the Dimbles are all in their ways refugees from the depredations of the N.I.C.E., as are, in their ways, Mark and Tom. The relationship between all these people is strongly democratic, with the servant Maggs and the gardener MacPhee present in positions of full equality.

What, then, has caused the sharp response given to this book by Kath Filmer? Clearly her quarrel is not specifically with Lewis's use of the phrase "some women." Rather, she deeply disapproves of Ransom's requirement of "obedience" in marriage, and, in a world of local equality but ultimate hierarchy, in all relationships. As with "some" and "certain," which seem to be equivalent but also skip between the opposites unspecific and specific identities, the dictionary presents deeply ambiguous and oppositional definitions of "obedience." Obedience is defined as "obeying" and as "submission." Its synonyms are "docile, tractable, compliant, and amenable." In *That Hideous Strength*, the members of the Company are anything but these! They are all in their ways individual, feisty, independent, fully developed people whose agreement is given from positions either of personal or of genuine need, even in some cases with deep reluctance. The word "submit" suggested by the dictionary as an equivalent for "obey" gives several senses which are closer to the behavior of the people of St. Anne's, even though its echoes of "submissive" would at first suggest otherwise. "Submit" can mean the following: "to present or refer to others for decision or consideration; to yield to the action, control, power [...] of another; to offer as an opinion, suggest, propose; and only finally, to be submissive, obedient, humble."

I rather suspect that affairs at St. Anne's were as Lewis thought they ought to be at a truly well arranged academic institution; he devotes a portion of his first chapter to showing how Bracton College's affairs are ill-arranged, and to the consequences, all unsuspected, of the way they make their decisions. I spent most of my adult life as an academic, and found quite a range of forms of behavior for which the word "submit" would be appropriate in the various senses I have outlined above, but in my personal behavior at any of the universities of my experience, I was never submissive, obedient, or humble, nor was I asked to be. The same can be said for St. Anne's Manor. The sense in general is of people living cooperatively in the presence of a leader with whom they have cast their common lot. They are constantly engaged in consultation, discussion, analysis, shared life, group participation, and mutual aid.

The crucial scene in the novel for this subject takes place during Jane's first interview with Ransom. As she describes her unhappy marriage to him, she suddenly experiences "a novel sense of her own injustice and even of pity for her husband" (THS 144; ch. 7). She has never been, in their sexual relationship, welcoming and responsive to him, but instead has been withdrawn and reluctant, admittedly in the face of his clumsy and importunate approaches to her. Ransom points out that "obedience—humility—is an erotic necessity" (THS 146; ch. 7). Strong stuff, but true for both partners. The completely successful physical expression of erotic love does require willing participation and a considerate attention to one's partner. Ransom explains that "obedience [is ...] more like a dance than a drill—specially between man and woman where the roles are always changing" (THS 147; ch. 7). In my experience of a marriage which began in 1951, this has been true in every aspect of the relationship. There is a later conversation on this subject between Jane and Margaret Dimble, a long-married woman, which Filmer does not quote; Jane says:

> "I think that what's puzzling me is that when I saw [the Director…] he said something about equality not being the important thing. But his own house seems to be run on—well on very democratic lines indeed."
>
> "I never attempt to understand what he says on that subject," said Mother Dimble. "He's usually talking either about spiritual ranks—and you were never goose enough to think yourself *spiritually* superior to Ivy—or else about marriage."
>
> "Did you understand his views on marriage?"
>
> "My dear the Director is a very wise man. But he *is* a man, after all, and an unmarried man at that. Some of what he says […] about marriage does seem to me to be a lot of fuss about something so simple and natural that it oughtn't to need saying at all" (THS 165; ch. 8).

In my opinion the whole book is directed toward these interlocked and complementary concepts of equality and reciprocity in social relationships and in marriage as a dance of mutual and shared obedience.

Fully half of *That Hideous Strength* is told from the point of view of Jane Studdock, and the story begins with her meditation upon matrimony, "ordained," as she remembers, "for the mutual society, help, and comfort that the one ought to have of the other" (THS 11; ch. 1). The thesis of the book is thus set forth, that marriage ought to be a state of mutuality. On the first page we conclude that the relations between Jane and her husband Mark are strained; on the last page, Jane is again the subject, and the whole story of the book is reprised, as, walking toward her reunion with a greatly chastened and humbled young man who awaits her arrival with bashful hope, she is said to be "descending the ladder of humility" too (THS 380; ch. 17). She is descending, that is, from the organization he described, which is based on a hierarchy of authorities and levels of mastery and obedience. But the passage itself subverts its apparent structure.

Jane thinks first of "the Director," the man called Ransom, whose community she has at last joined willingly because through him she has encountered wonder. She thinks next of "Maleldil," which is the name used in *That Hideous Strength* for God. Her contact with Ransom has led to her contact with God, in which she has known herself as a created being, contingent and dependent. This novel contains a number of extremely convincing and insightful depictions of women, not least that of Jane, but in the passage in which Jane encounters God, we have, not the woman's experience, but the man's; in fact, the experience of C.S. Lewis himself. He several times wrote that all people are feminine in relationship to God, which in an androcentric model gives a certain spin to the relationship between divinity and humanity.

She is on her way to rejoin the husband who has already been sent to await her, and, in this situation, "she thought of children, and of pain and death," in short of the whole human inheritance, and in particular of the way of women. "And now she was half-way to the lodge, and thought of Mark and of all his sufferings" (THS 380; ch. 17). Meditation upon God, then upon the human condition, and finally, last of all, upon her husband; this is the descent of her ladder of humility, with Mark as least and last, and hence, in Christian terms, the one most immediately in need of her "society, help, and comfort." This model for human relationship echoes that described in Matthew: "just as you did it to one of the least of these who are members of my family, you did it to me" (Matthew 25.40 NRSV).

If marriage is—and Lewis says so—a model of the soul's relationship with God, what would a marriage based on reciprocity tell us about the relationship between God and humankind? For that, I will look to a letter written by another major twentieth century Christian novelist, Dorothy L. Sayers, written in 1946 and first published in 1993:

> God is a Person from the beginning (the same Person that was manifested as a man in Christ), and He has made us persons in His own image […] He wants to call us His friends […]; we are privileged to stand with Him on terms of mutuality and exchange …"[16]

This is what Elisabeth Schüssler Fiorenza means by "a community of friends," and this is the picture offered by the Company of St. Anne's in *That Hideous Strength*. A Church based on this concept has from the time of Jesus's earthly life been struggling to emerge. Lewis's book, framed by the ancient structures of hierarchy, nevertheless expresses, in the interaction of its characters, a glimpse of that Church and a call for a relationship between women and men, and between God and humanity, which could truly be called a community of friends. Or so I've always read him.

Notes

[1] Kath Filmer, *The Fiction of C.S. Lewis, Mask and Mirror* (New York: St. Martin's Press, 1993) 99.
[2] Filmer 88.
[3] Filmer 88.
[4] Filmer 89.
[5] Filmer 102.
[6] Margaret Hannay, *C.S. Lewis* (New York: Frederick Unger, 1981) 105.
[7] John Le Carre, interviewed by James Kelly, "We distorted our own minds," *Time* 142.1 (July 1993): 32.
[8] Elisabeth Schüssler Fiorenza's study *But She Said: Feminist Practices of Biblical Interpretation* (Boston, MA: Beacon Press, 1992) 42.
[9] Schüssler Fiorenza 94.
[10] Schüssler Fiorenza 94.
[11] Schüssler Fiorenza 94.
[12] Schüssler Fiorenza 95.
[13] Schüssler Fiorenza 95.
[14] Schüssler Fiorenza 94.
[15] Schüssler Fiorenza 95.
[16] Barbara Reynolds, *Dorothy L. Sayers: Her Life and Soul* (London: Hodder and Stoughton, 1993) 369.

11. Archetypes of the Feminine in *That Hideous Strength*

> Because of those divine meanings in our materials it is impossible we shd. ever know the whole meaning of our own works, and the meaning we never intended may be the best and truest one.
>
> —C.S. Lewis to Sister Penelope, 20 February, 1943

Patterson explores C.S. Lewis's representation of the feminine and masculine in the Space Trilogy, and specifically in That Hideous Strength, *by first clarifying his treatment of gender as metaphors for matter and form, and body and spirit with reference to* Arthurian Torso *and the* Bible. *She then discusses the symbolic pairs of Bracton College and Bragdon Wood, and St. Anne's Manor and garden as archetypes of the feminine that stand in opposition to Belbury and in relation to aspects of Jane and Mark Studdock's character and transformation. Her annotations of these symbolic pairs, which include references to the Chronicles of Narnia, show the garden as an archetype of the center and of wholeness. She concludes that Lewis's much quoted statement about the God that "is so masculine that we are all feminine in relation to it" is fully balanced, if not thoroughly contradicted, by his imaginative development of the feminine in the Space Trilogy. Patterson makes her most explicit use of Jungian terminology in this paper and "Guardici Ben." The last section includes a discussion of the dinner at St. Anne's, which contrasts sharply with the banquet at Belbury analyzed in her paper of the same title.*

This paper was included in Patterson's proposed anthology of papers on Lewis's fiction under the title "The Unfathomable Feminine Principle: Images of Wholeness in That Hideous Strength.*" A slightly altered version was published under the same title in* The Lamp-Post of the Southern California C.S. Lewis Society *9.1-3 (1986): 3-38. Some of the discussion of the Quadrangle in this paper was also published as "On The 'Lady Alice' Quadrangle in* That Hideous Strength,*" in* The Lamp-Post of the Southern California C.S. Lewis Society *9.4 (1986): 22. Parts of the section on St. Anne's were included in the paper "Anti-Babels: Images of the Divine Center in* That Hideous Strength*" in* Mythcon II: Proceedings *(1972): 6-11.*

In *Out of the Silent Planet* C.S. Lewis presents Mars/Malacandra as essentially masculine: it is under the tutelage of a masculine deity and the action there concentrated on the traditionally masculine traits of heroism, intellectuality, creativity, and communication. In *Perelandra*, he presents Venus/Perelandra as a traditionally feminine world, ruled by a feminine deity and populated for almost the whole of the book by an unfallen Eve. The traits of the feminine are shown as those of softness, malleability, rich sensuality, watery unconsciousness, and intuitive and instinctive innocence. While he may have intended to give the feminine this same characteristic Western form in *That Hideous Strength*, the power of the symbol itself emerges in this final novel in all its multivalence and wholeness.

Lewis's use of gender imagery throughout the Space Trilogy may be better understood with reference to *Arthurian Torso*, to which Lewis contributed; the Bible, which Lewis knew well; and the four functions described by C.G. Jung: Thinking, Feeling, Sensation, and Intuition, which elucidate the archetypes that Lewis elaborated on in *That Hideous Strength. Arthurian Torso* has been cited by some to show how much Lewis learned from Charles Williams and by others to show how he misinterpreted him![1] Whatever we may think about such judgments, we can certainly agree that the book reflects Lewis's reading of Williams, and that is what concerns us here. Williams, Lewis says, used in his Arthurian poems "the Greek doctrine that Form is masculine and Matter feminine."[2] This doctrine expresses the fact that "the material of anything, the wood or clay, is full of possibility: the imposition of form makes it into a table or chair, a statue or a cup."[3] This, Lewis says, is "the true significance of Woman."[4] I like to think that Lewis did not mean to say that women—actual human persons of female gender—derived their "true significance" from acting as a sort of clay upon which human men can somehow impose a shape or form. I don't see any possible way, either physical or psychical, in which this could be true. What Lewis meant, I hope, is that "the Greek doctrine that Form is masculine and Matter feminine" is what the concept of Woman stands for in Williams's poems. Lewis goes on to explain: "the body, the world of the senses, is feminine in relation to […] the Spirit."[5] That is, the body and the senses are the material upon which the spirit imposes form.

Why doesn't he say so? Aren't body and spirit or matter and form sufficiently clear without using the metaphor of gender? But of course we cannot see matter unless it has form, and we cannot see spirit unless it is embodied in matter. To have being in our world, the use of the metaphor of gender tells us, matter and form—body and spirit—must be united. When they are divided, as in death, we have only the dissolution of the one and the disappearance of the other. The relationship between the sexes presents us with exactly this situation inside out.

In our world male and female always appear as separate. Only when engaged in sexual union can they be one. And in that situation, from the point of view of the participants, neither can see from the outside what their union—their state of wholeness—is like. Voyeurs are left out: what they see is not what really happens. And real lovers locked in a truly conjugal embrace do not resort to mirrors or similar mechanical contrivances. No: lovers do not see at all in the physical sense, or rather, their bodies do their seeing for them. The union is invisible, even, as it were, spiritual, the kind of seeing which is beyond seeing. The moment when one's femaleness or maleness is truly melded with the other's maleness or femaleness is beyond the capacities of any metaphor but a spiritual one to express it.

It is, then, no surprise that the Scriptures suggest a symbolism of gender in which male and female are, in their nuptial role, truly interchangeable. Isaiah 61.10 (RSV) is a good example of this balanced imagery:

> I will greatly rejoice in the LORD,
> my soul shall exult in my God;
> For he has clothed me with the garments of salvation,
> he has covered me with the robe of righteousness.
> As a bridegroom decks himself with a garland,
> and as a bride adorns herself with her jewels.

The principle of Hebrew poetry, that ideas are presented in matching couplets, in which meanings are reiterated, makes the equality of bridegroom and bride in this passage clear. God gives the "robe of salvation" to bridegroom and bride alike. Indeed, his action in doing so is compared to the act of the bridegroom in decking himself and the bride in adorning herself.

In *Arthurian Torso*, Lewis, who borrowed his bridegroom imagery from what he had learned at Mother Kirk's knee, commented on the meaning of female imagery:

> In the soft fertile earth of the ploughed fields, in the waters of sea and river, in shadows and darkness, in the clouds that make sunlight visible while receiving visibility from it, in all that receives, responds, brings forth and is enformed, but most of all in a beautiful and wise woman [...] Nature sets before us for our delight the unfathomable feminine principle.[6]

As C.G. Jung pointed out, all real symbols are reversible; and, just so, the Western imagery of gender emphasized in the Space Trilogy novels can be turned exactly about. Hints concerning the sister and the Sura in India are clues of what is to come, for in certain forms of Hindu symbolism, the female is the image of divine energy and action, and the male is the symbol of divine stability and contemplation. Just as Mars is masculine in *Out of the Silent Planet* and Venus is feminine in *Perelandra*, so Thulcandra–Tellus–Earth combines both genders in *That Hideous Strength* in an image of wholeness, given ultimate embodiment in the *heiros gamos* or sacred wedding of Jane and Mark. In mutual charity and delicately withdrawn beyond the end of the novel, they close the circle of exchange that completes the Trilogy.

In setting forth his vision of wholeness in *That Hideous Strength*, Lewis uses two closely related and balanced symbolic pairs that, in a sense, embody on Earth the same elements that are embodied in the first two novels in outer space, but with one notable difference: the pair he describes first is doomed to destruction.[7] Bragdon Wood lies adjacent to Bracton College and is the secret site of Merlin's tomb. Lewis means us to love this Wood and College, to be distressed by the prospect of their destruction, and to mourn their ultimate loss. They are associated, like Malacandra, with literature, learning, and long years. Nearly all the human names associated with Bracton and Bragdon are masculine, but the College itself, like all Alma Maters, and the Wood, like all woods, are feminine.

The garden and St. Anne's Manor are even more clearly united symbolically,[8] as the feminine—in the form of a garden and a house—is even more emphatically embodied, while the human occupants are almost exactly balanced as regards their gender. Indeed, this household reaches beyond humankind to include animals and angels. Like Perelandra, it is a younger world, full of the potentiality of birth and rebirth. Perhaps it is because of this degree of wholeness that St. Anne's triumphs and survives.

Belbury, temporary headquarters of the N.I.C.E. and the hideous strength of the title, is a third symbolic structure which sets its face, as it were, against both Bracton and St. Anne's. It also has animals, but they are in a laboratory zoo, and angels, who are fallen. Its humans are almost all male. It has a garden, but it is as ugly and artificial as human effort can make it. The Institute knows about and desires to get hold of Bracton College and Bragdon Wood, and in the course of the novel this desire is amply fulfilled. Perhaps the N.I.C.E. would have had worse luck with St. Elizabeth's College, from which Jane Studdock graduated, but of course, that was across the tracks and did not abut on Bragdon Wood! Of St. Anne's, on the other hand, the N.I.C.E. knows nothing. Even as Feverstone carries the hapless Mark toward Belbury, Jane, the woman the Institute seeks, is taking the train to St. Anne's. In *That Hideous Strength*, Belbury stands for the tendency Neil Ribe (1982) has called "the modern scientific world-picture [which] represents an extreme masculinization of nature and a banishing of the feminine. [...] The men of Belbury, by denying nature and the feminine, reap what they have sown and are destroyed."[9]

If we relate the two sets of pairs—Bracton College / Bragdon Wood and St. Anne's Garden / St. Anne's Manor—to Jung's concept of the four functions, and arrange them to accord with the scholarly mind, the mind, in my opinion, of Lewis himself, we create this diagram:

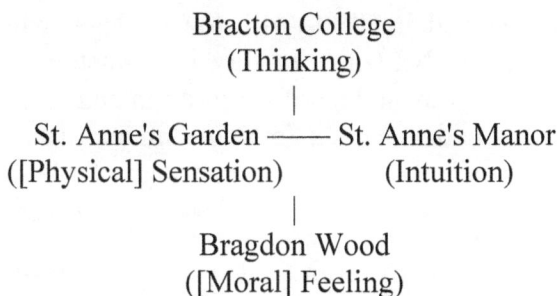

Bracton College
(Thinking)
|
St. Anne's Garden —— St. Anne's Manor
([Physical] Sensation) (Intuition)
|
Bragdon Wood
([Moral] Feeling)

Bracton College presents an image of Thinking, of the intellectual life as Lewis knew and loved it. He was the kind of person for whom Thinking is the superior function, the method by which he consciously met and knew the world. In Bragdon Wood, we see the profoundly didactic morality deeply buried in the psyche, where for a personality in which the superior function is Thinking, Feeling (Jung meant moral judgment) forms the inferior, that is, the hidden function. In Lewis's description, the Wood is full of heroic defenders and is the object of eager moralizers. Its occupant Merlin, whose presence Jane sees by the unconscious route of her dreams, comes up out of his burial chamber as a tremendous psychic force. This is what the inferior function is likely to do.

On the other hand, the Garden of St. Anne's is a symbol of the body: Lewis tells us so himself. Here, it becomes the function of Sensation, one of the two functions that a person with a superior Thinking function will find to be easily managed, perfectly balanced with Intuition. When the intuitive Jane confronts and accepts the physical aspect of herself, through her husband and the sensation-dominated Mark recognizes the value of his profoundly intuitive wife thinking and judgment will become balanced in their lives.

Finally, St. Anne's Manor is an image of Intuition, of the innate capacity for "seeing around corners," to use Jung's phrase. It is full of spirits and animals who know things directly, and its human occupants have assembled spontaneously and freely, each one arriving in the nick of time. The psychological situation expressed in this arrangement is worked out in the plot of the novel, in which an outburst of psychic force or libido emerges from the inferior function of moral Feeling which is buried in the unconscious, and overthrows the excessively rationalized intellect—Bracton College, which has sold itself to the scientistic N.I.C.E. Stability is ultimately re-established by a combination of body and spirit—Sensation and Intuition—which St. Anne's, garden and manor, a feminine image of wholeness, expresses, and for which the new-made marriage of Mark and Jane is the fulfillment.

The Grove of Academe, Bracton College, and Bragdon Wood

I still remember my first reading of the passage describing Bragdon Wood—I was quite ravished by the slow procession through the many enclosing walls and courts to the walled wood with its watery center. Years later, on visiting Oxford, I seemed to be seeing a place already familiar—or rather, to be catching glimpses, though the stones and trees of the real Oxford, of that place of which Bracton College and Bragdon Wood are themselves a symbol. As J.E. Cirlot (1962) says of the forest:

> Within the general symbolism of landscape, forests occupy a notable place, and are often found in myths, legends, and folktales. Forest-symbolism is complex, but it is connected at all levels with the symbolism of the female principle or of the Great Mother. The forest is the place where vegetable life thrives and luxuriates, free from any control or cultivation [...] Since the female principle is identified with the unconscious in Man, it follows that the forest is also a symbol of the unconscious. It is for this reason that Jung maintains that the sylvan terrors that figure so prominently in children's tales symbolize the perilous aspects of the unconscious, that is, its tendency to devour or obscure the reason.[10]

The forest is clearly an ambivalent symbol and Lewis associates it with Merlin, whose magic, formerly neutral, is made the subject of suspenseful anticipation: will he side with the N.I.C.E. as they hope or will he choose the Company of St. Anne's Manor?

Lewis begins the passage in which he describes the Wood:

> Very few people were allowed into Bragdon Wood. The gate was by Inigo Jones and was the only entry: a high wall enclosed the Wood, which was perhaps a quarter of a mile broad and a mile from east to west. If you came in from the street and went through the College to reach it, the sense of gradual penetration into a holy of holies was very strong. (THS 18; ch. 1)

We learn here that the Wood is walled and elongated. Lewis compares it to the most sacred part of the Tabernacle in the Wilderness and of the Temple of Jerusalem, the most sacred part of each of which was reached by a gradual approach through a series of increasingly restricted enclosures.

In saying that the gate is by Inigo Jones (1573–1652), Lewis gives us not only the date of the enclosure but its style, and even, perhaps, a hint of its meaning, which would be that of a perfect moment in the history of architecture. In the late sixteenth century, England was still in the Tudor period: Queen Elizabeth I sat on the throne from 1558 until 1603. When the Tudors began their reign England was essentially medieval; it was Inigo Jones who brought the Renaissance manner in its Palladian form to England. At the Queen's House at Greenwich (1616–1635) and the Banqueting House, Whitehall (1619–1622), he created a "Mediterranean classicism" which was both elegant and pure.[11] Walled woods, of course, predate even the middle ages. In the ancient Near East, for example, the enclosed plantation of trees equaled the enclosed garden in importance as a symbol of Paradise.

Lewis, having described his goal, the walled Bragdon Wood with its Inigo Jones gate, details the approach to this "holy of holies":

> First you went through the Newton quadrangle which is dry and gravelly; florid, but beautiful, Georgian buildings look down upon it. (THS 18; ch. 1)

The narrator's approach to the Wood consists of a series of widenings and narrowings, and passes through a hierarchy of values. The outermost court, like the outer courtyard of the Temple, is most open to the world. In Jerusalem, people could enter and see the burning of sacrifices on the outdoor altar and wash in the great Brazen Sea. But Lewis wishes to be more specific still: he places us in the early eighteenth century in a period which he finds "dry and gravelly."

Sir Isaac Newton (1642–1727), for whom this quadrangle is named, was a student of "natural philosophy." His ideas were developed, in the period after his death, toward applications he might not have approved. Voltaire wrote a study of him, translated into English in 1738, which praised him in terms that suggest science fiction: he dedicates his study to a lady, and asks her;

> How hast Thou dar'd , in spite of Custom's Force,
> To move so boldly, thro' so vast a Course?
> To follow *Newton* in the Boundless Road,
> Where Nature's lost, and ev'ry Thing but God?[12]

This suggests an answer to C.S. Lewis's famous pamphlet, "Will We Lose God in Outer Space?" (1958). One thinks of the Starship Enterprise which "boldly goes where no man has gone before!"

The glossary of Voltaire's work includes a definition of a "Planet" which would have satisfied equally Eustace Scrubbs in *The Voyage of the Dawn Treader*, and the youthful Lewis who wrote so loftily to his friend Arthur Greeves. Voltaire's definition is this:

> PLANET is a dark Globular Body, revolving about the Sun, or some other Planet, which being illuminated by the Sun, appears luminous as the Planets Jupiter, Saturn, Mars, Venus, that appear like fixed Stars, but are not.[13]

So much for the glorious and gleaming planets, whose tutelary Intelligences descend from the heavens in *That Hideous Strength*!

Born on Christmas Day 1642 as the son of a yeoman father who had died two months previously, Newton was baptized on New Year's Day, 1643.[14] He was reared in an austere biblical Anglicanism with a God who was *Dominus*, *Imperator*, and Master, rather like the God of Lewis's own terrible boyhood. A commentator on Newton's religious position says that he "proclaimed his belief in a personal God of commandments with plain words that harked back to the primitive sources of Judaic and Christian religion."[15] In his *Principia*, Newton wrote of God:

> This Being governs all Things, not as a *Soul of the World*, but as *Lord of the Universe*: and upon Account of his Dominion, he is stiled *Lord God*, supreme over all.[16]

For Newton, "the activities of the scientist were subject to moral and religious commandments."[17] Nevertheless he took part in the work which changed the traditional date of Christ's crucifixion,[18] and made his contribution thereby to the shift from a Christological emphasis—toward power, away from love—which was to be the religion of the "scientific age," as one commentator puts it, "a religion of great power and knowledge and precious little love."[19] The devil, like Christ, became diminished in "psychic potency" during Newton's lifetime "leaving God alone in His majesty, with Newton as His interpreter."[20] Oddly, Newton once wrote, in an essay entitled "Of the Day of Judgement and World to Come," "Do Men convers with Beasts and Fishes, or Angels with Men?"[21] Lewis apparently wanted to see what it would be like if they did, in his Space Trilogy.

The eighteenth century religious attitude was based on a kind of "*descriptive* or *observational* science,"[22] in which God is the "Creator or ultimate Efficient Cause." Newton had concluded that concepts or principles could not be observed but only assumed, that science is "an *interpretation* of what was observed." The Enlightenment concluded from these two lines of method that neither God nor divine principles could be proven by science. A commentator on these later derivations of Newton's thought concludes that "For a century [...] Newton the symbol drove thinkers with religious interests to some form of philosophical Idealism."[23] This is the position the young Lewis, newly arrived at Oxford, tried to hold. In *That Hideous Strength*, he characterizes the eighteenth-century world of Georgian thought as "florid but beautiful," and his narrator self does not linger in it.

And the vista he describes narrows: "Next you must enter a cool tunnel-like passage, nearly dark at midday unless either the door into Hall should be open on your right or the buttery hatch on your left, giving you a glimpse of indoor daylight falling on panels, and a whiff of the smell of fresh bread." The "indoor daylight" falls upon the interior of the Hall, where meals were served, and the "smell of fresh bread" came through the buttery hatch from the kitchen where the meals were prepared. Obviously this is a place of refreshment, light, and peace, a little annex to Paradise. And so it proves to be:

> When you emerged from this tunnel you would find yourself in the medieval College: in the cloister of the much smaller quadrangle called Republic. The grass here looks very green after the aridity of Newton and the very stone of the buttresses that arise from it gives the impression of being soft and alive. Chapel is not far off: the hoarse, heavy noise of the works of a great and old clock comes to you from somewhere overhead. (THS 18; ch. 1)

This is the original College building, built sometime after its foundation in 1300 "for the support of ten learned men whose duties were to pray for the soul of Henry de Bracton and to study the laws of England" (THS 15; ch. 1). Clearly it is a world much to Lewis's liking, not least in contrast to the "aridity of Newton." Its living stones and green grass suggest a combination of the Heavenly City of Revelation and the fresh turf of Paradise in Genesis. We know that after his conversion Lewis attended chapel every day, and here it is not far off.

The ponderous sound of the clock reinforces the sense of long, slow time, of a church of great antiquity and length of years. If Lewis felt the attraction of a medievalizing Christianity, perhaps even toward the Roman Catholicism of his period or of some Anglo-Catholic dream, where "the grass looks very green," he expressed it in this passage. And I think the name of this beautiful medieval college, Republic, must be derived from Plato's *Republic*; after all, it's "all in Plato, all in Plato," as the aged Digory says in *The Lion, the Witch and the Wardrobe*.

But now we approach the quadrangle that most clearly enjoys Lewis's favor. "You went along this cloister, past slabs and urns and busts that commemorate dead Bractonians, and then down shallow steps into the full daylight of the quadrangle called Lady Alice" (THS 18; ch. 1). Plenty of time is accounted for in this second narrow passage; many Bractonians lived and died between the fourteenth and the seventeenth centuries. The name of this quadrangle, Lady Alice, is most likely taken from Lady Alice Egerton, who as "a girl of fifteen" performed the role of "The Lady" when Milton's play *The Masque of Comus* was first enacted by herself and her brothers John and Thomas at Ludlow Castle in Wales in 1634.[24] This Lady Alice, born June 13, 1618, was the youngest daughter of John, first Earl of Bridgewater, and was the second of his children to bear that name: her sister, also Lady Alice Egerton, was born in 1613 and died in 1614. The second Alice became Countess Carberry. She has been described as "This accomplished young woman [...] an excellent pupil [...] who had already participated in court masques."[25] Her choice for the role was more than a "lovely compliment"; it was "intended to help repair the reputation of the entire family by making the last unmarried Egerton daughter act out her resistance to dangerous sexual temptation."[26] There had been a truly shocking scandal involving Lady Alice's cousin who, at the age of twelve, had been debauched by servants at the pleasure of her voyeurist husband. In the context of this pathetic case of child abuse, the play as a defense of chastity becomes extremely poignant.

A study written in 1847 of *English Churchwoman of the Seventeenth Century* includes some interesting remarks about the role of women during that period:

> The religious ladies of the seventeenth century whose names have come down to us, may fairly be regarded as samples of a much larger number like themselves. Of persons who lived and died in the privacy of domestic life, only a small proportion could meet with any kind of personal memorial: of these, necessarily the greater part would belong to the higher rank of society.[27]

Lewis probably intended the name Lady Alice, as applied to his beautiful college quadrangle and to its buildings, to evoke a sense of stately seventeenth-century pageantry in a somewhat rural, even familial setting, in which the idea of a virtuous, talented, and well-protected woman forms a central image.

We learn a little elsewhere in *That Hideous Strength* about Lady Alice's buildings: their common room was for three hundred years "one of the pleasant quiet places of England." This room in Lady Alice was "on the ground floor beneath the soler, and the windows at its eastern end looked out on the river and on Bragdon Wood" (THS 88; ch. 4). The East is the ceremonial position of the altar in a Christian church, a parallel with the placement of the holy of holies in the Temple, and Lewis was to reiterate its symbolic significance—that it is the direction from which the rising Sun casts its light—in *The Voyage of the Dawn Treader*.

It is against this East Window of the common room in Lady Alice that the ultimate outrage toward Bracton College property is committed while we look on, when "the Henrietta Maria window" is smashed in by the heavy equipment of the N.I.C.E. (THS 104; ch. 5). Henrietta Maria (1609–1669), who in the novel is said to have written her name on that window with her diamond, was the Roman Catholic wife of Charles I, the martyred king with whom Lewis's sympathies—to judge by his depiction of Cromwell's men in a passage to which we shall come presently—apparently lay!

When the narrator Lewis enters the quadrangle of Lady Alice, as he tells us,

> The buildings to your left and right were seventeenth-century work: humble, almost domestic in character, with dormer windows, mossy and grey-tiled. (THS 18; ch. 1)

Lewis wrote a letter to his father, postmarked December 8, 1918, about a visit he had made to Cambridge:

> several little quadrangles I remember, with tiled gables, sundials, and tall chimneys like Tudor houses, were charming.[28]

There can be no doubt that this was the sort of architecture Lewis liked best. For him to say that something was "humble, almost domestic," was to praise it.

And now he expresses the strongest praise to be found anywhere in his writings for his own denomination and chosen form of churchmanship. It is true that he denied himself public preference in these matters. He was too eirenic as well as too modest to praise his own particular mansion in the house of Mother Kirk in public. But here we have his authentic word on the matter: "You were in a sweet, Protestant world. You found yourself, perhaps, thinking of Bunyan or of Walton's *Lives*" (THS 18; ch.1).

Lewis was nothing if not ecumenical: John Bunyan (1628–1688), upon whose spiritual masterpiece, *The Pilgrim's Progress*, he had based his early allegory of his conversion, *The Pilgrim's Regress*, was a Baptist, not a very popular thing to be in the England of the seventeenth century. But the people in Izaak Walton's book, *The Lives of Dr. John Donne, Sir Henry Wotton, Mr. Richard Hooker, Mr. George Herbert* (1670), were Anglicans, and some of the Anglicans Lewis liked best. A commentator on "the making of Walton's Lives" explains that "Since he [Walton] was responsible for the first biographies of Donne and Wotton, and for the first accounts of Hooker, Herbert, and Sanderson which were more than sketches, he, more than anyone else, has been responsible for our conception of these men."[29] He adds, echoing what was almost certainly the opinion of Lewis, that Walton's *Lives* are, along with Boswell's *Life of Johnson*, "among the masterpieces of life-writing that belongs to the literature of the world."[30]

Now the narrator Lewis passes along to his third narrowing of the field of vision:

> There were no buildings straight ahead on the fourth side of Lady Alice: only a row of elms and a wall: and here first one became aware of the sound of running water and the cooing of wood pigeons. The street was so far off by now that there were

> no other noises. In the wall there was a door. It led you into a covered gallery pierced with narrow windows on either side. Looking out through these you discovered that you were crossing a bridge and the dark brown dimpled Wynd was flowing under you. (THS 18-19; ch. 1)

I don't know exactly where Bracton College was supposed to be located, but a town with Birmingham to the east, Wales to the west, hills to the north, and London to the south, is not very far from Malvern, where Lewis went to school just before he was joyously reprieved to the tutorship of Kirkpatrick.

The Wynd River itself is that ideal river which meanders in spirit through Oxford and Cambridge alike and which has been apotheosized not only in *The Wind in the Willows* but in numerous novels with university settings. Lewis wrote prose which surpassed his poetry, and "the dark brown dimpled Wynd" must be one of his most evocative lines.

We are not surprised to learn after this, that

> Now you were very near your goal. A wicket at the far end of the bridge brought you out on the Fellows' bowling green, and across that you saw the high wall of the Wood, and through the Inigo Jones gate you caught a glimpse of sunlit green and deep shadows. (THS 19)

With Lewis, nothing is a mere throwaway. I do not mean that one can construct a strict allegorical relationship for every word or phrase, but every image in these passages is freighted with allusive meaning. This bowling green is not merely a motif in an English university campus scene. It is England. An Edwardian study of *The Complete Bowler* informs us that "Sir Francis Drake was supposed to be surprised by [the news of] the Armada when playing a game of bowls!"[31]

In the traditions clustered about this "oldest of outdoor games"[32] is one that Thomas Beckett (who died in 1190 as the martyr who is commemorated at Canterbury Cathedral where his death took place) had played at "casting of stones" as a lad,[33] though one writer admits that this is probably a reference to the shot-put, not Bowls. A thirteenth-century drawing does depict a game of Bowls, however, and "the green of the Southampton Town Bowling Club was laid down towards the end of the reign of Edward I, before 1299,"[34] just in time for the game to be played by members of the newly formed Bracton College! In the play of the Southampton club, the President is called the "Master" and the chief medalist is called the "Knight" and dubbed "Sir" in victory, [35] suggesting that Bowls had become a sort of surrogate for ritual combat, and using the same terminology as that of the knights attending the Holy Grail. Early kings are reported to have disapproved of all this, and a series of enactments attempted to curb the game, to little avail, although "strictly speaking" the game was actually illegal until 1845.[36]

Whether legal or not, Shakespeare bowled, and referred to the game of Bowls in his plays. In *King Richard II*, Act III, Scene 4, the queen and her ladies at waiting play, as suggested by this conversation:

> Queen. What sport shall we devise here in this garden,
> To drive away the heavy thought of care?
> Lady. Madam, we'll play at bowls.

And finally, Sir Isaac Newton, "in the warmest pursuit of his discoveries, when going out, left a candle upon his table amongst his papers, and went down into the bowling green,"[37] with the result that the papers were set afire and he had to begin his project again! At this point, I am sure I can rest my case, but I cannot resist adding that the object of Bowls is to roll the bowls as close as possible to the Jack, a stone thrown out by the winner of an initial toss at the beginning of the game, giving the nickname of C.S. Lewis a place in our meditations on this passage. Interestingly, the Jack is also called the "mistress" and even the "kitty," which our Edwardian source gently informs us is a generic term for "woman."[38] In a word, the goal of Bowls is female!

Now, Lewis writes of Bragdon Wood:

> I suppose the mere fact of being walled in gave the Wood part of its peculiar quality, for when a thing is enclosed, the mind does not willingly regard it as common. As I went forward over the quiet turf I had the sense of being received. The trees were just so wide apart that one saw uninterrupted foliage in the distance but the place where one stood seemed always to be a clearing; surrounded by a world of shadows, one walked in mild sunshine. Except for the sheep whose nibbling kept the grass so short and who sometimes raised their long, foolish

> faces to stare at me, I was quite alone; and it felt more like the loneliness of a very large room in a deserted house than like any ordinary solitude out of doors. I remember thinking, "This is the sort of place which, as a child, one would have been rather afraid of or else would have liked very much indeed." A moment later I thought, "But when alone—really alone—everyone is a child: or no one?" Youth and age touch only the surface of our lives. (THS 19; ch. 1)

This beautiful paragraph presents us with a woodland entirely different from any in Tolkien and utterly different from the Broceliande of Charles Williams, with which it has sometimes been compared. Like all of them, however, it is a figure for the unconscious, that part of us in which youth or age have little meaning.

Interior solitude is for Lewis a reiterated theme—he wrote that he was the product of "indoor silences," where he had spent long hours reading alone. The visit to the upstairs solitude in the magician's house by Lucy in *The Voyage of the Dawn Treader* presents a similar image, as do the "Wood Between the Worlds" and the mountaintop orchard in *The Magician's Nephew*. Bragdon Wood, with its "quiet turf," "uninterrupted foliage," "mild sunshine," and "nibbling" flock of "sheep," is a place of endless possibilities, which is simultaneously enclosed and infinitely open, a place to be "rather afraid of" and yet "liked very much."

Not surprisingly, this holy place has a holier center:

> Half a mile is a short walk. Yet it seemed a long time before I came to the centre of the Wood. I knew it was the centre, for there was the thing I had chiefly come to see. It was a well: a well with steps going down to it and the remains of an ancient pavement about it. It was very imperfect now. I did not step on it, but I lay down in the grass and touched it with my fingers. (THS 19; ch. 1)

Of course the center is a well. A well is both the source of life and the entrance to the underworld, that passage toward which life is always tending. This is in every culture a feminine image, just as a woodland is feminine. A wood with a well in its center is certainly holy ground.

> For this was the heart of Bracton or Bragdon Wood: out of this all the legends had come and on this, I suspected, the very existence of the College had originally depended. (THS 19; ch. 1)

The word "heart" is reiterated in *That Hideous Strength* as an image of the center or place of deepest meaning. "Edgestow lay in what had been the very heart of ancient Logres" (THS 245), we are told, and "the village of Cure Hardy preserved the name of Ozana le Coeur Hardi." One commentator thinks this last is a little joke of Lewis's because the particular knight who bore this name is a Norman figure post-dating the elder mythologies of the Arthuriad. But surely this is not the point. The point is the word "*coeur*," heart, and Cure Hardy the village is presented as a figure for, indeed as itself embodying the "strong heart" of England. The diversion of the Wynd that leaves Edgestow a waterless desert will flood Cure Hardy to make "a new water supply for Edgestow" (THS 83; ch. 4). The beautiful little village, to be destroyed along with its "sixteenth-century almshouses and a Norman church and all that" (THS 83; ch. 4), will be re-named Jules Hardy or Wither Hardy, after the Director and Deputy Director of the N.I.C.E. No wonder Mark cannot bring himself to tell Jane what fate has been planned for Cure Hardy!

At the heart of Bragdon Wood, Lewis places the druid Merlin, the native Briton.

> The archaeologists were agreed that the masonry was very late British-Roman work, done on the very eve of the Anglo-Saxon invasion. How Bragdon the Wood was connected with Bracton the lawyer was a mystery, but I fancy myself that the Bracton family had availed themselves of an accidental similarity in the names to believe, or make believe, that they had something to do with it. Certainly, if all that was told were true, or even half of it, the Wood was older than the Bractons. I suppose no one now would attach much importance to Strabo's *Balachthon* though it had led a sixteenth-century Warden of the College to say that "We know not by ancientest report of any Britain without Bragdon." But the medieval song takes us back to the fourteenth century.

> *In Bragdon bricht this ende dai*
> *Herde ich Merlin ther he lai*
> *Singende woo and welawai.* (THS 19; ch. 1)

The *Balachthon* of Strabo (c. 63 BC–19 AD) is the work of a Greek geographer: I do not know what it said that impressed the sixteenth-century warden, but the fourteenth-century song can be translated thus: "In Bragdon bright this last day I heard Merlin where he lay Singing woe and well-away."[39] The words "*ende dai*" mean last day in the special sense of the day of one's death, and "*welawai*" means something like "alas!"

Merlin lies lamenting because he has been imprisoned by the last love of his life, "one of the damosels of the lake, that hight Nimue." He had foreseen, and predicted to Arthur, that "for all his crafts he should be put in the earth quick"—that is, buried alive. After long travels, the lake-lady grows tired of the importunate Merlin:

> And so on a time it happed that Merlin showed to her in a rock whereas was a great wonder, and wrought by enchantment, that went under the great stone. So by her subtle working she made Merlin to go under that stone to let her wit of the marvels there, but she wrought so there for him that he came never out for all the craft he could do. And so she departed and left Merlin.[40]

A goddess of the underwater world imprisons him in the earth where his powers have no efficacy. The location of his tomb is appropriate to elements of Celtic culture: "A widespread form appears to have been a sacred wood or tract of land on which stood groves of trees."[41] This is the *nemeton,* which served as a site for both shrines and places of burial.

Lewis does not conclude with the arrival of his narrator-self in this place. He continues:

> It is good enough evidence that the well with the British-Roman pavement was already "Merlin's Well," though the name is not found till Queen Elizabeth's reign, when good Warden Shovel surrounded the Wood with a wall "for the taking away of all profane and heathenish superstitions and the deterring of the vulgar sort from all wakes, may games, dancings, mummings, and baking of Morgan's bread, heretofore

> used about the fountain called in vanity Merlin's Well, and utterly to be renounced and abominated as a gallimaufrey of papistry, gentilism, lewdness and dunsicall folly." Not that the College had by this renounced its own interest in the place. (THS 20; ch.1)

Warden Shovel is an invention of Lewis's, like the de Bracton family. But the gallimaufrey of practices the Warden condemns is not. A gallimaufrey is a hash or hodge-podge, and "gentilism" is paganism, or, to put it into our own pejorative terminology, heathenism. The pagan components of European Christianity, remnants of the indigenous cultures which have been brought into Christianity there as everywhere else, have become from time to time the object of scorn and efforts at eradication. We know from his treatment of Bacchus in *Prince Caspian* and of Emeth in *The Last Battle* what Lewis actually thought about non-Christian religions and their meaning in a Christian context.

It is useful to see what practices Lewis places in his pre-Elizabethan woodland. First of all, wakes are not, in this context, occasions for mourning the dead. Rather,

> The Patronal Festival of any parish church is primarily a religious occasion, but in many villages it is, and had been for centuries, a local secular holiday as well, celebrated with sports and games, and sometimes an unofficial "fair" to which travelling showmen come with their swings and roundabouts. In northern and midland England, this holiday is usually known as the Wake, or Wakes; [...] the word "wake" in this connection really means a vigil, and springs from the ancient custom, now obsolete of "waking," or watching in the church during all or part of the night before a holy day.[42]

We are not told to what saint it was dedicated, but the Norman church in Edgestow stood near the corner of Bragdon Wood, which would before it was walled, have provided a delightful natural site for this kind of holiday-making.

"May games," on the other hand, were clearly associated with May Day, a festival derived from the Celtic quarterly festival of Beltane. On this festival, which had begun as a time for bringing out the cattle to pasture and causing them to pass between rows of bonfires, it had become customary in medieval England to gather and give out sprays of hawthorn blossom to prepare garlands of flowers and leaves, to carry about hoops of flowers on tall poles, sometimes with dressed and beribboned May-dolls displayed within (as images, no doubt, of the Mother Goddess), and to dance about a maypole, which of course represents the axis of the sky and is a World Tree, itself beflowered and beribboned, while the oxen who dragged it into place were equally bedizened with nosegays of flowers tied to the tips of their horns.[43]

The term "dancings" suggests sword-dances and morris-dances, very archaic forms. Dancing would have accompanied wakes and May games. Dancing is also associated with "mumming," which has a very specific application: "The seasonal round of life in England was once marked by ceremonies performed exclusively by men wearing a 'disguise' not only to preserve their temporary anonymity, but also to mark them as beings set apart from their community. […] One of the most persistent is the Mummers' play […] These performances usually occur during the Christmas period, though they are a feature of the winter months from All Souls [November 2] to Easter."[44] They are "a men's seasonal Ritual intended to promote fertility, expressed basically in terms of an action of revitalisation."[45] What the players say varies from play to play, but what they do remains constant and invariable. There is always a ritual combat in which one of the combatants dies, to be resurrected by a figure often called the Doctor, who acts in the manner of a shaman. The fertility element applies to the anticipated crops, but the season of mumming—at the Winter Solstice and during the season from the Celtic Samain (Halloween) to Easter, which falls sometime after the Vernal Equinox, suggests that it relates to the death and return of the light of the Sun as well as to the annual planting and growth of the crops.

"Morgan's bread" refers to the triple Celtic goddess called in one of her forms the Morrigan. This is the lady who appears in Malory as Morgan Le Fay. She was worshiped especially at Samain, as mate of the Dagda or all-competent god,[46] when the divisions between underworld and overworld were temporarily broached, as they still are on Halloween. As a goddess of death she was especially associated with the carrion birds—ravens or crows—which haunt the field of battle, so Morgan's bread would suggest the bodies of the dead.[47]

On All Souls' Day there is a British custom of eating Soul Cake, with a clear reference to the fact that these are the souls of the dead. In Mexico on the same date, confections take the form of little sugar skulls and bones, decorated with people's names in icing sugar, and in 1985 I myself was able to purchase a large chocolate skull on a sucker-stick, sold to celebrate Halloween by an eminently respectable Canadian candy company! As Edgestow possesses a windmill, and in the past, market towns found their mills essential (since although grain could be stored for long periods, flour could not), the flour for making Morgan's bread may have been ground in the mill that Jane glimpses on her way home from the Dimbles's house. The practices the wall of Bragdon was meant to prevent were yet again to be the object of attack:

> Old Dr Shovel, who lived to be nearly a hundred, can scarcely have been cold in his grave when one of Cromwell's Major Generals, conceiving it his business to destroy "the groves and high places," sent a few troopers with power to impress the country people for this pious work. (THS 20; ch. 1)

The reference to "groves and high places" comes from the Old Testament injunctions against the holy places of the Canaanites, and the troopers intended not to make an impression on the country people but to impress or draft them to help in this act of ritual destruction. Lewis was not, I think, especially friendly to iconoclastic activity whether it was against stained glass windows or sacred woodlands.

And he did not hold with the killing of kings or the doing away with the monarchy:

> The scheme came to nothing in the end; but there had been a bicker between the College and the troopers in the heart of Bragdon, and the fabulously learned and saintly Richard Crowe had been killed by a musket ball on the very steps of the Well. He would be a brave man who would accuse Crowe either of popery or "gentilism"; yet the story is that his last words had been, "Marry, Sirs, if Merlin who was the Devil's son was a true King's man as ever ate bread, is it not a shame that you, being but the sons of bitches, must be rebels and regicides?" (THS 20; ch.1)

This is an intentionally comic passage, with Crowe's learned and witty retort a debonair seal on his martyrdom, undergone "in the heart of Bragdon." It is a play upon the tradition of Merlin's diabolical descent as compared to the doggish descent of his murderers, and pictures a brave and dashing man who dies for a cause with a jest on his lips, laughing, as it were, in the face of death.

The notion that Merlin was "the devil's son" comes from the *Historia Regum Britanniae* (1136) written by Geoffrey of Monmouth, which tells how King Vortigern calls upon his magi for aid in attempting to build a fortress against the Saxons. "In South Wales the King's envoys find such a youth, whose name is Merlin. His mother conceived him when visited one night by an incubus, a demon inhabiting the aery space between moon and earth."[48] One assumes that Merlinus Ambrosius must have renounced his diabolical parent, since he does not choose to join the N.I.C.E.

The narrator Lewis presses on:

> And always, through all changes, every Warden of Bracton, on the day of his election, had drunk a ceremonial draught of water from Merlin's Well in a great cup which both for its antiquity and for its beauty, was the greatest of the Bracton treasures. (THS 20; ch. 1)

This "great cup" must have been a Celtic cauldron or a medieval vessel in the same tradition. Presumably it perished in the destruction of Bracton College when Edgestow was overthrown. Lewis was quite well aware of the scholarly conceptualizations of the early twentieth century, which associated the Holy Grail symbolism with the Celtic cauldron in which the Goddess boiled the dead and revivified them.

The narrator now concludes with a paragraph full of references to public figures who had lain, like himself, in Bragdon Wood, in contemplation of Merlin's Well:

> All of this I thought of, lying beside Merlin's Well, beside the Well which must certainly date from Merlin's time if there had ever been a real Merlin: lying where Sir Kenelm Digby had lain all one summer night and seen a certain strange appearance: where Collins the poet had lain, where George the Third had cried: where the brilliant and much-loved Nathaniel Fox

> had composed the famous poem three weeks before he was killed in France. (THS 20; ch. 1)

Now, Sir Kenelm Digby (1603–1665) was a seventeenth-century collector of medieval manuscripts, known as an enthusiast for scientific and alchemical works. He had obtained his library in 1632 from his tutor at Oxford, like himself an enthusiast for things occult. It is appropriate, therefore, that he has seen a "strange appearance" "beside Merlin's Well." People who look for strange appearances are likely to see them. But he was also a poet and a Roman Catholic, a supporter of Charles I, and he wrote a poem about that king, his "Icon Basilica," or "Image of the King," on the occasion of the monarch's execution. His position would be that of one who was a papist and perhaps even a gentilist, who like the murdered Bractonian Crowe had favored the King.

"Collins the poet" is William Collins (1721–1759) who was an early Romantic and wrote a study of the superstitions of the Scottish highlands. One is not surprised that this student of folk-life had paid a visit to Merlin's Well. "George the Third" for his part, was given not only to crying—we all know of his bouts of recurrent madness—but to a preoccupation with farming and similar homely and benign activities, so that he had earned the soubriquet of "the farmer King" and even "Farmer George." It seems rather to his credit that the sight of Merlin's Well had made him weep.

As for Nathaniel Fox, he is, with Warden Shovel and Richard Crowe, an invention of Lewis's. He may have been modeled after Rupert Brooke, whose poignant poem, "The Soldier," written in 1914, contains the famous lines:

> If I should die, think only this of me:
> That there's some corner of a foreign field
> That is forever England. There shall be
> In that rich dust a richer dust concealed;
> A dust whom England bore, shaped, made aware,
> Gave, once, her flowers to love, her ways to roam,
> A body of England's, breathing English air,
> Washed by the rivers, blest by suns of home.
> And think, this heart, all evil shed away,
> A pulse in the eternal mind, […][49]

Rupert Brooke died the next year on April 23, 1915, as a member of the British Expeditionary Force in the Aegean, and is buried on Scyros.

Lewis himself was styled a "soldier poet" when his first book of poems, *Spirits in Bondage*, appeared in 1919, and he actually carried a notebook of poems with him into battle in France. Happily, he did not die there, but his book concludes with the beautiful "Death in Battle," which contains lines that now read like a prefiguration of Aslan's Country:

> Ah, to be ever alone,
> In flowery valleys among the mountains and silent
> wastes untrod.
> In the dewy upland places, in the garden of God,
> This would atone.[50]

It is possible that Lewis associated Bracton College, with its doomed denizens, with his youth at Cherbourg House in Malvern and at Oxford. In describing Malvern (which he disliked and called Wyvern, after a medieval heraldic monster, though his brother Warren was happy there), he tells not only of the "bloods" or members of the "inner ring," a motif of considerable importance in *That Hideous Strength*, but of the elaborate practice of pederasty to be found among some of the students. He remarks that he was not tempted in like manner to the second of these, and then comments poignantly that nearly all of them—"bloods" and "tarts" alike—perished in France.

It was wartime Oxford to which the young Lewis later went and where he waited to be sent overseas in his turn, and where he made his promise to Paddy Moore to look after his mother Janie should his friend not return, in return for a promise that Paddy would look after Lewis's father in case he should die in France. As we know, this promise to his friend who indeed died in European combat, made at a time of absolute crisis in the lives of these two young men, was honored by Lewis to the last hour of Mrs. Moore's life.

It is no wonder that the college setting, with its exquisite quadrangles and dreaming woodland, forms an image drenched in nostalgia. A sense of both the deep past and of impending and inexorable doom hangs over the entire sequence, drowsing, incantatory, almost drugging, like magic Nimue used to bind Merlin under the ground.

Lewis concludes this powerful and hallucinatory sequence in the same mood:

> The air was so still and the billows of foliage so heavy above me, that I fell asleep. I was wakened by my friend hallooing to me from a long way off. (THS 20; ch. 1)

"Venus at St. Anne's": The Garden and the Manor

While the passages describing Bracton College and Bragdon Wood are written from the point of view of the narrator, Lewis, the sequences at St. Anne's Manor are given from Jane's point of view. She is the seer who goes there to bring the knowledge the Company needs in order to prevail. The reader sees what she sees at St. Anne's.

St. Anne's is exactly the opposite sort of establishment that Belbury is, which we see through Mark's eyes. As a garden, it is also, in many respects, the opposite of the forest associated with the College. As Cirlot explains it,

> The garden is the place where Nature is subdued, ordered, selected and enclosed. Hence it is a symbol of consciousness as opposed to the forest, which is the unconscious, in the same way as the island is opposed to the ocean. At the same time, it is a feminine attribute because of its character as a precinct. A garden is often the scene of processes of "Conjunction" or treasure-hunts—connotations which are clearly in accord with the general symbolic function we have outlined.[51]

Lewis himself emphasizes the subtle distinctions between forest and garden in the speech he gives to the effete Filostrato:

> "Oh yes, yes," replied Filostrato. "The pretty trees, the garden trees. But not the savages. I put the rose in my garden, but not the brier. The forest tree is a weed. But I tell you I have seen the civilised tree in Persia [...] It was made of metal. [...]" (THS 169; ch. 9)

Filostrato emphasizes the contrast, but as in all symbols, the opposites are really parts of a whole, for the conscious and unconscious are not separated in human experience, and both forest and garden are opposed to the Waste Land tower of Belbury.

Lewis followed the precedent of the biblical Tower of Babel in making Belbury a malign symbol, and has added his own compression by making the tower into an overblown Edwardian mansion with an excrescence of concrete buildings at its sides. He gives us a number of Mark's glimpses of its interior: we read of "the wide staircase" with its mirror (THS 50; ch.3); of the "large room furnished as a lounge where coffee was being served," with its "many tables," where Mark turns over the "glossy pages of an illustrated weekly" (THS 54; ch. 3); of the "noise and the agreeable smells which came from the folding doors" of the lunchroom (THS 54; ch. 3); of Mark's bedroom "with its bright fire and its private bathroom attached" (THS 66; ch. 3); and we find that "The pleasantest of the rewards which fell to Mark for his obedience was admission to the library" (THS 124; ch. 7). But behind all this rather public and impersonal, though physically luxurious facade, there is the Blood Transfusion Office, and Lewis powerfully evokes the transition from one to the other:

> It was all dark at this hour in the morning, and they went by the light of Miss Hardcastle's torch—on through carpeted and pictured passages into blank passages with rubberoid floors and distempered walls and then through a door they had to unlock, and then through another. (THS 159; ch. 8)

Perhaps this combination of forced elegance and chilly laboratory ambience is most perfectly evoked in Lewis's description of Belbury's grounds:

> But they were not the sort of grounds that anyone could walk in for pleasure. The Edwardian millionaire who had built Belbury had enclosed about twenty acres with a low brick wall surmounted by an iron railing, and laid it all out in what his contractor called Ornamental Pleasure Grounds. There were trees dotted about and winding paths covered so thickly with round white pebbles that you could hardly walk on them. There were immense flower beds, some oblong, some lozenge-shaped, and some crescents. There were plantations—slabs would be almost a better word—of that kind of laurel which looks as if it were made of cleverly painted and varnished metal. Massive summer seats of bright green stood at regular intervals along the paths. The whole effect was like that of a municipal cemetery. (THS 99; ch. 5)

The whole apparition sounds like something designed by a precursor of Filostrato! Clearly, Lewis does not care for this sort of garden and he counters its death-invoking image with the image of the walled garden at St. Anne's, whose inhabitants eventually call down benign spiritual powers which signal the destruction of Belbury. The Garden at St. Anne's is made to suit Lewis's tastes: "To a medieval poet," he wrote in *English Literature in the Sixteenth Century*, "the typically pleasant place out of doors is a garden, usually a garden well walled or hedged."[52] There was a garden like that in Lewis's experience: he wrote about it in a letter to his father, composed in a hospital in London when he was convalescing after being wounded in the war (June 6, 1918). It was the garden of his beloved tutor, Kirkpatrick:

> I opened the gate of Kirk's garden almost with stealth, and went on past the house to the vegetable garden and the little wild orchard with the pond where I had sat so often on hot Sunday afternoons, and there among the cabbages in his shirt and Sunday trousers, sure enough was the old man, still digging and smoking his horrible pipe.[53]

Kirkpatrick was the prototype of MacPhee, the resident skeptic of St. Anne's Manor, where he functions as the gardener. Before we actually meet MacPhee. Mrs. Maggs says of him, "He's out gardening hours ago" (THS 136; ch. 7).

It is St. Anne's garden which first gives to Jane a picture of what kind of place St. Anne's is: the passage which describes it is much shorter than the description of Bracton College and Bragdon Wood, but it is if anything even more evocative. It begins with "a high wall on [her] right that seemed to run on for a great way; there was a door in it and beside the door an old iron bell-pull." After Jane is admitted, by Camilla as it turns out, the description of the garden she enters continues simply enough:

> The woman led her along a brick path beside a wall on which fruit trees were growing, and then to the left along a mossy path with gooseberry bushes on each side. Then came a little lawn with a see-saw in the middle of it, and beyond that a greenhouse. Here they found themselves in the sort of hamlet that sometimes occurs in the purlieus of a large garden—walking in fact down a little street which had a barn and a sta-

> ble on one side and, on the other, a second greenhouse, and a potting shed and a pigstye—inhabited, as the grunts and the not wholly disagreeable smell informed her. After that were narrow paths across a vegetable garden that seemed to be on a fairly steep hillside, and then, rose bushes, all stiff and prickly in their winter garb. At one place they were going along a path made of single planks. (THS 59; ch. 3)

I have read this part of the passage over and over since I first came upon it more than thirty years ago, savoring the details: I like to think about the "brick path" and the "mossy path" and the "little lawn" and the "little street" and the "narrow paths" and the "path made of single planks." I am prepared to contemplate for hours the "fruit trees" espaliered on "the wall," the "gooseberry bushes," the "see-saw," the two greenhouses, the barn and stable and potting shed and even the pigstye, the vegetable garden on the steep hillside and the rose bushes, "prickly in their winter garb." I wish I could see it, in any season: white with snow, soaking wet in the spring, richly appareled and ready for harvest in late summer and early fall.

No literary or historical passages are needed to enhance this passage, but Lewis has allusions upon which he wishes to call, and he allows Jane's well-trained mind (one rather similar in its broad knowledge to his own), to meditate upon these matters as she negotiates the variety of pathways from the bottom of this garden to the door of the manorhouse. The sequence is a series of progressive psychic jumps or layers, rather like the ziggurat to which Lewis refers at the culmination of the sequence. It begins:

> This reminded Jane of something. It was a very large garden. It was like—like—yes, now she had it: it was like the garden in *Peter Rabbit*. (THS 60; ch. 3)

This garden, from Beatrix Potter's (1866–1943) book *The Tale of Peter Rabbit* (1902) is actually "Mr. McGregor's Garden." It is indeed remarkably large, like the garden at St. Anne's, and as it is revealed in Miss Potter's inimitable illustrations, which include those for *The Tale of Benjamin Bunny* (1904) and *The Tale of the Flopsy Bunnies* (1909), it resembles that garden in a great number of ways, the major exception being that it is not located on a "fairly steep hillside."

Mr. McGregor's garden has two entrances through its enclosure: one is the wooden gate in a hedge, under which Peter is able to squeeze; the other, sadly, is in a brick wall, and will admit a mouse but not a rabbit. The beds in this garden are evidently edged with low and well-trimmed boxwood borders; the plants mentioned in *The Tale of Peter Rabbit* include lettuces, French beans, radishes, parsley, cucumbers, cabbages, and gooseberries—the last exactly as Jane sees them at St. Anne's. Later, after Peter has visited the tool-shed and upset the pots of three geraniums, we read of peas, beans, onions, and finally black currant bushes. The garden has a large goldfish pond at the center, attended by a watchful white cat, and *The Tale of Benjamin Bunny* depicts Peter and Benjamin daintily progressing along a path composed exactly like Jane's, of "single planks."

The Tale of the Flopsy Bunnies add vegetable marrows and depicts apple trees and a multitude of colorful flowers. This third book appeared in print the year before Lewis's mother died, when he was probably too old to read it, at least until his adulthood when like Mark he became able to consider children's literature again. But he tells us himself in *Surprised by Joy* of his discovery of beauty through *The Tale of Squirrel Nutkin*, which was published in 1903, when he was five years old. Presumably Lewis read *The Tale of Peter Rabbit* soon afterwards, since it had been published a year previously. Jane will have read it as a child too: she was probably born in the 1920s.

Mr. McGregor's garden is what the British call a "cottage garden." The contents of such gardens were established in Elizabethan times and included—according to an observer of that period—"asparagus, beans, beets, cabbage, carrots, cucumbers, globe artichokes, gourds, leeks, onions, parsnips, peas, pumpkins, radishes, skirret, spinach and turnips."[54] Medieval countryfolk kept their pigs inside the cottage with the family, but during the nineteenth century, "In a small garden, there was always a pig, certainly some poultry, and often bees. [...] The pig was the staple of cottage economy all through the nineteenth century, just as it had been in the Middle Ages."[55] Pigs provided manure for the garden and ate table-scraps and discarded vegetation, as well as providing ham, sausage, head-cheese, trotters, and roast pork. The garden at St. Anne's is a very old-fashioned garden indeed, just as Lewis intended it to be. The ambience is like that in which Princess Irene of George MacDonald's *The*

Princess and the Goblin (1872) was "brought up by country people in a large house, half castle, half farm-house."[56] Symbolically, this garden reaches from the lowest parts of the earth to the highest parts of the heavens.

And now we read "Or was it like the garden in the *Romance of the Rose*? No, not in the least like really. Or like Klingsor's garden? Or like the garden in *Alice*? Or like the garden on top of some Mesopotamian ziggurat which had probably given rise to the whole legend of Paradise? Or simply like all walled gardens?" (THS 60; ch. 3). In this passage, Jane's mind flashes across French, German, and English literary masterpieces from the Middle Ages to the nineteenth century, just as we have seen that this garden does, with its deeply traditional plantation.

The Romance of the Rose, begun by Guillaume de Lorris in 1237 and completed by Jean de Meun in 1277, describes a Dreamer who relates that "I saw a garden, large and fair, enclosed with battlemented wall."[57] During the long course of this dream, he receives a variety of instructions, including one which describes "the life of the blest in Paradise,"[58] in which we read that "along the narrow paths / Bordered with blooming flowers and fresh herbs / So little trodden that they're not bent down,"[59] the blessed make their way, like Jane along her "narrow paths."

In the end of the poem we follow the Dreamer—who is of course a lover, "So near the rose tree that I could at will / Lay hands upon her limbs to pluck the bud,"[60] and are told in erotic detail of the success of this adventure. Lewis has placed roses in the garden of St. Anne's, but as befits a Waste Land situation they are "all stiff and prickly in their winter garb." It would be hard to imagine Jane, at this point in her life, imitating the rose in *The Romance*: "That never did this sweet bud turn from me / or think it any harm, but e'er complied / And let me do whatever she supposed I ought to do most to delight myself."[61]

The particular species of rose that presented this voluptuous image to medieval France had been brought to Europe from Mesopotamia, where "the culture of Islam [...] developed the idea of a watered garden as the ideal of Paradise."[62] Traditionally, it is said that the King of Navarre brought this rose back from the Crusades of 1239–1240: *Rosa Gallica officinalis*, or the Apothecaries' Rose. This is the very rose which figured in the War of the Roses,[63] and forms the basis of the special iconography of the "heraldic rose." The famous depiction of Arthur's Round Table at Winchester Cathedral shows a rose of this type at its center, and Shakespeare describes the quarrel beginning in a London garden as Somerset and Warwick order one another: "Pluck a red rose from off this thorn with me " (*Henry VI Part I*).[64] The Badge of England depicts what is called "a Tudor Rose,"[65] and Jane's maiden name was Tudor. No wonder, as a seer, that she is moved to meditation by the rose bushes of St. Anne's garden.

The third image of Jane's musings—"Or like Klingsor's garden?"—refers to the garden of the magician as he first appears in Wolfram von Eschenbach's (1170–1220) *Parzival*, where he is described as "a famous sorcerer."[66] His name is thought to be related to the Old French *clencheor*, "one who locks," and if so, he is actually "the deity of death."[67] This motif suggests the Underworld element present in gardens, where the roots reach down below the soil, and where the various tubers must be unearthed in order to harvest them. Klingsor, having been made impotent like the time-god Cronus of Greek mythology, has taken up the sorcerer's life. In one part of *Parzival* Sir Gawain spends an amorous night with a lady in Klingsor's castle. In the nineteenth century the German Romantic writer Novalis described the garden of Klingsor's castle thus:

> Most splendid of all stood out the garden in the great square before the palace, which consisted of metal trees and crystal plants and which was sown with jewel-blossoms and fruits.[68]

Even the fountain in this garden is frozen solid. One is reminded that the garden at St. Anne's is in its "winter garb." Klingsor in *Parzival* is a doublet for the Fisher-King; it is thus appropriate that his garden is cold and metallic, like the trees from Persia which Filostrato would like to use to cover the Earth after he has cleansed it from all natural growth, and like the leaves on the laurels in the funereal garden at Belbury. There is a little cold breath from the Waste Land in this reference.

The garden in *Alice* appears as a vision of Paradise in *Alice's Adventures in Wonderland*: "Alice opened the door and found that it led into a small passage, not much larger than a rat-hole: she knelt down and looked along the passage into the loveliest garden you ever saw. How she longed to get out of that dark hall, and wander among those beds of bright flowers."[69] And with this image of lost and unattainable loveliness, we are ready for the "garden on top of some Mesopotamian ziggurat which had probably given rise to the whole legend of Paradise."

The Ziggurat was a cosmic mountain, and the particular structure that some scholars identify as the "Tower of Babel" was the temple of Marduk in Babylon. This seven-story tower, called Etemenanki, "the Temple Foundation of Heaven and Earth," was capped by bricks of "resplendent blue enamel"[70] and on its top there was a shrine where the divinity was provided with a dwelling chamber.[71] Here the god was furnished with "a fine large couch, richly covered, and a golden table beside it [...] and no one spends the night there except [...] one Assyrian woman, all alone, whoever it may be that the god has chosen," according to the account by Herodotus.[72] In such a chamber, the connubium, the sacred marriage of king and queen, was carried out, beneath decorations of greenery; the union was intended "to reinforce the creative powers in nature."[73]

This wedding of cosmic and vegetable cycles is accomplished by Lewis in the single image of the garden on top of the mountain, an image that is consistent with historical precedent, and also provides a counterpart to the malignant aspects of the ziggurat—that of the Tower of Babel—suggested by Belbury.[74] As Elizabeth Moynihan, author of *Paradise as a Garden* (1979), explains

> the idea of Paradise as a garden is one of man's oldest ideals. Since the beginning of history [...] societies [...] shared the concept of Paradise as an ideal garden, a secure and everlasting garden.[75]

The earliest written account of Paradise indeed appears in the Middle East, in proto-literate Sumer in the account of Dilmun, the "pure, clear, and bright" land.[76] The famous "hanging gardens of Babylon" to which Lewis is probably referring in this passage, were raised gardens which were irrigated above the water level of the nearby Euphrates: recent reconstructions of Babylon do not show them on top of the great ziggurat which gave rise to the idea of the Tower of Babel, but they are certainly associated with it, and Mesopotamian paintings and carvings of sacred mountains, sacred trees, and floral motifs, form a part of these conceptualizations. Dante placed his Paradise garden on top of a mountain, and so did Milton.

All of these images will have been in Jane's mind as she walks through the garden on the steep hillside leading up to St. Anne's Manor. Finally, she thinks:

> Or simply like all walled gardens? Freud said we liked gardens because they were symbols of the female body. But that must be a man's point of view. (THS 60; ch. 3)

We have seen that the garden in *The Romance of the Rose* is precisely a symbol of the female body, which medieval readers did not need to have interpreted by Freud. Jane, whose feminist thoughts Lewis describes, thinks:

> Presumably gardens meant something different in women's dreams. Or did they? Did men and women both feel interested in the female body and even, though it sounded ridiculous, in almost the same way? (THS 60; ch.3)

"All walled gardens" are part of the image of the *hortus conclusus*, the enclosed garden, which is a significant symbol of the Blessed Virgin and forms one of her titles in the Litany in her honor. This association derives from the Song of Solomon 4.12: "A garden enclosed is my sister, my spouse."

The garden is a fundamental symbol of the feminine. It presents the natural world as a creation perfectly ordered, beautifully formed, and enclosed in a protective wall, into which one enters with care, and out of which one emerges with regret. It is a figure of the female who is the mother, source, haven, and protection of all humanity, male and female alike. It is also a symbol of the divine center. In *A Preface to Paradise Lost*, Lewis, writing about one of the greatest evocations of Eden in literature, discusses Milton's method of describing the garden of Paradise:

> [...] he does not begin with a particular image, rather with an idea—*in narrow room Nature's whole wealth.* The "narrow room," the sense of a small guarded place, of sweetness rolled into a ball, is essential. God had *planted* it all. Not created it, but planted it—an anthropomorphic God out of Ezekiel xxxi,

> the God of our childhood and man's, making a toy garden as *we* made them when we were children. The earliest and lowest levels are being uncovered. And all this realm was studded once with rich and ancient cities; a *pleasant soil*, but the mountain of Paradise, like a jewel set in gold, *far more pleasant* so that an emotion stolen from the splendour of the cities now flows into our feeling of Paradise. Then come the trees, the mythical and numinous trees, and *vegetable gold* from the garden of Hesperus […] and the hard, bright suggestions of *pearl* and *gold.*
>
> […] These references to the obvious and immemorial are there not to give us new ideas about the lost garden but to make us know that the garden is found, that we have come home at last and reached the centre of the maze—our centre, humanity's centre, not some private centre of the poet's.[77]

The center is the abode of God. The *mandala*, to use the Sanskrit word chosen by Jung for all manifestations of the divine center, appears again and again in literature and art. Love says to Dante in *The New Life*: "I am the centre of a circle to which all parts of the circumference are in a similar position." St. Bonaventure writes: "God is a circle whose centre is everywhere and whose circumference nowhere." And Charles Williams says, "The two formulae together cover almost the whole of the Way of Images—and indeed of the Way of Rejection of Images also."[78] Sr. Mary Laurentia Digges summarizes the idea in *Transfigured World* (1957):

> He [Christ] is (in T.S. Eliot's phrase) the "still point of the turning world." He is God, and here is Dante's description of his vision of the Godhead: "I saw a Point which radiated light [and] around the Point a circle of light whirled […] On that Point, the heavens and all of nature depend." (Paradiso 29.16 ff)[79]
>
> And again:
>
> All things find in him their origin, their impulse, the centre of their being; to him be glory. (Rom. 11.36)

> I saw God in a Point ... [sic] by which sight I saw that He is all things [...] for He is the mid-Point of all things.[80] (Julian of Norwich)

C.S. Lewis used the image of the sacred center in each of the interplanetary novels. In *Out of the Silent Planet* it is the abode of Oyarsa:

> [...] right below him lay an almost circular lake—a sapphire twelve miles in diameter set in a border of purple forest. Amidst the lake there rose [...] an island of pale red, smooth to the summit, and on the summit a grove of such trees as man had never seen. [...] Flowers indeed they were, not trees, and far down among their roots he caught a pale hint of slab-like architecture. He knew before his guide told him that this was Meldilorn. (OSP 132; ch. 17)

In *Perelandra* it is the place where Ransom encounters the Oyarsa of Malacandra (Mars) and Perelandra (Venus) together:

> He saw a valley, a few acres in size, as secret as a valley in the top of a cloud: a valley pure rose-red, with ten or twelve of the flowing peaks about it, and in the centre a pool, married in pure unrippled clearness to the gold of the sky. The lilies came down to its very edge and lined all its bays and headlands. (PER 165; ch. 15)

The image of the garden in the Trilogy may also owe something to Lewis's childhood memories, as he writes in *Surprised by Joy*

> Once in those very early days my brother brought into the nursery the lid of a biscuit tin which he had covered with moss and garnished with twigs and flowers so as to make it a toy garden or a toy forest. That was the first beauty I ever knew.[81]

As he says, "What the real garden had failed to do, the toy garden did [...] as long as I live my imagination of Paradise will retain something of my brother's toy garden."[82]

Not surprisingly, Lewis also incorporated the image into his children's stories. In *Prince Caspian* Aslan appears to Lucy: "A circle of grass, smooth as a lawn, met her eyes, with dark trees dancing all round it. And then—oh joy! For *he* was there: the huge Lion, shining white in the moonlight, with his huge black shadow underneath him"

(PC 140; ch. 9). In *The Voyage of the Dawn Treader*, the Table of Aslan becomes a shrine: "What they now saw was a wide oblong space flagged with smooth stones and surrounded by gray pillars but unroofed" (VDT 207; ch. 13). The familiar jewels and fruits—so strongly evoked in the Malacandrian and Perelandrian sacred centers described above, are here spread on a table:

> there were nuts and grapes, pineapples and peaches, pomegranates and melons and tomatoes. There were flagons of gold and silver and curiously-wrought glass; and the smell of the fruit and the wine blew toward them like a promise of all happiness.
>
> "I *say*!" said Lucy. (VDT 208; ch. 13)

The most explicit Narnian usage appears precisely where it belongs—in *The Magician's Nephew*—where the creation of Narnia quite properly includes a garden. Here the boy Digory finds a silver apple which cures his dying mother. The imagery is borrowed from Milton who borrowed it, Lewis has reminded us, from its original place in Genesis:

> And the Lord God planted a garden eastward in Eden; and there he put the man whom he had formed. And out of the ground made the Lord God to grow every tree that is pleasant to the sight, and good for food; the tree of life also in the midst of the garden, and the tree of knowledge of good and evil. (Genesis 2.9–10)

This paradise garden, given an exquisite Narnian coloring, is all we hope it will be—approached by Digory on the back of a flying (and talking) horse, Fledge, in the manner that Milton's Paradise is approached, it is set upon the top of a "green hill":

> All round the very top of the hill ran a high wall of green turf. Inside the wall trees were growing. Their branches hung out over the wall; their leaves showed not only green but also blue and silver when the wind stirred them. (MN 170; ch. 13)

The garden is to be entered by a pair of "high gates of gold, fast shut, facing due east," and "You never saw a place which was so obviously private. You could see at a glance that it belonged to someone else" (MN 170; ch. 13). Having entered alone, Digory advances to the center: "Everything was very quiet inside. Even the fountain, which rose near the middle of the garden made only the faintest sound." Then:

> He knew which was the right tree at once, partly because it stood in the very center and partly because the great silver apples with which it was loaded shone so and cast a light of their own on the shadowy places where the sunlight did not reach. (MN 172; ch. 13)

This is a sacred tree, of course, like the Tree of Life in Sumero-Babylonian literature:

> In Eridu there is a black *kiskanu*-tree
> growing in a pure place,
> its appearance is lapis-lazuli.[83]

And the grove is a sacred grove:

> In its holy temple there is a grove, casting its shadow,
> therein no man goeth to enter.[84]

This is that forest through which Dante passed in the *Purgatorio*: "Now eager to search out through all its maze / The living green of the divine forest."[85] For the mind, as Andrew Marvell says in "The Garden," on contemplating the splendors of the natural garden and forest,

> [...] creates, transcending these,
> Far other Worlds, and other Seas;
> Annihilating all that's made
> To a green Thought in a green Shade.[86]

This is the garden/forest we have been reading about:

> A garden enclosed is my sister, my bride:
> A spring shut up, a fountain sealed.

> A garden is a secret place, at once closed, alive with a concentration of natural forces, and open to the sky. Its secrecy may result from its being a small place between high walls, or from its being surrounded by forest, or simply from its being difficult to find. One archetypal garden is the secret herb-garden of Artemis [...] to this correspond the Roman vegetable-garden, the monkish herb-garden, and our own

> kitchen-garden, all of which are laid out in severe rectangles and serve a practical purpose. Another archetype is the apple-orchard, which even now still has vestiges of its archaic sacred character. Another is the clearing, the grove, a place graven out of the forest, which is the *nemeton* of the ancient Celts, a place of light, a place apart, a temple of air.[87]

It is, of course, the forest clearing in Bragdon Wood where Merlin's Well (and tomb) are reached through a complex maze of college buildings, preliminary enclosures that tell us, long before we learn it for sure, that Merlin will join with St. Anne's Manor and not with Belbury.

It is also the closed garden—"difficult to find"—that meets Jane, when, after a railway journey which is meticulously described in terms of townspeople, farm animals, and finally a long walk, she stands outside its door:

> She was on the highest ground in all that region. Presently, she came to a high wall on her right that seemed to run on for a great way: there was a door in it and beside the door an old iron bell-pull. (THS 49; ch. 2)

The garden, to Jane, is an initiation, a first suggestion of that fuller initiation she must undergo before she comes fully into the Company of St. Anne's Manor, but for the moment, she meditates on the country and as she does, a sentence rises in her memory.

> "The beauty of the female is the root of joy to the female as well as to the male, and it is no accident that the goddess of Love is older and stronger than the god." Where on earth had she read that? (THS 60; ch. 3)[88]

This passage is seen in advance by Jane through her special capacities as a seer, just as she has seen Grace Ironwood in her mind, accurately, before actually meeting her. She will pick up a book from a table inside the Manor, like Mark fingering the illustrated magazines at Belbury, and unlike him will read a passage of profound significance.

This passage was actually invented by Lewis, and embodies an idea he had derived from Coventry Patmore's book *The Angel in the House*. Lewis wrote to his close friend Owen Barfield on June 10, 1930, about "the lover as primarily the mechanism by which a woman's beauty apprehends itself. [...] Venus is a female deity, *not* 'because men invented the mythology, but because she *is*.'"[89] A mirror is a primary symbol of Venus, so much so that the sign for "woman" even in our own culture is based on the Mirror of Venus. We note that the Un-man gives a mirror to Tinidril in *Perelandra*, to tempt her to enjoy a vision of herself in her own, responsive, reflected face; and we learn in *That Hideous Strength* that in the great Wardrobe room of St. Anne's Manor, where the women deck themselves in the treasures of Logres, there is no mirror. A woman must know herself in the mirror of the other's eyes. The fact that it is other women who see these costumes, and that he also provides costumes for the men in the household which reveal them as the others see them, shows that Lewis really knew that each lover, male and female alike, must be known by reflection in the eyes of the other. These matters are beyond gender.

This knowledge is too much for Jane:

> what frightful nonsense she had been thinking for the last minute or so! She shook off all these ideas about gardens and determined to pull herself together. A curious feeling that she was now on hostile, or at least alien, ground warned her to keep all her wits about her. (THS 60; ch. 3)

And now we have one last view of the garden before she enters the house:

> At that moment, they suddenly emerged from between plantations of rhododendron and laurel, and found themselves at a small side door, flanked by a water butt, in the long wall of a large house. Just as they did so a window clapped shut upstairs. (THS 60; ch. 3)

The "plantations of rhododendron and laurel" are large, dark-leaved masses of growth used extensively as decorative shrubbery around the foundation of houses when a sense of relationship to the landscape, and the ornament of bushes which will not lose their leaves in winter are deemed desirable. This hint of landscape gardening in the English manner fits with the fact, not revealed until much later in the narrative, that the full extent of this garden as a model of the cosmos has not yet been made manifest. Jane's initiation inside the house is part of that manifestation: layer after layer of defensive sophistication is pierced as she passes through it. When she leaves the house, it is "not by the little door in the wall at which she had come in but by the main gate which opened on the same road about a hundred yards further on" (THS 70; ch. 3). She later returns to "a lighted doorway" (THS 156; ch. 7), tortured, exhausted, and awakes inside to safety, with the words "I am the gate to all good adventure" hovering in her still-sleepy mind (THS 160; ch. 9).

After she finally joins the company at St. Anne's Manor, MacPhee talks with Jane about the silent planet situation, and the part the company is to play in its remedy. "[W]e're going to defeat a powerful conspiracy by sitting here growing winter vegetables and training performing bears" (THS 189; ch. 9), he says disapprovingly. He is interrupted by Camilla, who, having come to take Jane "Away out to the garden" (THS 191; ch. 9), replies to MacPhee's objection with a line from Charles Williams's *Taliessin Through Logres*: "Fool, All lies in a passion of patience, my lord's rule." MacPhee, offended, says "If you're going to the garden, don't let me delay you, ladies" (THS 191; ch. 9).

At this point, Jane and Camilla go "to the front door" and there meet an "apocalyptic" sight. The image they confront presents Lewis's special vision of the Moon: "not the voluptuous Moon of a thousand southern love-songs, but the huntress, the untameable virgin, the spear-head of madness" (THS 191; ch. 9). And they see, too, "the stars severe and bright." This vision of the stars is repeated at least twice elsewhere in the novel. When the company returns from finding the deserted site from which the Tramp has encountered Merlin, "It had turned into a fine night: Orion dominated the whole sky" (THS 247; ch. 12). And when Mark finally escapes from Belbury, he sees "Sirius bitter green" (THS 349; ch. 16). The star motif is a reinforcement for a novel with an earthly setting, of the larger, interplanetary dimensions of the Trilogy and its illimitable heavens. Lewis says of the scene in the upper regions of the garden at St. Anne's, "The wildness crept into Jane's blood" (THS 191; ch. 9). She is with Camilla, the warrior maiden who had first escorted her through the garden.

And here we learn that the garden is so very large that it encompasses the Manor but extends beyond and above it:

> "That Mr MacPhee ..." said Jane, as they walked steeply uphill to the very summit of the garden." (THS 191; ch. 9)

As they walk, they speak of what MacPhee has told Jane about Ransom. "That is what people are like who come back from the stars," Camilla says, reinforcing the star motif. "Paradise is still going on there" (THS 192; ch. 9). Paradise, in other words, is somewhere upwards beyond the top of the garden of St. Anne's. And the Pendragon, she continues, is to be taken there again, when his interplanetary escorts return for him.

> "This house, all of us here, and Mr Bultitude and Pinch, are all that's left of the Logres: [...] Go on. Let's go right to the top. How it's blowing! They might come for him tonight." (THS 192; ch. 9)

This incident, with its rushing mighty wind like the breath of the Paraclete, occurs almost exactly halfway through the book, and presents an image of how it will conclude.

There is one other feature in the garden, not mentioned in the first catalogue of out-buildings, which gives a final dimension to its meaning, but like Lewis, I shall wait to the end of my narrative to discuss its existence and meaning. At the conclusion of his first description of St. Anne's garden, Lewis makes Jane and Camilla arrive at "a small side door [...] in the long wall of a large house. Just as they did so a window clapped shut upstairs" (THS 60; ch. 3). It is thus that the house announces itself. St. Anne's Manor is "a large house," and it is occupied. Somebody has been watching Jane's progress up the labyrinthine paths of the garden, and now claps shut the window in preparation to meet her: one suspects that the watcher is Grace Ironwood.

Jane is ushered, for the first time, into "a large sparely furnished room with a shut stove to warm it. Most of the floor was bare, and the walls, above the waist-high wainscotting, were of greyish white plaster, so that the whole effect was faintly austere and conventual" (THS 60; ch. 3). This room is indeed like the reception room at a convent, where cloistered nuns live. It is a religious house, and very different from the richly furnished lounge at Belbury. A single book lies "on the table in the middle of the room" and Jane sees in surprise the very quotation she had "remembered" in the garden. The reiteration of this passage continues with additional sentences:

> To desire the desiring of her own beauty is the vanity of Lilith, but to desire the enjoying of her own beauty is the obedience of Eve, and to both it is in the lover that the beloved tastes her own delightfulness. As obedience is the stairway of pleasure, so humility is the—" (THS 61; ch. 3)

And here the passage is interrupted. The mention of the stairway reminds us, however, that the house, too, is presented in feminine terms.

Jane's rather class-conscious mind notes, as she is escorted from this reception room, that "the narrowness and plainness of the passages" suggest that "they were still in the back parts of the house, and that, if so, it must be a very large house indeed" (THS 61; ch. 3). The largeness of the house is a continual theme in Lewis's descriptions of it. These narrow and plain passages are images of humility, not empty and threatening like the "blank passages with rubberoid floors and distempered walls" (THS 159; ch. 8) of Belbury's laboratory extension: merely the humble servants' quarters in a house where Jane is to find that since everybody is a servant, nobody is inferior.

When Camilla ushers her into the presence of the lady of St. Anne's Manor, Grace Ironwood, she does so "'like a servant,' Jane thought." This assumption is contradicted by the symbolic associations of the names Anne and Grace Ironwood. The name "Anne" also means "grace" and Grace's name is meant literally, for she only is able to cure Jane of her terrifying nightmares, by urging her to admit their reality. "Ironwood" chimes with the "rose bushes, all stiff and prickly in their winter garb" (THS 60 ch. 3), but there may be a further meaning. The entire episode of Jane's first visit to St. Anne's Manor is set within an account of her husband Mark's encounter with Fairy Hardcastle, the ogreish female head of the N.I.C.E.'s secret police. This dreadful Shelob of a woman is later to torture Jane with a lighted cigar in an openly Freudian scene, forcing her at last to go to St. Anne's and take up her vital and predestined role. As Miss Ironwood is the "austere and conventual" feminine center of St. Anne's so Fairy Hardcastle is the malign feminine center of Belbury and director of its most ugly activities. It was *Mrs.* McGregor, one remembers, who put Peter's father into a pie; and Fairies cannot abide iron. The name

"Hardcastle," beside its faintly phallic motif, is synonymous with the Tower of Babel, a very hard castle, which becomes a Castle Perilous for Mark. Lewis discusses the malign form of Fairy in his chapter on the *longaevi* in *The Discarded Image*: the female image can appear in either guise.

Fairy Hardcastle is countered in *That Hideous Strength* by a whole household of women, who are perhaps modeled after "Some Ladies at Wantage," Lewis's dedication for *Perelandra*). These women represent many different life styles: Ivy Maggs, the lively former servant girl with her easy democracy and loyal decency; Camilla Denniston, the handsome, athletic aristocrat whom Jane finds instantly attractive; Mother Dimble, the don's motherly wife whose nightly prayers embarrass Jane severely; and Jane Studdock herself, the passionate young bluestocking around whom the novel is centered. Her visions, which are apparently telepathic episodes, provide the means by which the N.I.C.E. is defeated. Also part of this group is the male celibate, MacPhee, the red-haired atheist saint who appears in several of Lewis's novels and is modeled on his beloved tutor The Great Knock; the redeemed bear, Mr. Bultitude, and Baron Corvo, the Jackdaw. The entire household, like a convent, revolves around the powerful masculine presence of the Director, Ransom, who is their image of Christ. Of him and of Jane's first encounter with him, Lewis writes: "Jane looked, and instantly her world was unmade" (THS 139; ch. 7). He is described in terms of Arthur and Solomon, and called "Mr. Fisher-King." The wintery condition of the roses in the garden are explained by this title.

After a very uncongenial interview with Grace Ironwood, who tells her what we have begun to suspect, because of the passage in the book which she has foreseen, and because we have also learned that Jane has dreamed of Grace Ironwood before she meets her—that her dreams are true and she cannot be cured of them—Jane is ready to make her angry departure. When she is escorted out by Camilla, Jane finds herself going "by the main gate which opened on the same road as the "little door in the wall at which she had come in by about a hundred yards further on" (THS 70; ch. 3). St. Anne's has a main gate as well as a small gate, but Jane has made the best, because the most humble, entrance at the beginning.

We are given absolutely no information about the appearance of the Manor at St. Anne's (beside the fact that it is "on-the-Hill"), except that at the rear it is enclosed by rhododendron and laurel. The contrast between this laconic information and the architectural detailing of Bracton College is notable. We learn nothing about the Manor's style, period, manner of roofing, or façade, only that it has at least a front and a rear entrance and that it is a very large house. This is a building of which it can truly be said that the inside is bigger—and far more significant—than the outside.

On the other hand, we learn a great deal about the vista that may be seen from its lofty position. When Jane visits next, the whole of Edgestow is enveloped in fog, but St. Anne's on its hilltop is above the fog. Other visible heights are "the wooded hills above Sandown where she had picnicked with the Dennistons; and the far bigger and brighter [island …] to the North [which] was the many-caverned hills—mountains one could nearly call them—in which the Wynd had its source" (THS 135; ch. 6).

Clearly the picnic spot is a holy place, a high place where Jane could have been expected to see clearly. And the North (which to Lewis was a symbol of the sacred) is the source, in "many-caverned hills" of the Wynd, which brings life down from its holy source, to Edgestow. The association of caves, rivers, and high places with the Earth Goddess is deeply set in the British Isles. Harvest hills were "recognized forms of the pregnant goddess probably employed in first fruits ceremonies,"[90] according to Michael Dames (1976): perhaps St. Anne's was on a hill like that, raised as it was from "the timbered midland plain" (THS 49; ch. 2), as Lewis identified the location, to be "the highest ground in all that region" (THS 49; ch. 2), and so sited as to be related to "the wooded hills above Sandown" and the "many-caverned hills […] in which the Wynd had its source" (THS 135; ch. 6).

Distant hills have been shown to function in the siting of temples in Greece and of henges in Britain: the sacred River Kennet arises from a small cave—Swallowhead Spring—close by to Silbury Hill and Avebury.[91] The reference by Lewis to "the timbered midland plain" is not merely descriptive but geographical, for the Midlands is a region in Britain, of which Birmingham, several times mentioned in *That Hideous Strength*, is the major city. Edgestow probably means "edge place," and it is apparently located near the edge of the Midlands, not far from the border of Wales.

On this second visit, Jane is taken not only to Grace Ironwood, but also to the Director. In this passage, Lewis creates the sense of a setting from Classical Greece, as if one entered by a gradual approach into a sacred precinct built in the Attic manner. Here, as in his discussion of Bracton College, he refers to "Georgian" architecture, but this is an architectural interior, and this Georgian is "fine" rather than "florid":

> They passed out into the plain, narrow passage and thence up shallow steps into a large entrance hall whence a fine Georgian staircase led to the upper floors. The house, larger than Jane at first supposed, was warm and very silent, and after so many days spent in the fog, the autumn sunlight, falling on soft carpets and on walls, seemed to her bright and golden. (THS 139; ch. 7)

Warmth, silence, a flight of stairs leading upwards to a higher level, and bright golden sunlight; these suggest the *temenos* or sacred enclosure of some unfaded Grecian temple. We may assume that the whole house is Georgian, which means that it had a Palladian Neo-classical manner, somewhat rustic, perhaps, and thus very simple and rectangular in form but with beautiful refinements of proportion and detail: such houses often had generous windows, a central doorway with a graceful fanlight above it, and a large entrance hall with a noble staircase.

The next portion of the description refers to the "first floor"—this means the first floor above the ground floor. St. Anne's is evidently composed of a ground floor with the servants' quarters and kitchens, a middle or "first floor," and a topmost floor where the great Wardrobe room is located.

> On the first floor, but raised above it by six steps, they found a little square place with white pillars where Camilla, quiet and alert, sat waiting for them. There was a door behind her. (THS 139; ch. 7)

The steps suggest a temple *stereobate*, a stepped substructure which in Greek temples had three steps, but in Roman temples six or more. The "little square place with white pillars" is like the porch or *pronaos* which formed the entrance to the *cella* or inner chamber of Greek temples.[92] The figure of Camilla, ever the door-keeper, elsewhere described in terms suggesting a vigilant warrior-goddess, creates the picture of a priestess or high devotee guarding a sacred portal.

Inside, "It was light—it seemed all windows. And it was warm—a fire blazed on the hearth" (THS 139; ch. 7). This interior is as much throne room as temple. And here Jane meets the first animal member of St. Anne's company:

> On one of the long window sills a tame jackdaw was walking up and down. The light of the fire with its weak reflection, and the light of the sun with its stronger reflection, contended on the ceiling. (THS 139; ch. 7)

Lewis had written to Arthur Greeves on October 30, 1916, of the culmination of a "glorious walk" he had taken:

> best of all, when we came down to the little inn of the village and had tea there with—glory of glories—an old tame jackdaw hopping about our feet asking for crumbs. He is called Jack, and will answer to his name.[93]

Evidently one of Lewis's favorite events is memorialized here.

The reflected firelight and sunlight, and the sense of warmth, are emphasized to express the contrast of St. Anne's with the dark, cold, fog-shrouded environs of Edgestow on the plains below. As Jane takes in more of this beautiful room, she becomes aware that she is not alone:

> The sofa was placed on a kind of dais divided from the rest of the room by a step. She had an impression of massed hangings of blue—later, she saw it was only a screen—behind the man, so that the effect was that of a throne room. (THS 140; ch. 7)

And of course it is by the sight of "the man" on that enthroning sofa that Jane's world is "unmade." She has met the Director, Mr. Fisher-King, the Pendragon of Logres, Elwin Ransom of the Third Heaven. Lewis has prepared us very carefully for this revelatory moment.

But even this life-changing experience does not end in Jane's remaining in the sanctuary of St. Anne's. She is sent away again to seek her husband's permission to return there, perhaps to persuade him to come too. Instead, she meets the Chief of the Secret Police of the N.I.C.E., whose cruel interrogation of her is mercifully interrupted by the engineered riot of Edgestow. Hours later, Jane is rescued and taken to St. Anne's again, exhausted, injured, and without Mark.

There, she awakens indoors, "with winter morning sunlight falling across her bed" (THS 160; ch. 8). On her previous visit, it was "autumn sunlight"; now it is "winter morning sunlight." She is again "upstairs," apparently on the "first" or middle floor, where there are bedrooms as well as the quarters of the Director. Jane is told by Ivy Maggs that there is "a pretty large library in the house," presumably the place where Ransom and Dimble carry out their research, aided by Arthur Denniston, and "a bathroom next door almost" (THS 161; ch. 8). This room contains the resident bear, Mr. Bultitude, and Jane is faced with two equally egalitarian relationships: one with Mrs. Maggs, whose tone "seemed to imply a closer relation than Jane had envisaged between them" (THS 160; ch. 8) and one with "a great, snuffly, wheezy, beady-eyed, loose-skinned, gar-bellied brown bear" (THS 161; ch. 8). One can learn humility above-stairs as well as below-stairs, apparently!

When I first read of Jane's awakening at St. Anne's, I was powerfully struck by the books with which she planned to entertain herself while spending the day recuperating from her torture. She is allowed to choose, from the "pretty large library," whatever she wishes, and she asks for "the Curdie books," *Mansfield Park*, and Shakespeare's Sonnets. Presumably these reflect her elevated, not to say eclectic taste in reading, of which we have already had a good sample as she walked uphill through the garden on her first visit, and they suggest a mind rather like that of C.S. Lewis. We have already seen, however, that every detail in *That Hideous Strength* is a strand in the web of Lewis's expressive technique.

Of the three choices, that of the Curdie books is the most self-evident. These are George MacDonald's *The Princess and the Goblin* (1872) and *The Princess and Curdie* (1883). The first tells of little Princess Irene, who lives in a house which is—as I have said—part castle and part farmhouse. In the topmost chamber of this house lives a lady for whom the name "goddess" would not be too strong a word, and in the underworld below lives a race of threatening goblins who are trying to break into the cellar and take her captive. Most dreadful among these is the Goblin Queen, a figure who could have furnished a model for Fairy Hardcastle. One cannot wonder at Jane's desire to read of these matters when she awakens from her visit to the police cells at Belbury.

But what of *Mansfield Park*? Jane Austen's novel of 1814 is the story of a young girl, Fanny Price, who like Princess Irene is brought up in a great house far from her family. This house embodies "the static values of control, stability, endurance,"[94] according to one commentator. This trio of qualities is precisely that which Ransom and his company require as they wait in a "passion of patience." Fanny Price comes to the house to be reared by Sir Thomas and Lady Bertram. At first shy, sad, and little valued by her cousins, she is befriended by one of them—Edmund—and after long sequences of stately and complex courtship with all the wrong people, Fanny and Edmund finally marry and move to a nearby parsonage, where "the happiness of the married cousins must appear as secure as earthly happiness can be."[95] This patient abiding, rewarded at length by a happy marriage, is a figure of Jane's future.

Shakespeare's Sonnets would seem to be a less obviously related choice, but Lewis writes in *English Literature in the Sixteenth Century* that "the sonnets are the very heart of the Golden Age, the highest and purest achievement of the Golden way of writing."[96] Indeed, *That Hideous Strength* includes a discussion in which Dr. Dimble praises Shakespeare for his capacity to produce variety by slight changes in the extremely orderly sonnet form, when he and Grace Ironwood are considering the relationship of miracle to divine love.

The meaning of the Sonnets lies beyond this for Jane, however. While their subject matter comes, as Lewis frankly states, from the love of Shakespeare for a beautiful young unmarried man, their message is universal: "from extreme particularity there is a road to the highest universality." Lewis states that "the greatest of the sonnets are written from a region in which love abandons all claims and flowers into charity."[97] We know that Charity is exactly what *That Hideous Strength* is about: that special love called Charity which Jane must learn to show to Mark. Lewis defines what kind of love this is: "This patience, this anxiety (more like a parent's than a lover's) to find excuses for the beloved, this clear-sighted unembittered resignation."[98] This is the humility of charitable love which Jane in fact achieves at the end of the novel.

Later in the day of her third and final arrival at St. Anne's, Jane rises from her rest and goes out to explore the house. Here, Lewis uses his favorite image of the best of all possible places:

> She passed down one long passage, through that silence which is not quite like any other in the world—the silence upstairs, in a big house, on a winter afternoon. (THS 162; ch. 8)

This is the same sort of silence as that which filled Bragdon Wood, you will recall, and is based on Lewis's childhood. Continuing her explorations, Jane

> came to a gallery whence she looked down the staircase into a large hall where daylight mixed with firelight. On the same level with herself, only to be reached by descending to a landing and ascending again, were shadowy regions which she recognized as leading to the Director's room. (THS 162; ch. 8)

She is becoming familiar with the house already. And indeed,

> When she reached the hall she saw at once where the back premises must lie—down two steps and along a paved passage, past a stuffed pike in a glass case and then past a grandfather clock, and then, guided by voices and other sounds, to the kitchen itself. (THS 163; ch. 8)

The location of the kitchen on the ground floor is in accordance with British practice. This is the "downstairs"—the servants' part of the house. On Jane's first visit she entered at the bottom of the garden and climbed upwards as far as Grace Ironwood's chambers. On her second visit she achieved the upper floor and the Director's quarters. This time she begins on that floor and of her own will descends to the humbler portions of the house.

There, she sees "a wide, open hearth with burning wood," with "a chair at one side of it," and "a doorway which doubtless led to the scullery." The welcoming old-fashioned hearth is suggestive of beginnings and antiquities. Mother Dimble sits contentedly, like a goddess of the hearth, beside it. The scullery is the humblest part of a kitchen, where the washing up is done, where the pots and pans are scoured and stored, and the roughest and dirtiest kitchen work takes place. There is a nightmare scullery in the King's castle in *The Princess and Curdie*; Merlin is to enter the house by this route, the place of utmost humility, for he too must curb his pride in order to serve the Pendragon.

Since Merlin figures so frequently in Jane's dreams—he appears in four of the eight which Lewis describes—he is an important *animus* image for her, an image of the masculine elements in her own personality: magical, archaic, visionary, powerful, needing to be tamed and domesticated, sweetened, and benignly brought to a voluntary humility in order that he (and she) may become the channel of a fiery and cleansing Charity.

Only three other rooms in the house are described by Lewis. One of them is the "little room on the ground floor at the Manor which [MacPhee] called his office" (THS 186; ch. 9). It is in "this tidy but dusty apartment" (THS 186; ch. 9) that the faithful old skeptic explains the interplanetary situation of the company and its Director to Jane. In the scene in which members of the company choose ceremonial garments for one another, MacPhee is provided with something like a monastic habit, and it is appropriate that he has a little cell of his own to go with it. We have already seen the conventual quarters used by Grace Ironwood, another celibate, which are equally appropriate to her vocation.

In considerable contrast to these austere settings, we read that "Mother Dimble and the three girls were upstairs in the big room which occupied nearly the whole top floor of one wing at the Manor, and which the Director called the Wardrobe" (THS 359; ch. 17). This room Lewis describes in detail:

> If you had glanced in, you would have thought for one moment that they were not in a room at all but in some kind of forest—a tropical forest glowing with bright colors. A second glance and you might have thought they were in one of those delightful upper rooms at a big shop where carpets standing on end and rich stuffs hanging from the roof make a kind of woven forest of their own. In fact, they were standing amidst a collection of robes of state—dozens of robes which hung, each separate, from its little pillar of wood. (THS 359; ch. 17)

This vivid description of the upper room at a big shop full of carpets and rich stuffs may come from a memory of Lewis's, perhaps of being taken by his mother as a child to such an establishment. The "woven forest" suggests a web-like image like that of the Great Dance forming the culminating sequence in *Perelandra.* As for the "'tropical forest," this is some indoor forest of the mind, a glimpse of a feminine universe seen by a boy who enters as an outsider.

The three young women and their older companion are dressing to attend a dinner prepared by the men of the household. Later on we see them in the last room to be described, the dining room of St. Anne's Manor:

> Dinner was over at St. Anne's and they sat at their wine in a circle about the dining-room fire. As Mrs Dimble had prophesied, the men had cooked it very well; only after their serving was over and the board cleared had they put on their festal garments. Now all sat at their ease and all diversely splendid: Ransom crowned, at the right of the hearth; Grace Ironwood, in black and silver, opposite him. It was so warm that they had let the fire burn low, and in the candlelight the court dresses seemed to glow of themselves. (THS 365; ch. 17)

This festival scene is the farthest possible from the blood-soaked horror which concludes the banquet at Belbury. The company seated in its circle, men and women together with Ransom at the right of the hearth and Grace Ironwood on the left, presents an image of wholeness which must derive from the Arthurian Round Table, and which embodies the relationship of the sexes at St. Anne's. Hierarchy and equality have met together here, servitude and courtliness have kissed each other! In Tantric thought, the male principle represents "cosmic consciousness," static and transcendental, while the female principle represents "cosmic energy," active and immanent.[99] Ransom plays this kind of masculine role in his "passion of patience," as the still center of St. Anne's Manor. As he lies on his sofa, despite his flashes of pain, Jane sees the "tranquility of his countenance." This is a man who entertains himself by feeding crumbs to mice, who sustains himself on a diet of bread and wine, and who is a "very light sleeper since [he] travelled in the Heavens" (THS 291; ch. 13). He is tied by the frailest strands to the Earth, while pouring all his being into a state of perfectly tuned consciousness as he awaits the will of his interplanetary masters.

Who, then, plays the role of the active feminine principle? Ransom calls her "that Old Woman" (THS 311; ch. 14), and Jane calls her "the Huge Woman" (THS 313; ch. 14). She is the "terrestrial Venus," of whom Ransom says "I have long known that this house is deeply under her influence" (THS 314; ch. 14). Jane has met this lady on the threshold of "the Lodge—a little stone house beside the garden door at which Jane had been first admitted to the Manor" (THS 298; ch. 14). Here we come to that extremely significant element of the garden which Lewis neglects to mention when he gives his elaborate depiction of Jane's upward progress through it on her first visit to St. Anne's-on-the Hill. The Lodge and its placement, which is at the very foot of the garden, hard by the door Jane first enters, are mentioned for the first time about a hundred pages before the end of the novel, and form the setting for its final scene.

Jane is helping Mother Dimble prepare it as a marriage chamber for the long-awaited return of Ivy Magg's Tom when we first see the Lodge. The process is described with almost as many allusions to traditional culture as were lavished by Lewis upon his descriptions of Bragdon Wood. We read of

> things out of sixteenth-century epithalamiums: age-old superstitions, jokes, and sentimentalities about bridal beds and marriage bowers, with omens on the threshold and fairies upon the hearth. (THS 298; ch. 14)

Deliciously, Lewis compares all this to Jane's vague memories of "helping at Christmas and Easter decorations in church when she had been a small child" (THS 298; ch. 14).

Three immemorial female activities are their attendance at the childbed, the marriage bed, and the death bed. To receive, wash, and wrap the child, to drape the marriage bed, to wash and again wrap the body of the dead: these were, until very recently, especially the task of women. The draping and adorning of the church echoes this role of women's attendance at the ultimate events of human life, reminding us of the presence of the midwives in the apocryphal birth narratives associated with Christmas, and of the women at the tomb in the biblical resurrection narratives associated with Easter.

On the threshold of this bridal chamber, clearly declared to be a sacred place, the decking of which can be compared to the decking of a church for its most holy festivals, Jane experiences her first vision of the novel. She has undergone a series of dreams, and has confronted the apotheosized Ransom in his private chambers. But this is neither dream nor face-to-face encounter. It is a vision:

> Jane saw that someone was sitting on a little seat just inside the door. This person was only a few yards away, and she must have been sitting very quiet for Jane not to have noticed her. (THS 301; ch. 14)

The description of this personage associates her with "a Minoan priestess," like the hierophantic images of bare breasted devotees in flounced dresses discovered in ancient Crete; with "a cow," suggestive of the Egyptian cow-goddess Hathor, giver of the substance of life; and with "Mother Dimble" herself, whom Jane has already compared in her mind to "impossible old women in ruffs or wimples" in Elizabethan or even medieval times.

The apparition bears "a torch in her hand. It burned with terrible, blinding brightness, crackling, and sent up a cloud of dense black smoke, and filled the bedroom with a sticky, resinous smell." When she wields this formidable weapon, "Jane noticed that what was curling up from everything the torch had touched was not flame after all, but vegetation" (THS 302; ch. 14). Venus behaves in the same way in *The Romance of the Rose*, when, answering the protestations of Shame on behalf of the maiden whom the Lover is courting, cries:

> The whole enclosure I will set on fire; Turrets and towers I will raze to earth. I'll burn your fences, walls, and columns down.[100]

The weapon is the one Lewis has depicted, "the waxen torch, whose smoking flame / Sets fire to all the world."[101]

> Venus spreads the fire
> Until aloft it's borne upon the wind
> And every female body, heart, and mind
> Is as intoxicated with its smell.[102]

This vision so frightens Jane that she seeks out the Director's aid, and he identifies the lady as if she were an old friend. But when the goddess Perelandra herself descends upon St. Anne's, even Ransom is "blinded, scorched, deafened," by the approach of embodied

Charity: "So Perelandra, triumphant among the planets, whom men call Venus, came [...]" (THS 321; ch. 15).

Between her encounter with the earthly Venus and the arrival of the triumphant planetary Venus, Lewis has taken care to arrange for Jane an encounter with that deity of whom the feminine principle (like the masculine principle) is but an aspect. This "religious experience" takes place, as is appropriate, in the garden.

> For one moment she had a ridiculous and scorching vision of a world in which God Himself would never understand, never take her with full seriousness. Then, at one particular corner of the gooseberry patch, the change came.
>
> What awaited her there was serious to the degree of sorrow and beyond. There was no form nor sound. The mould under the bushes, the moss on the path, and the little brick border, were not visibly changed. But they were changed. A boundary had been crossed. She had come into a world, or into a Person, or into the presence of a Person. (THS 315; ch. 14)

In a real sense, this is the climax of the novel. All symbols, all surrogates, all images fall away.

> Something expectant, patient, inexorable, met her with no veil or protection between [...] In this height and depth and breadth the little idea of herself which she had hitherto called *me* dropped down and vanished, unfluttering, into bottomless distance, like a bird in space without air. (THS 315; ch. 14)

A moment later, the experience is over. "The largest thing that had ever happened to her had, apparently, found room for itself in a moment of time too short to be called time at all" (THS 316; ch. 14). Indeed, it has found room for itself "at one particular corner of the gooseberry patch," in the garden with which Lewis has so carefully and elaborately prepared the setting for this absolute moment.

It is notable, but little noted, that the triumphant Goddess in that garden makes a second appearance in the novel, this time to Mark. He has approached St. Anne's, like Jane on her second visit, through the fog. As he struggles upward, "This mist grew softly luminous [...] above him, as though the light rested on St. Anne's" (THS 378; ch. 17). The breath of Paradise steals toward him down the hill: "health and youth and pleasure and longing seemed to be flowing towards him from the cloudy light upon the hill" (THS 378; ch. 17). As he walks on, his past relationship to Jane is shown to him, as if he were like the Lover in the *Romance of the Rose*, now repentant. "He was discovering the hedge after he had plucked the rose, and not only plucked it but torn it all to pieces and crumpled it with hot, thumb-like, greedy fingers" (THS 379; ch. 17). And now,

> He looked up and perceived a great lady standing by a doorway in a wall. It was not Jane, not like Jane. It was larger, almost gigantic. It was not human, though it was like a woman divinely tall, part naked, part wrapped in a flame-coloured robe. Light came from it. The face was enigmatic, ruthless, he thought, inhumanly beautiful. It was opening the door for him. (THS 380; ch. 17)

And he goes in to wait for Jane, into the little stone house at the bottom of the garden of St. Anne's Manor, to which his wife comes down "into the liquid light and supernatural warmth [...] and across the wet lawn [...] and past the see-saw and the greenhouse and the piggeries, going down all the time, down to the lodge, descending the ladder of humility" (THS 380; ch. 17).

The Goddess whom Mark and Jane have met is no mere feminine "matter" in need of masculine "form," whatever Lewis makes Ransom say to Jane about "the loud, irruptive, possessive thing—the gold lion, the bearded bull—which breaks through hedges and scatters the little kingdom of your primness" (THS 312; ch. 14). His novel tells us something else as well. What can we make, in the context of these encounters, of his famous statement, "What is above and beyond all things is so masculine that we are all feminine in relation to it"? In *That Hideous Strength*, all the power of Lewis's imagination has been poured into creating a sequence of feminine images of divine wholeness: Alma Mater, sacred woodland, enclosed garden, protective house, Earthly Venus, Heavenly Charity. In these images, he shows that "What is above and beyond all things" must also be so feminine that we are all masculine in relation to it. Again and again in *That Hideous Strength*, "the imaginative man" in Lewis (who said that this part of him was older than "the rational man") has been telling and telling us so!

Notes

[1] Stephen Medcalf, "Objections to Charles Williams (Part I)," *The Charles Williams Society Newsletter* 33 (Spring, 1984): 10. Medcalf says that "I think that more harm has been done to Williams' reputation by the advocacy of two of his personal friends than by any attack. I mean here Dorothy Sayers and, alas C.S. Lewis." Readers will no doubt choose for themselves who is right in this dispute.
[2] C.S. Lewis, "Williams and the Arthuriad," *Arthurian Torso*, by C.S. Lewis and Charles Williams (London: Oxford UP, 1948) 147.
[3] C.S. Lewis, "Williams and the Arthuriad" 147.
[4] C.S. Lewis, "Williams and the Arthuriad" 147.
[5] C.S. Lewis, "Williams and the Arthuriad" 148.
[6] C.S. Lewis, "Williams and the Arthuriad" 148-49.
[7] Editor's note: In "Anti-Babels," Patterson quoted the description of Bracton Wood from *That Hideous Strength* in full (18-19; ch. 1), and also that from the abridged version which Lewis himself created (1955).
[8] Editor's note: In "Anti-Babels," Patterson quoted the description of the garden at St. Anne's in full (59-60; ch. 3), and also that from the abridged version.
[9] Neil Ribe, "That Glorious Strength: Lewis on Male and Female," *The New York C.S. Lewis Society Bulletin* No. 157 14.1 (Nov. 1982): 9.
[10] J.E. Cirlot, *A Dictionary of Symbols* (New York: Philosophical Library, 1962) 107.
[11] Trewin Copplestone, ed., *World Architecture* (New York: Chartwell Books, 1963) 280.
[12] Francois Marie Voltaire, *The Elements of Sir Isaac Newton's Philosophy*, 1738, trans. John Hannah (London: Frank Cass and Col., 1967) vii.
[13] Voltaire, *The Elements of Sir Isaac Newton's Philosophy* 361.
[14] Frank E. Manuel, *The Religion of Sir Isaac Newton* (Oxford: Clarendon Press, 1974) 4.
[15] Manuel 16.
[16] Manuel 16.
[17] Manuel 47.
[18] Manuel 62.

Notes

[19] Manuel 62.
[20] Manuel 64.
[21] Manuel 100.
[22] John Herman Randall, Jr., "The Religious Consequences of Newton's Thought," *The Annus Mirabilis of Sir Isaac Newton 1666–1966*, ed. Robert Palter (Cambridge, MA: MIT Press, 1967) 337.
[23] Randall 342.
[24] Violet O'Valle, "Milton's *Comus* and Welsh Oral Tradition," *Milton Studies XVIII* (Pittsburgh, PA; University of Pittsburgh Press, 1983) 25-44, passim. I owe this identification of "Lady Alice" to Professor Nettie Lutton, whose many useful comments during the original reading of this paper are gratefully acknowledged.
[25] Barbara Breasted, "*Comus* and the Castlehaven Scandal," *Milton Studies III* (Pittsburgh, PA; University of Pittsburgh Press, 1971): 207.
[26] Breasted 202.
[27] *English Churchwomen of the Seventeenth Century* (New York: Stanford and Swords, 1847) iii.
[28] *The Letters of C.S. Lewis*, ed. W.H. Lewis (London: Geoffrey Bels, 1966) 52.
[29] David Navarr, *The Making of Walton's Lives* (Ithaca, NY: Cornell UP, 1958) viii.
[30] Navarr 3.
[31] James Alexander Manson, *The Complete Bowler: Being the History and Practice of the Ancient and Royal Game of Bowls* (London: Adam & Charles Black, 1912) 3.
[32] Manson 4.
[33] Manson 4.
[34] Manson 6.
[35] Manson 7.
[36] Manson 11.
[37] David Brewster, *Memoirs of the Life, Writings and Discoveries of Sir Isaac Newton*, vol. 2 (Edinburgh: Thomas Constable and Co, 1855) 138.
[38] Manson 173-74.

Notes

[39] I am indebted to Professor Harry Logan for this translation and its explication.
[40] Sir Thomas Malory, *Le Morte d'Arthur*, vol. I, bk IV, ch. 1 (Harmondsworth, UK: Penguin, 1969) 118.
[41] T.G.E. Powell, *The Celts* (London: Thames and Hudson, 1980) 166.
[42] Christina Hole, *A Dictionary of British Folk Customs* (1976; London: Granada, 1978) 312.
[43] Hole 192-206.
[44] Alex Helm, *The English Mummer's Play* (Bury St. Edmund: D.S.I. Brewer, 1980) 1.
[45] Helm 6.
[46] Powell 146.
[47] Patricia Monaghan, *The Book of Goddesses and Heroines* (New York: E.P. Dutton, 1981) 207.
[48] Nikolai Tolstoy, *The Quest for Merlin* (London: Hamish Hamilton, 1985) 2.
[49] *The Collected Poems of Rupert Brooke* (New York: John Lane Co., 1915) 111.
[50] C.S. Lewis, *Spirits in Bondage* (New York: Harcourt Brace Jovanovish, 1984) 74.
[51] Cirlot, *A Dictionary of Symbols* 110.
[52] C.S. Lewis, *English Literature in the Sixteenth Century* (London: Oxford UP, 1954) 58.
[53] *The Letters of C.S. Lewis*, ed. W.H. Lewis 42.
[54] Anne Scott-James, *The Cottage Garden* (Harmondsworth, UK: Penguin, 1981) 64. Skirret has tubers which are sweet, white, and about "a finger thick: the Emperor Tiberius had them brought from Germany: Waverly Root, *Food* (New York: Simon and Schuster, 1980) 462.
[55] Scott-James (1981) 42.
[56] George MacDonald, *The Princess and the Goblin* (1872) ch. 1.
[57] *The Romance of the Rose*, trans. Harry W. Robbins (New York: E.P. Dutton, 1962) 5, section 2, lines 2-3. [Editor's note: In "Anti-Babels," Patterson added "Lewis commented upon this garden in *The Allegory of Love*, writing, 'of course, its classical and erotic models

Notes

only partially account for it. Deeper than these lies the world-wide dream of the happy garden—the island of the Hesperides, the earthly paradise, Tirnanogue.'" *The Allegory of Love* (New York: 1936; Oxford UP, A Galaxy Book, 1958) 119-20.]

[58] *The Romance of the Rose* 423, title of section 92.

[59] *The Romance of the Rose,* 423-24, section 92, lines 26-28.

[60] *The Romance of the Rose* 462, section 100, lines 2-3.

[61] *The Romance of the Rose* 463 section 100, lines 33-36.

[62] Allen Paterson, *The History of the Rose* (London: Collins, 1983) 41.

[63] Paterson 44.

[64] Paterson 48.

[65] Paterson 49.

[66] *The Parzival of Wolfram Von Eschenback*, trans. Edwin H. Zeydel and Bayard Quincy Morgan (Chapel Hill, NC: University of North Carolina Press, 1951) 270, line 16.

[67] *The Parzival of Wolfram Von Eschenback* 365, book 13 note 10.

[68] Novalis, "Klingsor's Fairy Tale," *Hymns to the Night and Other Selected Writings* (New York: The Liberal Arts Press, 1960) 17.

[69] Lewis Carroll, *Alice's Adventures in Wonderland, The Annotated Alice*, Intro. and Notes by Martin Gardner (Harmondsworth, UK: Penguin, 1970) 30. [Editor's note: In "Anti-Babels," Patterson added "Gardner's note on the garden passage in *The Annotated Alice* assumes a Paradisal meaning also: 'As sublibrarian of Christ Church, Carroll used a small room overlooking the deanery garden where the Liddell children played croquet. How often he must have watched them, longing to escape from the dark halls of Oxford into the bright flowers and cool fountains of childhood's Eden!'" (30).]

[70] Georges Roux, *Ancient Iraq* (1964; Harmondsworth, UK: Pelican, 1969) 358.

[71] E.O. James, *From Cave to Cathedral* (New York: Praeger, 1965) 138.

[72] Herodotus, *The Histories*, trans. Aubrey de Sélincourt (Harmondsworth, UK: Penguin, 1954) 86.

[73] James 145-46.

Notes

[74] Editor's note: In "Anti-Babels" Patterson elaborated on the association between Belbury and its biblical prototype, the Tower of Babel. "Belbury is a new Babel, and like its Biblical prototype, it ultimately falls through a doom of tongues. In the story of the Tower of Babel in Genesis 11.1–9, after the tower has been built 'whose top may reach heaven' (Genesis 11.4), God, observing that 'now nothing will be restrained from them, which they have imagined to do' (Genesis 11.6), scatters them abroad by confounding their language—causing the builders to become mutually unintelligible. This story is, of course, the origin of the word 'babble,' but the name originally referred to Babylon, where there was a great tower which deeply impressed the captive Israelites: this gigantic ziggurat, an imposing example of the characteristic 'high temple' of ancient Mesopotamia, was one of the wonders of the ancient world. This many-leveled tower actually existed and was itself a concrete image of the primeval myths of the people who built it. Its purpose was that given to it in the Bible, for the priests mounted the consecutive levels of this world-mountain to commune with their cosmic divinities upon its summit."

[75] Elizabeth B. Moynihan, *Paradise as a Garden: In Persia and Mughal India* (New York: George Brazillier, 1979) 2.

[76] Moynihan 3.

[77] C.S. Lewis, *A Preface to Paradise Lost* (1942; London: Oxford UP, 1961) 50-51.

[78] Charles Williams, *The Figure of Beatrice* (London: Faber and Faber, 1963) 24.

[79] Sr. M. Laurentia Digges, S.S.J., *Transfigured World* (New York: Farrar, Strauss and Cudahy, 1957) 81.

[80] Quoted in Digges 87.

[81] C.S. Lewis, *Surprised by Joy: The Shape of My Early Life* (1955; Harcourt, Brace, Jovanovich, 1966) 7.

[82] C.S. Lewis, *Surprised by Joy* 7.

[83] Quoted from G. Widengren, *The King and the Tree of Life* (Uppsala: 1951), by John Armstrong, *The Paradise Myth* (London: Oxford UP, 1969) 10.

[84] Quoted from Widengren, *The King and the Tree of Life*, by Armstrong, *The Paradise Myth* 10.

Notes

[85] Dante Alighieri, *Purgatorio*, trans. Lawrence Binyon, quoted in J.W. Johnson, *Utopian Literature* (New York: Modern Library, 1968) 120.
[86] Andrew Marvell, "The Garden," quoted in Johnson 180.
[87] Eithne Wilkins, *The Rose-Garden Game* (New York: Herder and Herder, 1969) 118-19. [Editor's note: the opening lines are cited in Wilkins as from The Song of Solomon 4.12.]
[88] The internal quotation is given again a few pages later, in an expanded form. The rest of this expanded version is given below in the quotation beginning "To desire the desiring of her own beauty is the vanity of Lilith […]"
[89] *Letters of C.S. Lewis*, ed. W.H. Lewis 141.
[90] Michael Dames, *The Silbury Treasure* (London: Thames and Hudson, 1976) 142.
[91] Michael Dames, *The Avebury Cycle* (London: Thames and Hudson, 1977) 36-38.
[92] Gisela Richter, *A Handbook of Greek Art* (London: Phaidon, 1959) 22.
[93] *Letters of C.S. Lewis*, ed. W.H. Lewis 32.
[94] Jane Austen, *Mansfield Park* (1814; Harmondsworth, UK: Penguin, 1960) 35. [Editor's note: I have been unable to identify the commentator to whom Patterson is referring, possibly because of some variation in the editions of the novel.]
[95] Austen, *Mansfield Park* 473; vol. III ch. 17 (ch. 48).
[96] C.S. Lewis, *English Literature in the Sixteenth Century* 502.
[97] C.S. Lewis, *English Literature in the Sixteenth Century* 505.
[98] C.S. Lewis, *English Literature in the Sixteenth Century* 505.
[99] Ajit Mookerjee and Madhu Khanna, *The Tantric Way* (London: Thames and Hudson, 1977) 15.
[100] *The Romance of the Rose* 439, section 95, lines 39-40.
[101] *The Romance of the Rose* 439, section 94, lines 298-99.
[102] *The Romance of the Rose* 439, section 94, lines 300-304.

Bibliography

Ackerman, Phyllis. "Stars and Stories." *Myth and Mythmaking*. Ed. Henry A. Murray. Boston: Beacon Press, 1968. 90-101.

Andersen, Hans Christian. *The Snow Queen*. 1844. Gutenberg ebook #442.

Appleton, LeRoy, and Stephen Bridges. *Symbolism in Liturgical Art*. New York: Charles Scribner's Sons, 1959.

Armstrong, John. *The Paradise Myth*. London: Oxford UP, 1969.

Beowulf. Trans. Michael Alexander. Harmondsworth, UK: Penguin, 1973.

Black, Maggie. *The Medieval Cookbook*. New York: Thames and Hudson, 1992.

Bockel, Otto. *Handbuch des Deutschen Volksliedes*. 1908. Hildesheim, Germany: Georg Olms Verlagsbuchhandlung, 1967.

Brandon, S.G.F. *Religion in Ancient History*. 1969. London: George Allen and Unwin, 1973.

Breasted, Barbara. "*Comus* and the Castlehaven Scandal." *Milton Studies III*. Pittsburgh, PA: University of Pittsburgh Press, 1971. 201-24.

Brewster, David. *Memoirs of the Life, Writings and Discoveries of Sir Isaac Newton*. Vol. 2. Edinburgh: Thomas Constable and Co., 1855.

Brown, Judith. "Pilgrimage from Deep Space." *Mythlore* 4.3 (March 1977): 13-15.

Burnett, Frances Hodgson. *The Secret Garden*. 1911. New York: J.B. Lippincott Co., 1938/1949.

Butterworth, Edric A. Schofield. *Some Traces of the Pre-Olympian World in Greek Literature and Myth*. Berlin: De Gruyter, 1966.

Carroll, Lewis. *Alice's Adventures in Wonderland and Through the Looking Glass*. 1865. Harmondsworth, UK: Puffin Books, 1975.

—— *Alice's Adventures in Wonderland*. In *The Annotated Alice*. Introduction and Notes by Martin Gardner. Harmondsworth, UK: Penguin Books, 1970.

Cirlot, J.E. *A Dictionary of Symbols*. New York: Philosophical Library, 1962.

Coles, Robert. *Dorothy Day: A Radical Devotion*. Boston, MA: Da Capo Press, 1989.

The Collected Poems of Rupert Brooke. New York: Dodd and Mead Co., 1915.

Como, James. "Spirit in Bondage." Rev. of *All My Road Before Me, 1991. CSL: The Bulletin of the New York C.S. Lewis Society* 22.8 (June 1991): 3-4.

Copplestone, Trewin, ed. *World Architecture*. New York: Chartwell Books, 1963.

Coren, Michael. "A Different Light on George Woodcock." *The Globe and Mail.* Toronto, ON. Monday 23 May 1994: C2.

Cosman, Madeleine Pelner. *Fabulous Feasts: Medieval Cookery and Ceremony.* New York: George Brazillier, 1976.

Cox, John D. "Epistemological Release in *The Silver Chair*." *The Longing for* a *Form: Essays on the Fiction of C.S. Lewis.* Ed. Peter J. Schakel. Kent State, OH: Kent State UP, 1977. 159-70.

Crawford, Fred D. "Charles Williams and C.S. Lewis." *Mixing Memory and Desire: The Waste Land and British Novels*. University Park, PA: Pennsylvania State UP, 1982. 90-102.

Cumont, Franz. *Astrology and Religion Among the Greeks and Romans*. New York: Dover, 1912.

Dames, Michael. *The Avebury Cycle*. London: Thames and Hudson, 1977.

—— *The Silbury Treasure*. London: Thames and Hudson, 1976.

Dante Alighieri. *The Divine Comedy of Dante Alighieri, The Florentine*. *Cantica I, Hell*. Trans. Dorothy L. Sayers. Harmondsworth, UK: Penguin, 1949.

—— *The Comedy of Dante Alighieri, The Florentine. Cantica II Purgatory*. Trans. Dorothy L. Sayers. Harmondsworth, UK: Penguin, 1955.

—— *The Divine Comedy of Dante Alighieri, The Florentine. Cantica III Paradise*. Trans. Dorothy L. Sayers and Barbara Reynolds. Harmondsworth, UK: Penguin, 1962.

Darrah, John. *The Real Camelot: Paganism and the Arthurian Romances*. 1914. London: Thames and Hudson, 1981.

Davidson, H.R. Ellis. *Gods and Myths of Northern Europe*. Harmondsworth, UK: Penguin, 1964.

Dean, John. *Blind Ambition.* New York: Simon and Schuster, 1976.

De Castillejo, Irene Claremont. *Knowing Woman: A Feminine Psychology*. New York: G.P. Putnam's Sons for the C.G. Jung Foundation for Analytical Psychology. 1973.

De Troyes, Chretien. *The Story of the Grail*. Trans. Robert White Linker. Chapel Hill, NC: University of North Carolina Press, 1952.

Digges S.S.J., Sr. Mary Laurentia. *Transfigured World.* New York: Farrar, Strauss and Cudahy, 1957.

Dodds, E.R. *The Greeks and the Irrational*. Berkeley, CA: University of California Press, 1951.

Downing, David C. *Planets in Peril: A Critical Study of C.S. Lewis's Ransom Trilogy.* Amherst, MA: University of Massachusetts Press, 1992.

Eliade, Mircea. *Rites and Symbols of Initiation*. New York: Harper Torchbooks, 1958.

Eliot, T.S. "Burnt Norton." *Four Quartets*. London: Faber and Faber, 1959.

—— *The Waste Land and Other Poems.* London: Faber and Faber, 1978.

Ellul, Jacques. *Anarchy and Christianity.* Grand Rapids, MI: Eerdmans, 1988.

Ellwood, Gracia Fay. "Both God's and Mary's Son." *Queen of All Hearts*. January-February, 1976. 15-16.

English Churchwomen of the Seventeenth Century. New York: Stanford and Swords, 1847.

Euripides. *The Bacchae*. Trans. Donald Sutherland. Lincoln, NE: Nebraska UP, 1968.

Fairbrother, Nan. "Gardens Since Eden." *Horizon* 1.5 (May 1959): 24-53.

Filmer, Kath. *The Fiction of C.S. Lewis, Mask and Mirror*. New York: St. Martin's Press, 1993.

Frankfort, Henri. *Kingship and the Gods*. Chicago, IL: University of Chicago Press, 1948.

Frye, Northrop. *The Secular Scripture*. Cambridge, MA: Harvard UP, 1976.

Fulton, Margaret. *Encyclopedia of Food and Cooking*. London: B. Mitchell, 1984.

Funk, Robert W., Ray W. Hoover, and the Jesus Seminar. *The Five Gospels: The Search for the Authentic Words of Jesus*. New York: Macmillan, 1993.

Gardner, Martin. *The Annotated Alice*. Harmondsworth, UK: Penguin Books, 1970.

Geertz, Clifford. "Religion as a Cultural System." *The Interpretation of Cultures*. New York: Basic, 1973. 87-125.

Goffar, Janine. *C.S. Lewis Index: Rumours From the Sculptor's Shop*. Riverside, CA: La Sierra UP, 1995.

The Golden Ass of Apuleius. Trans. Robert Graves. Farrar, Straus and Young, 1951. New York: Farrar, Straus and Giroux, 2009.

Grahame, Kenneth. *The Wind in the Willows*. New York: Ariel Books, 1980.

Gray, John. *Near Eastern Mythology*. London: Hamlyn, 1969.

Grimm, Jacob. *Teutonic Mythology*. 4 Vols. 1883. Gloucester, MA: Peter Smith, 1976.

Guthrie, W.K.C. *The Greeks and Their Gods*. Boston, MA: Beacon Press, 1950.

Hannay, Margaret Patterson. *C.S. Lewis*. New York: Frederick Ungar, 1981.

Harding, M. Esther. *The Way of All Women.* New York: Harper and Row, 1970/Colophon Edition, 1975.

—— *Women's Mysteries: Ancient and Modern.* Boston, MA: Shambhala Publications, 1971.

Hawkins, G.S. *Stonehenge Decoded.* New York: Dell Publishing, 1966.

Heidel, Alexander. *The Babylonian Genesis.* 1942. Second Edition 1951. Chicago, IL: University of Chicago Press, 1963.

Helm, Alex. *The English Mummer's Play.* Bury St. Edmund: D.S.I. Brewer, 1980.

Herodotus. *The Histories.* Trans. Aubrey de Selincourt. Harmondsworth, UK: Penguin, 1954.

Hieatt, Constance J. and Sharon Butler. *Pleyn Delit: Medieval Cooking for Modern Cooks.* Toronto, ON: University of Toronto Press, 1976.

Hobart, Mark. "Is God Evil?" *The Anthropology of Evil.* Ed. David Parkin. Oxford: Blackwell, 1985.

Hole, Christina. *A Dictionary of British Folk Customs.* 1976. London: Granada, 1978.

Homer. *The Odyssey.* Trans. W.H.D. Rouse. 1937. New York: New American Library, I960.

Hooper, Walter. *C.S. Lewis, A Companion and Guide.* London: HarperCollins, 1996.

—— Personal Letter to Nancy-Lou Patterson. 2 May 1971.

Horne, Brian, ed. *Charles Williams: A Celebration.* Leominster, UK: Gracewing, 1995.

Ingersoll, D.W. "Why a Yellow Ribbon?" *Anthropology and Humanism Quarterly* X (February 1985): 7-15.

"In His Own Image." [Theater Program]. *Peter Luke, Hadrian Vll.* Haymarket: Theatre Royal, 1969. np.

James, E.O. *From Cave to Cathedral.* New York: Praeger, 1965.

Johnson, J.W. *Utopian Literature.* New York: Modern Library, 1968.

Johnson, Robert A. *She: Understanding Feminine Psychology.* New York: Perennial Library, Harper and Row, 1977.

Jung, C.G. "Anima and Animus." *Two Essays in Analytical Psychology.* 1953. New York: Meridian/World Publishing, 1956.

—— *The Archetypes and the Collective Unconscious*. Princeton, NJ: Bollingen, 1959.

—— "Commentary." *The Secret of the Golden Flower.* Trans. Richard Wilhelm. 1931. London: Routledge and Kegan Paul, 1969.

—— *Symbols of Transformation*. Princeton, NJ: Bollingen, 1956.

—— *Synchronicity*. Princeton, NJ: Bollingen, 1952.

Jung, Emma. "On the Nature of the Animus." *Animus and Anima.* 1957. Zurich: Spring Publications, 1972. 1-43.

Karkainen, Paul A. *Narnia Explored.* Old Tappan, NJ: Fleming H. Revell Co., 1979.

Kaster, Frank S. "C.S. Lewis's John Milton: Influences, Presence, and Beyond." *CSL: The Bulletin of the New York C.S. Lewis Society* 24.9-10 (July/August 1993): 1-12.

Kerenyi, C. *Eleusis, Archetypal Image* of *Mother* and *Daughter.* New York: Bollingen Foundation/Pantheon Books, 1967.

Kipling, Rudyard. *The Jungle Book.* 1894. New York: Grosset and Dunlop, 1950.

Knight. Bettie Jo. "Paradise Retained: *Perelandra* as an Epic." Dissertation, Oklahoma State University, 1983.

Kramer, Samuel Noah. *Mythologies of the Ancient World.* Garden City, NY: Anchor Books, 1961.

Lacy, Morris J., ed. *The Arthurian Encyclopedia.* New York: Peter Bedwick Books, 1986.

Larousse Encyclopaedia of Mythology. New York: Prometheus Press, 1960. New Edition: Putnam, 1968.

Le Carre, John. Interviewed by James Kelly. "We distorted our own minds." *Time* 142.1 (July 1993): 32.

Lewis, C.S. A Grief Observed. London: Faber and Faber, 1961.

—— *The Allegory of Love*. 1936. New York: Oxford UP, 1958.

—— *All My Road Before Me: The Diary of C.S. Lewis, 1922-1927.* Ed. Walter Hooper. London: HarperCollins, 1991.

—— *A Mind Awake*. Ed. Clyde S. Kilby. London: Geoffrey Bles, 1968.

—— "Answers to Questions on Christianity." 1944. *God in the Dock: Essays on Theology and Ethics*. Ed. Walter Hooper. Grand Rapids, MI: Eerdmans, 1970. 48-62.

—— *A Preface to Paradise Lost*. 1942. London: Oxford UP, 1961.

—— *The Collected Letters of C.S. Lewis, Volume I: Family Letters, 1905–1931*. Ed. Walter Hooper. New York: HarperCollins, 2004. [Editor's Note: This source has been added because it includes a copy of a letter referred to by Patterson in "The Host of Heaven" 141 note 92.]

—— *C.S. Lewis's Letters to Children*. Eds. Lyle Dorsett and Marjorie Mead. 1985. New York: Touchstone, 1995.

—— "De Descriptione Temporum." *Selected Literary Essays*. Ed. Walter Hooper. Cambridge: Cambridge UP, 1969. 1-14.

—— *The Discarded Image: An Introduction to Medieval and Renaissance Literature*. Cambridge: Cambridge UP, 1964.

—— *English Literature in the Sixteenth Century, Excluding Drama.* London: Oxford UP, 1954.

—— *The Four Loves.* 1960. New York: Harcourt Brace, 1988.

—— *The Great Divorce.* 1946. New York: HarperCollins, 1973.

—— *The Letters of C.S. Lewis*. Ed. W.H. Lewis. London: Geoffrey Bles, 1966.

—— *Letters to an American Lady*. Ed. Clyde S. Kilby. Grand Rapids, MI: William B. Eerdmans, 1967.

—— *Letters to Malcolm: Chiefly on Prayer*. 1963. London: Geoffrey Bles, 2002.

—— *Mere Christianity*: *A Revised and Amplified Edition.* 1952. San Francisco, CA: Harper, 2001.

—— *Miracles: A Preliminary Study*. 1947. London: HarperCollins, 2001.

—— *Of Other Worlds: Essays and Stories.* Ed. Walter Hooper. London: Geoffrey Bles, 1966.

—— "On Three Ways of Writing for Children." *Of Other Worlds: Essays and Stories*. Ed. Walter Hooper. New York: Harcourt Brace Jovanovich, 1966. 22-34.

—— *Present Concerns.* London: Collins, Fount, 1986.

—— *Reflections on the Psalms.* London: Geoffrey Bles, 1958.

—— *Selected Literary Essays*. Ed. Walter Hooper. Cambridge: Cambridge UP, 1969.

—— "Sometimes Fairy Stories May Say Best What's To Be Said." *Of Other Worlds: Essays and Stories*. Ed. Walter Hooper. New York: Harcourt Brace Jovanovich, 1966. 35-38.

—— *Spirits in Bondage*. 1919. New York: Harcourt Brace Jovanovish, 1984.

—— *Surprised by Joy: The Shape of My Early Life*. 1955. New York: Harcourt Brace Jovanovich, 1966.

—— *Timeless at Heart.* Ed. Walter Hooper. London: Collins, Fount, 1987.

—— *Transposition and other Addresses*. London: Geoffrey Bles, 1949.

—— "Why I am not a Pacifist." *Timeless at Heart.* Ed. Walter Hooper. London: Collins, Fount, 1987.

—— "Williams and the Arthuriad." *Arthurian Torso*. London: Oxford UP, 1948. 93-200.

—— *The World's Last Night and Other Essays.* New York: Harcourt, 1960.

Lindsay, David. *A Voyage to Arcturus*. 1920. New York: Ballantine, 1968.

Lobdell, Jared. Cited in "That Hideous Strength: Report of the 41st Meeting, March 9, 1973." *The New York C.S. Lewis Society Bulletin* 4.5 (March 1973): 1-5.

——"Petty Curry: Salvation by a taste for Tripe and Onions." *Orcrist* 6 (Winter, 1971–1972): 11-13.

Logan, Darlene. "Battle Strategy in *Perelandra*: *Beowulf* Revisited." *Mythlore* 9.3 (1982): 19, 21.

Lowenberg, Susan. *C.S. Lewis, A Reference Guide, 1972-1988*. New York: G.K. Hall, 1993.

Lutton, Jeannette Hume. "Wasteland Myth in C.S. Lewis's *That Hideous Strength.*" *Forms of the Fantastic*. Eds. Jan Hokenson and Howard D. Pearce. Westport CT: Greenwood, 1986. 69-86.

MacDonald, George. *At the Back of the North Wind.* 1868. Gutenberg ebook #225.

—— *The Princess and Curdie*. 1883. Gutenberg ebook #709.

—— *The Princess and the Goblin*. 1872. Gutenberg ebook #708.

—— Cited in "Lewis on Communion." *The Lewis Legacy* (Winter 1997): 1-5.

McKenzie, Patricia Alice. *"The Last Battle:* Violence and Theology in the Novels of C.S. Lewis." Dissertation, University of Florida, 1974.

Malory, Sir Thomas. *Le Morte d'Arthur*. Harmondsworth, UK: Penguin, 1969.

Manlove, Colin. *Christian Fantasy from 1200 to the Present.* Notre Dame, IN: Notre Dame UP, 1992.

Manson, James Alexander. *The Complete Bowler: Being the History and Practice of the Ancient and Royal Game of Bowls*. London: Adam & Charles Black, 1912.

Manuel, Frank E. *The Religion of Sir Isaac Newton.* Oxford: Clarendon Press, 1974.

Marshack, Alexander. *The Roots of Civilization*. New York: McGraw-Hill, 1972.

Mayo, Jeff. *Astrology*. London: St. Paul's House, 1964.

—— *The Planets and Human Behavior.* London: L.N. Fowler, 1972.

Medcalf, Stephen. "Objections to Charles Williams (Part I)." *The Charles Williams Society Newsletter* 33 (Spring 1984): 10.

Miles, Clement C. *Christmas Customs and Traditions*. 1912. New York: Dover, 1976.

Milton, John. *Paradise Lost*. Ed. Merritt Y. Hughes. Indianapolis, IN: The Odyssey Press, 1962.

Monaghan, Patricia. *The Book of Goddesses and Heroines*. New York: E.P. Dutton, 1981.

Mookerji, Ajit, and Madhu Khanna, *The Tantric Way*. London: Thames and Hudson, 1977.

Moorman, Charles. *Arthurian Triptych*. Berkeley, CA: University of California Press, 1960.

Moynihan, Elizabeth B. *Paradise as a Garden: In Persia and Mughal India.* New York: George Brazillier, 1979.

Myers, Doris T. "The Compleat Anglican: Spiritual Style in the Chronicles of Narnia." *Anglican Theological Review* 66.2 (April 1984): 148-60.

Navarr, David. *The Making of Walton's Lives*. Ithaca, NY: Cornell UP, 1958.

Neuleib, Janice Witherspoon. "The Concept of Evil in the Fiction of C.S. Lewis." Dissertation, University of Illinois, 1974.

Neumann, Erich. *The Great Mother.* Bollingen Series XLVII. Princeton, NJ: Princeton UP, 1955.

Novalis. "Klingsor's Fairy Tale." *Hymn to the Night and Other Selected Writings.* New York: The Liberal Arts Press, 1960.

Otto, Rudolf. *The Idea of the Holy*. New York: Oxford UP, 1923.

O'Valle, Violet. "Milton's *Comus* and Welsh Oral Tradition." *Milton Studies XVIII*. Pittsburgh, PA; University of Pittsburgh Press, 1983. 25-44.

The Parzival of Wolfram Von Eschenback. Trans. Edwin H. Zeydel and Bayard Quincy Morgan. Chapel Hill, NC: University of North Carolina Press, 1951.

Paterson, Allen. *The History of the Rose*. London: Collins, 1983.

Patterson, Nancy-Lou. [Including her major *Mythlore* papers, the papers she wrote and which she also cited in papers included in *Ransoming the Waste Land*, and other major papers that specifically address the work of the Inklings.]

—— "'A Bloomsbury Blue-Stocking': Dorothy L. Sayers' Bloomsbury Years in Their 'Spatial and Temporal Content [sic]." *Mythlore* 19.3 (1993): 6-15.

—— "'A Comedy of Masks': Lord Peter as Harlequin in *Murder Must Advertise*." *Mythlore* 15.3 (1989): 22-28.

—— "'All Nerves and Nose': Lord Peter Wimsey as Wounded Healer in the Novels of Dorothy L. Sayers." *Mythlore* 14.4 (1988): 13-16.

—— "'Always Winter and Never Christmas': Symbols of Time in Lewis's Chronicles of Narnia." *Mythlore* 18.1 (Autumn 1991): 10-14. [See *Ransoming the Waste Land Volume II.*]

—— "An Appreciation of Pauline Baynes." *Mythlore* (Autumn 1980): 3-5.

—— "Angel and Psychopomp in Madeleine L'Engle's 'Wind' Trilogy." *Children's Literature in Education* 14.1 (1983): 195-203.

—— "Anti-Babels: Images of the Divine Centre in *That Hideous Strength.*" *Mythcon II, Francisco Torres, Santa Barbara, CA, 1971.* Ed. Glen Good Knight. Los Angeles: The Mythopoeic Society, 1971. 6-11. [See *Ransoming the Waste Land Volume I.*]

—— "Archetypes of the Mother in the Fantasies of George MacDonald." *Mythcon I, Harvey Mudd College, Claremont, Ca., 1970.* Glen GoodKnight. Los Angeles: The Mythopoeic Society, 1970. 14-20.

—— "Artist's Statement about the Cover: The Merry Party." *The Lamp-Post of the Southern California C.S. Lewis Society* 19.4 (Winter 1995-96): 4-6.

—— "'A Ring of Good Bells': Providence and Judgement in Dorothy L. Sayers' *The Nine Tailors.*" *Mythlore* 16.1 (1989): 50-52.

—— "Art in the English Classroom: An Interdisciplinary Approach." *English Quarterly* 6.4 (Winter 1973): 345-49.

—— "Artist's Statement on This Month's Cover." *The Lamp-Post of the Southern California C.S. Lewis Society* 8.4 (December 1994): 4.

—— "'Banquet at Belbury': Festival and Horror in *That Hideous Strength.*" *Mythlore* (Autumn, 1981): 7-14, 42. [See *Ransoming the Waste Land Volume I.*]

—— "Beneath That Ancient Roof: The House as Symbol in Dorothy L. Sayers' Busman's Honeymoon." *Mythlore* 10.3 (1984): 39-46.

—— "'The Bolt of Tash': the Figure of Satan in C.S. Lewis's *The Horse and His Boy* and *The Last Battle*." *Mythlore* 16.4 (Summer 1990): 23-26. [See *Ransoming the Waste Land Volume II.*]

—— "Bright-Eyed Beauty: Celtic Elements in Charles Williams, J.R.R. Tolkien, and C.S. Lewis." *Mythlore* 10.1 (Spring 1983): 5-10.

—— "Cat o' Mary: The Spirituality of Dorothy L. Sayers." *Studies in Sayers: Essays Presented to Dr. Barbara Reynolds on her 80th Birthday*. Dorothy L. Sayers Society, 1994. 28-32.

—— "'Changing, Fearfully Changing' [Polarization and Transformation in Dorothy L. Sayers's Strong Poison]." *University of Waterloo Courier* (Sept. 1985): 11-17.

—— "Charles Williams." *Modern British Essayists. Second Series*. Ed. and Foreword Robert Beum. Detroit: Gale, 1990. 316-25.

—— "C.S. Lewis and the Dragon." *The Lamp-Post of the Southern California C.S. Lewis Society* 27.1 (Spring 2003): 21-25.

—— "Death by Landscape." *Niekas* 45 (July 1998): 22-25.

—— "'Eve's Sharp Apple': Five Transgressing Women in the Novels of Dorothy L. Sayers." *The Sayers Review* III.3 (April 1980): 1-24.

—— "'The Glorious Impossible': Mystery and Metaphor in the Fantasies of Madeleine L'Engle." Archives, University of Waterloo.

—— "The Green Lewis: Inklings of Environmentalism in the Writing of C.S. Lewis." *The Lamp-Post of the Southern California C.S. Lewis Society* 18.1 (Mar. 1994): 4-14. [See *Ransoming the Waste Land Volume II.*]

—— "Guardaci Ben: The Visionary Woman in C.S. Lewis' Chronicles of Narnia and *That Hideous Strength*." *Mythlore* in 6.3 (Summer; 1979): 6-10; and 6.4 (Autumn 1979): 20-24. [See *Ransoming the Waste Land Volume I.*]

—— "'Halfe Like a Serpent': The Green Witch in *The Silver Chair*." *Mythlore* 11.2 (Autumn 1984): 37-47. [See *Ransoming the Waste Land Volume II.*]

—— "The Holy House of Ungit." *Mythlore* 21.4 (Winter 1997): 4-15. [See *Ransoming the Waste Land Volume II.*]

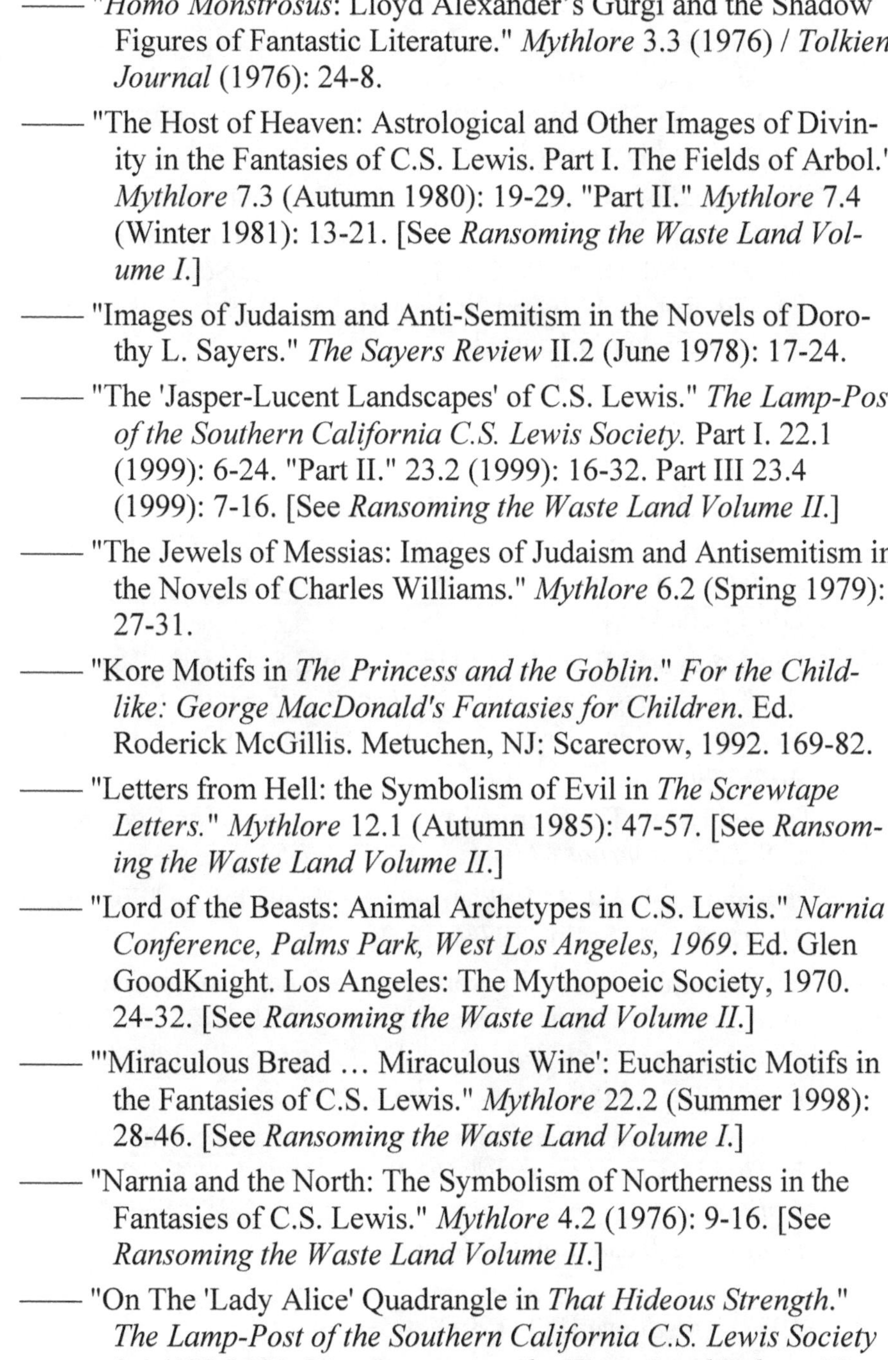

—— "*Homo Monstrosus*: Lloyd Alexander's Gurgi and the Shadow Figures of Fantastic Literature." *Mythlore* 3.3 (1976) / *Tolkien Journal* (1976): 24-8.

—— "The Host of Heaven: Astrological and Other Images of Divinity in the Fantasies of C.S. Lewis. Part I. The Fields of Arbol." *Mythlore* 7.3 (Autumn 1980): 19-29. "Part II." *Mythlore* 7.4 (Winter 1981): 13-21. [See *Ransoming the Waste Land Volume I.*]

—— "Images of Judaism and Anti-Semitism in the Novels of Dorothy L. Sayers." *The Sayers Review* II.2 (June 1978): 17-24.

—— "The 'Jasper-Lucent Landscapes' of C.S. Lewis." *The Lamp-Post of the Southern California C.S. Lewis Society.* Part I. 22.1 (1999): 6-24. "Part II." 23.2 (1999): 16-32. Part III 23.4 (1999): 7-16. [See *Ransoming the Waste Land Volume II.*]

—— "The Jewels of Messias: Images of Judaism and Antisemitism in the Novels of Charles Williams." *Mythlore* 6.2 (Spring 1979): 27-31.

—— "Kore Motifs in *The Princess and the Goblin.*" *For the Childlike: George MacDonald's Fantasies for Children.* Ed. Roderick McGillis. Metuchen, NJ: Scarecrow, 1992. 169-82.

—— "Letters from Hell: the Symbolism of Evil in *The Screwtape Letters.*" *Mythlore* 12.1 (Autumn 1985): 47-57. [See *Ransoming the Waste Land Volume II.*]

—— "Lord of the Beasts: Animal Archetypes in C.S. Lewis." *Narnia Conference, Palms Park, West Los Angeles, 1969.* Ed. Glen GoodKnight. Los Angeles: The Mythopoeic Society, 1970. 24-32. [See *Ransoming the Waste Land Volume II.*]

—— "'Miraculous Bread ... Miraculous Wine': Eucharistic Motifs in the Fantasies of C.S. Lewis." *Mythlore* 22.2 (Summer 1998): 28-46. [See *Ransoming the Waste Land Volume I.*]

—— "Narnia and the North: The Symbolism of Northerness in the Fantasies of C.S. Lewis." *Mythlore* 4.2 (1976): 9-16. [See *Ransoming the Waste Land Volume II.*]

—— "On The 'Lady Alice' Quadrangle in *That Hideous Strength.*" *The Lamp-Post of the Southern California C.S. Lewis Society* 9.4 (1986): 22. [See *Ransoming the Waste Land Volume I.*]

—— "Ransoming the Wasteland: Arthurian Themes in C.S. Lewis's Interplanetary Trilogy, Part I." *The Lamp-Post of the Southern California C.S. Lewis Society* 8.2-3 (November 1984): 16-26. "Part II." 8.4 (December 1985): 3-15. [See *Ransoming the Waste Land Volume I.*]

—— "'Some Kind of Company': The Sacred Community in *That Hideous Strength.*" *Mythcon XVI, Wheaton College, Wheaton, Ill., 1985*. Ed. Diana Pavlac. The Mythopoeic Society, 1985. 247-70. Rpt. in *Mythlore* 13.1 (1986): 8-19. [See *Ransoming the Waste Land Volume I.*]

—— "Some Women in C.S. Lewis's *That Hideous Strength.*" *The Toronto Pilgrimage C.S. Lewis Society* 1.1 (Jan.1994): 1-7. [See *Ransoming the Waste Land Volume I.*]

—— "Thesis, Antithesis, Synthesis: The Interplanetary Trilogy of C.S. Lewis." *CSL: The Bulletin of the New York C.S. Lewis Society* 16.8 (June 1985): 1-6. [See *Ransoming the Waste Land Volume I.*]

—— "'This Equivocal Being': The Un-Man in C.S. Lewis's *Perelandra.*" *The Lamp-Post of the Southern California C.S. Lewis Society* 19.3 (Fall 1995): 6-24; 19.4 (Winter 1996) 7-19. [See *Ransoming the Waste Land Volume I.*]

—— "Trained Habit: The Spirituality of C.S. Lewis." *The Canadian C.S. Lewis Journal* 87 (Spring 1995): 37-53.

—— "Tree and Leaf: J.R.R. Tolkien and the Visual Image." *English Quarterly* 6.4 (Spring 1974): 10-26.

—— "The Triumph of Love: Interpretations of the Tarot in Charles Williams' *The Greater Trumps.*" *Mythcon III, Regency Hyatt House, Long Beach, Ca., 1972*. Ed. Glen GoodKnight. Los Angeles: The Mythopoeic Society, 1974. 12-32.

—— "The Unfathomable Feminine Principle: Images of Wholeness in *That Hideous Strength.*" *The Lamp-Post of the Southern California C.S. Lewis Society* 9.1-3 (1986): 3-38. [See *Ransoming the Waste Land Volume I.*]

—— "Why We Honor the Centenary of Dorothy L. Sayers (1893–1957)." *Mythlore* 19.3 (1993): 4-5.

Patmore, Coventry. *The Rod, the Root, and the Flower*. New York: Books for Libraries Press, 1968.

Patrick, James. *The Magdalene Metaphysicals: Idealism and Orthodoxy at Oxford, 1901–1945*. Macon, GA: Mercer UP, 1985.

Pinsent, John. *Greek Mythology*. London: Hamlyn, 1969.

Plank, Robert. Contribution to "*That Hideous Strength*." *The Bulletin of the New York C.S. Lewis Society* 3.7 (May 1972): 8.

—— "Some Psychological Aspects of Lewis's Trilogy." *Shadows of Imagination, The Fantasies of C.S. Lewis, J.R.R. Tolkien, and Charles Williams*. Ed. Mark Robert Hillegas. Carbondale, IL: Southern Illinois UP, 1969. 26-40.

Potter, Beatrix. *The Tale of Peter Rabbit*. 1902. Gutenberg ebook #14838.

Powell, T.G.E. *The Celts*. London: Thames and Hudson, 1980.

Randall, Jr., John Herman. "The Religious Consequences of Newton's Thought." *The Annus Mirabilis of Sir Isaac Newton 1666–1966*. Ed. Robert Palter. Cambridge, MA: MIT Press, 1967. 333-43.

Rawson, Ellen. "The Fisher King in That Hideous Strength." *Mythlore* 9.4 (Winter 1983): 30-32.

Reid, Susan. "The Kwakiutl Man Eater." *Anthropologica* XXI. 2 (1979): 247-75.

Reynolds, Barbara. *Dorothy L. Sayers: Her Life and Soul*. London: Hodder and Stoughton, 1993.

Ribe, Neil. "That Glorious Strength: Lewis on Male and Female." *The New York C.S. Lewis Society Bulletin* No. 157 14.1 (Nov. 1982): 1-9.

Richter, Gisela. *A Handbook of Greek Art*. London: Phaidon, 1959

Robertson, Seonaid M. *Rosegarden and Labyrinth: A Study in Art Education*. London: Routlege and Kegan Paul, 1963.

The Romance of the Rose. Trans. Harry W. Robbins. New York: E.P. Dutton, 1962.

Root, Waverly. Food. New York: Simon and Schuster, 1980.

Roux, Georges. *Ancient Iraq*. 1964. Harmondsworth, UK: Pelican, 1969.

Said, Edward W. *Orientalism.* 1978. New York: Vintage Books, 1994.

Sammons, Martha. *A Guide Through C.S. Lewis' Space Trilogy.* Westchester, IL: Cornerstone Books, 1980.

Sansom, William. *A Book of Christmas.* Toronto, ON: McGraw-Hill, 1968.

Scholem, Gershom G. Major *Trends in* Jewish Mysticism. New York: Schocken Books, 1961.

Schüssler Fiorenza, Elisabeth. *But She Said: Feminist Practices of Biblical Interpretation.* Boston, MA: Beacon Press, 1992.

Scott-James, Anne. *The Cottage Garden.* Harmondsworth, UK: Penguin, 1981.

Seznec, Jean. *The Survival of the Pagan Gods.* 1953. Princeton, NJ: Bollingen, 1972.

Sibley, Agnes. *Charles Williams.* Boston, MA: Twayne Publishers, 1982.

Sister Sylvia Mary C.S.M.V. *Nostalgia for Paradise.* London: Darton, Longman, and Todd, 1965.

Spivak, Charlotte. "Images of Spirit in the Fiction of Clive Staples Lewis." *Mythlore* 14.2 (Winter 1987): 32-38.

Stewart, J.I.M. "Floating Islands." *Critical Essays on* C.S. *Lewis.* Ed. George Watson. Aldershot: Scolar Press, 1992.

Stoker, Bram. *Dracula.* 1897. New York: Bantam Classic, 1981.

Sturch, Richard. "Common Themes Among the Inklings." *Charles Williams: A Celebration.* Ed Brian Horne. Leominster, UK: Gracewing, 1995. 153-75.

Sutherland, Donald, trans. *The Bacchae of Euripides.* Lincoln, NE: University of Nebraska Press, 1968.

Tanakh, The Holy Scriptures. New York: The Jewish Publication Society, 1988.

Taylor, Donald. "Theological Thoughts about Evil." David Parkin, *The Anthropology of Evil.* Oxford: Basil Blackwell, 1985.

"That Hideous Strength." *The Bulletin of the New York C.S. Lewis Society* 3.7 (May 1972): 8.

Timmerman, John H. "Logos and Britain: the Dialectic of C.S. Lewis's *That Hideous Strength.*" *The Bulletin of the New York C. S. Lewis Society* 9.9 (Nov. 1977): 1-8.

Tolstoy, Nikolai. *The Quest for Merlin*. London: Hamish Hamilton, 1985.

Trible, Phyllis. *God and the Rhetoric of Sexuality*. Philadelphia, PA: Fortress Press, 1978.

Urang, Gunnar. *Shadows of Heaven: Religion and Fantasy in the Writing of C.S. Lewis, Charles Williams, and J.R.R. Tolkien.* Philadelphia, PA: Pilgrim Press, 1971.

Vanauken, Sheldon. *A Severe Mercy, With Letters by C. S. Lewis*. San Francisco, CA: Harper and Row, 1977.

Vastokas, Joan M. "The Shamanistic Tree of Life." *artscanada* (Dec. 1973/Jan. 1974): 125-49.

Visser, Margaret. *The Rituals of Dinner*. Toronto, ON: HarperCollins, 1992.

Voltaire, Francois Marie. *The Elements of Sir Isaac Newton's Philosophy*. 1738. Trans. John Hannah. London: Frank Cass and Col., 1967.

Von Franz, Marie-Louise. *On Divination and Synchronicity*. Toronto, ON: Inner-City Books, 1980.

Von Matt, Leonard, and Francis Trochu. *St. Bernadette*. London: Longmans Green and Co., 1957.

Waggoner, Diana. *The Hills of Faraway—A Guide to Fantasy*. New York: Atheneum, 1978.

Walton, Izaak. *The Lives of Dr. John Donne, Sir Henry Wotton, Mr. Richard Hooker, Mr. George Herbert*. Menston, UK: The Scholar's Press, Ltd., 1969.

West, J.A., and J.G. Toonder. *The Case for Astrology*. New York: Coward-McCann, 1970.

West, Richard. Contribution to "*That Hideous Strength.*" *The Bulletin of the New York C.S. Lewis Society* 3.7 (May 1972): 8.

Weston, Jessie L. *From Ritual to Romance*. 1920. Garden City, NY: Doubleday Anchor Books, 1957.

Whitmont, Edmund C. *Return of the Goddess*. New York: Crossroads, 1984.

Wilkins, Eithne. *The Rose-Garden Game: The Symbolic Background to the European Prayer-beads.* New York: Herder and Herder, 1969.

Williams, Charles. *The Arthurian Poems of Charles Williams*. Cambridge, UK: D.S. Brewer, 1982.

—— "The Figure of Arthur." *Arthurian Torso*. London: Oxford UP, 1948. 5-90.

—— *The Figure of Beatrice.* London: Faber and Faber, 1963.

Yeats, W.B. "The Second Coming." *The Collected Poems of W.B. Yeats.* New York: Macmillan, 1958.

Index

Nancy-Lou Patterson. "The Destruction of Edgestow." First published as the cover of *Mythlore* 16.2 (Winter 1989). Further publication prohibited.

www.ingramcontent.com/pod-product-compliance
Lightning Source LLC
Chambersburg PA
CBHW020332270326
41926CB00007B/146

* 9 7 8 1 9 8 7 9 1 9 0 3 5 *

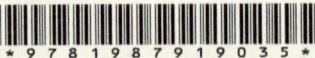